Investment Banking

FOR DUMMIES®

A Wiley Brand

by Matthew Krantz
and
Robert R. Johnson, PhD, CFA, CAIA

Investment Banking For Dummies®

Published by: **John Wiley & Sons, Inc.,** 111 River Street, Hoboken, NJ 07030-5774, www.wiley.com

Copyright © 2014 by John Wiley & Sons, Inc., Hoboken, New Jersey

Published simultaneously in Canada

No part of this publication may be reproduced, stored in a retrieval system or transmitted in any form or by any means, electronic, mechanical, photocopying, recording, scanning or otherwise, except as permitted under Sections 107 or 108 of the 1976 United States Copyright Act, without the prior written permission of the Publisher. Requests to the Publisher for permission should be addressed to the Permissions Department, John Wiley & Sons, Inc., 111 River Street, Hoboken, NJ 07030, (201) 748-6011, fax (201) 748-6008, or online at http://www.wiley.com/go/permissions.

Trademarks: Wiley, For Dummies, the Dummies Man logo, Dummies.com, Making Everything Easier, and related trade dress are trademarks or registered trademarks of John Wiley & Sons, Inc., and may not be used without written permission. All other trademarks are the property of their respective owners. John Wiley & Sons, Inc., is not associated with any product or vendor mentioned in this book.

For general information on our other products and services, please contact our Customer Care Department within the U.S. at 877-762-2974, outside the U.S. at 317-572-3993, or fax 317-572-4002. For technical support, please visit www.wiley.com/techsupport.

Wiley publishes in a variety of print and electronic formats and by print-on-demand. Some material included with standard print versions of this book may not be included in e-books or in print-on-demand. If this book refers to media such as a CD or DVD that is not included in the version you purchased, you may download this material at http://booksupport.wiley.com. For more information about Wiley products, visit www.wiley.com.

Library of Congress Control Number: 2013954075

ISBN 978-1-118-61577-5 (pbk); ISBN 978-1-118-61570-6 (ebk); ISBN 978-1-118-61571-3 (ebk); ISBN 978-1-118-61588-1 (ebk)

Manufactured in the United States of America

10 9 8 7 6 5 4 3 2 1

Contents at a Glance

Table of Contents

Part II: Digging In: Performing Investment Banking 93

Chapter 6: Finding the Data: Documents and Reports 95

Chapter 7: Making Sense of Financial Statements 113

Introduction

*I*nvestment banking is the fuel of capitalism.

Human progress takes money and ideas. But more times than not, the people with the money aren't the same ones with the ideas. Having a mound of cash and no creative ideas only creates a mound of money. Meanwhile, an entrepreneur with all kinds of dreams can't even break ground if there's no cash to break ground with.

Enter investment banking. Investment banking has been mankind's solution to pairing up the people with money and the people with ideas. The combination of money, or *capital*, and entrepreneurship is a dynamic marriage that's behind some of mankind's greatest accomplishments. Investment banking has financed 'round-the-world trade expeditions and built railroads and bridges.

Given the great role investment banking plays in the financial system, it has taken on a larger-than-life mystique with the masses. Many people suspect that investment banks are pulling the strings of the economy, but they may not know enough to realize exactly what investment banks do.

Get ready to take a peek into the private and important world of investment banking. This book could just have easily been called *Wall Street For Dummies,* because it's your guide into the complex but pivotal world that Wall Street plays in making the financial system work.

We wrote this book not only to help you understand what's done on Wall Street, but also to show you how to use some of the financial tools that help measure financial performance. After reading this book, you'll know how Wall Street works, and how to put its secrets to work for you.

About This Book

Believe it or not, investment banking affects you.

You may not live in Manhattan, under the shadow of the giant skyscrapers of Goldman Sachs and Morgan Stanley. You may not even be involved in the financial industry — your only dealings with a bank may be when you stop to take money out of the ATM.

But investment banking is so much a part of the financial system that, whether you realize it or not, you fall into its shadow. The fact of the matter is, if you're like most people, managing your money is falling increasingly on your shoulders. Gone are the days when you could work at a company for 40 years and expect to have a fat pension waiting for you in retirement.

Today, managing your money and making sure you have enough to pay for life's biggest investments — including homes, cars, college, and retirement — is up to you. You can't do it alone, though. Stuffing your money into a box and burying it in the backyard definitely won't cut it. If the termites don't eat up your life's savings, inflation will. Each year, prices for goods and services rise, eroding the power of your savings.

The only way to keep up with the ravages of inflation is to invest your money. And that's where Main Street usually becomes acquainted with Wall Street. Main Street has money in search of returns, and Wall Street is busy cooking up financial investments that it says will deliver those returns.

Typically, investment banking is a pretty heady topic that's discussed in MBA classes or in important-sounding books with long and intimidating titles. But in *Investment Banking For Dummies,* we break down the topic into understandable pieces.

Keep in mind that this book, like all the books in the *For Dummies* series, doesn't have to be read cover-to-cover (although we'll be flattered if you read it all). Each of the topics is broken down into easy-to-digest parts and chapters. Feel free to skip around the book to areas that interest you most, and save the parts that seem irrelevant until you're curious about them later.

While reading this book, keep in mind that we're trying to explain the topic, not impress you with how complicated the topic is. To help signal when a topic is about to get hairy, look for the Technical Stuff icon in the margin. When you see that icon, it means the information is great if you sleep with a calculator on your pillow instead of a teddy bear, but feel free to skip it if it's too much to handle right now.

The same goes for the gray boxes of text known as *sidebars.* In the sidebars, you'll find interesting but slightly tangential material that you can skip if you want. We found the information interesting enough to put it in the book, but it's not essential to your understanding of the topic at hand.

Within this book, you may note that some web addresses break across two lines of text. If you're reading this book in print and want to visit one of these web pages, simply key in the web address exactly as it's noted in the text, pretending as though the line break doesn't exist. If you're reading this as an e-book, you've got it easy — just click the web address to be taken directly to the web page.

Finally, we've written this book so it contains everything you need to know. If there's an obscure financial term or ugly-looking formula, we include the details and give instructions on how to use it. Although you're free to read other relevant financial titles in the *For Dummies* series, including *Fundamental Analysis For Dummies,* by Matt Krantz (Wiley), it's not necessary. If you're more interested in investing for yourself, rather than the process of investment banking, check out *Investing Online For Dummies,* 2nd Edition, also by Matt Krantz (Wiley). Okay, that's enough of the shameless self-promotion.

Foolish Assumptions

Because you have this book in your hands, we assume that you have a greater-than-average amount of curiosity about the way our financial system works. You probably read the financial press and know what the big financial players are doing in general, but you don't really understand how and why they're doing it.

We also assume you're not an investment banker, because we haven't met many investment bankers who would admit to being a dummy. But you're probably somehow who wants to know was investment bankers do and maybe even think about being one every time you watch *Wall Street.*

Icons Used in This Book

To draw your attention to certain kinds of information, we use a series of icons. Here's what the icons mean:

Investment bankers have no shortage of techniques that make their jobs easier. You'll find those marked with the Tip icon.

This book is a reference, which means you can turn to it again and again, to look up the information you need. However, occasionally, we tell you something that's so important, you'll want to commit it to memory, and when we do, we use the Remember icon.

 Danger! Danger! Investment banking is full of perils and possible screw-ups. We flag you to these pitfalls so you can avoid taking down a 100-year-old investment banking firm with a multi-billion-dollar blunder.

 Investment banking can be complicated stuff. And it's a shame that the complexity of investment banking can be a turnoff for some. When we talk about subjects that are especially gnarly, we mark the info with a Technical Stuff icon, so you can breeze on by.

Beyond the Book

In addition to the material in the print or e-book you're reading right now, this product also comes with some access-anywhere goodies on the web. If you're craving even more information on investment banking, check out the free Cheat Sheet at www.dummies.com/cheatsheet/investmentbanking. There, you'll find more on what investment bankers do, why companies buy other companies, and how to get in on an initial public offering, or IPO.

In addition, we've written several articles on topics ranging from how to read analyst reports to understanding cash flow. They're available at www.dummies.com/extras/investmentbanking.

Where to Go from Here

So, what are you waiting for? The world of investment banking is fascinating, and waiting for you to dive in. When you understand how Wall Street works, you'll know how to make investment banking work for you, instead of getting worked over by the world's biggest banks. Flip through the book, and start reading anywhere you see something interesting!

Part I
Getting Started with Investment Banking

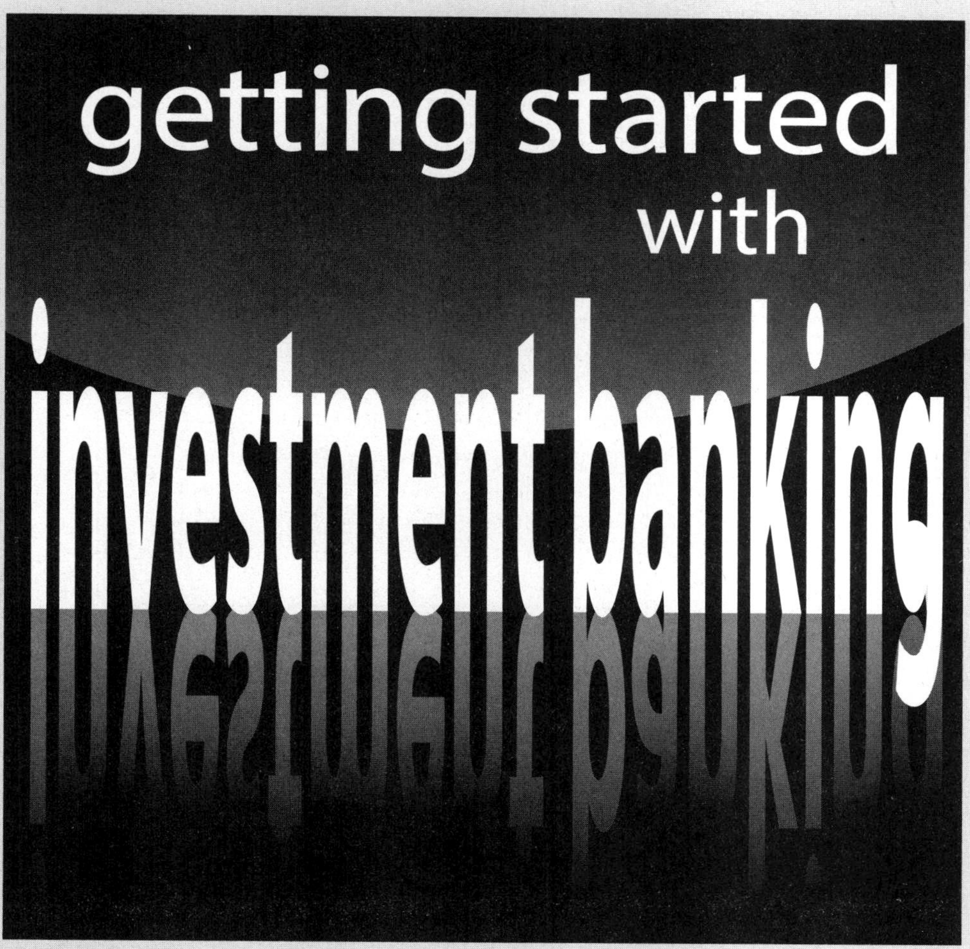

In this part . . .

✔ Discover the role investment banking plays in the financial system so you can understand the types of services that are provided in the economy.

✔ See how investment bankers interact with investors in order to appreciate the primary job of moving money from those with extra cash to those who need it.

✔ Look at the process of selling a company to investors so you can see the purpose of one of the key functions served in investment banking.

✔ Recognize what goes on in merger activity so you can see how deals are done and what your job may be as an investment banking professional.

Chapter 1

Introducing Investment Banking

*I*f you're like most people, when you hear the term *investment bank,* one of a few things may cross your mind. Your eyes may glaze over as you think about mind-numbingly detailed financial statements and valuation metrics. Yawn. Or, you may think of exciting high-stakes financial maneuvers, like those out of the movie *Wall Street,* where well-dressed bankers treat companies like Monopoly squares to be dispassionately bought and sold.

But maybe you're attracted to investment banking by the mental gymnastics required and the promise of big bonuses and riches to those who are in the know. And that may be why you picked up this book.

As you can see, there are many preconceived notions about investment banking and investment bankers. Many of these ideas, though, are often pieces of fiction blended with stories of larger-than-life personalities of high finance that spill out of the pages of the money section of financial publications.

In this book, we tell you what *really* happens in the investment banking world. This chapter introduces you to the high-level reality of what investment banking is. Here, you see how Wall Street really works. In this chapter, you see that although investment banking can be extremely lucrative, it's also an important facilitator of economic growth and traces its roots to the idea of putting money into the hands of the dreamers and creators.

What Investment Banking Is

If you're like most people, you probably figure investment banking got its start in a towering office skyscraper in New York City. But the real story of the origin of investment banking is far less metropolitan, yet arguably even more interesting. Investment banking traces its roots to the age of kings and queens. Many of the most commonly used financial instruments trace their origins to centuries ago when bankers navigated the edicts of rulers and, believe it or not, religious leaders. If you're interested in the very early days of investment banking, check out the appendix for a quick history lesson.

But for now, just know that investment banking is, at its very core, pretty straightforward. Investment banking is a method of controlling the flow of money. The goal of investment banking is channeling cash from investors looking for returns into the hands of entrepreneurs and business builders who are long on ideas, but short on bucks.

Investment bankers raise money from investors, by selling securities, and then transfer that money to people who need cash to start businesses, build buildings, run cities, or bring other costly projects to reality.

There are many aspects of investment banking that muddy this fundamental purpose. But in the end, investment bankers simply find opportunities to unlock the value of companies or ideas, create businesses, or route money from being idle to having a productive purpose. (In Chapter 2, you discover the purpose of investment banking.)

The role investment banking plays

Investment bankers get involved in the very early stages of funding a new project or endeavor. Investment bankers are typically contacted by people, companies, or governments who need cash to start businesses, expand factories, and build schools or bridges. Representatives from the investment banking operation then find investors or organizations like pension plans, mutual funds, and private investors who have more cash than they know what to do with (a nice problem to have) and who want a return for the use of their funds. Investment banks also offer advice regarding what investment securities should be bought or the ones an investor may want to buy.

One of the trickiest parts of understanding investment banking is that it's typically a menu of financial services. Some investment banking operations may offer some services, but not others.

The services offered by investment banks typically fall into one of a few buckets. One of the best ways to understand investment banks is to examine all the functions that some of the biggest investment banks perform. For example, Morgan Stanley, one of the world's largest investment banks, has its hands in several key business areas, including the following:

- **Capital raising:** This part of the investment banking function helps companies and organizations generate money from investors. This is typically done by selling shares of stock or debt.

- **Financial advisory:** In this role, the investment banking operation is hired to help a company or government make decisions on managing their financial resources. Advice may pertain to whether to buy another company or sell off part of the business. A common business decision tackled by this type of investment banking is whether to acquire another company or divest of a current product line. This is called *mergers and acquisitions* (M&A) advisory.

- **Corporate lending:** Investment banks typically help companies and other large borrowers sell securities to raise money. But large investment banks are also frequently involved in extending loans to their customers, often short-term loans (called *bridge loans*) to tide a company over while another transaction is in the works.

- **Sales and trading:** Investment bankers are a creative and innovative lot, in the business of constructing financial instruments to be bought and sold. It's natural for investment bankers to also buy and sell stocks and other financial instruments either on the behalf of their clients or using their own money.

- **Brokerage services:** Some investment banking operations include brokerage services where they may hold clients' assets or help them conduct trades.

- **Research:** Investment banks not only help large institutions sell securities to investors, but also assist investors looking to buy securities. Many investment banks run research units that advise investors on whether they should buy a particular investment.

The terms *investments* and *securities* are pretty much interchangeable.

- **Investments:** Investment banks typically serve the role of a middleman, sitting between the entities that need money and those that have it. But periodically, units of investment banking operations may invest their own money in promising companies or projects. This type of investment, often made in companies that don't have investments that the public can buy, is called *private equity*.

Investment banking operations at one firm may be engaged in some of the preceding activities, but not all. There's no rule that demands investment banking operations must perform all the services described here. As investment firms grow, though, they often add functions so they're more valuable to their clients and can serve as a common source for a variety of services.

How investment banking differs from traditional banking

The critical part of the investment banking process is in the way cash is funneled from the people who have it to the people who need it. After all, traditional banks do essentially the same thing investment banks do — get cash from people who have excess amounts into the hands of those who have productive uses for it.

Traditional banks take deposits from savers with excess cash and lend the money out to borrowers. The main types of traditional banks are *commercial banks* (which deal primarily with businesses) and *retail banks* (which deal mostly with individuals).

The difference between traditional banks and investment banks, though, is the way money is transferred between the people and institutions that need it and the ones who have it. Instead of collecting deposits from savers, as traditional banks do, investment bankers usually rely on selling *financial instruments* (such as stocks and bonds), in a process called *underwriting*. By selling financial instruments to investors, the investment bankers raise the money that's provided to the people, companies, and governments that have productive uses for it.

Because banks accept deposits from Main Street savers, those deposits are protected by the Federal Deposit Insurance Corporation (FDIC), which guarantees bank deposits. To protect itself, the FDIC along with the federal government puts very strict rules on banks to make sure they're not being reckless.

On the other hand, investment banks, at least until the financial crisis of 2007 (see the appendix), were free to take bigger chances with other people's money. Investment banks could be more creative in inventing new financial tools, which sometimes don't work out so well. The idea is that clients of investment banks are more sophisticated and know the risks better than the average person with a bank account.

The meaning of the term *investment bank* got even more unclear after the financial crisis that erupted in 2007. Due to a severe shock to the bond market, many of the dedicated investment banks went out of business, including venerable old-line firms such as Lehman Brothers and Bear Stearns, or were bought by banks. Many of today's largest investment banks are now units of banks or technically considered commercial or retail banks, although they still perform investment banking operations. Meanwhile, these banks will often say they perform investment banking functions. The term *investment bank* is somewhat of a misnomer, because the major financial institutions are now technically considered banks.

Now that you see that the chief role of investment banks is selling securities, the next question is: What types of securities do they sell? The primary forms of financial instruments sold by investment banks include the following:

- **Equity:** If you've ever bought stock in a company, be it an individual firm like Microsoft or an index fund that invests in companies in the Standard & Poor's (S&P) 500, you've been on the investor end of an equity deal. Investment bankers help companies raise money by selling ownership stakes, or *equity,* in the company to outside investors. After the securities are sold by the investment bank, the owners are free to buy or sell them on the stock market. Equity is first sold as part of an equity offering called an *initial public offering* (IPO).

- **Debt capital:** Some investors have no interest in owning a piece of the company, but they're more than willing to lend money to it, for a price. That's the role of debt capital. Investment banks help companies borrow money by issuing bonds, or IOUs, that are sold to investors. The company must pay the prearranged rate of interest, but it doesn't give up any ownership of the company. If a company falls onto hard times, though, the owners of the debt have a higher claim to assets than do the equity owners if a liquidation of the company is necessary.

- **Hybrid securities:** Most of what investment banks sell can be classified as either debt or equity. But some securities take on traits of both, or are an interesting spin on both. One example is *preferred shares,* which give investors an income stream that's higher than what's paid on the regular equity. But preferred shares don't come with as high a claim to assets as bonds, and this income stream can be suspended by the company if it chooses.

The services investment banks provide

Investment banks do much more than just raise capital by selling investments. Although selling securities to raise money is arguably the primary function of investment banks, they also serve several other roles. All the functions of investment banks typically fall into one of two primary categories: selling or buying.

- ✔ **The sell side:** Investment banks are best known for the part of their business that sells securities, or the *sell side*. This function of the investment bank is responsible for finding investors to buy the securities being sold, which raises the money needed by businesses and governments to grow and prosper.

- ✔ **The buy side:** Investment banks may also take the role of advising the large investors who are interested in buying financial instruments. Serving in its role on the buy side, the investment bank can offer suggestions to large institutional investors like mutual funds, pension plans, or endowments on which securities may be appropriate for it to buy in order to meet return targets.

The dual role played by investment banking operations, serving both buyers and sellers of securities, raises constant worries of double dealing and conflicts of interest. Some people rightly question whether it's possible for the same investment bank that makes money selling shares of an IPO, for instance, to give honest and unbiased investment advice to investors trying to decide whether they should buy or sell. The question of conflicts of interest in investment banking operations has become paramount since the financial crisis began in 2007.

How investment banks are organized

Investment banks may seem like financial behemoths that have their hands in just about any matter that involves large sums of money. And to a large degree, that's true. Investment banks are usually involved in some fashion when it comes to financing major projects, conducting trading in financial instruments, or developing new ways to generate capital.

With that said, nearly all major investment banks divide their operations into several key areas, including the front office, middle office, and back office. When you talk to someone about investment banking, or even listen to the heads of investment banks talk, they'll often refer to these three common parts of a traditional investment bank:

- ✔ **The front office:** The *front office* is exactly what it sounds like. It's not only the part of the investment bank that sells investments, but also the part that courts companies looking to do deals. Traditionally, companies that are looking to find a fast way to turbo-charge growth may think about buying another company (say, a rival with similar customers or complementary technology).

From the front office, investment banks help usher along the M&A process by pairing up buyers and sellers. The front office is also the part of the investment bank that conducts *trading* (frenetic buying and selling of securities to take advantage of any mispricings — even if the holding period is for only a few seconds). This type of trading, done using complicated mathematical formulas and using the firm's money (not the clients' money), is often called *proprietary trading.* Many investment banks operate a business where they buy and sell securities themselves. Proprietary trading tends to be quite profitable for investment banks.

Another part of the front office is the part of the business involved in conducting research on companies. The front office often employs sell-side analysts, whose job it is to closely monitor companies and industries and produce reports used by large investors trying to decide whether to buy or sell particular securities. (You can find out more about research analysts in Chapter 2.)

✔ **The middle office:** The *middle office* of an investment bank is generally out of the limelight. It's the part of the bank with the job of cooking up new types of securities that can be sold to investors. Some innovations in investment banking are useful, but others can wind up putting investors and the markets in general in an unfavorable light. Some of the infamous financial instruments cooked up in the middle office of investment banks that came back to haunt the system include *auction-rate securities* and *credit default swaps.*

Auction-rate securities are debt instruments that promise investors higher rates of return than are available in savings accounts. Instead of selling debt at a prearranged interest rate, the investment bank would conduct auctions, and the rate would be set by a bidding process. That's great as long as there are willing buyers and sellers. But the auction-rate market relied on auctions, many of which weren't successful during the financial crisis that erupted in 2007. Many investors holding the securities found they couldn't sell them because the market had dried up, causing a huge headache for the investors and investment banks. Credit default swaps are tools that allow lenders to sell the risk that borrowers won't be able to meet their obligations. Credit default swaps operate as a form of unregulated insurance policies. These instruments got so complicated, though, that they exacerbated the financial interdependencies between giant financial firms, worsening the financial crisis that erupted between 2007 and 2009.

✔ **The back office:** The *back office* is the part of the investment bank that is far from the glamour of the front office. It's primarily made up of the systems and procedures that allow investment bankers to gather the data they need to do their jobs well. The back office, for instance, maintains the computer systems used by investment bankers to gauge interest in certain securities and provides traders the ability to make short-term bets on market movements. The parts of investment banking considered more operational in nature tend to fall into the back office.

REMEMBER

Investment banking operations are rarely identical between firms. Some banks and investment banks are engaged in some front-office areas, while others steer clear of them completely. There are also some peripheral areas of business some banks and investment banks include as part of their services that don't fall in one of the traditional "offices." One example of a service that is often grouped in investment banking is *investment management.* In an investment management unit, investment professionals are paid to invest money on behalf of individual clients or institutions.

The current lay of the investment banking land

After the tumultuous changes in the investment banking business following the financial crisis of 2007 through 2009, the entire landscape changed. Following the banking crisis, investment banks needed capital. Some of the most storied investment banks, unable to raise money, merged with other banks or became commercial banks themselves. Suddenly, the financial system was comprised of behemoth banks that have the deposit-taking abilities of banks but also engage in investment banking. The result is the formation of several mega-institutions that many people fear are "too big to fail," including the ones shown in Table 1-1.

Table 1-1	Among the Last Banks Standing
Firm	*2012 Revenue ($ billions)*
JPMorgan Chase	91.7
Wells Fargo	79.5
Bank of America Merrill Lynch	75.2
Citigroup	59.3
Goldman Sachs	34.2
Morgan Stanley	26.1

Source: S&P Capital IQ (www.capitaliq.com)

Types of investment banking operations

Insiders in the investment banking business use all sorts of terms, some decidedly derogatory, to classify the players in the business. Some classifications that investment banks fall into include the following:

- ✔ **Bulge bracket:** Bulge bracket investment firms aren't the ones that ate too many slices of cheesecake. Instead, *bulge bracket* is a commonly used slang term to describe the biggest of the big investment banking operations. The bulge bracket firms are the behemoths, like the ones in Table 1-1. They have their hands in most areas of investment banking.

- ✔ **Boutique:** Boutique investment firms are smaller investment banks and traditional banks that choose to focus on one or a select few areas of the business. Some firms, for instance, focus on selling securities for smaller companies.

- ✔ **Regional:** Regional firms typically focus on a particular part of the country. Whereas the bulge bracket firms continually try to grow and take market share from rivals, there seems to be plenty of room for smaller players like these. Some regional firms also often concentrate on a particular type of investment banking service, be it trading services or underwriting of securities.

How investment banks get paid

As you can imagine, although investment banking plays an important role in funding economic progress, there's also lots of money to be made. Investment bankers can't afford those fancy suits if they're not getting paid.

Investment bankers perform services for customers and collect money in a number of ways, include the following:

- ✔ **Commissions:** Investment banks sometimes collect fees in exchange for conducting a financial transaction between a buyer and seller. One of the more common forms of commissions is often collected in the brokerage operations by some traditional banks and investment banks. For instance, Merrill Lynch, the brokerage and investment banking unit of Bank of America, charges commissions when purchasing stock for its customers. But that's just a small example.

- ✔ **Underwriting fees:** A lucrative area of investment banking generates fees for selling securities in the *primary market* (the collection of buyers' and sellers' interest in trading brand-new securities). When a company sells stock to the public for the first time, for instance, the investment banker who handles the deal, called the *underwriter,* collects a fee. (You can read more about companies selling stock to the public for the first time in IPOs in Chapter 3.)

- **Trading income:** Investment banks usually handle other people's money. But many investment banking operations also include a trading division. This unit attempts to take advantage of temporarily mispriced financial instruments. This high-risk proprietary trading is designed to generate profits for the firm.

- **Asset management fees:** Some investment banks help their clients make decisions on how to invest their money. Investment banks generate asset management fees when they help clients decide which securities they should buy or sell.

- **Advisory fees:** Companies often look to their investment banks for advice, especially in the cases of M&A deals. And in these cases, the investment bankers are brought in to provide in-depth, numerical analysis of a proposed deal. The companies pay substantial fees for this high-level assistance. (Read more about M&A deal making in Chapter 4.)

Dissecting an investment banking operation: Using Goldman Sachs as an example

Of all the investment banks, few are as well known — and even as infamous — as Goldman Sachs. The firm's long history in investment banking and its seeming omnipresence in markets around the world cement its recognized role as a premier investment bank.

Remember: It's important to note that Goldman, too, found itself in a world of hurt during the financial crisis, and it had to turn to famed investor Warren Buffett to invest billions to help the company avoid a liquidity crisis. Goldman also borrowed billions from taxpayers, too. Nonetheless, those hoping to learn about investment banking, what it is, and how it works, are well served to look at the way Goldman Sachs structures its business and the size of those pieces, including the following:

- **Institutional client services:** The biggest part of Goldman's business is what it calls *institutional client services*. Here, the firm arranges and helps conduct transactions for clients who want to buy and sell everything from bonds to foreign currencies and commodities, in a process called *market making*. Typically, the clients of this part of the business include big financial institutions, governments, and companies.

- **Investing and lending:** Goldman may consider itself to be an investment bank, but it also makes loan to businesses and governments. Most of the loans Goldman is involved in are long term; they may involve everything from financing real estate deals to building power plants.

- **Investment management:** Here's where Goldman serves the role of helping its clients put their money to work. Goldman offers financial advice to institutions through mutual funds, accounts it manages on behalf of clients, wealth management services, and financial counseling. Goldman serves some very wealthy individuals and families in this part of its business.

✔ **Investment banking:** This part of Goldman is the one most interesting to readers of this book. Here, Goldman guides companies embarking on M&A, provides assistance in bringing companies public, and conducts financial restructurings.

You can see how the different parts of Goldman rank in order of importance to revenue in the following table.

Business Unit	2012 Revenue ($ millions)	2011 Revenue ($ millions)	2010 Revenue ($ millions)
Institutional client services	18,124	17,280	21,796
Investing and lending	5,891	2,142	7,541
Investment management	5,222	5,034	5,014
Investment banking	4,926	4,355	4,810

Source: Goldman Sachs 2012 annual report
(www.sec.gov/Archives/edgar/data/886982/000119312513085474/d446679d10k.htm)

How Investment Banking Is Done

Investment banking isn't just a theory or subject. Investment banking isn't just an economic function, either. Investment banking is a profession that requires the efforts and expertise of armies of trained financial experts. You may have studied English in college, for instance, but you don't "do" English. But you can practice investment banking (which is something you find out about in Chapter 6). At this point in the book, you go from understanding what investment banking is to how it's applied in the business world.

Finding the financial statements

Chocolate factories need milk, sugar, and cocoa to produce their delicious products. But the raw materials used by many investment banking firms is the information contained on the *financial statements*. These documents released by companies provide investment bankers with much of the information they need to start analyzing companies and looking for investment banking opportunities.

But these important documents can't do you any good if you can't find them. That's what you find out how to do in Chapter 6. There you discover tools that make it easy for an expert investment banker to retrieve and find all the relevant data from the financial statements, even information the companies may not realized is as valuable as it is.

Understanding the importance of financial statements and ratios

Investment bankers in the movies may be best known for roaming the concrete alleys of Wall Street, ears glued to their cellphones, constantly on the hunt for deals. But much of the most important work done by investment bankers is done in front of a computer screen, examining rows of numbers and statistics using spreadsheets and other financial analysis tools. In Chapter 7, you find out how to make sense of all the information that's contained in financial statements and why these documents are so precious to investment bankers and vital to their success.

Investment bankers know it's not necessary to read financial statements from cover to cover like a book. Financial statements, like *For Dummies* books, can be read in sections — you jump to areas that interest you at the time. Additionally, some of the best insights that come from the financial statements result from putting the numbers through the paces by applying financial ratios, which we introduce you to in Chapter 8.

Zeroing in on past transactions

Putting a price tag on companies and other investments is a big part of what investment bankers do. Talk about *The Price Is Right* on a grand scale! Luckily, you don't have to play Plinko and guess what companies are worth. There's no shortage of analysis tools that investors can use to calculate the value of companies. Investment bankers use ratios, such as the price-to-earnings ratio and price-to-book ratio, discussed in Chapter 8, to value companies.

Sometimes, though, the best yardstick of a company's value isn't what an investment banker can calculate, but what the market will bear. Understanding how to obtain and analyze past transactions is one way investment bankers can accurately gauge the value that investors will likely put on a company. In Chapter 10, you see how investment bankers handle the process of studying past transactions, and what that means for the value of investments.

Seeing the value of fixed income

Splashy debuts of new companies and their stocks often grab the attention of individual investors. Who can't resist the success story of an entrepreneur with a dream who brings a company to sell shares to the public for the first time and becomes an instant millionaire? That's the American way.

But although equity IPOs may get all the attention, much of the heavy lifting of the financial markets is done using *fixed-income instruments,* also known as debt. Investment bankers are critical cogs in the process of helping companies borrow money at attractive rates in the bond market. You see the role investment bankers play in the bond market and how fixed income fuels the capitalistic system in Chapter 11.

Turning Into an Investment Banking Pro

Investment banking is one of those disciplines that you can delve into for decades and still not master. There are corners of investment banking that go well beyond the understanding of the capital markets and even the mechanics of gathering information about companies and their needs for investment to continue to grow.

If you're willing to put in the time and effort, you can discover very profound ways to understand companies, how they're valued, and the ways they use financial engineering and investment banking products to maximize their returns.

Putting the discounted cash flow analysis to work

When it comes to the top skills that serious investment bankers must hone, the discounted cash flow analysis is certainly high on the list. The *discounted cash flow* is a culmination of many of the tools beginning investment bankers have to create in-depth and comprehensive models of what companies are worth.

The concept of a discounted cash flow may be something you can learn in school. But it's the assumptions and the quality of the inputs embedded in the analysis that make this technique essential to the investment banker. In many ways, investment bankers can show off everything they know when they create a detailed discounted cash flow analysis, which you find out about in Chapter 12.

Seeing how leverage becomes a force in investment banking

Light a stick of dynamite, and you pretty much know what's going to happen. Bang! But sometimes that explosive power can be used to build as well as to destroy. Explosive power can be used to clear mountains to make way for freeways or tunnels. But dynamite can have some predictable negative uses, too.

In many ways, the use of debt, in a process called *leverage,* can be much like dynamite. When used prudently, leverage can be a creative force that gives companies the power to grow and create wealth faster than they would have otherwise. But at the same time, leverage can be abused and lead to great destruction of wealth, jobs, and enterprise. The graveyard of companies is littered with examples of businesses that lit the leverage bomb and didn't know how to harness the power.

In Chapter 13, you see how investment bankers can prudently apply leverage to deals as a way to get very positive results. Success with leverage requires extreme caution, knowledge, and discipline.

Pinpointing buyout targets

Investment bankers often find themselves playing the role of a corporate matchmaker. A big part of the job description is finding new ways to raise money and help companies restructure themselves in a way that makes them more profitable for their owners.

There are many tools companies can use to boost profits, one of which is pushing along M&A deals. Sometimes the investment bankers are contacted by a company eager to sell themselves by looking for so-called *strategic alternatives.* But other times, the investment bankers are called on by big companies with money to burn looking for a deal. The big companies in the hunt call investment bankers to help identify and court targets.

Investment bankers, in large part, are hired due to their contacts in the business community and their ability to use financial modeling analysis to find deals that make economic sense. In Chapter 14, we explore many of the tools used by investment bankers to identify companies that are ripe for a buyout and discover ways to pair them up with the buyers.

Putting Investment Banking to Work

CEOs may be good at the things they do — such as controlling costs, finding new products, tapping new markets, and playing golf — but when it comes to investment banking operations, including tapping investors for money or cooking up M&A deals, CEOs often find themselves well out of their comfort zone.

Only the largest companies can afford to maintain an in-house staff dedicated to analyzing the company's investment banking options. It's most common for a company's board of directors or top management to contact an investment banking firm to lend expertise.

Because investment bankers are dedicated being the conduit between companies and investors' money, they're expected to be the experts on all things financial. Investment bankers must be able to go beyond just what a company's management team is telling them in order to independently understand a business situation. Starting in Chapter 15, you discover some of the most advanced skills that the best investment bankers have.

Staying in compliance with the rules

Perhaps the most important thing for investment bankers to do is stay out of jail. And these days that seems to be tougher than it sounds, as regulators are routinely fining investment bankers for not complying with the rules. It's a sensitive area because the investment banking business is filled with rules and regulations. Running afoul of these regulations is usually a one-way ticket to jail, or at least enough to be prevented from engaging in investment banking in the future. You find out how to avoid wearing jailbird pinstripes in Chapter 15.

Looking beyond the published financial statements

Financial statements can sometimes be the only things investment bankers can trust. Company management has a big incentive to puff their chests and try to act like their companies are performing better than they really are. And even investors can be misleading, aggravating for change at the company even if things are going fine.

Investment bankers must be extremely comfortable diving into the financial statements. These statements, which must adhere to strict rules and be overseen by independent accountants, may be the only unbiased pieces of information that investment bankers get.

But despite the value of financial statements to investment bankers, these documents, too, need to be looked at with at least an ounce — and at times pounds — of skepticism. Although it's not common, executives at companies sometimes attempt to fudge the numbers to mislead investors or (gasp!) investment bankers. When a company's performance is faltering, and investors are likely to be disappointed, some dishonest executives and accountants may decide to distort the financial results through liberal interpretations of accounting or outright fraud.

Individual investors, who may not take the time to read the financials, can often fall for such accounting gimmicks. But investment bankers are held to a much higher standard and are generally considered to be above the tricks. In Chapter 16, you find out some of the ways investment bankers can look for accounting sleight of hand in the financial statements and avoid getting duped.

Making adjustments to financial statements for comparability

Accountants don't like surprises. Some accountants may be startled if a pen they thought had blue ink turns out to be black. But although the predictability of accountants may be subject for good-natured ribbing at cocktail parties, that uniformity is essential in financial analysis.

To accurately compare and contrast companies in different industries — something investment bankers have to do frequently — the companies' financials must be subject to the same ground rules. Accounting rules usually do a pretty good job aligning the financials of different companies. *Generally accepted accounting principles* (GAAP) are a set of accounting standards that attempt to create a measure of performance that is somewhat comparable across industries.

But despite the value of GAAP, it's up to investment bankers to take greater efforts to make sure that the financial results of companies are truly apples-to-apples comparisons.

In Chapter 17, you find out ways that investment bankers are able to modify and adjust the financial results of companies to make their results comparable. These techniques, as well as everything you read about in this book, all come into play when you try your hand at an investment banking analysis case study in Chapter 18.

Chapter 2

The Purpose of Investment Banking: What Investment Bankers Do

*I*nvestment banking is the grease that oils the capitalistic machine. Businesses, entrepreneurs, governments, schools, and other institutions that hope to build and expand need cash to make it happen. But in the financial version of the chicken-and-the-egg dilemma, sometimes the people with the great plans don't have the cash to get started.

And that's exactly where investment bankers come in. Investment bankers find ways to put together investors with money, who would like a return on that money, with the people building projects.

Investment bankers play an interesting role in that they're usually just the money people. The officials from the city or government are in charge of the project, be it building a bridge or building a power plant. But investment bankers are the critical financial players that make sure the project is adequately funded, but at the same time, generates adequate returns to make the investors happy.

This chapter isn't designed to get into the nitty-gritty yet. The gory details of what investment bankers do comes in later chapters in this book. This chapter is more of a bird's-eye view that shows you some of the ways investment bankers get involved in key financial transactions. You'll read examples where investment banking plays a big role in making things happen with companies and investors. Perhaps one of the most high-profile ways investment bankers are seen in modern finance is in mergers and acquisitions (M&A), transactions where big companies decide to buy a rival or another company with advantages it would like to have. You also find out about leveraged buyouts (LBOs), which are unique transactions where buyers use large amounts of borrowed money to buy a company. Another primary driver of investment banking activity are initial public offerings (IPOs), where companies raise money by selling pieces of ownership to the public for the first time. Tying many aspects of investment banking together are the disciplines of research and valuation. Lastly, in this chapter, you get a sense of the importance of trading at many investment banking units, and appreciate the risks and potential rewards.

Putting the For-Sale Sign on Corporate America

Investment bankers are the ultimate corporate matchmakers. They're like the friends you had when you were single, who were always trying to fix you up. When companies or investors are on the prowl to buy other companies, or put themselves up for sale, they often turn to investment bankers for a hand. We cover the M&A process in more detail in Chapter 3, but for now, know that investment bankers play several important roles in the M&A process, including the following:

- **Performing due-diligence services:** Investment bankers can help the buyers and sellers determine a reasonable price for the company. The value is put on the company by comparing with other companies that trade on stock markets or based on the fundamental profitability of the company.

- **Matchmaking services:** Investment bankers are only as good as their source list. When a company is looking to do a deal, investment bankers start working their personal relationships trying to find companies that may be in play or open to a bid.

- **Lining up investors:** When a company is looking to raise money by selling securities, the deal hinges on being able to actually find buyers for those securities. Investment bankers are often looked to in order to find investors willing to buy the securities.

You discover the wide array of ways investment bankers help put companies on the market in the rest of this section. These deals range from everything including mergers and acquisitions to leveraged buyouts and private business sales.

Mergers and acquisitions

Typically when two people get married, there are two willing adults. From time to time, though, things may feel a little forced — a shotgun and an angry father may be involved.

The same goes when companies get together and combine. Usually, the terms of a deal are fairly straightforward. Typically, a larger company is looking to bolster a part of its business. The company could hire a team of people to build that company from scratch, pairing up researchers to design the product, finance people to price it right and control costs, marketing people to whet the consumers' appetite, and operations people to get the product. But all that takes time and money. So, instead, companies often buy already existing companies, saving themselves a lot of work.

Why companies buy other companies

Making widgets and selling them for a profit is why most companies exist. Microsoft, for instance, is in the business of making and selling computer software and hardware. So, why do so many companies during the course of business wind up buying and selling businesses?

There are many reasons why companies may consider using M&A, including the following:

- ✔ **Getting big fast:** Building a business takes time. There are people to hire, distribution to set up, and products to sell. Sometimes the time it takes to get up and running is too long, and the delay gives the rivals with the first-mover advantage an even bigger lead.

  A great example of a merger done for speed was Coca-Cola's 2007 purchase of Energy Brands Glaceau, maker of Vitamin Water. Coca-Cola bought the company, which made flavored water and energy drinks, in 2007 for $4.1 billion in cash. By buying Glaceau, Coca-Cola was instantly a player in the low-calorie flavored-water business with an already established brand name.

✔ **Filling out a product line:** Some companies may have been hugely successful in a narrow product line. But to find growth, which investors are always clamoring for, companies may need to fill in some gaps.

A classic example of using M&A to fill in a product-line hole came in 2001. Leading jelly maker J.M. Smucker bought the Jif peanut butter brand (along with Crisco oil) from Procter & Gamble for $813 million in stock. The deal solved a problem for J.M. Smucker — now the company could sell all the ingredients for a tasty peanut-butter-and-jelly sandwich. Talk about synergy. But at the same time, Procter & Gamble also wanted to reduce its holdings in the food business.

✔ **Geographic expansion:** Business is going global, and companies need to have a worldwide presence or risk getting beaten by rivals. M&A deals are a quick way to spread into other countries.

The biggest proposed M&A deal of 2012 (see Table 2-1) was a great example of a company looking to M&A deals for a geographic expansion push. Japan-based telecommunication firm, Softbank, made a nearly $60 billion offer for U.S. wireless carrier Sprint Nextel. Softbank looks to the deal as a way to get a beachhead in the United States in the fast-growing area.

Table 2-1	Biggest U.S. Merger Offers of 2012		
Target	*Buyer*	*Transaction Value ($ billions)*	*Select Investment Banks Involved*
Sprint Nextel	Softbank	59.5	Merrill Lynch, Rothschild, UBS, Citigroup, Mizuho
Plains Exploration	Freeport-McMoRan Copper & Gold	11.4	JPMorgan Chase, Credit Suisse, Jefferies, Barclays
NYSE Euronext	IntercontinentalExchange	10.8	Perella Weinberg, Citigroup, Goldman Sachs, Morgan Stanley, Wells Fargo

Target	Buyer	Transaction Value ($ billions)	Select Investment Banks Involved
Hudson City Bancorp	Wilmington Trust	3.8	Evercore Partners, JPMorgan Chase
McMoRan Exploration	Freeport-McMoRan Copper & Gold	3.7	JPMorgan Chase, Credit Suisse, Jefferies, Barclays

Source: S&P Capital IQ (www.capitaliq.com)

Notice that more than one investment bank is usually involved in big merger deals. Both the buying and selling companies may consult and recruit the services of multiple investment banking operations.

The advantages of building versus buying

Some large companies may decide it's better to just buy another company to get in the new market quickly. Large companies that buy for this reason are called *strategic buyers*. Investment banks are often brought in during these typical M&A deals to advise on whether it makes sense or help come up with the money to make it happen.

Sometimes the *target* — the company being eyed — doesn't want to be bought. And that's when deals often turn *hostile,* where the investors or management of the strategic buyer are hoping to make the deal happen, but the target is resisting. Again, investment banks are often pivotal in hostile M&A deals because the buying of a company that doesn't want to be bought often requires more brinkmanship and cash.

Pitfalls of ill-conceived mergers

One of the reasons companies engaged in merger activities call in so many investment banks and advisors is that they don't want to blow it. Mergers are often big bets that cost a great deal of money, either consuming cash or requiring the company to borrow or sell debt. Companies, and their shareholders, don't want companies to blow it on deals that don't work out. You can read more about botched M&A deals in Chapter 4.

Leveraged buyouts

Leveraged buyouts are another area where investment bankers can really put their skills to use. LBOs are a form of corporate buyout, but the high-octane version. In an LBO, the acquiring company typically buys the company with a large amount of debt. The acquired company then pays off the debt over time using the cash flow generated by the business.

You can find more details about LBOs in Chapter 5. For now, just know that leveraged buyouts are typically done by specialized firms, called *financial sponsors.* One of the most common forms of financial sponsors are *private-equity firms.* These investment firms typically have a host of limited partners, or investors, who provide money to the private-equity firm. The private-equity firm uses the cash from the limited partners, plus a heap of debt, to buy companies, fix them up, and then sell them for a tidy profit. Sometimes, the management of a company, including the CEO, may look to use a leverage buyout to buy the company from investors. These management lead deals are called *management buyouts.*

Some of the biggest private-equity firms include Bain Capital, Blackstone, Carlyle Group, a unit of Goldman Sachs, Kohlberg Kravis Roberts, and TPG Group. These firms often work alongside investment banks to not only raise money by selling debt, but also conduct the transaction. Investment banks typically get involved in leveraged buyouts later, when the private-equity firms want to exit.

How leverage changes the nature of a deal and a firm

Private-equity firms are looking to own the companies for a relatively short period of time. Debt is a way to drive higher profitability from the company that was bought. By boosting profit, the buyer, the private-equity firm, can sell the acquired company for a big profit later. Here are some ways private-equity firms sell companies:

- ✔ **IPOs:** One way for private-equity firms to get out of a buyout deal is by selling the company to the public. This is done by carving the company up into shares that are sold to public investors. During raging bull markets, IPOs become a popular way for private-equity firms to exit deals because they can get top dollar.

- ✔ **Sales to strategic buyers:** If a private-equity firm wants to sell its position in a company, and the stock market is depressed, it may court big companies that may be interested in the deal.

- ✔ **Recapitalizations:** If a private-equity firm can't find a buyer for a business, or if the timing isn't right, it may consider restructuring the makeup of the company's financing. The company, for instance, may take on an additional investor as a way to reduce the amount of debt.

Private equity: Not the ticket to riches

Private equity firms had their absolute heyday in the mid-2000s. One of the key ingredients to private-equity firms is access to cheap money. And in the mid-2000s, private-equity firms could borrow from just about anyone with a pulse at extremely low interest rates. Banks and bond investors were more than willing to lend and buy bonds offering private-equity firms practically unlimited amounts of money to buy companies. Meanwhile, pension plans and other large institutions were lining up to invest in the private-equity firms' investment funds used to hunt down and buy companies.

Some of the biggest LBOs of all time took place during the boom years of 2005, 2006, and 2007. Car rental firm Hertz, technology services firm SunGard Data Systems, retailer Toys "R" Us and retailer Neiman Marcus were all bought up by private-equity firms in 2005.

The crescendo of the private-equity boom was capped off when one of the top LBO firms,

Blackstone, decided to sell stock of itself in an IPO. Individual investors saw the IPO of Blackstone as a way to get on the inside track of the world of high finance. But how wrong they were. In fact, Blackstone was selling out at the peak of the LBO craze.

The company sold shares in an IPO at $31 a share on June 22, 2007. But sadly, individual investors who bought the deal were paying up just as the LBO business was about to hit a wall. Shortly after the IPO of Blackstone, the financial crisis of 2007 hit. Suddenly, banks were too nervous to lend to LBO firms and bond investors didn't want to lend money to the speculative ventures. Shares of Blackstone fell from $31 a share to less than $5 a share in early 2009. As of early 2013, shares of the private-equity firm were still trading for less than the $31-per-share IPO price.

Why leverage is used

Private-equity firms and investment banking operations have a tight relationship because they're very mutually beneficial. Private-equity firms are constantly looking to buy and sell firms, which is exactly in the wheelhouse of investment bankers. Meanwhile, because private-equity firms rely on financial events like IPOs to exit positions, investment banks can make money on these deals when they're opened and closed.

The pros and cons to debt in deal making

Debt can be like dynamite for investment bankers and private-equity firms. When companies borrow, they can invest in new capacity or equipment using other people's money. The investment can push up profit without asking shareholders to put more money into the business. That's the upside of debt.

But debt comes with a big downside. The company must pay an interest rate to borrow the money. That interest rate is a cost that must be less than the returns being obtained from the assets bought with the debt. Also, if the interest gets too onerous and the company can't keep up with the payments, the company may be forced into bankruptcy protection.

Private business sales

Much of what investment banks do is out in the open and public. When a giant company like Softbank buys Sprint Nextel, there's no secret about it. For one thing, Sprint Nextel is a *publicly traded company,* meaning the shares are held by the public and free to trade on a public marketplace, called a *stock exchange.*

But sometimes investment banks work behind the scenes to help sell off or allow private companies to conduct sales. These deals take a bit more massaging because there are no publicly traded securities from which to glean a value of the company. When dealing with publicly traded companies, there's really no secret in terms of what price tag investors are putting on the firm. The value of a public company is its *market value,* which is the per-share stock price multiplied by the number of shares outstanding.

But with private companies, there is no objective and dispassionate way to measure the value of the company. The value is, plainly stated, a meeting of minds between what potential buyers are willing to pay and how much the seller is willing to accept.

Appreciating the rationale of private sales

It's a classic American story. A young entrepreneur invents a technology in a garage or dorm room and knows he or she is onto something big. Some entrepreneurs, like Bill Gates of Microsoft, may stick with the idea and build and expand and create a giant publicly traded company.

Other entrepreneurs, though, know that building a company takes time and a string of not just one-hit products, but several, to fend off competition. Additionally, building a company requires the ability to tap many business skills, ranging from marketing to finance, not just research and development.

For that reason, it's not uncommon for young fledgling companies with a hot technology to simply sell themselves to bigger companies that already have an organization in place to put the technology to use right away. In deals like this, investment bankers are called in to put a price tag on the company and technology being bought.

Some of these private company sales can be significant bets. In May 2013, for instance, Internet firm Yahoo! bought a young website called Tumblr for $1 billion. Tumblr, a blogging platform used to share photos and other digital musings, was a private company founded by David Karp, who was a 19-year-old high-school dropout when the company started.

Seeing where private transactions are the best choice

During the Internet boom of the late 1990s, *going public* was the ultimate goal of many companies. The dream of creating a company, selling the shares to the public and becoming instantly fabulously wealthy was the reason many Internet companies existed.

But some companies actually want to do just the opposite. There are major, short-term pressures associated with being a publicly traded company. The biggest obligation is that public companies must provide the investors a complete rundown of their financial performance during the quarter, disclosures you can read about in Chapter 7. This required disclosure is fine when the company is doing well — kind of like plastering a grade-school paper with an "A" on it on the refrigerator door.

When a company is suffering, though, and needs to make major changes in a painful restructuring, the quarterly reporting can be an exercise in humility. And this is one reason why some companies look to *going-private transactions,* where investment banks assist in allowing private investors to buy back all of a company's shares.

One classic example is computer maker Dell. The company had been struggling with slower sales of personal computers. It wanted to go private to give it the time to restructure its business. Dell's management team offered to take the company private for nearly $25 billion in a bid in early 2013. Going private would allow the company to make the necessary long-term investments (which short-term investors may not like) to make it more competitive in a world where mobile gadgets have become a big threat to traditional desktop computers and laptops.

Understanding the unique traits of private deals

IPOs may get all the attention. Splashy sales of stock to the public, such as Facebook in May 2012, grab headlines and investors sometimes line up to buy shares.

But sometimes companies raise money in more subtle and private ways. One example of a way investment banking pairs up companies and investors, away from the prying eyes of the public, is with a *private placement.* In a private placement, a company can sell stock directly to investors even if there's no public offering or shares listed on an *exchange* (a regulated marketplace for securities to be bought or sold). Companies may use private placements because they offer a few advantages:

- ✔ **Lighter regulation:** IPOs are heavily monitored by regulators. Every risk the company faces must be disclosed along with audited financials, meaning the books have to be studied by an accounting firm. But because private placements are not offered to the public, the securities don't have to be registered with the Securities and Exchange Commission (SEC). This means the company and investment banks don't have to jump through all the hoops to get the sale done.

- ✔ **Limited to sophisticated investors:** Private placements can't be offered to the general public. Instead, they must be extended only to *accredited investors* (typically, professional investors like mutual funds or high-net-worth individuals). These investors are the ones who are supposed to know how to research risky investments, or have the wherewithal and understanding to take losses.

- ✔ **Lower costs:** Because a private placement doesn't require as much regulatory oversight, the costs of putting out the offering tend to be lower. Fewer lawyers are needed because there are fewer documents to create. And there's less cost associated with investment banking, because private sales tend to be smaller and don't require the lining up of a massive group of investors to get the deal done.

Private placements may seem like a dream come true for companies. After all, who wouldn't like having fewer regulators breathing down his neck? But private placements come with their drawbacks, too. Because these offerings aren't made to as many investors, companies tend to get lower price tags on their stock than they would if they sold shares to the public. Academic studies show that companies that sell stock in private placements tend to be valued about 30 percent lower than public companies. There's also a limit to the number of private shareholders a company can have (500) before it must register with the SEC. After a company accumulates more than 500 private investors, which includes employees who get shares of the company, it must file with the SEC. Triggering this rule was a big reason Google conducted an IPO when it did, in 2004.

Initial public offerings

The IPO still remains one of the pinnacles of what a company can achieve in its early life. When a company sells stock to the general public for the first time, it's a sign that the company has a compelling enough story that it can attract outside investors to buy a piece of the company.

IPOs are a financial transaction that requires the heavy involvement of investment banks. You'll read more details about these important deals in Chapter 4.

In this section, you find out the basics of IPOs. In a traditional IPO, the investment banking operation gets involved very early. The investment bankers are critical partners in allowing a company to go public.

The lifecycle of a company: When going public makes sense

When a company is young, financing can get pretty dicey. It's not unheard of for very early investors to pay for equipment and salaries of employees with any money they can get their hands on. Charging up credit cards, hitting up family members for loans, and tapping retirement savings are all ways that an entrepreneur with the burning passion to start a company gets the process started. Starting a company takes a tremendous amount of money.

If the company proves to be successful, the options for raising money, or *financing,* grows. Prior to going public with an IPO, a growing company may consider a few options to raise money, including the following:

- **Venture capitalists:** *Venture capitalists* are investors who pool money from other investors looking for very high potential returns, and are willing to suffer huge losses in the process. Venture capitalists take the money they gather, usually from large institutions like insurance companies or pension funds, and bet money by buying stakes of young companies that have great prospects. Although many of these bets don't pan out, if the venture capitalists hit it big with a few of their bets, the returns can be huge. You don't need to invest in many Googles (which ultimately sold stock to the public in a huge payday for venture capitalists) to make the gambles worthwhile.

    Although venture capitalists can be a critical place for young companies to raise money, it comes at a steep price if the company pans out. The venture capitalists end up owning a big slice of the company, which reduces the ultimate payout for the entrepreneur.

- **Bank loans:** Commercial banks are in the business of lending to companies that need capital. Periodically, a bank may extend a line of credit to a small business, especially if the business is stable. Banks, though, tend to be skittish and won't lend if there's even a scent of risk with the company. Internet companies, which have little in the form of assets, for instance may be turned away for bank loans because there isn't anything to be used as collateral.

- **Crowdfunding:** The idea of crowdfunding is very new but likely to become more important. Currently, an entrepreneur with an idea can use websites like Kickstarter (www.kickstarter.com) to explain to the public what her idea is and how much money she needs to make it happen. Consumers interested in making the product come to life are able to pledge a dollar amount on the crowdfunding site. As soon as enough money is raised, the company can use the cash to build the product.

Crowdfunding is currently only a way for consumers to donate money to new businesses, not invest in them. Typically, these crowdfunding donors are given a token of appreciation for their contributions, usually early dibs on the product after it's released. Currently, though, companies aren't allowed to sell stock using crowdfunding. That's changing though. The 2012 Jobs Act contains a provision that opens the future to the idea of *stock-based crowdfunding* where companies can sell stock to the public. The SEC is tasked with the job of allowing companies to raise money with crowdfunding, while protecting investors.

For much more information on crowdfunding, check out *Crowdfund Investing For Dummies,* by Sherwood Neiss, Jason W. Best, and Zak Cassady-Dorion (Wiley).

There may be options for companies not ready for an IPO to raise money. But at some point, the companies with the best prospects outgrow the venture capitalists, don't want to pay the onerous terms of bank loans, or need more capital than can be raised casually. When these things happen, it's time for the company to go public. Going public is a relatively long and costly process that requires preparing statements for regulators and investors, getting the company's story out, and actually selling the shares.

IPOs tend to be lagging indicators, meaning investors are more willing to take a wager on a newly public company when the broader stock market is doing well. IPOs tend to ebb and flow quite a bit, as Table 2-2 shows.

Table 2-2	Number of U.S. IPOs, 2008–2012	
Year	*Number of U.S. IPOs*	*Proceeds Raised*
2012	128	$42.6 billion
2011	125	$36.3 billion
2010	154	$38.9 billion
2009	63	$21.8 billion
2008	31	$24.5 billion

*Source: Renaissance Capital (*www.renaissancecapital.com*)*

The role of the investment banker in IPOs

Investment bankers are involved in the very onset of a company going public, and they're the keys to making the deal happen. When investment bankers assume the role of selling securities, especially in an IPO, they're often called the *underwriters.*

A typical IPO usually follows these steps:

1. **The company produces information about its stock sale.**

   The company must give investors an extremely detailed outline of its opportunities, financial results, and risks. This filing is called the *prospectus*. Investment bankers assist in making sure the company includes all the material information investors need to know about the offering. You'll learn more about what's in the prospectus in Chapter 4.

2. **The company takes its story to the streets.**

   If companies are going to ask investors to pony up millions of dollars for the company, they're going to have to convince them to buy. That's the role of the roadshow. *Roadshows* are events and meetings investment bankers arrange between companies selling stock and prospective investors.

3. **The investment bankers gather up the investors in the book-building process.**

   The traditional IPO is a process shrouded in a bit of secrecy. During the roadshows, investment bankers get an idea of how likely it is for specific investors to buy stock, how many shares, and at what price. The investment bankers record this *indicated interest,* or general idea of how much buyers want to invest, to gauge how many shares are likely to be bought when the IPO is sold. This process of tallying up how much interest there is in the stock is called *book building*. The book-building process is critical because it tells the investment banks selling the deal at what price the shares should be sold.

4. **Underwriters price the deal.**

   Underwriters typically work late into the night before the stock starts to trade, assembling all the orders of investors. The underwriters look at all the orders for the stock and at what prices investors are interested. The underwriters then find the highest possible price at which all the shares would sell. The IPO is priced, or the initial price charged to these initial investors is set.

5. **Underwriters support the IPO.**

   The initial price of the new stock is set by the investment bankers the night before, and all the shares are sold to the initial investors. The initial investors in IPOs are typically the friends and business partners of the underwriting firms. For instance, large institutions that use the investment bank's other services are often given access to IPOs, as are wealthy individuals that may be clients of the investment banks.

   After the deal is priced, these initial investors are free to sell on the open market, in what's called *aftermarket trading*. And it's during the first day of regular trading when regular investors, customers of brokerages like TD Ameritrade and Charles Schwab of the world, are able to buy the stock.

What matters in an IPO

Underwriters stay involved in the process during this tenuous first day of trading. Investment banks want to do whatever they can to make sure the shares of the newly public company don't *break* (close below the initial price). A broken deal is often looked at negatively by investors; plus, a broken deal makes it look like the investment bank didn't set the initial price correctly.

Investment bankers try to balance the needs and wants of the buyers and sellers. If the price of the IPO zooms upward, the investors who sold their shares may feel like they were shortchanged and missed out on gains. However, if the price drops after the stock starts trading, the buyers may feel cheated and avoid that investment banking firm's deal in the future. There's also a risk that if an investment bank prices shares too high, it might need to step in and buy the shares to stop them from falling too much. On the first day of trading of Internet stock Facebook in May 2012, for instance, underwriters had to step up and buy to hold the stock from closing below the $38-per-share offering price.

Lastly, several months after the IPO has been trading, the investment bank's research unit will *initiate coverage* on the new stock. A research analyst at the bank will write a report describing the company and the stocks, advising the investment bank's clients on whether to invest in the new stock. This investment research capability of investment banks is covered in the next section as well as in Chapter 3 in greater detail.

Helping Investors Decide Whether to Buy or Sell

Investment banks make most of their money helping companies and governments raise money by selling securities. But most important, the investment bankers act as middlemen between buyers and sellers. Investment bankers not only help the sellers prepare securities to be sold, but also interact with potential investors. One of the great values offered by investment bankers to their customers selling securities is their ability to find buyers.

The importance of research

Even if there were thousands of companies lined up to sell securities, that wouldn't necessarily translate into big profits for investment banks. The fees, generated by underwriting securities, only materialize if there are ample buyers to soak up the stock being offered. And that's the role of the research unit of investment banks. By tasking research analysts with closely following developments in industries or by individual companies, the investment bank can assist investors on deciding whether to buy into securities. Chapter 3 describes this process in more detail, but here you can find out why research is so important.

Sell-side and buy-side analysts

Most large investment banks have entire research divisions that employ armies of research analysts. These research analysts pick apart the prospects of a company and tell investors whether to buy the stock. These analysts are called *sell-side analysts* because it's their job to highlight stocks they say are worthy of investment, but they don't actually invest in the stocks themselves. Sell-side analysts typically are creating research to be used by investors actually doing the buying, called *buy-side analysts*. These research reports are also often provided to individual investors who are clients of the firm for free, or sometimes made available through discount brokerage firms or for purchase.

Buy-side analysts are the ones who will be actually plunking down cash if they decide to purchase a security. These analysts consider the demands of the investors who have given them money to invest, be it mutual fund investors or pensioners with money in the pension plan. Buy-side analysts typically work for large mutual funds, which have pooled money from smaller investors to build a diversified portfolio. Buy-side analysts rely primarily on their own in-house research, which is not typically available to individual investors. Buy-side analysts, though, also use sell-side research to bolster their own insights about potential investments.

How an analyst's research can make money for investors

Investment bankers, looking to sell shares of a security they're pitching for a client raising money, will often seek out buy-side analysts to stoke demand. The buy-side analysts are the ones who decide whether the risk of a particular investment is worthwhile given the potential returns. There are massive potential conflicts of interest here, because there's the danger that the buy-side analysts at an investment bank may issue positive reports on IPOs sold by that investment bank. For that reason, sell-side analysts at investment banks that did an IPO must wait 40 days before issuing a research report on that company.

What do the analysts do?

Sell-side analysts are billed as industry experts who follow companies closely and provide insights. These professionals typically build *financial models* that tell them how much a stock is worth and what investors should be willing to pay. These financial models aren't made with plastic parts and model glue; instead, they're made from spreadsheets and quantitative analysis.

What recommendations are and why they are important

Typically, sell-side analysts provide a recommendation on a stock, on whether investors should buy, sell, or hold the shares. Most sell-side analysts also put a *price target* on the shares, putting their best guess on what the shares may be worth a year from now. Some sell-side analysts also do *channel checks* from time to time. In channel checks, the analysts find out how much demand for products there is by examining orders from end-users and customers.

How the sell side interacts with the buy side

Sell-side analysts are also often given the role of providing buy-side analysts access to the management teams of a company. Most large investment banks put on conferences or presentations that allow potential investors to hear CEOs of companies talk about the prospects of their firms.

How sell-side analysts make money for the investment bank

Research continues to be one area in which making money can be somewhat problematic. With the money-raising functions of investment baking, the ways investment banks generate fees is pretty straightforward. A company pays the investment bank a charge for handling an IPO, for instance.

Getting paid for research is a bit more elusive, though. There are some instances where buy-side investors pay an investment bank to access the research from its sell-side research team. But more often than not, research is paid for in less direct methods.

One of the most common ways that investment banking operations are paid for research is through trading commissions. Sell-side analysts try to pitch investment ideas to buy-side analysts. Instead of paying for the research reports, the buy-side analysts may instead place trades for the investment through the investment bank's trading desk. By trading through the investment bank's trading desk, the buy-side analyst's firm pays a trading commission, which acts as payment for the research services.

Digging Into the Role of the Trading Desk

Traders sitting in their living rooms with their pajamas may be the image conjured by the term *active trader*. But it turns out, a vast majority of the millions of orders to buy and sell stocks and bonds each day don't come from the keyboards of ambitious day traders, but the massive trading operations of the world's largest investment banking operations.

Most major investment banks maintain trading desks. These trading desks are responsible for buying and selling securities. The trading operations of investment banks are typically involved in buying and selling everything from stock to bonds, *futures contracts* (contracts that allow buyers to take delivery of an asset at a certain time in the future at a preset price), *commodities* (claims on real assets ranging from energy to agricultural products), and foreign exchange contracts.

The trading desk of an investment bank often sits at the epicenter of its operations. On one hand, the investment bank is tasked with selling securities to help raise money for clients; on the other hand, it's in charge of helping to find buyers. The buyers and sellers often intersect at the trading operations.

Why investment banks are into trading

Investment banks' trading operations are designed to serve several purposes. At the source, the trading operations are made to handle the demands of customers of the firm who need to purchase or unload large amounts of stock or other investments.

The trading desks of investment banks can assist customers, including pension plans and mutual funds, to build large positions in a financial asset or unload it. Investment banks, though, also trade with their own money. The investment banks attempt to use the knowledge of its employees and insights of its operations to find mispriced assets and use the information to make profits on trades.

Many investment banks get involved in trading to generate money from a variety of sources, including the following:

- **Trading financing:** Many investment banking operations lend lines of credit to other financial institutions, usually on a short-term basis. These loans can be used by the investment bank's clients who want to place trades.

- **Trade facilitation:** Companies that use big investment banks usually aren't buying or selling 100 shares of a stock. Hundreds of thousands of shares may be bought or sold by these mega players. There are so many moving parts that having an investment bank can help in the transactions, including offering insurance services where a client can be protected if there's an unforeseen drop in portfolio values. Investment banking operations often serve the role of *market maker* (a position where they buy and sell securities). As a market maker, investment banks stand ready to buy or sell lots of stock just to make sure there's adequate trading in a security.

✔ **Creating securities to be traded:** Investment banks are routinely cooking up new securities, typically those that have value based on other investment like stocks, for investors to trade. These invented securities are called *derivatives,* because they derive their value based on another asset.

How investment banks turn pennies into billions

Next time you log onto your online brokerage account to buy a stock, don't think there's a human on the other end selling to you. More likely than not, you're buying the stock from a computer that trades in and out of stocks millions of times a day.

Wall Street has been taken over by an army of computers that buy and sell stocks as easily as you may shoot down aliens in a video game. Some sources estimate that nearly 70 percent of the trading on the major stock market exchanges is being done by computer programs. These programs, often referred to as *algorithmic trading, program trading,* or *automated trading,* are a big area of interest for many investment banking operations.

Computerized trading can be used for a number of reasons, including the following:

✔ **Serving needs of clients:** Sometimes computers are employed to serve the customers of investment banks, helping them sell large positions of stock. Selling for big customers takes a bit of finesse — if all the stock is dumped at one time, the stock price can be pushed lower and cause the seller to reduce his or her own proceeds. Investment bankers have systems in place to help them sell more gradually to avoid these problems.

✔ **Part of market-making responsibilities:** Computerized trading may also be part of investment banks' role as market makers. Investment banks certainly trade to try to make a profit, looking for chances to buy and sell stocks for a gain. But in some cases investment banks can also serve a secondary role. When making a market, investment banks aren't necessarily trading to make a profit (although they probably don't complain when they do). They're the buyer of last resort, standing on the market looking to buy and sell when there are people looking to sell and buy. They're providing *liquidity.*

✔ **To make speculative bets:** Investment banking operations may look to conduct *proprietary trading,* where they trade with their own money, using their own research. These strategies get pretty obscure, with investment banks typically looking to make a fast buck when different assets are mispriced, even for a few milliseconds, relative to each other.

The type of analysis used in trading operations

Investment banks aren't very transparent about the trading they're doing — and that's no mistake. One of the greatest downsides of proprietary trading is that when other investors get wind of the strategy and start to copy it, the strategy doesn't work anymore.

Imagine that an investment bank figured out that stocks tend to soar on the first trading day of January. Talk about an easy way to make money. The trading operation would simply buy stocks on December 31 and sell them on January 1, or whatever the first day of trading is. But if the secret got out, other traders would buy stocks on December 31, too, which would spoil it for everyone. Why? The stock prices would be pushed up on December 31, essentially eliminating the January 1 pop.

Due to the value of keeping trading secrets quiet, you don't often hear what investment bankers have been doing until the strategy blows up on them. But investors can see that typically trading strategies fall into several categories, including

- **Cross-market arbitrage:** *Arbitrage* is a fancy word used to describe a situation when assets are temporarily mispriced relative to each other. These cross-market arbitrage strategies can get pretty complicated, because computers are programmed to find unexplained relative differences in price between stocks, bonds, exchange rates, and currency prices. The computers can locate mispriced assets and theoretically make risk-free trades.

- **Event arbitrage:** Some trading operations try to anticipate and place bets ahead of major market-moving events. Events that may move stocks include a company being included in the popular Standard & Poor's 500 stock market index, which is usually a boon for the stock. Another example may be a company being ripe to be bought or a small biotech firm getting approval to market a new blockbuster drug.

- **High-frequency technical trading:** Another area of trading that investment banks are turning to is a type of high-frequency trading where they take advantage of different trading speeds. It's becoming increasingly common for large trading operations to develop light-speed networks that will let them place that buy or sell order just a millisecond or less before competitors, giving them an edge. This area of trading has proved to be lucrative for many investment banking operations and one that regulators have been monitoring.

High-frequency technical trading is attracting attention from regulators. There's a concern that some investment bankers are taking advantage of the trading systems to get an unfair advantage.

Chapter 3

How Investment Bankers
Sell Companies

In This Chapter

▶ Digging into the specific tasks investment banks undertake when selling a company

▶ Finding out what's included in an IPO prospectus

▶ Identifying the keys to a successful IPO

▶ Understanding how sell-side research aids in the process of selling a stock

▶ Determining who sell-side research analysts serve

▶ Diving into a sample sell-side research report to understand its purpose

*I*nvestment banking isn't exactly a glamorous business. When was the last time you heard a 6-year-old say she wants to be an investment banker when she grows up? Much of what investment bankers do is lucrative, but it's behind the scenes and tucked in the back rooms of the financial system.

If there's an area where investment bankers really shine, it's in the process of selling a company to the public for the first time in an initial public offering (IPO). The IPO is one of the few times when the general public has a chance to see and interact with investment banks and the financial products they're selling and see the role investment bankers play in the economic machine.

We introduce the importance of the IPO in Chapter 2. In this chapter, we delve more deeply into the IPO process, taking a look at what investment banks look for when selling a company in the public markets. One of the key jobs of investment banks in bringing a company to the public markets is assisting in creating a document that spells out the details of an offering, called the *prospectus*. Here, we explore the prospectus in detail, along with the ways investment bankers can make sure an IPO goes off smoothly.

Closely linked to the IPO process is the sell-side analysis function of many investment banks. These operations help complete the process of selling the company that investment banks are often tasked with.

Also in this chapter, you get an understanding of the types of research that go into a research report. We dissect and analyze a sample report to illustrate how investment banks dig into a company's financials and prospects so they can either recommend a security or advise against it.

Getting Companies Ready for Sale on Public Markets

There comes a time in a company's life when going public is often the best option. When a company gets big enough, and a broad enough audience of investors is lined up to buy a piece of a company, it's time to strongly consider an IPO.

When a company goes public, it carves itself into pieces that investors in the general public can buy. Just about every stock you can invest in, at one point, first sold its stock in an IPO.

Companies often turn to IPOs when

- **Bank loans are too expensive.** When a company gets bigger, borrowing from the bank becomes a relatively costly form of raising money.

- **Venture capitalists are too onerous.** *Venture-capital firms* are great sources for young companies that don't have many options. But these investors insist on big ownership stakes, stripping the entrepreneur's ownership in the companies. Venture-capital funds are pools of money from private investors who are looking to hit it big.

- **Venture capitalists or other private investors want to cash out.** Venture capitalists often buy companies with the idea they they'll sell them once they get big enough to attract public investors. The IPO is a way for venture capitalists to cash in on their investment, so they can put that money into another small company. Private investors, such as private-equity firms, also urge companies to sell shares to the public so they can cash in.

- **Bonds are too expensive.** Young companies can sell bonds to raise money. But bond investors are a nervous lot, and they tend to demand high rates of return on companies that don't have a long-term, proven track record. Borrowing this way, especially for relatively unproven companies, can often be prohibitively expensive. Also, bonds must be repaid with interest. A young company may be reluctant to sign up for a deal that requires it to make routine interest payments when its cash flow may be uncertain.

After companies exhaust their normal avenues for raising money, that's when IPOs come into play. IPOs are a way for companies to get investment capital from investors, who want to be owners. These owners are happy to get a piece of the company and don't even require a routine payment of cash.

Don't think that conducting an IPO is free. Those investment bankers need to eat, too, right? IPOs do have costs, which typically involves hiring a team of investment bankers to put together all the necessary documents to appease investors and put on meetings with investors, called *roadshows*. You can read about the importance of the roadshow, to whet investors' appetites for the stock in Chapter 2. In this section, you find out about all the moving parts investment bankers may watch when selling a company's stock to the public for the first time.

Meeting the requirements to make an IPO happen

Investment bankers can concoct just about any financial product out of thin air. And some of these products indeed make investors' money go poof (as you find out in Chapter 19). But IPOs aren't created out of nothing. An IPO at its core requires a willing company that's looking to raise money by selling part of itself to willing investors.

And for an IPO to be successful — in that it attracts ample investors to pay a healthy price for the stock — the bar is even higher. A few characteristics of a company that is often a prime candidate for a successful IPO includes being in the following:

- **An industry investors are interested in:** IPO investors often get infatuated with certain investment themes. When an industry catches the attention of investors, there's usually ample appetite for several key players to go public as investors lap up the shares like hungry wolves.

  The best example of an industry that IPO investors couldn't get enough of was the Internet. During the late 1990s and early 2000s, just about any company with an *e* before its name or a dot-com after it was able to sell stock to the public and get a huge valuation. Table 3-1 shows how Internet companies ruled the IPO market in 1998 through 2000.

Table 3-1	When Internet IPOs Ruled the Market		
Year	Total Number of IPOs	Number of Internet IPOs	Percentage of IPOs That Were Internet Companies
1998	322	40	12.4%
1999	504	272	54.0%
2000	397	149	37.5%

Source: Jay Ritter, University of Florida (`http://bear.warrington.ufl.edu/ritter/ipodata.htm`)

✔ **A fast-growth period of its lifecycle:** Companies often love IPOs because they can raise money without actually agreeing to ever give that money back or even pay interest on it. IPOs can be a great deal for the company compared with other ways of raising money, which require interest payments. That said, investors are a fickle bunch. If they're not going to get paid a predictable return, they generally want the promise of something else. And that something else is usually a piece of a company with explosive growth. Investors routinely examine a company's growth rate to make sure it's expanding faster than the average company to see if it's worth investing in.

Hopes for rapid growth was one of the keys of the May 17, 2012, IPO of Internet sensation Facebook. The online social-networking company raised more than $16 billion from investors, making it the third largest U.S. IPO of all time and the biggest technology IPO ever, according to Renaissance Capital. Facebook was certainly putting up huge growth. The company posted 154 percent revenue growth in 2010 and 88 percent revenue growth in 2011. Those massive rates of growth were more than enough to get the attention of investors. But sometimes companies go public when they're peaking so they can sell their shares at a rich price. More than a year after its IPO, shares of Facebook were still below the price they fetched when they were initially sold to initial investors.

✔ **Strong competitive advantage:** If investors are going to take a risk on shares of a newly established public company, they want to make sure they're protected a bit. One way investors can feel good about their investment is betting on a company that has scarce competitors and very high *barriers to entry* (meaning, it would be costly for a competitor to take on the company in the product marketplace).

Many massive IPOs fit this category. Visa and UPS are the no. 1 and no. 11 largest U.S. IPOs ever, having raised $17.9 billion and $5.5 billion, respectively. Both of these companies really only have a handful of serious competitors and are protected by the fact that massive investments in equipment would be needed for anyone to even dream about taking them on.

Writing the prospectus

The most important document the company and the investment bankers must produce to make an IPO happen is the prospectus. The prospectus is the massive document that lists all the opportunities, risks, and financial details about the company that's selling stock to the public. It's available to investors, regulators, and other interested parties.

For most IPOs, the prospectus can be an immense document that spans hundreds if not thousands of pages. Creating the document is one of the major tasks that investment bankers are paid to do when bringing an IPO to market. The prospectus typically contains a wealth of information that falls into several key sections, which we outline in this section.

Summary

At the top of a prospectus, the investment bankers lay out the main details an investor should be concerned with. Here, in the summary section, investors learn about the company's intentions from the deal. Of most interest to investors — and investment bankers — is how many shares the company plans to sell and at what price.

In this part of the prospectus, investment bankers also try to demonstrate why the company is looking to sell stock. It's pretty typical for the investor to get a taste of the size of the company's target market. The summary is also a common place for the company's management team to lay out their broad objectives for the company.

Risk factors

If there is a "cover yourself" section of a prospectus, it's the risk factors area. In this part of the prospectus, the company and its investment bankers warn investors of all the possible things that could go wrong and cause the value of the new stock to crumble. Investment bankers may not list the risk of a zombie invasion, but they list just about everything else.

Here, companies are practically preparing their "I told you so" defense in case the stock doesn't work out. You'll find references to just about anything that could possibly happen in this section, along with loads of canned, boilerplate warnings that appear to be cut-and-pasted from filings.

Although most of the risk factors are boilerplate, you can find some gems in there. This can be an area on which investment bankers spent quite a bit of time, so pay attention.

Industry data and other metrics

Just as a rising tide lifts all boats, investors know that companies are often only as good as the industries they're in. If you invest in a grocery store company, investors know to expect relatively thin profit margins (meaning, the company will likely only retain a small slice of its total revenue as profit, because that's how the industry works).

And because the performance of the industry has such a large bearing on how well a company does, it's a critical aspect of the prospectus. Investors will find a description of the financial measures that are most important in the industry, as well as an outline of how the company going public stacks up.

Use of proceeds

When a company goes public, it can raise hundreds of millions if not billions of dollars overnight. Literally. Isn't capitalism wonderful? But hopefully the money isn't being raised so the CEO can throw a heck of a party or buy a billion black hoodies. The money being generated by the IPO is for some sort of corporate purpose, and it's in this section of the prospectus that this purpose is revealed to investors.

Normally, a young company going public is raising money because it needs cash to expand and grow. But there are other reasons why a company may go public, including to pay off part of its debt, to purchase another company, or to allow its employees to sell their shares and raise money. Whatever the reason, it must be outlined in detail here.

IPO investors usually look askance at IPOs where the money raised isn't being used by the company. Investors are especially skeptical when many of the shares being sold in an IPO are being sold not by the company itself, but by the CEO and other company executives. After all, these insiders know the company better than anyone. If they're bailing out, why would investors with less information jump in?

Capitalization

The capitalization structure of a company is critical to IPO investors. The *capitalization structure* is a description of the types of financing that were used by the company to raise money. The typical company has a blend of forms of financing ranging from bank loans to outstanding bond debt and perhaps *preferred stock* (a special type of stock that typically pays a supersized dividend and has greater claims to the company than the regular, *common stock* that's issued by companies).

Financial data

Some hard-core financial types skip past many of the sections of the prospectus listed earlier and go straight for this part. Here's where you find the company's *financial statements* (detailed financial records that show how much the company made in profit and revenue, as well as everything it owns and owes). You can find more information about these financial statements, including the income statement and balance sheet, in Chapter 7.

Management's discussion and analysis of financial condition

Wow, that's a mouthful. But that's the section's official name. Most investment bankers refer to this important section of the prospectus by its acronym, MD&A. It's in this section of the prospectus that the company's management team, with the help of the investment bank, steps through the financial statements, almost line-by-line, with full description. Any numbers that are a little offbeat or unusually large or small should be detailed in this section.

Business

If investors are seriously considering forking over money to buy a piece of a company, they'd better know at least what the company does. The business section of the prospectus is the place where the company explains its reason for being. The company often explains the products it makes or the services it provides and why customers deem them worthy to be bought.

Management

A company is only as good as the people running the place. And that's not a detail missed by IPO investors. The management team of a young company is critical. Decisions made by the top brass will largely determine if the company is able to head off the inevitable challenges. In the management section of the prospectus, you find a listing of all the top management team members — usually the chief executive officer (CEO), chief operating officer (COO), chief financial officer (CFO), and the members of the *board of directors* (the group of experts who are supposed to look out for the interests of investors and oversee the management). In the management portion of the prospectus, you also find a short biography on all the top people at the company, including their ages. Want to feel old? Facebook CEO Mark Zuckerberg was just 27 according to the company's prospectus when the company was going public.

Executive pay

The CEO and other members of the management team aren't running the company you're looking to invest in out of the goodness of their hearts. The managers of top companies are paid, usually huge sums of money, for taking on the job. In this section of the prospectus, investors find out exactly how much these people are being paid.

Reading the executive pay of CEOs can be like trying to solve some kind of financial puzzle. These top executives get paid in all sorts of ways, not just a base salary but a tangled quilt of bonuses and stock-based pay. Getting bogged down in the details is easy. Luckily, regulators have leaned on companies and forced them to simplify the way they explain executive pay. If you just want to get an idea of what the CEO was paid, head for the *summary compensation table,* where you find each executive listed along with his or her salary, bonus, stock awards, and all other pay listed clearly.

Related-party transactions

Double-dealing may be typical in mystery novels, but that's exactly the kind of thing you don't want going on at a company you're looking to invest in. The trouble with IPOs, though, is that many of these companies trace their roots to being practically family business. Many young companies, even after going public, may have complicated business relationships between founders, their families or friends. All these tangled dealings must be highlighted and explained as *related-party transactions.*

Principal and selling shareholders

When you buy shares of an IPO, you're buying those shares from someone. If a company is private, it doesn't have to tell anyone who its investors are. But when a company seeks to raise money from the public, in an IPO, the rules of disclosure get really strict. As an investor, you have the right to know who is selling. Most of the time, the shares of a company are being issued by the company itself. But in some cases, you'll see selling by early investors — often venture capitalists — who want to cash out of the investment. If you see lots of insiders selling, that generally isn't a good sign.

Underwriting

When you're in school, you want to see your name on the perfect attendance list or maybe the dean's list. But when you're an investment banker, the goal is to be part of the underwriting list on as many IPOs as possible. When a company goes public, it must list all the investment banks and advisors that helped bring the shares to market. For big IPOs, the list can be a long one and is often a who's who of investment banks.

Legal matters

If you want to get sued, one of the best ways to make it happen is to start a business. Companies of all sizes are constant targets of lawsuits, and young companies looking to go public are no exception. Most of these suits are nuisances or minor, but periodically outstanding litigation can be significant, especially if it pertains to the product or service being sold. This section of the prospectus must outline any pending suits against the company. The company itself usually gives a little bit of commentary on how significant it thinks the litigation is.

Supporting the IPO: Making success last

When IPOs fail, it makes investment bankers look bad. If shares of an IPO can't stay above the *offering price* (the price at which the shares are sold to initial investors) it reflects poorly on the investment bankers. After all, if the shares were priced too high, that meant that the investors overpaid or the investment banker didn't understand the business well enough. When a stock starts to trade on an exchange, such as the New York Stock Exchange, following the IPO that's called *aftermarket trading.* If the price of the IPO, in aftermarket trading, falls below the offering price, it's called a *broken deal.* Not good for investment bankers or investors.

And that's why keeping a company on the right track, even after its IPO, is viewed as part of the responsibility of the investment banker. To be clear, the investment banker can't do anything to change the way the company is being run — that's up to the management team of the company. Still, there are levers that the investment bankers can pull to keep the IPO working for all parties, at least in the very short term.

Holding the insiders hostage with lockups

Just about the last thing IPO investors want to see is all sorts of selling by officers and directors the second after a company goes public. Think of it this way: Stock prices are set by supply and demand. If after a company goes public, employees and officers start dumping their stock, the market will be swamped with a supply of stock and push down the price of the shares. This unleashing of supply could create an avalanche of selling, not to mention spook investors by the strong negative signal it sends.

To prevent this downward spiral, investment bankers help companies create a *lockup period* (a set period of time during which the officers and directors are prohibited from selling shares). Lockup periods come in all types and can be customized by the company and its investment bankers.

Modern IPOs are increasingly using a style of lockup period that expires gradually over time. Usually, the investment banks want to lock up all insider sales for at least 90 days after the IPO to give the fledgling stock a good period of time to find a natural equilibrium between buyers and sellers. After 90 days, the first group of insiders will get the green light to sell. After that first lockup comes off, another group of shares may be released after 180 days and another group after 365 days. By spacing out the lockup expiration dates like this, the investment bankers can somewhat control the flow of stock into the market.

Quiet periods

Regulators get a bit touchy when companies start looking to sell stock to the public for the first time. Securities regulations are in place to curb any activities that will fool investors into buying investments where the sellers know they're a bust. Regulators and investment bankers work together to control the information that a company and its officers parse out to investors prior to an IPO and right after it's done.

A company is prohibited from engaging in promotional activity to push up the value of its IPO, usually prior to the IPO and up to three months afterward. Investment bankers, too, must watch what they say and stick to the facts and not use promotion. It's a fine line, for sure. After all, part of the IPO process includes *roadshows* (visits with potential investors). Talking about the IPO or the company is not illegal. In fact, it's essential — full disclosure is the point of the IPO process. But the key is that the company and investment bankers can't get promotional and make misleading promises about the company's prospects.

Follow-on and secondary offerings

Raising money from the capital market can be like plastic surgery in Hollywood: Once someone gets started, it can be hard to stop. Similarly, once a company raises money from investors by selling stock to the public, that's usually not the end of the process.

Companies, with the help of their investment bankers, can come back another time to raise money with a *follow-on offering*. During a follow-on offering, companies can sell additional shares to the public. These offerings can generate more capital for the company, which may help it turbocharge its growth. But in the process, the company is also creating new shares and selling them. And when the additional shares hit the market, they *dilute* the value of the existing shares, or make them worth less because the company is carved into more pieces. The underwriter is closely involved in these follow-on offerings.

The word *dilution* is like poison with investors. Any move by a company that increases the number of shares and reduces the value of each share is typically frowned upon by existing investors.

Another time additional shares may go to market is in a *secondary offering*. Secondary offerings allow significant current investors to sell their shares in an organized fashion, after the IPO. Secondary offerings are not dilutive because no new shares are created. The shares existed before — they were just held by insiders. Insiders are simply selling shares they had before.

Seeing What Sell-Side Analysts Do

When companies decide to go public, there's no shortage of investment bankers who are lining up to get the job. The fees associated with underwriting an IPO can be significant, so just about every investment banking firm would be happy to get the piece of the deal.

Because of the intense competition for deals to bring companies public, investment bankers often have to sweeten the pot and pitch all the support they can provide to the deal.

One thing nobody wants to happen, and that includes companies and investment bankers, is for the IPO to break, or fall below the offering price. Companies worry that if they become just one of the thousands of stocks available for trading, they may get lost in the Wall Street shuffle.

One way investment bankers allay this concern is by offering aftermarket research support. Most large investment banking operations employ teams of sell-side analysts who research companies, including many of the ones that the investment bank brought public, and produce reports to tell investors if the stock is worth a look.

The goals of the sell-side analyst

The sell-side analyst at a firm that does investment banking has a somewhat complicated job. Their primary job is to use *fundamental analysis* (the ability to determine the value of a company examining the details of the business) to help investors decide whether to invest. But here's where things get complicated. Sell-side analysts are writing about companies that just so happen to be some of the investment bank's best clients and generate large fee income from IPOs, mergers, or follow-on offerings.

Given the conflicts that sell-side analysts face, it's important to understand the roles that these professionals serve, including the following:

- ✔ **Protecting new stocks from being lost and forgotten:** When a company goes public, it's suddenly in competition with thousands of other publicly traded companies. There are massive companies with huge market values, like Microsoft and Exxon Mobil, in addition to small and midsize companies. Investors have no shortage of choices when it comes to finding stocks to buy.

Reminding investors to take a look at a newly public company is one role of the sell-side analyst. By providing *research coverage* on a newly public company, the sell-side analyst is drawing attention to that stock. And having analyst coverage from a major Wall Street firm is a way for a company to avoid being an *orphan* (forgotten stock) with investors.

✔ **Performing surveillance for investors:** Pity the poor mutual fund manager. These buy-side investors need to scour Wall Street for the very best investments that will help them beat the market and justify the fees they charge their investors. But even for large mutual funds, with sizeable teams of analysts, doing in-depth research on every stock out there is virtually impossible. That's why buy-side investors often look to the sell-side analysts for help. The sell-side analysts are laser focused on a somewhat limited universe of stocks. This specialization helps them establish an expertise in certain industries. Their research summarizes the risks and opportunities of a certain company, saving the buy-side investors lots of time and potential mistakes. Reports from sell-side analysts may highlight stocks that buy-side investors weren't even following or aware of. Buy-side analysts rely mostly on their own research, but sell-side research might be something they would consider, too.

✔ **Highlighting anomalies:** Because sell-side analysts are so focused on certain companies, they're able to pinpoint stocks that may be attractive, but overlooked, because other investors aren't paying attention to the full story. Sell-side analysts can afford the time to really dig into a company and see, for instance, that revenue may have fallen not due to a problem with the business, but because it sold off a business unit.

What investors look to sell-side analysts for

Sell-side analysts are the line into the company for some investors. Sell-side analysts take the time to read the reports companies put out and listen into all the earnings conference calls, where the management teams discuss the performance of their company during the previous three months.

And for that reason, investors have some pretty high demands of their sell-side analysts, including the following:

✔ **Research reports:** The primary product from sell-side analysts is the research report. These reports (covered in more detail in the "Examining a Sample Research Report" section, later in this chapter) are where sell-side analysts spell out everything they know about the company and communicate their findings to investors.

✔ **Instant updates:** Following any big news from a company, investors expect sell-side analysts to be on top of the development. Instant updates are rapid dispatches from the sell-side analysts explaining what the takeaway from the new development is and whether it changes their opinion on the stock.

✔ **Industry analysis:** Although sell-side analysts primarily concern themselves with individual companies, most recognize the importance of industry factors. Many top sell-side analysts produce an industry analysis where they look at the larger forces at play in the industry and how they could affect companies within the industry.

Spreading the word: Disseminating sell-side research

Research doesn't do anyone any good if it's just sitting on an investor's shelf. Getting the word out, and sharing research ideas, are how sell-side analysts get noticed. When sell-side analysts make a name for themselves, they often draw attention to their firms. Sometimes a sell-side analyst gets so well known in an industry that companies looking to go public look to the firm as an underwriter. It's much how real-estate agents who focus on specific neighborhoods often win many of the listings in that area.

The dangers of conflicts

Sell-side analysts have to walk a fine line between serving the wants of the companies going public and the demands of investors who rely on the research being accurate and truthful. This divide is so blurred that periodically an analyst or firm steps over it.

Perhaps the biggest crackdown in the failure of investment banks to preserve the integrity of their research reports came in 2003. The Securities and Exchange Commission (SEC) and other regulators penalized ten of the largest investment banks at the time for conflicts of interest between their investment banking units and their research teams. This incident is covered in more detail in Chapter 19. For now, just know that regulators found that the investment

banks were more interested in currying favor with companies looking to go public, and generate big IPO fees, than providing helpful and accurate information to investors. And huge changes were made to the research business as a result. For instance, research analysts were no longer allowed to join in any pitches (including at the roadshows) to get investment banking business.

Two analysts, Jack Grubman and Henry Blodget, formerly of Salomon Smith Barney and Merrill, Lynch respectively, were personally named in the global settlement. Both were fined and permanently barred from the securities business.

Investment banks get out the research from their sell-side analysts in a number of ways, including through the following:

- ✔ **Thebroker network:** Most of the large firms with investment banking operations — the Bank of Americas and Morgan Stanleys of the world — employ armies of brokers around the globe. These brokers provide investment help and guidance to clients. The brokers often refer to the research of sell-side analysts when making investment recommendations.

- ✔ **Buy-side connections:** Big mutual funds and other institutions tend to have ongoing relationships with certain large investment banks. It's a tangled relationship with the buy-side investors looking to the investment banks as a source of all sorts of services, including trading and research. Big investment banks typically forward all their research to these large customers.

- ✔ **Electronic distribution:** As more individual investors try their hand at picking stocks themselves, there's been increased demand for them to obtain sell-side research. Most of the large online brokerage firms, including TD Ameritrade and Charles Schwab, provide research reports from some of the big investment banking operations.

Examining a Sample Research Report

Research reports aren't exactly the kinds of things you start reading and can't put down. J. K. Rowling probably doesn't worry much about competing with the latest research report on IBM from a major investment bank. That said, oodles of important information about a company can be stuffed into a research report. And knowing how to read research reports has elements of both art and science.

What to look for in the document

Research reports don't have to follow a specific formula. Analysts at different investment banks have some latitude in determining the look and feel of their reports. But more often than not, research reports follow a certain protocol of what investors expect them to look like.

Many of the research reports from major research organizations follow somewhat of a pattern that contain key elements, making them easy for investors to find information they need. Figure 3-1 is a reprint of the first page of a research report from S&P Capital IQ.

To be clear, S&P Capital IQ is not an investment bank, but a well-known and independent provider of stock research. What S&P Capital IQ provides is technically *independent equity research,* not sell-side research, because the company doesn't do any investment banking. Still the format of S&P Capital IQ's reports adhere to industry standards and are illustrative for that reason.

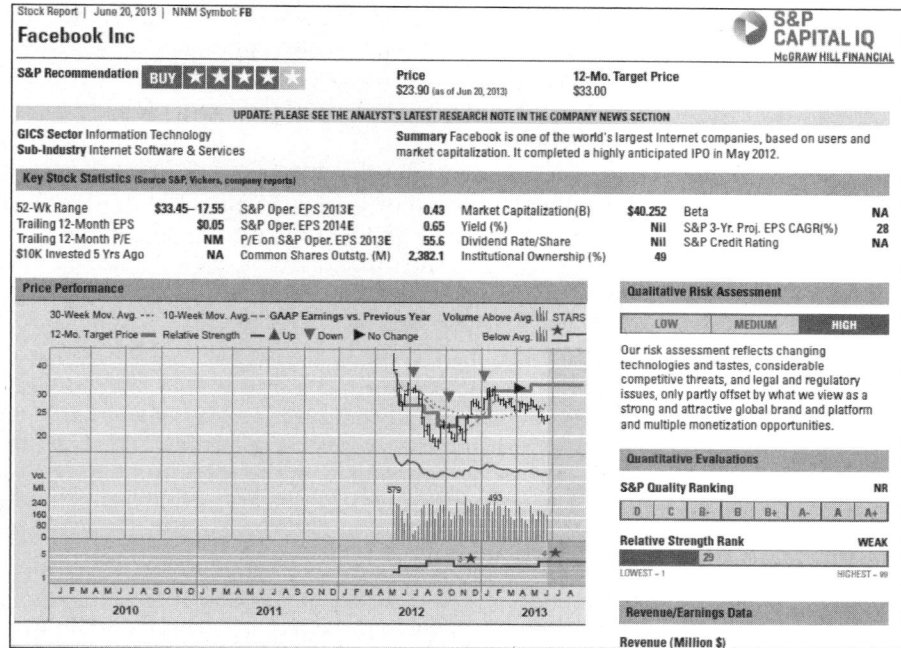

Figure 3-1: A page of a research report from S&P Capital IQ.

Courtesy of S&P Capital IQ

The main sections of a research report

Investors are busy people. They don't have the time to read through a research report that buries the findings and disguises the analysts' decisions. Research reports are designed to be highly functional and percolate to the top the information that's most important so investors can find it quickly.

Again, there's no standard or required format for research reports to follow. But most of the time, they contain a number of key elements, including the following:

✔ **Recommendation:** Analysts don't hide how they feel about stocks. Right at the top of most research reports is the *recommendation,* typically a phrase that tells investors what the analysts think about buying the investment. Most analysts use one of the following terms: "strong buy," "buy," "hold," "sell," or "strong sell."

Many beginning investors tend to place too much emphasis on the recommendation. Sure, it's easy to just see if the analyst rates the stock a "strong buy" and then run out and buy it. But savvy investors know that most of the value of the research report is in the analysis of the company and the industry, and they don't blindly follow the recommendation.

✔ **Price target:** If you visit a research analyst's office, you may expect to find a crystal ball. Most analysts make a bold prediction of where they think the stock could be trading in the future, usually 12 months from the time of the report. The price target is usually derived using different techniques, some of which are covered later in this book, including discount cash-flow analysis.

✔ **Key statistics:** Buy-side analysts use research reports to save them time. Many investors are looking for quick, at-a-glance information to help them get a feel for a company's future. The key statistics portion of a research report typically gives investors a summary of all the numerical data points that matter, ranging from the stock price to financial ratios such as price-to-earnings ratios. In this area of the report, you'll also find the analyst's forecast of the company's future earnings, a key part of creating a price target.

✔ **Highlights/summary:** Research reports can get lengthy, sometimes spanning ten pages or even more if it contains in-depth information about the industry. The highlights or summary area attempts to boil all this information down to the bare essentials.

✔ **Investment opinion:** In the investment opinion area, the analyst gets some room to expound a bit on the rationale behind the recommendation. If the stock is a strong buy, the analyst makes a case for that recommendation in the investment opinion section.

✔ **Business summary:** Believe it or not, some investors just know companies by the trading symbol. In this part of the report, analysts usually show investors that the investment is backed by a company that generates profits and earnings. The business is summarized in this portion of the report so investors can understand the key drivers of the company.

✔ **Ratio analysis and financials:** One of the best ways for investors to really dig into a company to see if it's a good investment is by using ratio analysis. Dozens of critical financial ratios help investors assess the value and trajectory of a company. You can find out how to calculate these ratios yourself in Chapter 8. But you can save yourself some trouble, too, because most analysts calculate many of the key ratios for you in this section.

✔ **Industry outlook:** One of the influences on the profitability of a company is the industry that it's in. Stocks in the grocery-store industry, for instance, typically keep a small portion of revenue as profit, while technology companies that make software and Internet services tend to keep a much higher percentage of their revenue. This part of the research report explains the industry and goes into what bearing that line of business has for the company.

Ways to look beyond the "buy" or "sell"

Sell-side analysts working at firms that do investment banking sometimes get looked at somewhat suspiciously. There's a concern, sometimes warranted, that the sell-side research analysts are being overly bullish on companies because they're clients of the firm. And in the past, such wrongdoing has been found.

But ignoring the work of sell-side analysts, simply because of a risk of conflict is a mistake. ***Remember:*** Sell-side analysts have the time to really dig into a company. Most sell-side analysts also follow several companies in the industry so they can spot broad trends that have ramifications on short-term movements of the stocks.

Anyone who uses the research coming out of investment banks can put these reports to best use by

✔ **Focusing on everything but the recommendation:** Sure, it's easy to just look at the front page of a report and scan for the buy or sell. But doing so leaves out much of the most valuable information sell-side analysts provide. Look at how the price target is arrived at. What assumptions is the analyst making? The thinking behind the recommendation is more valuable than the recommendation itself.

Sell-side analysts are often criticized for never meeting a company they didn't like and have a "buy" rating on seemingly every company in existence. And it's true that sell-side analysts traditionally rank many more companies as strong buys than strong sells. That's just a natural bias of the industry that anyone working with the investment banking industry needs to keep in mind. Also, remember that sell-side analysts rarely call stocks a "sell." With many analysts, *hold* is actually the euphemistic term for "sell."

✔ **Not overlooking independent research:** Although large Wall Street firms with giant investment banking operations dominate research, they're not alone. There are firms, like S&P Capital IQ and Morningstar, that generate research that aren't connected with any investment banking. Compare the opinions of independent analysts with those of sell-side analysts to see where they differ.

✔ **Concentrating on larger industry analysis reports:** Many leading sell-side analysts periodically (sometimes once a year) put out monstrous reviews of an industry. These reports are usually the best work many analysts put out. Because the reports are broad, the analysts don't have to be as mindful about potentially upsetting companies that happen to be big clients of the firm. These reports also give the analysts more freedom to share their insights about the business. And don't overlook the research from *boutique investment banking firms,* which typically focus on a narrow number of industries. These firms can share profound insights about an industry you don't want to miss.

Chapter 4

How Investment Banking Is Used in Mergers and Acquisitions

. . . .

In This Chapter

▶ Understanding the thinking behind the decision for firms to buy rivals

▶ Seeing what kinds of firms make good acquisitions targets

▶ Finding out how hostile acquisitions differ from friendly ones

▶ Analyzing M&A deals and understanding the nuances of what makes them work

▶ Understanding why some M&A deals fail

. . . .

*B*uyers and sellers of companies engage the services of investment banking experts to try to make sure that in any mergers and acquisitions (M&A) transaction, a fair deal is struck. In this chapter, we tell you how investment banking is used to source potential business combinations and how price tags are put on a company that is being acquired. We examine why some firms want to be acquired and try to make themselves more attractive to potential suitors and why other firms don't want to be acquired and actually try to make themselves less attractive to suitors. Finally, we show you why some business combinations are wildly successful and others fail miserably.

Come Here Often? The Basics of Mergers and Acquisitions

The basic goal of all M&A activity is value creation and growth. The rationale behind M&A activity is that the acquiring firm can more efficiently achieve value creation through acquisition rather than organic growth. Underlying nearly all M&A activity is the premise that some form of synergy exists in the transaction. *Synergy* is simply explained as 1 + 1 = 3. That is, the two firms combined are worth more than either firm is worth alone.

The premise behind M&A is that the combined firm is worth so much more than the two firms separately that the acquiring firm can even pay a substantial premium for the target firm and still realize a value increase. That's the theory. Unfortunately, in practice, synergy isn't always borne out, and acquisitions aren't always successful.

Kinds of mergers

Fundamentally, there really is no difference between a *merger* and an *acquisition.* Both terms refer to a situation in which two companies combine and become one company. Typically, a transaction is referred to as a *merger* if it's a combination of equals — that is, if both firms are approximately the same size — and if both parties agree to the combination. A transaction is typically referred to as an *acquisition* when a larger entity buys a much smaller entity or when the decision to combine is not mutual (in which case, it's referred to as a *takeover*).

There are three basic kinds of mergers — horizontal, vertical, and conglomerate, referring to the business relationship between the two parties. Understanding the different kinds of mergers gives you insight into the motivations behind mergers.

Horizontal mergers

A *horizontal merger* is one in which a firm acquires another firm in its same industry and with similar or compatible product lines. Horizontal mergers often result in the combined firm having a more complete product line and often provide greater geographic coverage with the products. A horizontal merger may also allow the combined firm to realize *economies of scale* — that is, cost per unit of output declines as output increases.

Firms such as ExxonMobil, ChevronTexaco (now called Chevron), and ConocoPhillips are all examples of firms created as the result of horizontal mergers in the petroleum industry. The merger of Daimler-Benz and Chrysler is an example of a horizontal merger in the automobile industry.

Horizontal mergers are the most scrutinized for potential antitrust violations by the U.S. Department of Justice, because the combination of former competitors can serve to restrict competition and raise prices to the consumer.

Vertical mergers

A *vertical merger* takes place when two companies combine that previously sold to or bought goods from each other. A manufacturer may merge with a supplier of parts or producer of raw materials, or it may merge with a retailer who sells the products of the firm.

The goal of a vertical merger is not necessarily to grow or increase revenue, but to cut costs and realize a higher profit margin. Another reason for a vertical merger is to ensure that you have access to needed supplies in the production process.

One of the largest and most infamous vertical mergers (infamous because it was disastrous for Time Warner shareholders) took place when Internet provider America Online (AOL) merged with publisher Time Warner. This was considered a vertical merger because Time Warner produced content and AOL distributed content through its Internet service. Another example of a vertical merger involves the recent trend of both Coca-Cola and PepsiCo acquiring their bottling companies.

Conglomerate mergers

A *conglomerate merger* occurs when two companies with completely unrelated businesses combine. The primary motivation for a conglomerate merger is to diversify the firm and decrease risk. The idea is that when one part of the business is performing poorly, a completely unrelated business may be thriving. If the profits of the separate businesses are not highly *correlated* — that is, their sales don't tend to move together — then the earnings stream of the combined business will be more stable.

There are many examples of very profitable conglomerate firms, with General Electric perhaps being the poster child for a successful conglomerate because GE produces everything from refrigerators to jet engines. An example of a conglomerate merger was the combination of ABC and the Walt Disney Company.

Why companies merge instead of simply growing organically

Although there are only three basic kinds of mergers (see the previous section), firms have many motivations for seeking to combine with other firms. Some reasons are very sound and seek to maximize the value of the entity for its owners, while others are less so. In this section, we cover a variety of motives for firms to merge with other firms.

For synergy

As we explain earlier, *synergy* is defined as 1 + 1 = 3, but how are synergies realized? If a bank acquires another bank, the combined entity can eliminate duplicate branches in the same local markets. In this manner, it maintains the same customers and has a lower cost structure. The same logic exists for mergers in which the combined firm has a much more complete product line. For instance, when two car companies merge, the dealers can sell the vehicles of both firms and duplicative dealerships can be closed down, or when a soft-drink producer merges with a fast-food chain, an outlet for the product is secured. In the "Overstated synergies" section, later in this chapter, we explain that many synergies are illusory.

For speed

Growing organically is tough and takes patience. It's often quicker and more of a sure thing to buy growth via an acquisition than to patiently grow a business the good old-fashioned way. A company may not know how successful it will be in organically growing a business, but it knows exactly what it's buying in an acquisition — or at least it thinks it does.

Achieving organic growth is particularly challenging in industries that are in very mature stages, such as the petroleum industry. Growing organically is very difficult in some industries, and the acquisition route may represent the only viable option to achieve rapid growth.

For increased market power

Mergers can result in increased market power. In particular, in a horizontal merger, there is less competition following the merger, so the combined firm will likely have more pricing power. In fact, many horizontal mergers are closely scrutinized for antitrust violations for precisely this reason — because they can dampen competition. On the other hand, in vertical mergers, the result is less supply-chain uncertainty and a likely increase in product quality because the firm has more control over its supplies.

To gain access to foreign markets

Crossing borders can be very difficult for many businesses, and one of the easiest ways for a company to quickly and effectively access foreign markets is to merge with a firm from a different country. Crossing borders can be very difficult for a variety of reasons, most notably regulatory and cultural concerns, but merging with an existing firm can skirt many of those issues.

The creation of Latam Airlines Group — the result of a 2012 merger between Brazil's TAM Airlines and Chile's LAN Airlines — is an example of two firms merging to access markets beyond their home countries.

Because of the management's own interests

One of the dirty little secrets of merger activity is that some mergers are realized because it's in the best interests of the management — and not necessarily in the best interests of the shareholders — to merge and create a larger company. The fact is, bigger organizations pay their CEOs more than smaller organizations' leaders are paid. Size of the firm really does matter when it comes to CEO pay. And it isn't just CEO pay, but the pay of the entire executive team. Not surprisingly, CEOs seek to increase their compensation and influence by building a bigger empire.

To diversify

The primary motivation for conglomerate mergers is diversification and reduction of risk. If a *cyclical firm* (one that tends to see its profits rise and fall with the business cycle) acquires a *counter-cyclical firm* (one that tends to see its profits rise when the broad economy falters), for instance, the profit stream of the combined firms should be more stable.

For example, if an upscale restaurant chain acquires a staple food producer, the revenues of the upscale restaurant chain will be up when the business cycle is booming and will be down when the business cycle is depressed. The revenue streams of the combined firms should counterbalance each other to some degree and result in a more stable firm-wide income across the business cycle.

Diversification may be a good motivation for the management of a company but it isn't necessarily a good motive from the standpoint of the owners of the firm, those pesky shareholders. A conglomerate merger actually reduces the investor's ability to make choices among firms. For instance, say you're very bullish about the prospects of the firm producing staple foods and bearish concerning the prospects of the restaurant chain. If those two firms were to enter into a conglomerate merger, you couldn't invest only in the segment that produces the staple foods — instead, you could only invest (or not invest) in the entire combined firm. Reduction of risk may be good for the management of the firm, but it isn't good for the shareholders or their set of investment choices. In fact, the business combination reduces the investor's investment opportunity set.

For tax considerations

Some mergers take place because it simply makes good sense from a tax perspective. Specifically, if a firm has accumulated large tax losses, it may make an attractive acquisition target by a firm with a large tax bill. The combined firm will have a lower tax bill than the two separate firms. In addition, a firm that is able to increase its depreciation charges following an acquisition will save in taxes. These tax savings should result in an increase in firm value.

Rarely will a merger take place solely for the purpose of realizing tax savings, but it is a contributing factor.

For greater control

Many companies are acquired because the acquirer believes that there is hidden value in the assets of the acquired firm that can be unlocked if it gains control. In other words, the company is mismanaged and the new management team can turn the enterprise around. If a company truly is being mismanaged, the value of the assets is not being maximized. If those assets can be acquired at a depressed price that reflects the current use of the assets, and the acquirer can make more effective use of those assets, then the hidden value of the assets can be realized through a change in control.

You often hear about a firm being acquired for less than breakup value. In an *efficient market,* where stock prices reflect all publicly known information about a company, how can that happen? What that essentially means is that the value of the assets if the company is broken up and sold is greater than the market value of the firm as an ongoing entity. This kind of apparent under-valuation by the market is completely rational if the current management is squandering the use of the company's assets.

To capitalize on untapped borrowing capacity

Everyone has heard the saying "Capital is king," so simply having access to capital must be a member of the royal family. A source of hidden value is unused borrowing capacity. A firm may be an attractive takeover candidate if it has little or no debt on its balance sheet. An acquiring firm could acquire the assets of the firm and utilize the previously untapped borrowing capacity to acquire much needed capital and expand even further. If the firm can make more on the borrowed funds than those funds cost, it will realize an increase in value and add to the combined firm's return on equity, making both the shareholders and the management happy.

Firms that make attractive acquisition targets

The most attractive acquisition targets will have more than one of the qualities cited in the previous section. For instance, it would seem that an ideal target would be a mismanaged firm with significant unused debt capacity operating at either marginal profitability or at a loss and with unused tax credits. The belief is that the acquiring firm can acquire the company at a depressed price and subsequently improve the management of the firm and realize synergistic benefits that will improve profitability. The previously unused debt capacity can be tapped to increase the return on equity to the shareholders of the acquirer. If there are tax losses, those tax losses can be used to offset the profitability of the acquiring firm and lower the tax bill of the combined entity.

There is no single blueprint for the ideal acquisition candidate. An acquiring firm has specific requirements that are unique to its particular situation — and those requirements will vary from firm to firm. Before looking for acquisition targets, the acquiring firm should have in mind what it's trying to accomplish via the transaction — what its overall strategy is in relation to the acquisition. The firm can, with the help of its investment bankers, develop an acquisition profile or wish list of the criteria for an ideal acquisition candidate.

How companies identify firms to merge with

Typically, companies work with investment bankers to create an *acquisition profile* (a description of a firm that would be the ideal target). After that profile has been created, the investment bankers work with the firm to identify potential acquisition targets via several avenues:

- ✔ If a potential target firm is publicly traded, getting information from large databases and public filings is fairly easy.

- ✔ If a potential target is not publicly traded, a great deal of information about the firm is likely still publicly available via a search of industry publications, company websites, and news reports.

- ✔ Third-party reports, particularly those related to industry analysis, can also be helpful.

- ✔ If an industry is one that makes use of patents, an analysis of patents granted can provide promising leads.

- ✔ Both the investment bankers and firm principals likely have many personal contacts in the industry of interest. Tradeshows and industry conferences are terrific networking venues; many mergers were merely ideas that germinated at these events.

Any or all these means may be utilized to identify potential acquisition candidates.

Doing M&A Buffett-style

Famed investor Warren Buffett often goes about both his life and business a little unconventionally, and his identification of potential acquisition targets is no exception. Buffett makes public his acquisition profile by publishing it in the Berkshire Hathaway annual report to shareholders and has been doing so for many years. He basically advertises for principals from firms to come shopping their firms to Berkshire for potential sale, and he has been very successful with this unique strategy. In Berkshire Hathaway's 2012 annual report, Mr. Buffett stated that acquisition candidates should

- ✔ Be large purchases (with at least $75 million of pre-tax earnings)

- ✔ Be able to demonstrate consistent earning power

- ✔ Earn good returns on equity while employing little or no debt

- ✔ Have management in place

- ✔ Be simple businesses

- ✔ Have an offering price

Buffett states that despite these detailed and specific criteria, he is often approached about acquisitions that don't come close to meeting the criteria. "We've found that if you advertise an interest in buying collies, a lot of people will call hoping to sell you their cocker spaniels," he has said.

The nature of the merger: Friendly or hostile?

Business combinations can be characterized as either friendly or hostile. Although the end result is the same — the combination of two previously separate firms into one entity — the investment banking process differs substantially depending upon the nature of the transaction.

In a *friendly merger,* the two firms work together on the transaction, and the combination is approved by both the target firm's board of directors and the acquiring firm's board of directors. Essentially, there is a meeting of the minds, and both parties agree that the acquisition is beneficial to their respective shareholders.

Not surprisingly, academic research has provided evidence that friendly mergers are more likely to be synergistic than hostile takeovers are. It makes sense that integrating the operations of two companies is easier if both of them favor the combination — people who *want* to work together are more successful than people who *have* to work together.

In a *hostile takeover,* the transaction is opposed by the target company's board of directors and management. Not surprisingly, many acquisitions are opposed by the management of the target firm — after all, they may find themselves unemployed if the transaction takes place. Because the deal is opposed, the acquiring company must gain control of the acquired firm to get it to agree to the transaction. Because the board of directors isn't amenable to the business combination, in a hostile takeover the acquiring company will do one of the following to acquire the target company:

- ✔ **Make a tender offer.** A *tender offer* is simply a public offer to buy the shares of the target firm at a fixed price that represents a substantial premium to the current market price. The tender generally has stipulations that the offer is good only if 51 percent of the shareholders agree to sell at that price. If enough shareholders agree to sell — or *tender* — their shares, the acquiring firm can take control of the company, change the composition of the board of directors, and ultimately acquire control of the company.

    Tender offers are good news for the shareholders of the target company, because the typical market reaction to a tender offer is a dramatic increase in the stock price — reflecting the premium that the tender is to the current market price. Even if the tender offer doesn't succeed, it signals to the market that the target firm is "in play," and you may see other firms get into a bidding war.

Shark repellent

Some firms just don't want suitors coming after them — they don't want to date and certainly don't want to get married. Working with their investment bankers, corporations can take actions that make themselves less attractive to potential suitors. These actions have spawned the most colorful and descriptive language in the world of finance. In fact, the whole class of actions intended to discourage unwanted takeover overtures is sometimes referred to collectively as *shark repellent*, because it's meant to ward off the sharks. The term *killer bees* has even been used to describe the team of individuals employed to ward off takeover bids. The killer-bee team is composed of investment bankers, lawyers, accountants, and tax specialists.

Some defense mechanisms are put into place before a hostile takeover bid, and others are enacted after a hostile takeover has been attempted. These measures include the following:

- **Poison pills:** A *poison pill* allows shareholders the right to buy shares of the company at a substantial discount to market value if one shareholder acquires a certain percentage of a company's stock — say, 20 percent. Because the entity acquiring the large position is prohibited from participating in the purchase through the poison pill, the potential acquirer would suffer substantial dilution in percentage ownership, rendering the takeover prohibitively expensive and discouraging any takeover attempt.

- **Poison puts:** *Poison puts* are similar to poison pills, except that they grant the target firm's bondholders the right to sell their bonds back (or *put* them) to the company. This discourages takeovers because it raises the cost of the transaction — the acquirer must be prepared to refinance the firm's debt immediately after the acquisition. Additionally, the bondholders are often entitled to a substantial premium to current market value under the terms of the poison puts.

- **Golden parachutes:** *Golden parachutes* are compensation packages of the senior management of companies that provide for large payouts — often several times annual salary — in the event that the executive loses his job as a result of a change in corporate control. If these agreements extend further down in the organization, they're called *silver parachutes*. Either way, they serve to make the acquisition less attractive by raising the cost of the takeover by the amount of the agreements. The proponents of golden parachutes contend that they're necessary because corporate executives may be quick to abandon ship and seek employment elsewhere if their firm were being courted by another firm. In perhaps the most lucrative golden parachute in history, Duke Energy agreed to pay former Progress Energy CEO Bill Johnson $44 million in compensation, including $10 million severance, for essentially 20 minutes on the job as Duke CEO following the acquisition of Progress by Duke. Now, that's good work if you can get it.

- **Staggered boards of directors:** In lieu of electing the entire board of directors each year at the company's annual meeting, a firm may arrange to have board members appointed for longer terms and have only a portion of the directors sitting for election in any given year. The effect of this type of an arrangement is to discourage an unfriendly party from taking control of the board via a vote in any given year.

- **Supermajority voting:** Firms can, through changes in their bylaws, adopt a requirement that a higher percentage than a simple majority of shareholders must vote to approve a merger. This requirement could be as high as 75 percent or 80 percent. Additionally, the provision may enact an even higher standard by precluding the hostile acquirer from participating in the vote. This makes

(continued)

(continued)

it practically impossible for the acquirer to obtain enough votes to approve the takeover.

✔ **Acquiring debt:** Firms can simply make themselves less attractive to potential acquirers by leveraging up their own balance sheets, or borrowing heavily. By loading up with debt, companies exhaust some of the unused debt capacity that is so highly valued by acquiring firms. If a firm has little unused debt capacity, a potential acquirer has less flexibility if the firm were to be acquired. This would certainly seem to work against the interests of the current shareholders — taking on debt merely for the sake of becoming less attractive as a takeover candidate is definitely not in the best interests of the current shareholders.

✔ **Fair price amendments:** The bylaws of certain corporations require that a company seeking to acquire it must pay a "fair price" to targeted shareholders. The provisions vary from company to company, but one example is that the acquirer must pay at least as much as the highest price the target firm has traded for in the market for a given period of time. A second element of fair price amendments is the prohibition of a *two-tiered tender offer.* These tenders happen when the acquirer offers a higher price in the first tender offer and threatens a lower bid in a second step for those shareholders who fail to sell right away. This ensures that all shareholders receive the same amount per share.

✔ **Dual classes of shares:** The shareholder base of some corporations includes two different kinds of shares, each having different voting privileges. For instance, Warren Buffett's company, Berkshire Hathaway, has A and B shares. Berkshire Hathaway's B shares have a market value of approximately 1/1,500 of the A shares but only have 1/10,000 of the voting rights of the A shares. If there are two classes of stock with different voting rights, a corporate raider would have to gain control of the shares with the greater voting power — a daunting task.

✔ **Greenmail:** *Greenmail* essentially involves paying the potential acquirer to go away and not initiate a further attempt to acquire the target firm. The entity is generally paid a substantial premium for their stock, and it agrees not to try to gain control of the firm in the future. Greenmail became prevalent in the 1980s and made many *corporate raiders* (private investors who aggressively pursue buying companies that often aren't in the selling mood) a lot of money. One of the first examples of Greenmail happened in 1984, when Disney Productions paid Saul Steinberg $59 million to go away and drop his takeover bid.

✔ **White knights:** A proactive way to thwart a potential hostile takeover bid, or at least to make it less likely, is for the target company's board to seek a friendly investor — a *white knight* — to purchase the company or to take a substantial stake in the firm to discourage a takeover attempt. Warren Buffett has been referred to as Wall Street's White Knight because he has stepped in at different times and taken positions in very high-profile financial firms, including Goldman Sachs, Salomon, and Bank of America. Buffett's infusion of capital has strengthened these firms and made their ownership structure more stable and less likely to fall into the hands of a hostile bidder.

✔ **Pac-Man defense:** The *Pac-Man defense,* named for the once popular arcade game, involves the target firm turning around and making a bid to acquire the hostile bidder. This situation is fairly rare, because it generally involves a smaller company trying to acquire a larger firm. The first occurrence of the Pac-Man defense was in 1962 when Martin Marietta Corporation made an offer to buy Bendix after Bendix had made a hostile takeover offer for Martin Marietta.

A recent example was when Knight Capital Group — the stock-trading firm whose technology breakdown contributed to a major disruption of the U.S. stock markets in 2012 — was acquired by Getco after a bidding war with Virtu Financial. Knight shareholders ended up receiving a premium that was about 20 percent over market price for the troubled firm.

✔ **Engage in a proxy fight.** A proxy fight is a little different from a tender offer, but the goal is identical — to gain control of the target firm so that the acquisition is ultimately approved. A *proxy vote* is a situation in which a shareholder gives her vote (or *proxy*) to someone authorized to vote for her on a particular matter. In this case, it's to seek a change in control of the organization and establish a board and management team that is favorable to being acquired. With proxy authority, the acquiring corporation is able to take control of the target company, replace the directors with its own appointees, and approve the merger resolution.

An example of a successful proxy fight was Weyerhaeuser's 2002 acquisition of Willamette Industries. Upon rejection of two previous offers to buy Willamette, Weyerhaeuser secured control of the Willamette board via a proxy fight. This ended a protracted four-year process that began with a friendly merger offer and included two tender offers. Who said high finance was easy?

Tools Used to Analyze the M&A Deal

A separate team from different investment banking organizations works on opposite sides of any proposed acquisition deal. They serve as the representatives of each of the parties — the buyer and the seller — throughout the deal and work to ensure that a fair deal is reached. This is an important source of fee income for investment banks, and M&A activity represents a very profitable business for most investment banking firms.

The role of the buy-side M&A advisor

When an investment banking firm is advising a firm seeking to acquire another company, the investment banking firm is referred to as a *buy-side advisor*. The buy-side advisor is responsible for

✔ Helping the company identify potential acquisition targets

✔ Performing due diligence on proposed targets

✔ Valuing the proposed benefits of the acquisition

✔ Negotiating with target firms to establish the terms of the deal

✔ Closing the deal

We cover each of these responsibilities in the following sections.

Identifying potential acquisition targets

The buy-side M&A advisor will help identify potential target firms that meet the client's criteria. They will reach out to the potential target firms to gauge their interest and discuss the potential transaction.

The process of courting an M&A target is very confidential, because if it became public that a firm was targeting another publicly traded firm for acquisition — or even if a rumor started that it was happening — market participants would bid up the value of the target firm, making it more expensive to acquire. In fact, when a firm in a given industry is the target of an acquisition, other firms that fit a similar profile in that industry often see their stock prices bid up, because they may become the next acquisition targets.

Performing due diligence

Due diligence in the context of an acquisition refers to an in-depth analysis of the target firm in order to gain a true picture of the firm — its strengths and weaknesses, with particular emphasis placed upon the firm's financial condition. The process of due diligence involves gathering a great deal of information and analyzing and interpreting that information in order to determine if a deal could be potentially advantageous for the buyer and at what price a deal would make sense.

Much of this due process focuses on financial modeling in an attempt to determine the incremental value that would likely be created in the acquisition. The result of this modeling is the creation of *pro forma financial statements* (projected financial statements — such as balance sheets, income statements, and cash-flow statements — that attempt to show the financial performance of the firm if things go "as to form"). These projections are generally made several years out into the future and are used as inputs into the valuation process.

Inherent in the due diligence process is the requirement that the team of investment bankers evaluate the potential synergies of the business combination. Particular emphasis is paid to the target firm's competitive position in the industry, as well as the strategic fit within the acquiring company. A vital element of accurate (and, thus, successful) due diligence is the necessity to make some key and realistic assumptions regarding the potential synergies in the merger and the risks involved so that when the valuation models are applied, a realistic estimate (and not simply an optimistic or best-case estimate) of the value is obtained.

The due-diligence process should detail the strengths and weaknesses of the proposed transaction and highlight the significant risks of the transaction to the buyer, so that a reasoned decision can be made through consideration of all the relevant facts and conjectures.

Valuing the company

The goal of the due-diligence process should be an unbiased estimate of the true value of the target firm to the buyer. This is where young associates of investment banking firms — most often recent MBA graduates — cut their teeth in the field by applying a wide variety of valuation methods in marathon sessions to determine that value. These associates pore over reams of data and run multiple iterations of financial models.

Several different valuation methods are employed, but the primary method involves a *discounted cash-flow analysis,* in which the incremental earnings of acquiring the target firm are discounted back (or put) in *present value terms.* In theory, if the net present value of the acquisition is positive (if the present value of incremental earnings exceeds the purchase price), it should add to the value of the parent firm. The resulting valuation should not simply be a single point estimate, but should involve a sensitivity analysis that will provide the acquiring firm with a range of potential values, depending upon the realization of some of the key assumptions (such as future sales growth, cost efficiencies realized, and the appropriate risk level of the firm). In addition, the valuation exercise will make use of relative valuations — price to earnings, price to cash flow, and price to sales, to name a few. If this sounds complicated, don't worry — we cover discounted cash-flow analysis in more detail in Chapter 12.

A major portion of the valuation exercise involves the *accretion/dilution analysis.* This is a part of the analysis that determines whether the *earnings per share* (EPS) of the buying firm will increase or decrease after the deal is completed. As you may imagine, shareholders don't like transactions that will lower or dilute the EPS of the firm. In rare occasions, shareholders will support a dilutive acquisition, but only if it appears that the acquisition will result in a long-term increase in EPS.

Negotiating the terms of the deal

In addition to the price, the investment banking team will negotiate the specific terms of the acquisition with the target firm. This includes negotiating the composition of the board of directors and management team, as well as any necessary employment contracts. There will likely be several rounds of negotiation in any merger situation with a great deal of give and take between the two parties. The final deal often looks substantially different from the first pass of the deal.

With respect to price, a good investment banking firm will tell the client when to stop bidding. In their zeal to complete a deal, many firms lose sight of the necessity to not win at any cost.

Closing the deal

Both the acquirer and the acquired firm's board of directors meet to approve the transaction. In addition, both the buy-side and the sell-side's investment banks deliver a *fairness opinion* regarding the transaction to their respective clients. The fairness opinion states simply that the deal is fair and that no entity over- or underpaid. Shareholders of both firms look to the fairness opinion as third-party approval that the deal was, indeed, aboveboard. Finally, in order for the deal to be closed, the shareholders of both parties must approve the transaction.

The role of the sell-side M&A advisor

Although the sell-side M&A advisor will perform many of the same functions as the buy-side advisor, there are some fundamental differences, depending upon whether the firm wants to be acquired.

Preparing the company for sale

Many companies who are acquired were actually *looking* to be acquired — they welcome the overtures from potential buyers. In fact, increasingly, the dream of many entrepreneurs is to found a company, operate it successfully, grow the business, and then sell out to a major firm in the industry for a handsome profit. If that's the case, the sell-side investment banking advisor will prepare an analysis of the company and recommend steps that should be taken prior to the firm looking for potential suitors to make the firm more attractive.

Like buy-side advisors, sell-side M&A advisors prepare a detailed valuation report on the company, specifying a range of values that the firm should conceivably sell for. Where warranted, this analysis will also provide a summary of selling part of the company — certain product or business lines — in lieu of the entire company. In fact, the firm may find that by selling off parts of the firm, it may be able to command a higher price than by selling the entire firm to one buyer.

Marketing the firm

A major difference between buy-side and sell-side M&A advising is that the sell side focuses on marketing the firm. Therefore, sell-side advisors provide clients with advice on a business plan that makes the firm more attractive to potential buyers. This relationship may start several years in advance, because the company generally prepares for the day when it will be sold. Sell-side advisors also prepare detailed marketing materials for distribution to potential buyers.

A major part of marketing the firm involves initiating contact with potential buyers and gauging levels of interest. Connecting the buyer and seller is one of the most important functions of the sell-side M&A advisor; all the avenues detailed earlier for the buy-side advisor (see "Identifying potential acquisition targets") may be utilized by the sell-side counterpart.

If, on the other hand, the firm does not want to be acquired, the sell-side M&A advisor consults with firm management and the board of directors on a game plan to enact some of the takeover defense strategies outlined in the "Shark repellant" sidebar, earlier in this chapter.

Why Many M&A Deals Go Wrong

It may seem like much of the analysis of mergers and acquisitions involves the application of financial models and is very cut-and-dried, mathematical, and technical, but a great deal of art is involved in the deal. In fact, two investment banking teams can draw dramatically different conclusions even when presented with an identical set of facts and data to analyze. That is, in essence, what makes the financial world work — there is a buyer and a seller for every transaction.

Even though many very intelligent people work on M&A deals, the deals can and often do go bad for a myriad of reasons.

Misplaced incentives

Some mergers and acquisitions simply shouldn't see the light of day because they're basically bad ideas from the start. But there are incentives all around to get a deal done — a successful M&A deal results in many individuals getting paid and others, notably the management of the acquiring firm, building a bigger empire to oversee. So, some of the analysis may not be unbiased, but may be influenced by other factors. Recognizing when those factors are at play is difficult, however, because there is a great deal of judgment involved in the due-diligence and valuation processes. Plus, many investment bankers and their teams remind us of the time-worn joke about accountants: When asked what 2 + 2 is, the accountant replied "What do you want it to be?"

With the changing of an assumption, the investment banker can transform a deal from marginally unattractive to a must-do.

Some M&A deals fail to materialize when they actually should have been done. Some firm boards and management teams are so concerned with their personal positions — and livelihoods — that they fight potential suitors when it's in the shareholders' best interests to pursue the business combination. That's why many investors support management having large personal stakes in the equity of their own firms. Such an equity stake seeks to align the incentives of management with those of the shareholders and provides them with an incentive to act in the best interests of the shareholders.

Faulty analysis

The financial models that are used by investment banking firms are very standard discounted cash-flow and relative valuation models — standard fare in the industry. Rarely is the analysis faulty because improper models are being applied. A simple tweaking of an assumption here or there in the analysis — perhaps a sales growth rate that is a couple percentage points higher or a discount rate that is a couple percentage points lower — can make all the difference in the world when it comes to making a transaction appear profitable or unprofitable and providing the client with the answer they want to hear.

Forecasting future cash flows is very difficult, especially out several years in advance. Just ask that great American ballplayer and philosopher Yogi Berra, who once said, "It's tough to make predictions, especially about the future." Yet, much of the modeling in an acquisition setting requires investment bankers to do just that — predict the future.

Falling into a false sense of security when analyzing the numbers that result from the due-diligence process is quite easy. There is an "illusion of precision" because the modeling is so complex that people believe that the valuations arrived at must be accurate. This is the same situation that investors encounter when trying to determine if a particular share of stock is over- or undervalued. And it's precisely why many of the most successful value investors in the world demand a large *margin of safety* (essentially, a margin of error) before they commit their funds. They want to know that even if they were a little too optimistic in their assumptions, the deal will likely turn out in their favor. Many companies are so anxious to do a deal that they accept even marginal deals with little or no margin of safety. This kind of thinking is exacerbated when there is a lot of M&A activity — firms don't want to miss out on all the good deals.

Overstated synergies

Some mergers and acquisitions fail because the investment bankers and management teams are simply overly optimistic about the synergies that can be achieved. In fact, over-optimism may be the single biggest reason that shareholders are disappointed with the results of a merger or acquisition. The benefits described on paper are not realized and simply can't be translated into the real world.

 An example of overstating synergies is the purchase of Snapple Beverage Corporation by Quaker Oats for $1.7 billion in 1994. On paper, this seemed like a terrific pairing — Quaker Oats had a great deal of success with its Gatorade brand and believed that it could realize economies of scale and utilize the same marketing channels with the Snapple brand. A scant three years later, Snapple was sold by Quaker Oats to Triarc for $300 million — a fraction of what Quaker Oats paid. Talk about money down the drain.

Culture wars

Many mergers and acquisitions are unsuccessful because of the difficulty of integrating companies with distinctly different firm cultures. Bringing two firms together to operate under a single umbrella involves more than just combining assets and liabilities on a balance sheet — it also involves bringing people together to work productively with each other.

 *Corporate culture* can be thought of as the company's personality and is often embodied in "that's the way we do things here" mentality. Some firms' cultures are very bureaucratic and hierarchically oriented, while others emphasize teamwork and more worker autonomy. Integrating firms with distinctly different corporate cultures can be problematic and lead to the business combination failing to achieve the expected synergies.

 Many pundits believe that the failed merger of German-based Daimler-Benz and U.S.-based Chrysler failed not because there weren't synergies to be realized (the merger made sense in theory), but because the corporate cultures of the two firms were so distinctly different that the two parties didn't play well together in the corporate sandbox. Daimler paid a heavy price for this merger misstep — it paid $38 billion for Chrysler in 1998 and only received $7.4 billion nine years later when it sold Chrysler to Cerebus Capital. Daimler-Benz may engineer terrific automobiles, but they got derailed by a cultural chasm.

The winner's curse: Overpaying

Anyone who has participated in an auction has likely set a price at which they would feel comfortable buying a particular lot or item. You tell yourself you won't go beyond that price — "I'll pay $500 and not a single penny more!" Yet, when it comes time to bid on the item that you're interested in, you find that the bid quickly escalates and exceeds the price limit you set. You justify your change in strategy because you've waited and invested your entire day in the process, becoming emotionally invested in "winning," which you now define as ending up with the item, not ending up with the item at a reasonable price. You don't want to see that rival bidder outbid you for the item — how can you let him win? You end up paying much more than you intended, but you didn't go home empty-handed — you won! Or did you?

Just like the individuals in the popular TV series *Storage Wars* (where individuals bid against each other at auctions for abandoned storage lockers), corporate executives find themselves in bidding wars to acquire firms and go beyond the prices that they rationally set for the target company. Initially they set price limits at which the acquisition makes good economic sense for the shareholders. But, as soon as they get into a bidding war, it's no longer just about acquiring the firm for a price that makes economic sense — it's about winning . . . at virtually any cost.

Economists have coined the phrase "the winner's curse" to explain the phenomenon in which the winning bidder in an auction is the one who most overestimates the value of the item being auctioned. This explains why, on average, academic studies show that acquisitions are good for the shareholders of the *target firm* (the company being acquired) and bad for the shareholders of the acquiring firm.

History is replete with examples of the winner's curse, but perhaps the biggest example is when in October 2007, the Dutch bank ABN Amro was acquired by Royal Bank of Scotland for a cool $99.9 billion (at least they kept it under $100 billion) following a bidding war with Barclays. At the time, a *USA Today* headline trumpeted "Royal Bank of Scotland wins biggest financial takeover." What did they win? In January 2009, RBS announced a loss of £28 billion, of which £20 billion was due to the ABN Amro acquisition. This led to a £45 billion taxpayer bailout of RBS in October 2008, because the transaction degraded the bank's capital and exposed it to more troubled loans. And you thought that the Yankees overpaid for Alex Rodriguez!

Chapter 5

How Investment Banking Is Used in Leveraged Buyouts

*L*everaged buyouts (LBOs) are often viewed as the mystery thriller of the financial world. They've attracted the attention of the media and general public because of the high-profile players involved and the vast fortunes that have been made with them. The most famous LBO of all time was initiated by private equity firm KKR & Co. and involved the purchase of RJR Nabisco. This transaction was the subject of the book *Barbarians at the Gate*, by Bryan Burrough and John Helyar (Harper & Row), and spawned a movie with the same name.

Hollywood treatment of LBOs makes them seem full of intrigue, but most of the time, they're not all that complicated. Private equity firms pool investors' funds together and make investments in, among other things, leveraged buyouts and venture capital. The term *private equity* became widely known in the 2012 U.S. presidential campaign, because Mitt Romney was a principal in the private equity firm Bain Capital — a firm that engages extensively in LBOs. Much of the media focus was on the potential negative consequences of LBOs such as downsizing and job losses, but the media often neglected to focus on the very positive aspects of LBOs, which may include a more efficient allocation of resources, greater economic efficiency, and job creation in the long run. Like anything else, LBOs are neither universally good nor universally bad. In this chapter, we lay it out all out for you.

In This Corner: Introducing the Players

An LBO is conceptually a very simple transaction in which an undervalued or underappreciated company or a division of a company is purchased by a private equity or other sponsor firm. The purchased company is then transformed from being publicly traded — owned by shareholders who can freely buy and sell their shares of the firm — to one that is privately held by a much smaller group of investors who hold sizeable and largely illiquid — that is, very difficult to sell — ownership blocks.

As the name implies, leverage (or debt) plays a major role in this purchase and transformation. In fact, the primary source of funding is debt secured by the assets of the company being purchased — similar to how a homeowner borrows money via a mortgage to purchase a home. The home itself serves as *collateral* for the loan, and the lender's recourse is to seize the assets in the event of default. Collateral is the specific property that a borrower pledges to a lender to secure repayment of a loan. In much the same way that the automobile serves as collateral for a car loan, specific assets of the firm will be pledged as collateral for specific loans in an LBO.

There is another striking similarity between LBOs and the residential housing market. Some real estate speculators make a living by purchasing homes, fixing them up (painting, renovating bathrooms and kitchens, and putting in hardwood floors), and selling them for a handsome profit. Similar to people who "flip" homes, the sponsors of LBOs generally don't own the companies for a very long period of time. The goal of nearly all LBO sponsors — like KKR or Bain Capital — is to purchase a company that is temporarily depressed or undervalued by the public markets and make some significant changes in the company's operations, thus improving the profitability of the firm. Then, in a few years, the private equity firm can sell the new and improved company at a premium in the public markets or to another strategic buyer. The goal of the LBO is to dramatically increase the value of the target company.

Unlike home flippers, the changes made by LBO sponsors are not new kitchens and bathrooms; instead, they're often focused on cutting costs and making meaningful changes in the way the company operates. Some ways LBO sponsors may improve a company would be assembling the product overseas rather than domestically, or jettisoning certain divisions of the company or simply changing the way a product is distributed or marketed. This is where private equity and LBOs have a negative connotation with some in the media and popular culture, because LBOs are often associated with job losses and downsizing.

Hawkers at sporting events often shout "You can't tell the players without a program!" The same is true in the world of LBOs. The major players involved in LBOs are investment banks, big institutions, company management, and the company's stock and bond investors. They work together to transform the way companies operate and hopefully improve the way economies allocate scarce financial capital.

Investment banks

Investment banks are often accurately characterized as making money on all aspects of the investment process from helping take firms public through initial public offerings (IPOs) to advising those same firms as they become private through LBOs. In fact, some firms seem to be in an endless ownership cycle. They go public, private, and public again, often with the help of the same investment banks. It is, as they say, good work if you can get it and generates enormous fee income for investment banks.

Firms look to their investment bank to advise them when either they already have been identified as the target of an LBO or when they want to position themselves to be an attractive candidate for an LBO. There are many steps firms can take to put themselves in the best position to profit from an LBO and some of these characteristics are listed in the "Identifying companies that can work in a leveraged buyout" section, later in this chapter. Investment banks often utilize their extensive networks of contacts to gauge the interest of potential purchasers for firms who may be interested in being the target of an LBO.

Once the LBO has been successful and the company has been transformed, the private equity sponsor wants to reap the rewards of the endeavor. Investment bankers are called upon to play a pivotal role at this point. The investment banking expertise sought often involves putting a *valuation* on the shares of the company and lining up investors for an IPO. The valuation is a best guess as to what investors will be willing to pay for the newly issued shares of the firm. An IPO represents the first time that shares of a company are sold to the public, and because no shares trade in the market prior to the IPO, the valuation process truly is a bit of a guessing game.

Alternatively, investment bankers could be called upon to utilize their extensive network of contacts to find a *strategic buyer* who will pay top dollar for the new and improved firm. A strategic buyer is another firm that believes that when the company is merged into the strategic buyer's firm, it will be a good and profitable fit. Finally investment bankers may counsel the firm through a *secondary leveraged buyout,* effectively recapitalizing the firm once again. A secondary leveraged buyout simply takes the firm through another round of borrowing and transfers ownership to another private equity sponsor.

Big institutions

Private equity firms and leveraged buyout firms pool investors' assets and invest in a variety of companies. Sponsoring LBOs is a major activity of private equity firms. Some of the biggest private equity firms include TPG Capital, the Carlyle Group, the Blackstone Group, and Warburg Pincus. Some of the major investment banking firms such as Goldman Sachs and JPMorgan Chase are also major sponsors of LBOs and have private equity partnerships that their clients can invest in.

Investors generally don't invest directly in LBOs, but they'll invest through one of these LBO sponsors who set up specific funds. These specific funds invest in a variety of LBOs so that the risk for the investor is effectively spread out over several deals. In that way, these private equity funds are somewhat like mutual funds, but they invest in entire companies and are actively involved in the management and transformation of the firms. Some deals work out spectacularly and some are abject failures. By investing in several deals, the likelihood of achieving a reasonable return level is increased.

Almost all LBO and private equity sponsors set up their funds as *limited partnerships*. A limited partnership is a form of business organization that has at least one general partner, who manages the business and assumes legal debts and obligations. As the name implies, the partnership typically has many *limited partners* who are entitled to the cash flow from the partnership but are legally liable for debts only to the extent of their original investments. Thus, the investors in LBOs are typically limited partners in a fund set up by one of the private equity firms.

The LBO sponsor serves as the *general partner* and retains an ownership interest in the target firm. The general partner has management control of the limited partnership and shares in the profit of the partnership. But, unlike the limited partners, the general partner is responsible for the debts of the partnership, which means the general partner has much greater liability. Therefore, unlike most securities issued with the help of investment banks, the sponsor firms retain an ownership interest and have a major incentive to ensure that the deals are profitable. This alignment of incentives between investors and the private equity sponsors is often cited as a major advantage of the private equity form of ownership.

Unlike mutual funds, a private equity fund doesn't allow an investor to buy and sell shares on a daily basis. Although limited partners may be able to sell their partnership interests to another investor, the market is not very active and liquidity is very limited.

The commitments investors make are to a particular fund that makes specific investments. The typical private equity company will sponsor many different funds, and these funds are not comingled. Consequently, some funds of sponsors may be very successful, while others may suffer large losses. Also, unlike mutual funds, private equity funds are designed to be in existence for a limited time period — typically ten years.

Management

The typical LBO transaction involves a sponsor firm partnering with management of the target firm. That is, most LBOs are not "hostile" and do not involve an entity taking the firm over and replacing the management team with a new group of leaders. A *hostile takeover* is one in which another organization takes control of a corporation by purchasing a majority of the equity of the firm against the wishes of the current management. LBO sponsors specifically look for well-managed firms that are, for whatever reason, underappreciated by the financial markets as their typical targets. In fact, many LBOs are initiated by the management team and are referred to as *management buyouts* (MBOs). An MBO is just a form of an LBO that is initiated by the management team and results in the management team having a large proportion of the ownership in the target firm.

MBOs often happen when the founder of a company is looking to exit and realize his big payoff and the management team is interested in buying the company because they believe in the future prospects of the company and want to retain their positions in the firm. The management team may also want to take the company in a direction that the founder was not interested in going.

This isn't to say that the private equity sponsor is a *passive investor* – one who is hands off and simply allows the management team to control the firm. In fact, they're far from being hands off. Private equity sponsors often help bring additional management expertise to the firm and are actively involved in fundamental decisions that help unlock the value inherent in the target firm. They often serve as advisors to the management team and will have seats on the board of the reconstituted company.

Management is also typically given a share of the equity — often through *equity options* or *warrants* — to help incentivize them to make decisions that are in the best interest of creating long-term value for the owners of the firm. Equity options or warrants are a form of a *derivative* (a security whose value depends upon, or is derived from, the value of something else). In this case, the equity option or warrant values increase dramatically if the value of the company increases, but they have no value if the value of the company declines. Unlike publicly traded firms, the ownership of private firms is much more concentrated and has a much longer time horizon. In this type of ownership structure, management can focus on making decisions that are in the best long-term interest of the firm and not worry about the short term and the next quarter's earnings or meeting growth targets set by market analysts.

The stakes for management are generally much higher in an LBO structure than in the typical publicly traded firm. Because LBO firms have a much higher degree of financial leverage than the typical firm, there is a higher risk of failure. In the event of failure, managers of LBO target firms stand to lose a great deal — their jobs, their reputations, and the value of the equity stake they're provided in the firm. That's why many people consider this form of organization to be an efficient method of more closely aligning the interests of the owners with the interests of managers.

Stock and bond investors

Investing in LBOs has become commonplace for most institutional investors such as insurance companies, public pension funds, university endowments, and foundations. However, these institutions typically don't invest directly in LBOs — that is, they don't sponsor their own LBOs. Instead, they invest through funds sponsored by the plethora of private equity companies.

A private equity company's track record is extremely important to investors. The private equity sponsors who develop a strong track record of success often find that they don't have to actively market their new funds, because previous investors buy up the limited partnership interests of any new funds that they sponsor. In fact, it's often very difficult for new investors to invest in the funds of the most successful private equity companies because they're often oversubscribed by investors in current partnerships sponsored by the same firm.

Many institutional investors invest in private equity through *fund of funds*. A relatively recent innovation in the private equity landscape, a fund of private equity funds, as the title suggests, is a pool of money that invests in a wide variety of private equity limited partnerships. That way, the institutional investor doesn't have to concern itself with the detailed due diligence involved in the selection of the specific private equity fund. The strategy of gaining exposure to private equity through a fund of funds is particularly popular with smaller institutional investors who may not have the resources or expertise to undertake the due diligence involved with specific fund investing yet want exposure to this asset class. Of course, the downside of investing in a fund of funds is the additional layer of fees that the fund of funds sponsors extract.

In the early 2000s, with the success of the "Yale model" of investing popularized by investment guru David Swensen, more and more institutional investors flocked to so-called *alternative investments* and allocated a larger and larger percentage of their assets to these asset classes. Typically any asset class outside of stocks, bonds, and cash is referred to as an alternative investment. The most popular types of alternative investments include hedge funds, private equity, commodities, and real estate.

The Yale model advocates equity investment at the expense of fixed income commitments and doesn't consider the lack of liquidity inherent in these types of investments to be a major concern. The idea is that, over the long-run, these equity investments will provide higher returns and, because institutional investors have long time horizons, they should allocate the bulk of their investments to equity. During the recent financial crisis, that lack of liquidity due to the credit crunch became paramount and caused major problems at many institutions. This lack of liquidity led to substantial losses in the portfolios of many of these institutional investors as there was very little appetite for illiquid investments when the credit markets became frozen. As a result of this experience, many institutional investors have scaled back their investments in these types of relatively illiquid assets, but these asset classes still occupy a significant percentage of institutional investors' assets.

Aiming for the Right Targets in a Leveraged Buyout

Some companies make good LBO candidates while others are not positioned to be successful targets of an LBO sponsor. The bottom line of any potential LBO analysis involves the ability of the reconstituted firm to generate sufficient cash flow to not only make the required payments on the new debt but also to provide a substantial return to the new equity investors.

Interestingly, individual investors can somewhat benefit from LBOs by trying to identify, before the announcement, which firms will be the targets of future LBOs. If a company is the target of an LBO and there are firms in that same industry with similar characteristics, it's often beneficial to buy shares of those firms because they often rise in anticipation that the competitor firms might be the target of future LBOs. For instance, if there are several firms in the department store industry that have recently been the targets of LBOs, investors will speculate that other similarly positioned firms in the industry will be the subject of future LBOs.

Identifying companies that can work in a leveraged buyout

In some time periods in the financial markets, it seems like all firms are candidates for LBOs. There are boom and bust periods in LBOs much like there are cycles in other sectors of investment markets. For instance, in the late 1980s, the junk bond market fueled a bubble in LBOs and firms like Drexel Burnham

Lambert enjoyed tremendous success and individuals like Michael Milken amassed great fortunes and became titans of finance. At other times, most recently at the height of the financial crisis, the LBO market dries up and the limited partnership interests suffer a loss in value as investors flee this sector of the market.

Notwithstanding the boom and bust periods, there are certain underlying characteristics of companies that make them attractive targets for LBOs. The characteristics include the following:

- **Strong management:** Probably the most important characteristic of a firm that is a potential LBO candidate is high quality management who is willing to work closely with the LBO sponsor. After the firm undergoes the LBO, the management will be under the gun to generate high cash flows in order to pay both the interest and principal on the debt. Private equity sponsors are active investors and need to work hand-in-hand with management to enact the changes necessary to unlock the hidden value in firms.

- **Low leverage:** The sponsor wants to effectively replace equity with debt in an LBO, so firms that make good targets for LBOs should have little or no debt. Having unused debt capacity is a major element that sponsor firms find particularly attractive. Because interest payments to debt holders are tax-deductible expenses, while dividend payments to shareholders are not, much of the value of an LBO is realized through the potential tax savings (from making interest payments in lieu of dividend payments) afforded by the higher levels of debt. The U.S. tax code effectively encourages corporations to fund their operations by issuing debt instead of equity. In fact, the tax deductibility of interest payments is often referred to as a "tax shield," effectively protecting the target from paying corporate income taxes.

- **Strong asset base:** To induce lenders to lend money with the firm's assets as the collateral for the loan, the quality of assets must be strong and marketable. An asset is *marketable* if it can be sold very quickly, easily and without substantial loss of value. For instance, firms with a large percentage of assets booked as "goodwill" are not attractive LBO candidates, while firms with large tangible asset bases are coveted by LBO sponsors. That's because goodwill is an asset that cannot be bought or sold easily, but instead, is a line item on financial statements to reflect the value of brands and other trademarks. Also, firms carrying excessive amounts of cash and working capital are attractive candidates because those funds can be drawn upon to buy assets, pay down debt, and accomplish various other tasks.

- **Low business risk:** Firms that are seen as attractive LBO candidates tend to be in relatively staid, low-tech businesses that have minimal business risk. Firms like RJR Nabisco and the supermarket chain Albertsons were the targets of two of the biggest LBOs in history. These kinds of firms don't typically have the need for a high degree of research and development expenditures, because of their low-tech nature. Boring businesses make the best LBO targets.

✔ **Stable cash flows:** Because a sponsor firm seeks to reorganize the target firm and have it carry much more debt, the target firm should have predictable revenues and stable cash flows that will allow it to service the debt — paying the interest and principal. If a target firm's cash flows are unstable — high one year and low the next — lenders are likely to balk at committing funds because they'll be worried about the firm being able to pay down the debt during unprofitable periods.

✔ **Out of favor:** Private equity sponsors look to buy undervalued or out-of-favor companies. One of the best ways to identify undervalued companies is to look at their P/E ratios (see Chapter 8). A high P/E ratio means that the marketplace has high hopes for the future of a company and puts a premium on its valuation. On the other hand, a low P/E ratio generally means that a firm is out of favor with investors. Low-P/E firms offer the greatest upside for LBOs, because if the company can indeed be turned around and its fortunes reversed, the P/E ratio that the market places on the firm will likely increase.

✔ **Divisions that don't fit the firm:** Many LBO targets are not entire firms but are divisions of firms that really don't fit within the larger firm and may not be receiving the care and feeding necessary to maximize their potential. Conglomerates frequently spin off or sell unwanted divisions in LBOs and are often under pressure by shareholders to jettison businesses that aren't performing well for whatever reason. Once these divisions are operating as freestanding companies and get the attention they warrant, unlocked potential can be realized.

Appreciating the power of cash flow

We've all heard the phrase "Cash is king," and this really applies to LBOs. The ability to generate sufficient cash flow to make the required interest payments and to pay down the principal on the debt is of paramount importance to the success of any LBO. When prospective investors, prospective lenders and analysts alike scrutinize LBO deals they look at the expected return in cash flow terms on the investment. In addition, private equity sponsors focus on the *rate of return* (the percentage return) they expect to receive on their investment, as well as the rate of return the limited partners of their funds expect to earn.

We discuss the calculation of cash flow in detail in Chapters 7 and 12, but we offer a brief introduction here. Although *accounting profit* (or net income) is certainly important to companies and investors alike, cash flow is a more important concept. Accounting profit is the firm's total earnings calculated using the rules of accounting and takes into account all the firm's expenses. Accounting profit is used to figure out a company's tax bill and is useful for comparing the returns of companies. Quite simply put, however, you can't pay your suppliers, employees, or bondholders, or provide dividends to your shareholders, with accounting profits — but you *can* with cash. The concept of *cash flow* recognizes that certain noncash expense items (like depreciation and amortization) are deducted in computing net income but don't actually involve any outlay of cash. For example, firms are able to deduct a portion of the cost of a machine each year as depreciation, but no one writes a check for depreciation or has to pay someone for that charge. Consequently, a firm with a great deal of depreciation will have a substantially higher cash flow than accounting profit.

There are almost as many variations for computing cash flow as there are analysts out there, but the basic methodology is that you simply take a company's net income and add back all non-cash expenses. An important variation of cash flow is *free cash flow* (discussed in detail in Chapter *12*). Free cash flow is simply cash flow minus any required *capital expenditures* to maintain the firm's operations at the current level. Capital expenditures include things such as the purchase of new machines to replace machines that are worn out. Investment bankers often calculate the value of the firm as the *present value* of all future free cash flows to the firm.

Lenders often use *multiples* of a measure of cash flow to determine how much in total debt they are willing to provide to an LBO deal. The most common cash flow measure in this context is *earnings before interest, taxes, depreciation, and amortization* (EBITDA). Lenders generally gauge how much they're willing to lend as some multiple of EBITDA — for instance, five or six times EBITDA. The exact multiple of EBITDA varies over time. When LBOs are more popular and lenders have a more favorable view of equity markets, the multiple will increase.

Coming to terms with the return analysis: Internal rate of return

Rates of return are central concepts in the investment world. Investors often compare their performance to that of other investors, other investments and stock indexes by comparing rates of return. In the private equity world, rates of return are calculated by computing the *internal rate of return* (IRR) of an investment. The IRR is simply defined as the discount rate (or rate of return) that equates the present value of the projected costs (cash outflows) of an investment with the present value of the projected cash inflows from the investment. Another way of looking at IRR is that it's the interest rate that equates the present value of all cash flows (where a cash outflow is negative and a cash inflow is positive) to zero. The concept of present value is discussed in detail in Chapter 11.

To compute the IRR of an investment, you simply solve for the term IRR in the following equation:

$$CF_0 + \frac{CF_1}{(1+IRR)^1} + \frac{CF_2}{(1+IRR)^2} + \frac{CF_3}{(1+IRR)^3} + \ldots + \frac{CF_T}{(1+IRR)^T} = 0$$

For instance, if an investment required an initial cash outlay of $100 million the projected cash flows were $30 million in each of the next three years and $150 million four years from today, the equation for calculating the IRR is:

$$-\$100 + \frac{\$30}{(1+IRR)^1} + \frac{\$30}{(1+IRR)^2} + \frac{\$30}{(1+IRR)^3} + \frac{\$150}{(1+IRR)^4} = 0$$

In this case, the IRR for this investment is 33.1 percent. Not a bad rate of return. (By the way, IRR can be computed using any standard financial calculator or via an Excel spreadsheet.)

Expected returns for private equity deals are substantially higher than expected returns in the public equity markets. This reflects the fact that private equity deals are generally a good deal riskier than public equity investments on several fronts. They're generally much more highly leveraged than public companies, and they're less liquid than investment in public equities. Thus, to induce investors to commit funds to private equity, they must expect higher returns.

The exact percentage returns expected by private equity investors varies widely depending upon market conditions. For instance, when long-term U.S. government bonds are yielding 6 percent to 8 percent and publicly traded stock returns are in the 10 percent to 12 percent range, it would not be uncommon for LBO investors to expect returns in excess of 20 percent, perhaps in the mid 20 percent range. But if expected returns on other asset classes in the market are much lower, returns expected by private equity investors will generally be commensurately lower. The expected returns in the private equity markets are largely influenced by a combination of current market conditions and investors' appetites for risk.

Finding the Exit

Famed investor Warren Buffett's preferred holding period is "forever." He wants to identify investments that involve only one decision — the purchase decision. Buffett has very little turnover of holdings in his portfolio and seeks to invest in businesses that will be profitable for a long period of time. Private equity sponsors, on the other hand, know that even before they purchase a company, they'll be preparing for the day when they'll sell the firm. Identifying a proper exit strategy in both form and time are among the most important decisions made by any LBO sponsor. A well thought-out exit strategy can make or break a private equity deal.

Setting a target for exit in time

Private equity LBO sponsor firms generally have a relatively short timetable in mind when they purchase a firm through an LBO transaction. This is largely due to the fact that most of the private equity structures are limited partnerships that have a planned life of ten years or less.

On average, the holding periods for the sponsors of LBOs tend to be three to eight years. Many critics of the private equity process contend that private equity sponsors are like vultures that come in and strip down a company and quickly flip it like many real estate investors flip houses. This generally isn't the case with LBOs, as private equity sponsors add significant value by bringing in management expertise, reducing costs through process reengineering, and making meaningful changes to the target firm. These kinds of changes don't take place overnight — they generally require a time commitment of several years. If the changes were cosmetic and not substantive, the financial markets wouldn't be fooled and the returns to private equity wouldn't be attractive.

Considering how the exit will happen

As noted earlier, the exit is all-important, and not all LBOs are unwound in the same manner. There are three primary methods for LBO sponsors to exit their positions and realize the ultimate return on their investment: an IPO, a sale to a strategic buyer, and another LBO.

Initial public offering

The Holy Grail for LBO sponsors is often a successful IPO of the target firm. Of course, this is the case only if the resulting organization is seen by investors as a desirable individual company whose future prospects are bright and the firm can command a premium price in the financial markets. If timed properly, an IPO allows the LBO sponsor to effectively cash in on the investment in the firm and provides the desired cash flow to limited partner investors in the private equity sponsor firm. In addition, the IPO of an LBO target often allows a much need infusion of equity into the target firm that is likely still often highly leveraged, even several years after the LBO.

The LBO sponsor enlists the help of a lead investment bank to bring the company public. The lead investment bank is responsible for determining the value of the company and arriving at the IPO share price. Determining what the market will bear is an extremely important function of the lead investment bank, as a price that is set too high will result in an undersubscribed new issue and investors will see the share price decline upon initial trading in the public markets. This leads to very unhappy IPO investors and negatively impacts the reputation of the investment banking firm with investors of future IPOs. On the other hand, a significantly underpriced issue — one whose price increases dramatically upon public trading — results in an opportunity loss for the sponsor firm.

Investment banks generally strive to set an IPO price that is just a bit below what the market will actually bear. The prototype of a successful IPO is one in which the price in the secondary market — when the shares begin trading — is just slightly higher than the IPO price. If on the first day of trading the IPO closes up around 5 percent above the IPO price, the investment bankers feel that they've done their job.

There are horror stories — from the standpoint of the investment banks and the LBO sponsors — of firms that have gone public and the share price in the secondary market is soon multiples of the recent IPO price. For example, in May 2011, on the first day of public trading, the shares of social networking firm LinkedIn closed at $94.25, or more than double the $45 IPO price. Billions of dollars were left on the table by the private owners of LinkedIn. It was a windfall for the new shareholders who bought the firm at the IPO price. But such a result would give pause to other firms who were considering using those investment bankers to bring their deals public because they'd worry that their deal would be significantly underpriced.

Now, investment banks don't operate alone when bringing firms to market. Investment banks generally form a syndicate of other investment banks to ensure widespread distribution of the issue. A *syndicate* is simply a group of investment banks that gets together to help sell the shares in the IPO to its various customer bases. Each member of the syndicate agrees to be responsible to sell a certain portion of the issue. This makes distribution of the issue easier and spreads the risk among several investment banking firms.

The biggest disadvantage of this exit strategy is that IPOs generally involve high transaction costs. Those investment bankers don't buy their homes in the Hamptons and their luxury automobiles because they work for free. The investment banking infrastructure and due diligence necessary to ensure a smooth public offering is costly.

The best laid plans of LBO sponsors are, however, often thwarted by conditions in the financial markets. An LBO sponsor can have done everything correctly and have a firm primed and ready for an IPO only to find that the IPO market is soft due to prevailing market conditions. This was especially true during, and in the aftermath of, the financial crisis, as investors as a whole became very risk averse and market valuations (as reflected by P/E ratios) were at the low end of recent historical ranges. IPOs aren't greeted enthusiastically by potential investors during uncertain market periods. Much like a comedian's delivery, timing is everything when seeking an exit from an LBO via an IPO.

Sale to a strategic buyer

This exit strategy is the most common, and the one that is most preferred in the private equity industry because it's quick and simple. A strategic buyer is an entity that believes that the target company offers synergy to its existing business line. Simply put, *synergy* is the concept that one plus one can equal three, that some businesses are worth much more in the hands of one entity than another.

Synergies can be realized in any number of ways involving, for example, product line expansion, geographical expansion, or the purchase of suppliers or distributors. For instance, a soft drink company may purchase a sports drink manufacturer that underwent an LBO. The sports drink product line can be marketed and distributed through the same channels that the soft drink product line is currently utilizing.

From the seller's standpoint, this exit strategy is very clean because the LBO sponsor is negotiating directly with the strategic buyer and their investment banking advisors. The strategic buyer is also likely to pay a premium for the purchase because the buyer is likely in a position to realize the most value for the purchase. In essence the firm is worth much more in the hands of the strategic buyer because of the synergies that can be realized.

Another leveraged buyout

The exit strategy for a minority of private equity deals involves simply selling the company to another private equity firm that will essentially put the firm through a secondary LBO. This can happen when the original LBO sponsor needs to exit the deal, most likely because the partnership holding the deal is being unwound and capital is being returned to the limited partners.

The biggest disadvantage of exiting an investment using a secondary LBO is that the sponsor private equity firm is dealing with another professional private equity firm that will likely drive a hard bargain. The over-exuberance sometimes witnessed in the IPO market by individual investors is less likely to be realized in a market characterized by sophisticated buyers who realize that the seller is likely under some pressure to unwind the deal and realize their return.

Part II

Digging In: Performing Investment Banking

Source: U.S. Securities and Exchange Commission (www.sec.gov)

Find out more about looking past earnings to understand cash flow in an article at
http://www.dummies.com/extras/investmentbanking.

In this part . . .

✔ Discover which financial documents matter the most to investment bankers and how to obtain them so you can find the data needed for analysis.

✔ Analyze financial statements to find the data you need so you glean insights from the information and help contribute or understand the role of investment banking.

✔ Use financial ratios to compare financial data from different financial statements and across companies and industries.

✔ Figure out how to sell financial securities at prices that haul in proceeds for the sellers, but at prices where the buyers can still make money so you can see how a successful deal is structured.

✔ See how companies and governments sell bonds to raise money so you understand one of the key aspects of money raising in investment banking.

Chapter 6

Finding the Data: Documents and Reports

In This Chapter

▶ Discovering how to use the Securities and Exchange Commission's EDGAR database

▶ Putting financial data into a format that can be analyzed

▶ Keeping in touch with news and other important non-financial data

*I*nvestment bankers make a business out of knowing other companies' business. Part of being a dealmaker requires a deep knowledge of what companies are up to, what their CEOs are trying to accomplish, and what goals organizations have.

But investment bankers can't afford to sit in their high-priced skyscrapers and wait for CEOs to call them, looking to do a deal. Investment bankers need to be proactive, scanning the world for mergers that would make sense, divestitures that would save companies money, or financial instruments that don't yet exist, but could.

Part of this role of investment banking requires investment bankers to have a good grasp of the financial and non-financial information about the corporate world. It doesn't take much guesswork to know which companies need to grow to keep their shareholders happy, which ones could drive profit higher with a well-designed merger, or even which private companies could turbo-charge growth with an initial public offering (IPO).

But knowing what investment banking needs companies have — often even before the companies themselves realize it — takes a strong ability to unearth all the information possible about companies and industries. And that's the job of this chapter. Here, you find out how investment bankers can learn about companies in a hurry, getting up to speed on an industry and practically becoming experts without even leaving their desks.

Much of the data that investment bankers need are stored on the system operated by the chief securities regulator, the U.S. Securities and Exchange Commission (SEC). But getting your hands on the data is only part of the trick. Next, you need to know how to get the data into a format that can be put through the rigors of investment banking research. This chapter also shows you how to get your hands on the non-financial data, which can be as important (if not even more critical) to investment bankers.

Finding What You Need on the Securities and Exchange Commission's Website

Edgar Allan Poe may be known for his stories of mystery and suspense, but there's another Edgar, one that's much nearer and dearer to investment bankers' hearts (yes, they have hearts!). This Edgar has the job of removing mystery from company information.

The SEC, the unit of the government responsible for overseeing the securities business, operates a database known as EDGAR, short for Electronic Data-Gathering Analysis and Retrieval. The EDGAR database is the best friend of many investment bankers who are trying to research companies and understand the very fine subtleties of their businesses.

What types of information you can find

The SEC performs all sorts of functions to insure the smooth and efficient functioning of the financial system. The SEC inspects companies' accounting, looking for funny business, and supervises the issuance of new securities. The SEC's role of running the EDGAR database, though, is of utmost importance to investment bankers. This database is the wellspring for information that drives many investment banking activities.

The EDGAR database is essential for investment bankers because it contains

- ✔ **The key financial filings that companies provide:** Looking for a company's annual report or quarterly statement? These forms and many more are all stored on EDGAR and are accessible anytime and for free online.

- ✔ **Reports showing who owns large pieces of companies:** If you buy a stock, if you're like most people, that's a matter between you and your accountant. But large investors — those with $100 million or more of other people's money to invest — have to provide a report called a *13F,* showing their funds' holdings. These documents can be telling for investment bankers looking to monitor the movements of large and influential investors. Similarly, investors who own more than 5 percent of a company must disclose that holding in EDGAR on a *13D* filing.

✔ **News events and internal corporate details:** Popular media outlets can be vital sources of news. But when a new development is extremely significant, companies must disclose them in the EDGAR database as an *8-K* filing. Similarly, the juicy details about a company, including how much the executives are paid, are also available in EDGAR in the *DEF 14A* filings.

Remember the SEC typically only has detailed data on publicly traded companies or companies with debt owned by public investors. Private, or *closely-held,* companies are those owned by a relatively small number of private investors, where the shares aren't available on a public market.

The key types of documents

EDGAR is an enormous database. Every day, companies submit scores of electronic filings to EDGAR, where they're stored and made available to anyone in the public who wants to view them.

The filings pour into EDGAR because companies and other registrants are required to provide documents to investors and regulators and meet deadlines set by the SEC for compliance.

There's a massive number of possible forms that companies and investors may have to submit. Some of the regulatory forms are pretty obscure, so they're rarely filed. If you're glutton for punishment, or you're having trouble falling asleep, you can read a list of every single document that can be filed into EDGAR at `www.sec.gov/info/edgar/forms/edgform.pdf`. But to save you the trouble, in this section we tell you about the regulatory filings that matter most to investment bankers.

Annual report (10-K)

Companies' annual reports used to be beautiful colorful documents that were magazine-like and mailed to investors' homes. Those days are quickly fading away as the functional needs of real-time investors push aside the form of beautiful financial documents.

The term *annual report* is somewhat of a colloquialism. The actual document that matters, which companies release each year to describe how they're doing, is known by its regulatory name, the *10-K*. The 10-K is an often lengthy, comprehensive document that describes the company's performance over the past fiscal year. The 10-K is extremely detailed and must be looked over by an accounting firm before being submitted to EDGAR. The 10-K provides the numerical data showing the company's profits and the value of what the company owes and owns, as well as descriptive language highlighting how the company did.

Quarterly report (10-Q)

Publicly traded companies have several large burdens, one of the largest being to keep investors up-to-date on progress on a quarterly basis. The quarterly report, or *10-Q*, is the regulatory document in which companies give investors a rundown of their performance over a three-month period. The quarterly report isn't nearly as detailed as the annual report, but it gives the key data points from the period, including the *financial statements*. (We cover the financial statements in more depth in Chapter 7.)

Proxy statement (DEF 14A)

The proxy statement is one of the juicier regulatory filings. We're not talking *The Hunger Games* or anything here, but the proxy statement, known by its official name *DEF 14A*, is where companies put many of the more salacious details about their operations. The purpose of the proxy statement is to present investors with a list of all the items that are up for *shareholder approval*, or a vote at the annual meeting. But included in this filing are endless goodies, including details on what the top management are paid. (We offer more details on reading the proxy statement in Chapter 7.)

Prospectus (S-1)

When a company sells shares to the public for the first time in an IPO, the document that matters most is the prospectus, or *S-1*. The prospectus contains all the information that investors should know before investing in a new issue. (You can read more about the prospectus and what it contains in Chapter 3.)

Interim report of material events (8-K)

Companies are constantly changing and evolving organizations. New developments, such as getting approval to sell a new product or canceling a big project, are potentially important for investors to know about because they can significantly impact the value of the stock. Whenever a company has non-public and material information — in other words information that no one knows about but that's also important — it must be shared with the world. The way companies get the data out to everyone is the *8-K* filing in the EDGAR database.

How to use EDGAR to pinpoint information

One of the greatest things about EDGAR is that it contains just about every piece of data on publicly traded companies (those that have stock that trades on a public exchange) and firms that have sold debt to the public. But the second best thing about EDGAR is the fact that it's free. And even though EDGAR is operated by the government, you don't have to wait in line to use it. In fact, you can use it right now.

The EDGAR database is extremely easy to use, once you figure out where to go and what to do. And that's exactly what we explain in this section. It all starts at the SEC's website (www.sec.gov).

Instead of giving you theoretical instructions on how to find a company filing, you can discover how to do it using a typical situation. Let's say you're an investment banker who's trying to help a midsize healthcare company sell itself to a larger company. Your client wants to sell the company, rather than pursue an initial public offering, because there are other rivals working on similar technology. A delay in getting to market could mean the company could lose market share and not reach its potential.

That's your challenge. You now need to start your research on companies that may be interested in making a deal. As an investment banker, you start putting together your short list of possible bidders, one of which is General Electric. But you can use EDGAR to strengthen your case. Here are the steps you'd follow to research one possible bidder:

1. **Go to** www.sec.gov.

2. **Click the Company Filings link, located just below the Search SEC Documents box in the upper-right corner (see Figure 6-1).**

   You're taken to the EDGAR search page.

Figure 6-1:
The Company Filings link on the SEC home page.

Source: U.S. Securities and Exchange Commission (www.sec.gov)

3. **In the Fast Search box on the right side of the page, enter the name of the company (in this example, General Electric) or the stock symbol if you know it (in this case, GE), and click the Search button.**

4. **Click the See All Company Filings link.**

   A giant list of all the company filings that are in EDGAR appears. With a company the size and stature of GE, there are, not surprisingly, all sorts of filings, including the ones described in the previous section.

5. **Look through the list and start thinking about the filing with the information you seek.**

   When examining whether a company may be a potential buyer, what you want to know is how important the target's industry is to the possible bidder (in this example, GE). GE has a large business unit that serves the healthcare industry. Getting the full details on the importance of an industry to a company is exactly the type of thing a 10-K is for.

6. **Look through the list of results in the EDGAR database (and this may take quite a bit of scrolling), until you find the 10-K listing (shown in Figure 6-2).**

7. **Click the Documents link for the filing you're interested in.**

   You're taken to a listing of the data inside the 10-K filing. You can see what GE's looks like in Figure 6-3.

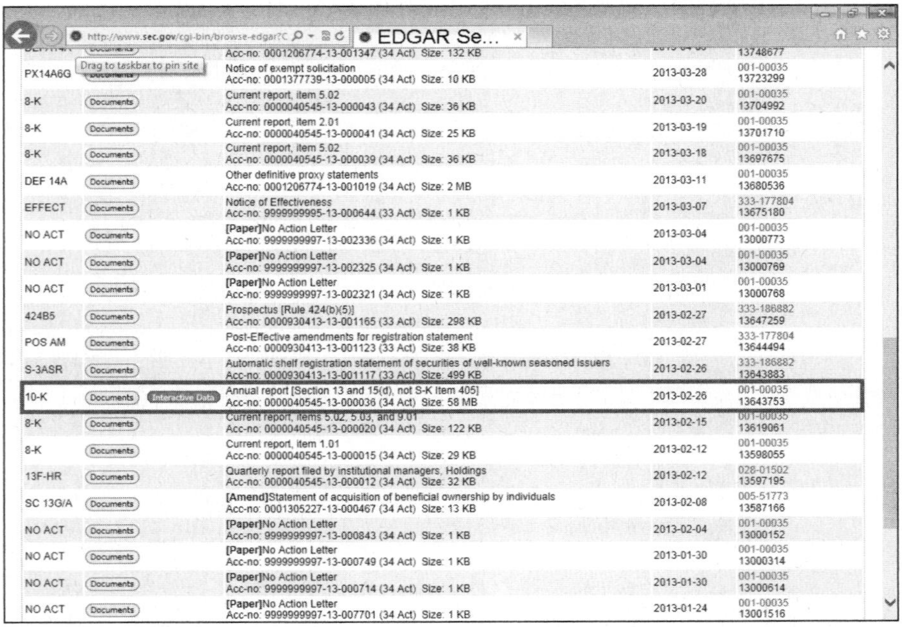

Figure 6-2: The EDGAR database listing shows you all the filings that are available for a company (in this case, GE).

Source: U.S. Securities and Exchange Commission (www.sec.gov)

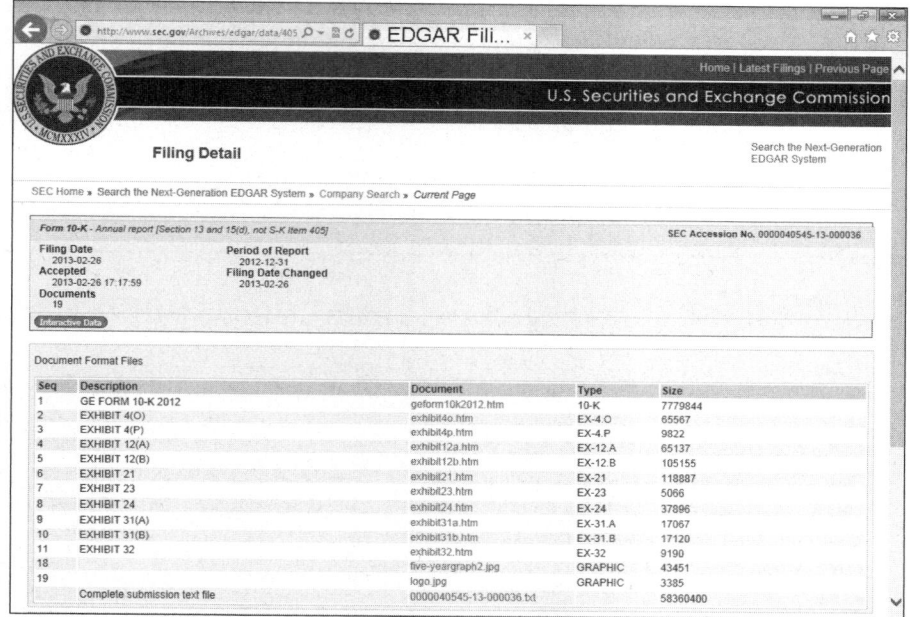

Figure 6-3: GE's 10-K filing contains a number of documents.

8. **Select the actual Form 10-K.**

   Don't be confused by the variety of documents. You want the Form 10-K, not one of the accompanying exhibits. In this case, click geform10k2012.htm. You're taken to the form.

9. **Drill down and find the relevant data.**

   After opening the document, it's time to start sleuthing. Be sure to use the search function on your computer to find keywords. With a little bit of searching, you'll soon find that GE describes its different industry units in a *footnote* (a detailed piece of financial data that doesn't fit in the financial statements). Specifically, in this case, footnote 28 is the one to home in on. This footnote, called "Operating Segments," describes GE's healthcare unit, including the products it makes (such as magnetic resonance imaging and computed tomography devices).

10. **Do the analysis.**

    Scroll down even further in the footnote and you'll see a financial breakdown of all GE's business units, including healthcare. It turns out, GE's healthcare business hauled in $18.3 billion in revenue in 2012, making it the company's third largest of eight business units. That's a significant fact and tells the investment banker that healthcare is of interest to GE. In fact, the healthcare unit grew by just 1.1 percent in 2012 — that's pretty slow growth, especially compared to the

14.8 percent growth in the transportation unit. Perhaps a manager of GE's healthcare unit would be up to discussing a merger that could reignite growth for them.

The preceding steps are just a hypothetical example, but they give you an idea of how the EDGAR database can be tapped to glean financial insights about companies of importance to investment bankers.

Watch out, EDGAR — here comes social media

For decades, EDGAR has been the official source of company information for investors and investment bankers. Investors have long learned that if they want to get information, and be completely sure it's official and accurate, EDGAR is *the* source. In fact, many of the professional tools investment bankers use pull in data from EDGAR.

But rapid changes in the way investors get information about companies are starting to take hold. In April 2013, the SEC gave companies the green light to start using social media sites like Facebook and Twitter to share and disseminate information to investors. The SEC says it's okay as long as the companies inform investors that they plan to use social media to share information ahead of actually doing so.

The SEC's acceptance of social media is a significant development. The shift prompts investors to broaden their tech skills to make sure they don't miss anything. Investors must take a close look at the official regulatory documents, including 8-Ks, 10-Ks, and 10-Qs, and see if companies disclose their plans to share information on Facebook and Twitter. If they do, investors will need to sign up to follow the companies on those social networks.

The SEC's change arose from a query into a Facebook post made by Reed Hastings, CEO of online video site Netflix. Hastings told his Facebook followers that the company was hitting a milestone in the number of hours being watched on the service. The SEC didn't find any wrongdoing, but it used the event as a teaching moment. Netflix subsequently told investors it may issue material information on five different social media venues, including the Netflix blog, the Netflix Tech blog, the Netflix Facebook page, the Netflix Twitter feed, and Hastings's public Facebook page.

So far, most companies are taking a wait-and-see attitude toward social media. Most of the companies that are using social media are simply posting links to their EDGAR filings or press releases. If you'd like more information on how to follow companies on social networking sites like Twitter and Facebook, check out *Facebook For Dummies,* 5th Edition, by Carolyn Abram (Wiley), and *Twitter For Dummies,* 2nd Edition, by Laura Fitton, Michael E. Gruen, and Leslie Poston (Wiley).

Remember: When dealing with investment information, be extremely careful about the source. In this age of instant information, faulty information can get disseminated quickly and spread rapidly. An infamous example of bad information spreading quickly came in August 2000 when a 23-year-old student from El Camino Community College concocted a fake press release about technology company Emulex. The press release falsely stated that the company's accounting was being investigated by the SEC. That fake press release hit an online press release dissemination service at 10:13 a.m. Eastern time, and shortly after, a news service reported on it. In just 16 minutes, 2.3 million shares of Emulex traded hands, and the stock price plummeted and destroyed $2.2 million in market value.

Getting Data in a Format You Can Work With

EDGAR can be a bit like catnip for investment bankers: They can't get enough. When you start diving into the regulatory filings of companies, it's not long before you're checking the annual reports of competitors or diving into the latest stock moves of Warren Buffett.

But if there's one shortcoming of EDGAR, it's that the data aren't exactly in the most perfect shape for analysis. The data contained in the regulatory filings aren't typically presented in a format that's easily analyzed. In a perfect world, the financial statements would be in a spreadsheet that could be crunched. But instead, the documents are stored in text files, which are fine for reading, but not so great for doing the kinds of analysis investment bankers are known for.

Don't lose heart, though. In this section, we tell you how to transform the data-laden files of EDGAR into files that are just begging to be analyzed. Before getting your hands dirty with Microsoft Excel, though, it's useful to see if any web-based tools can do much of the heavy lifting for you. If those tools fail, which may happen if your needs are unique, you need to understand how to import EDGAR data into an Excel spreadsheet.

Assembling the tools you need

Joe Friday of *Dragnet* fame would like EDGAR. EDGAR gives you the facts and just the facts. The SEC puts little to no effort into getting the data into a format that's easy to analyze. And that's by design. EDGAR is built to simply be a central storage place for all the documents filed by companies and investors.

Investment bankers need much more than comes out of EDGAR. Reading a regulatory filing word by word like a book isn't how analysis is done. The numbers must be examined and dissected, and making this happen takes some data mining.

But before you start building complex mathematical formulas and spreadsheets, it's always a good idea to see if you're able to get the data you need from a pre-built system. Here are examples from three of the most dominant players in the business that do much of the analysis of EDGAR data:

- ✔ **Bloomberg:** If knowledge is power on Wall Street, then investment bankers' go-to weapon is their Bloomberg machine. These devices, which you see perched on many investment bankers' desks, pull financial data from thousands of sources, including from EDGAR. All the data are organized and accessible with just a few keystrokes. You can find data about the specific company you're examining, but also the stock and bond data of the company's competitors. If you work at a firm that has Bloomberg access, you'll most likely be able to extract the data you need there.

- ✔ **S&P Capital IQ:** Standard & Poor's is a household name, but when it comes to ranking the creditworthiness of companies and governments, it's becoming more well known when it comes to data services. S&P Capital IQ is a web-based financial information system that provides in-depth access to just about anything you'd want to know about companies. The system calculates various financial ratios, like the ones you find out about in Chapter 8. S&P Capital IQ is especially good at pulling data out of EDGAR and presenting it in a way that makes analysis easy.

- ✔ **Thomson Reuters:** This data service has a long history of being invaluable for investment bankers, especially in Europe. It, too, contains a wealth of knowledge from companies, and if your office has access to the system, you can save yourself lots of time by pulling the data out here.

Keep in mind that Bloomberg, S&P Capital IQ, and Thomson Reuters are all, first and foremost, professional products. The subscription fees for these services are pretty steep, because they're not designed for consumer use. But if you work at a bank, brokerage firm, or investment banking operation, most likely you can gain access to one of these three systems.

Even if your workplace doesn't have Bloomberg or Thomson Reuters access, you can still gain from their wealth of information. Both Bloomberg (www.bloomberg.com) and Thomson Reuters (www.reuters.com/finance/stocks) operate robust public websites that contain a good helping of aggregated data from EDGAR. Thomson Reuters's website is particularly good at providing investors with a bevy of commonly used financial ratios. You can save yourself a ton of time by looking up financial ratios on Thomson Reuters's site as opposed to calculating them yourself. But if you still want to calculate the ratios, which is a good idea to know how to do, be sure to check out Chapter 8.

Importing financial information into Excel

If you don't have access to one of the big financial services commonly used by investment bankers (see the preceding section), don't fret. As long as you have access to a spreadsheet program, the most powerful of which is Microsoft Excel, you can do deep analysis of company data. The tricky part, though, is knowing how to get data from EDGAR into Excel. There are a few ways to help your data make the leap.

Copying and pasting EDGAR data

To copy and paste data from EDGAR into an Excel spreadsheet, follow these steps:

1. **Get the EDGAR financial document up on your screen.**

   See the "How to use EDGAR to pinpoint information" section, earlier in this chapter, for instructions.

2. **Hold down the left mouse button, and highlight the data you want to capture.**

3. **When all the data is highlighted, click your right mouse button and choose copy.**

4. **Open Excel.**

5. **Place your cursor in cell A1, and right-click.**

   A contextual menu appears. In newer versions of Excel, this menu has several Paste options (including Paste – Keep Source Formatting or Paste – Match Destination Formatting), and the one you choose varies on how the data was formatted in EDGAR, which varies by company. With some versions of Excel, including Excel 2013, you can see what the pasting will look like before you actually commit. Choose the paste option that keeps the columns in the best order and go for it. You'll know the best paste option because the data will line up neatly in rows and columns in the spreadsheet.

   If you don't like the way it looks after pasting, just press Ctrl+Z (⌘+Z on a Mac) to undo your work. Then right-click, and try another paste option.

6. **Clean up the spreadsheet.**

   When cutting and pasting from EDGAR into Excel, a few glitches are easy to spot. For example, you may find a strange column break or another weird formatting issue. You can clean them up as needed.

Importing directly into Excel

Copying and pasting into spreadsheets is usually the first thing that comes to mind when people think about analyzing EDGAR data. But sometimes the jump over the great divide doesn't go well. In those cases, or in more specialized instances where you want to automate the process, you can use a built-in feature of Excel that pulls in data from Edgar. It's Excel's Data From Web feature. Here's how to use it:

1. **Open a new Excel spreadsheet, and go to the EDGAR page you need.**

2. **Select the Data tab in Excel, and click the From Web option.**

    If you're using an old version of Excel (2003 or earlier), you won't see a Data tab. In that case, we suggest upgrading Excel. (You'll be better off in the long run anyway.)

    A box that looks like an Internet Explorer browser screen appears.

3. **Copy the EDGAR web page address and paste it into the New Web Query box in Excel, and click Go.**

    The New Web Query feature scans the EDGAR page for any table and places a yellow square with an arrow next to it.

4. **Click the yellow square with the arrow next to the table you want to pull into Excel.**

5. **Click the Import button at the bottom of the New Web Query window, and click OK in the Import Data box.**

    Excel does the rest.

Getting in tune with interactive data

The SEC has been on a push to help make it easier for investors to use EDGAR. One of the SEC's initiatives is designed to help get data to leap from EDGAR to Excel. Some companies choose to file their financial data on EDGAR in a special format called *interactive data*. Some companies may voluntarily add a function to EDGAR that allows investors to see financial data in tabular form.

To obtain a company's interactive data, follow the instructions in the "How to use EDGAR to pinpoint information" section, earlier in this chapter. When you see the list of available documents listed for the company (in Step 6), if that company makes interactive data available, you'll see an Interactive Data button next to the Documents button (refer to Figure 6-2). After clicking the Interactive Data button, all the company's financials will be presented in an special website that allows you to choose different ways to look at the data. And the data are presented in a table that makes it much easier to cut and paste into Excel than the standard electronic filing.

Paying Attention to the Non-Financial Information

Numbers, financial statements, and other quantifiable information are usually what people associate with investment bankers and investing banking. But it's pretty typical for investment bankers to have to pay close attention to non-financial data, too. Much of the art of a deal has to do with recent developments at companies, not to mention the personalities of the key players.

Doing your homework and analyzing the financial information of companies is certainly one of the primary things an investment banker needs to do. But don't overlook the importance of non-financial developments either. Just because a data point doesn't fit into the rows and columns of a spreadsheet doesn't mean it's not important.

Monitoring news streams for investment banking ideas

Investment bankers don't waste any time in reacting to corporate developments. The trading desk at many large firms is clearly reacting in real-time to changes in interest rates, exchange rates, and the stock market. But all areas of an investment banking operation need to be nimble and able to adjust the operation's offerings to reflect the current economic environment.

Investment bankers need to keep their eyes on developments at companies or markets to identify ways to best serve their customers. Doing so means constantly surveying the economic landscape for developments pertaining to key aspects of the financial system.

Monitoring the macro economy

Companies and investors like to think of themselves as free thinkers, but most are largely beholden to the vagaries of the economy. When the economy is rockin'-'n'-rollin' and the factories are humming, many companies look to get aggressive and expand, buy competitors, and file to sell stock to the public. But when the economy cools off and business gets slow, most companies completely retrench, lay off employees, and cut investment in plant and property.

Investment bankers need to keep a close eye on how the economy is performing so they can be in sync with the needs of clients. One aspect of watching the macro economy involves keeping tabs on *economic indicators*.

Economic indicators are statistical measures that sample the health of the economy. Oft-watched economic indicators include the following:

- ✔ **Consumer confidence:** When consumers are in the spending mood, it can drive demand for companies' goods and services. The University of Michigan releases monthly survey data on thousands of households to reveal how consumers are feeling about the economy.

- ✔ **Unemployment reports:** When jobs are hard to come by, companies aren't hiring and consumers aren't spending. This critical piece of economic data, from the Bureau of Labor Statistics and U.S. Department of Labor, is closely watched each month.

- ✔ **Retail sales:** The U.S. economy is consumer driven, so if consumers aren't spending, that's not good for growth. Investors closely watch the total receipts of retail outlets, generated by the Census Bureau of the Department of Commerce each month.

- ✔ **Inflation:** Inflation, or rising prices, can have a profound influence on the economy, companies, and investors. Inflation can be measured in several ways, including the Consumer Price Index (CPI), which is a monthly gauge of the cost of a representative basket of goods.

You can always go to the source of economic indicators. For instance, if you want, you can go directly to the website of the Bureau of Labor Statistics (www.bls.gov) to retrieve information on the unemployment rate or the CPI. But investment bankers often save time by using services that not only pull all the economic indicators into one place, but show what economists were expecting. The value of the indicator itself isn't as important as how it measures up to forecasts.

A great source for economic indicator data is Briefing.com, which maintains an economic calendar http://briefing.com/investor/calendars/economic/ and not only gives the data and dates of key reports, but tells you what was expected.

Monitoring the news

Don't forget that investment banking demands ebb and flow with developments in the business world. For that reason, it's critical to keep a close eye on developments in companies to know where the demands for financial services will likely be. Both Bloomberg and Thomson Reuters maintain dedicated news feeds that give investment bankers a good idea of the developments that matter most.

Bloomberg's and Thomson Reuters's websites are comprehensive data sources, so it's easy to get distracted. But if you're looking to monitor news key to investment banking, Bloomberg places much of that in the news area, www.bloomberg.com/news, and Thomson Reuters places it in its Global Markets area, www.reuters.com/finance/markets.

Don't overlook the major national newspapers and their websites — *The Wall Street Journal, The New York Times,* and *USA TODAY* closely watch business developments. All these sources also provide links to their stories using Twitter, which is fast becoming a handy way for investment bankers to measure scuttlebutt on news and the economy.

Monitoring the filings

One of the greatest things about EDGAR is that it contains just about every filing ever made by a company. But that's also one of its drawbacks. There's so much data being filed to EDGAR that you can easily overlook important filings that may slip in unnoticed. The investment banker's duty is to keep a close eye on what companies and investors are filing so nothing gets overlooked.

Most of the professional market information tools — Bloomberg, Thomson Reuters, and S&P Capital IQ — allow users to get notifications when a company of interest makes a filing. But there are free services that do the same thing for people who don't have access to these services. SECFilings. com (`www.secfilings.com`), for instance, allows you to set up alerts and be notified anytime a company, investor, or any other filers submits a document to EDGAR.

Quickly processing information with aggregators

If you pick up anything from this section, it's that investment bankers are constantly on the search for data. They're looking for clues about the economy's direction and closely monitoring the stock market and company filings. Any information about the financial markets can help an investment banker sense what kind of financial products will be in demand.

Because investment bankers are so focused on certain areas, it's especially important to keep a close eye on specific transactions. Trend information can be helpful when trying to figure out what companies and investors will need from their investment bankers in the future.

Keeping tabs on mergers and acquisitions

Two of the biggest money makers for investment bankers are buyouts and sellouts. When companies are on the hunt to buy rivals or other businesses (see Chapter 4), there are lots of fees for investment bankers to collect on. Luckily, there are ample tools for investment bankers to see who's buying whom.

One popular source for mergers and acquisitions (M&A) hounds is Mergermarket (www.mergermarket.com). The subscription service closely monitors deal making so investment bankers can see how active the M&A market is and try to figure out what companies may be in play and, therefore, in the market for an investment banker. Factset Mergers (www.factsetmergers.com), another subscription service, monitors M&A activity to keep investment bankers informed. And Dealogic (www.dealogic.com), another subscription service, keeps in-depth data on deals so investment bankers can mine for trends and try to see what's next.

Tracking the IPO market

Bringing companies public, and allowing them to raise money by selling stock to the public, has long been a cornerstone of investment banking. So, keeping an eye on what kinds of companies are going public and at what prices is a critical thing investment bankers should be watching.

A top source of IPO market data is Renaissance Capital (www.renaissancecapital.com); here, you find data on recent IPOs and in-depth and thoughtful resources regarding IPO trends. The *IPO calendar* is a listing of all the IPOs that are coming, and something investment bankers keep close tabs on; IPOScoop.com (www.iposcoop.com) lets you track the IPO calendar.

Watching corporate profits

When companies are swimming in profits, they don't jump into a money bin like Uncle Scrooge. These profit-rich companies can, though, afford to do many of the things investment bankers would like them to do. After all, the companies flush with profit can entertain ideas of buying another company or investing in a new plant or expanding overseas.

Given that profits are what fill a company's coffers, investment bankers need to monitor profits closely. There's no question that companies provide full details on their profitability in their financial statements on EDGAR. And in Chapter 7, we explain how to read companies' profit reports.

But investment bankers must also have an understanding of overall profit growth trends for companies at large. And S&P Dow Jones Indices maintains a treasure trove of profit data at http://us.spindices.com/indices/equity/sp-500. There, you can see corporate profit trends, using the Standard & Poor's 500 universe of large U.S. companies.

Doing research on the key players in a deal

Don't make the mistake of thinking that a deal is just about the numbers. The people behind the deal — for instance, the CEO and investors in a company being targeted for a buyout — can be very important.

Bloomberg, S&P Capital IQ, and Thomson Reuters all maintain comprehensive databases on all the players in finance, ranging from mutual fund managers to large investors. These services even allow you to e-mail some of these heavy hitters.

If your employer doesn't have access to one of these services, or you're an individual, you'll need to be a bit more creative to find the information you need. Again, EDGAR is your best friend.

 If you're looking for information about a large investor, for instance, you can use the same EDGAR search directions given in the "How to use EDGAR to pinpoint information" section, earlier in this chapter. But instead of using the Fast Search, you can use the Company Name search. Most big investors operate under a company name. For instance, if you want to track the moves of hedge-fund manager David Einhorn, you'll want to search for his investment firm — Greenlight Capital — in EDGAR. There, you'll find all Einhorn's moves that must be reported to the SEC.

Chapter 7

Making Sense of Financial Statements

*W*hen you go to the doctor, you end up sharing parts of your body or personal concerns you don't normally divulge to just anyone. It's the professional relationship you have with your doctor that makes you feel free to open the kimono, literally and figuratively.

A similar situation exists between investment banks and their clients. Companies commonly share detailed aspects of their business with close financial advisors. It's part of the relationship between investment banks and companies, and a big reason why the industry is so closely regulated — that information has great value.

But even though companies often share privileged information with investment bankers, investment bankers must do their part to research a company in order to understand it better. And when it comes to getting to know a company, even beyond what the CEO may tell an investment banker, the financial statements are hard to beat.

A company's *financial statements* break down exactly how the firm is performing financially, how it got there, what kind of economic condition it's in and even a little bit about how it's positioned for the future. Information contained in the financial statements is generally considered to be the base camp from which companies and their investment bankers must start before building more complex financial products and planning for the future.

In this chapter, you find out about the primary financial statements investment bankers pay the most attention to: the income statement, balance sheet, and statement of cash flows. And since the proxy statement is such a treasure-trove of company information, we explore that document, too, from an investment banker's perspective.

Income Statements

Individual investors are often fixated on the income statement. Every quarter, investors eagerly await *earnings season* (a roughly three-week period during which major companies report their quarterly results). During earnings season, investors pore over the financial documents released by companies, especially the income statement.

There's a good reason why investors pay such keen attention to the income statement: The income statement is what tells all interested parties, stock investors, bondholders, employees and, yes, investment bankers, how much the company earned during that quarter.

The income statement's basic task is to show investors how much the company brought in by selling goods and services, and how much was left in profit after paying expenses.

The income statement adheres to very strict accounting guidelines, called *generally accepted accounting principles* (GAAP). All companies that trade on U.S. exchanges and file financial statements with the Securities and Exchange Commission (SEC) are required to follow GAAP. By following the same set of accounting rules, investment bankers are able to compare the financial results of different companies against each other.

Although all companies must follow these rules, there is often room for interpretation of these guidelines, and comparing one firm to another may not be an "apples-to-apples" comparison. You can find more on this in Chapter 16.

The income statement is used by investment bankers primarily to

- ✔ **Gauge the trajectory of the business.** By reading the income statement, investment bankers can get a good idea where the company is on the spectrum of the firm's lifecycle. The income statement, for instance, can show investment bankers if it's a young company that's growing rapidly or a lumbering giant that's hitting the wall and struggling to find new businesses to tap.

✔ **Find out where a company's objectives lie.** If there's one reason why investment bankers pay close attention to the income statement, it's because other investors and company management pay close attention to it. If a company's management, including the CEO, can't find a way to drive profit higher, their high-paying jobs could be on the line. By scanning the income statement, investment bankers can in short order get a pretty good idea of what problems CEOs must solve in order to hang onto their lucrative jobs.

✔ **Understand the true drivers of the business.** Companies are often best known for their higher-profile businesses, but the true driver is something else. The income statement cuts away any preconceived notions about which businesses are most important to a company and gets down to the facts.

The true drivers of business

"Invest in what you know" is one mantra routinely repeated by individual investors. The renowned investor Peter Lynch repeated this refrain in his best-selling book *One Up on Wall Street* (Simon & Schuster). Many naïve investors feel that if they enjoy the products and services of a company, they should run home and invest in that company's stock.

Investment bankers need to avoid such simple thinking, though, and the income statement is a good way to stay objective. For instance, consider the Walt Disney Company. The entertainment company is perhaps best known for its worldwide theme-park empire, and many people assume that Disneyland and Walt Disney World are the biggest drivers of the business. But a quick examination of the company's income statement reveals that, although theme parks are very important to Disney, they aren't its largest business.

An examination of Disney's fiscal 2012 income statement, for the year ended September 29,

2012, shows that the company brought in total *revenue* (total payments for goods and services) of $42.3 billion during the period. After paying all its expenses, Disney turned a *profit* of $10.0 billion.

But looking into the matter with more detail using the income statement, it turns out that during 2012 at least, Disney's theme parks accounted for just 31 percent of the company's revenue and 19 percent of profit. The bulk of the company's revenue, 46 percent, and profit, 66 percent, actually came from Disney's media networks business, namely the ESPN sports network.

In this chapter, we show you how to analyze the income statement yourself. If you're interested, websites can do some of the analysis for you, too. For example, Trefis (www.trefis.com) examines companies' income statements and helps calculate which products have the biggest influence on the value of the business.

Locating the areas of interest to investment bankers

If you're an accountant or investor, you look at the income statement very differently than an investment banker does. Accountants look for inconsistencies or ways the companies may overstate their profits or appearance of success. Investors examine the income statement for clues on whether the company would likely be a good investment. But investment bankers look at financial statements trying to find ways to approach the companies with ideas of ways to improve results.

This chapter isn't intended to be a comprehensive primer on the line items on the financial statements. There are entire books dedicated to that topic, and they're pretty thrilling, as you can imagine. The point of this chapter is to explain the basics of the financial statements and how investment bankers, in particular, examine them. In Chapter 8, you find out how to glean insights from the numbers from the financial statements by turning them into financial ratios. If you're interested in finding out even more about reading financial statements to discover undervalued investments, here's our shameless plug for *Fundamental Analysis For Dummies,* by Matt Krantz (Wiley), which shows you some of the tricks.

For investment bankers, the focus is on certain line items on the income statement that are the most telling for their purposes, including

- **Revenue:** *Revenue* is the amount of total sales that's being hauled in by a company. Revenue is sometimes called *sales* or "the top line." Investment bankers pay very close attention to revenue because it's a measure of the amount of dollar volume running through the company. Revenue is also the basis for measuring how quickly a company is growing. Companies must follow strict guidelines that determine when they can count a sale as revenue, in a process called *revenue recognition.*

- **Cost of goods sold (COGS):** Companies don't get to keep all their revenue, as hard as they might try. There are costs associated with producing a product or service. Those *direct costs* include buying raw materials.

- **Gross profit:** A company's *gross profit* is how much is left of revenue after paying COGS. Gross profit is a good indication of how profitable a company's line of business is before mucking up the analysis with peripheral overhead costs, some of which are more controllable than direct costs are.

- ✔ **Selling, general, and administrative costs (SG&A):** Companies don't just need to buy raw materials to get a product to market. There are salespeople to pay, not to mention advertising costs and executive paychecks to deal with. These overhead costs are often *indirect costs* by investment bankers.

- ✔ **Operating income:** A company's *operating income* is how much it keeps from revenue after paying both direct and indirect costs. Operating income gives investment bankers a good indication of a company's profitability, excluding the bite from Uncle Sam in the form of taxes.

- ✔ **Interest expense:** Companies that borrow money from bondholders or other lenders typically need to make periodic interest payments on those loans. The portion of the expenses paid in the current period is shown in the interest expense line item.

- ✔ **Income taxes:** Companies must pay taxes, too. Taxes can be a significant cost for companies, and tax bills may even come into play when making decisions on business moves or where even to physically locate a business. One consideration in mergers, for instance, has to do with managing tax bills.

- ✔ **Net profit:** Investment bankers arrive at the bottom line, or *net profit*. Net profit tells the investment bankers how much the company earned after subtracting all the costs.

These line items apply to most manufacturing firms and even many service firms like restaurant chains. Financial companies are unique, and the line items on the income statement are read differently.

Tweaking the statement with different assumptions

Unlike many other users of financial statements, investment bankers rarely accept the financial statements at face value. To glean insights about where the business may be headed, and what kinds of financial products the company may need, investment bankers tweak the numbers for their own analysis purposes. All accountants must operate under the same rules, but those rules allow for some maneuvering.

Looking at financials in a new way: Pro-forma results

Investment bankers largely look at financial statements as ancient history. And it's true that even a quarterly statement may be a month old before it's filed to the SEC's EDGAR system (see Chapter 6), and by then, the business may have changed.

Given the backward-looking nature of financial statements, investment bankers try to use information from the past to tell something about the future. That's the role of so-called *pro-forma analysis*. In Latin, *pro forma* means "as a matter of form." In a pro-forma analysis, Investment bankers take the financial statements, including the income statement, and make hypothetical adjustments to them.

An investment banker thinking about pitching a buyout candidate to a company, for instance, may add that target company's revenue to the buyer's revenue on the income statement. By making estimates based on the past income statement, the investment banker can attempt to see how much the deal may add to the purchasing company's bottom line. Forming these hypothetical *financial models* can help investment bankers see how proposed changes to the business will likely affect its results.

Finding out all about net operating profit after tax

One of investment bankers' favorite adjustments to the income statement is net operating profit after tax (NOPAT). NOPAT is a way to look at a company's profit to remove the distortion of debt and interest costs. NOPAT is calculated as follows:

$$NOPAT = Operating\ Income \times (1 - Corporate\ Tax\ Rate)$$

Investment bankers like to look at NOPAT as a way to see how profitable a company is, leaving out the influence of the costs of debt financing. Examining NOPAT gives investment bankers an idea of how much debt a business can theoretically support before the interest payments become too onerous.

Finding investment banking opportunities

The income statement is fertile ground for investment bankers looking for holes in a business that may be filled with some financial products. Part of the magic investment bankers subject the income statement to is based on financial ratios (see Chapter 8). Another technique is comparing a company's financial statements to the industry (as shown in Chapter 9). But there are opportunities to spot just by glancing at the income statement, including the following:

✔ **Capacity to handle more debt:** Investment bankers love finding ways to get companies to take on more debt. Adding debt to a company, or *leveraging* it, creates different ways for the investment bank to make money, including the selling of the bond offering. When used properly, leverage can also boost a company's profitability. The income statement, particularly the interest expense line item relative to the company's net income, can be especially telling when an investment banker is going to suggest a company add more debt.

✔ **Ripe for a boost in growth:** When investment bankers see the revenue line either stalling or creeping higher at a snail's pace, they see opportunity. Investors usually demand that companies generate growth, which can get increasingly difficult as companies get bigger. But when CEOs are looking for a fast and easy way to grow, they may turn to investment bankers for buyout candidates that may help the company get the top line moving higher again.

✔ **Candidates for divestiture:** Sluggish growth in net income, even as revenue is expanding, is a possible indication that the company may be involved in a *low-margin business*. A low-margin business is one that generates substandard levels of net income relative to the revenue it brings in. Sometimes a low-margin business can act as an anchor around a company because it ties up employees and resources, with little payback. Enterprising investment bankers may identify these low-margin businesses as candidates to be sold to another company, to private investors, or even to the public as an initial public offering (IPO) or spin-off. Although these low-margin businesses may be anchors to the company, if operated as stand-alone businesses, by management that focuses on that business, they may become quite profitable. As evidence of that, researchers find that spinoffs perform quite well.

Balance Sheets

The *balance sheet* is a snapshot in time of the financial health of a company. In its simplest form, the balance sheet is a financial statement that shows all the assets the company owns and all the liabilities that it owes based primarily on historical cost or book value.

Investment bankers with a practiced eye and attention to detail can take a quick glance at a balance sheet and identify a company's financial strengths and weaknesses. The balance sheet gives investment bankers a look at the resources and liabilities a company has at its disposal, critical information when it comes to pitching financial products to the company.

Finding your way around the key parts

Investment bankers have a unique way of looking at the world, and that view extends to the balance sheet. In this section, you find out the key elements of the balance sheet to investment bankers.

Getting to know the assets

Investment bankers might crack open the balance sheet by first examining what the company has. All the companies' possessions are listed as assets and placed into understandable groups:

- **Cash and cash equivalents:** Cold, hard cash — or, as controversial football star Randy Moss put it, "Straight cash, homey." There's nothing like it, whether inside your wallet or on the balance sheet of a company. Investment bankers pay particular attention to cash because it's critical in many corporate maneuvers. Cash equivalents are extremely short-term investments that can be quickly and easily turned into cash.

- **Accounts receivable:** When companies sell goods and services, they usually don't get paid right away. Instead, the selling company takes an IOU from the customer for a short time. These IOUs are called *accounts receivable* on the balance sheet.

- **Inventory:** Companies that make products can't manufacture them out of thin air. Companies must buy raw material and other ingredients, which is included in inventory. But the inventory line item also counts the value of products waiting to be sold or in various stages of manufacturing.

- **Property, plant, and equipment:** Companies often make massive investments in equipment and other facilities to bring their products and services to market. Here investors can find out how much those investments cost the company, minus depreciation (see the next bullet point).

- **Accumulated depreciation:** When companies buy an asset, whether a machine or building, the passage of time takes a toll on that asset and typically reduces its value. Accountants require the companies to estimate how much value has likely evaporated due to the passage of time, and this is known as *depreciation*.

  Depreciation may be a cost, but it doesn't cost the company any of its cash. This characteristic is important to remember later in this chapter when you read about the statement of cash flows.

- **Long-term investments:** Assets that companies plan to keep for a while, typically more than a year, are included here. Generally, these investments are stocks, bonds, and real estate.

- ✔ **Goodwill:** *Goodwill* is one of those assets that investment bankers know have value but have trouble describing. Goodwill is a catchall term to describe assets that have value, but generally aren't tangible. Goodwill is often associated with copyrights, trademarks, and brand names, for instance.

  One of the most common ways for companies to accumulate goodwill is when they buy another company for more than the book value of the company on the balance sheet. The difference is goodwill.

- ✔ **Total assets:** Investment bankers tally up the value of all the assets the company controls, and that is the *total assets*.

Finding out about the liabilities

You have to spend money to make money. That's just the reality of business. And the bills companies face, or the things they owe, show up in the liabilities section of the balance sheet, which includes the following:

- ✔ **Accounts payable:** Just because a company buys something from another firm doesn't mean it actually has to pay for it right away. The accounts payable line item measures the sum the company owes.

- ✔ **Short-term borrowings:** Companies can borrow in many different ways. Here, accountants require companies to break out what portion of the debt the company owes is due in less than a year.

- ✔ **Long-term debt:** When companies borrow money that's not due for more than a year, the total must be tallied up in the long-term debt line item.

- ✔ **Current portion of long-term debt:** A company may have a long-term loan, but part of that loan is to be repaid in less than a year. That portion of the loan due in the short-term must be disclosed here.

- ✔ **Capital leases:** Being a renter can be convenient, even for companies. But some leases come with many strings attached, which put the company on the hook for the obligations of the leased property. Those cases must be documented on the balance sheet.

- ✔ **Pension and other post-retirement benefits:** If you're like most working Americans, you probably don't get a pension and have to settle for a 401(k) match. But some older companies still owe retirees pension benefits. And oftentimes, these are especially large obligations.

Understanding the equity

Equity is one of those words in finance that can have many different meanings. In investment banking, the term *equity* is often used synonymously with stock, for instance. But when talking about the balance sheet, the term *equity* usually refers to the value of the shareholders' ownership of the company. Another good way to think of equity in terms of the balance sheet is the different between assets and liabilities.

Understanding a company's financial strength

The balance sheet for an investment banker serves a similar role as blood work for a doctor. When you go to the doctor, and blood is drawn, the physician can get a snapshot of your health at the current time. The blood work tells the doctor more about long-term trends or attributes about your health. Similarly, investment bankers use the balance sheet to get a broad view of the health of a company.

If a company just released a hit product, it may be posting huge profits and the income statement may show the numbers of a highly successful company. But not until the company finds a way to extract that profit and put it in the bank or invest it do those riches show up on the balance sheet.

The primary way investment bankers pull apart the financial statements is by using financial ratios (see Chapter 8). But there are ways to glean insights into a company's financial health just using the balance sheet, including the following:

- **Common sizing analysis:** One of the key weapons of investment bankers is the technique of *common sizing,* a type of financial analysis that measures all the elements of a financial statement relative to the total. When common sizing the balance sheet, all the company's individual assets are divided by the total assets and each of the individual liabilities are divided by the total assets, too.

  This seemingly simple exercise can quickly put a company's balance sheet into perspective. Table 7-1 is a simple example of common size analysis using Hershey's 2012 balance sheet. Notice how the common sizing puts the numbers in context.

  An investment banker would look at this common size analysis, and several things would immediately jump out. First, notice that 15 percent of the company's total assets are held in cash. An investment banker may wonder if there might be better uses for that cash than sitting idly collecting interest. Another takeaway is that 35 percent of the company's assets are tied up in property, plant, and equipment. This indicates that the company is pretty capital intensive, meaning large investments in equipment are needed to compete.

Table 7-1   Putting Hershey's Balance Sheet into Perspective

Balance Sheet Line Item	2012 Value ($ millions)	Common sized Value
Cash and equivalents	$728.3	15.3%
Accounts receivable	$461.4	9.7%
Inventories	$633.3	13.3%
Property, plant, and equipment	$1,674.1	35.2%
Goodwill	$588.0	12.4%
Other assets	$669.70	14.1%
Total assets	$4,754.8	100%
Accounts payable	$442.0	9.3%
Short-term debt	$118.2	2.5%
Current portion of long-term debt	$257.7	5.4%
Long-term debt	$1,531.0	32.2%
Other liabilities	$1,357.6	28.6%
Total liabilities	$3,706.5	78%
Total equity	$1,048.4	22%

✔ **Comparing debt to equity:** One of the most telling exercises for investment bankers looking at the balance sheet is the relationship between a company's total debt and its equity. By simply dividing a company's total liabilities by its total equity, investment bankers can see how leveraged a company is, or how much of the cost of the company's assets are financed using debt and how much are financed using equity.

Using the Hershey example above, investment bankers see that the company relies much more heavily — more than three times more — on borrowings than on equity. Knowing this will help guide the investment bankers offering solutions to the company.

✔ **Studying book value:** A company's *book value of equity,* loosely speaking, is much like a person's net worth. The book value of equity of a company is a rough estimate of what the company's collection of assets is worth after paying all its liabilities. The key assumption, here, however, is that assets are liquidated at book value and liabilities are extinguished at book value. In reality, some assets, such as land, may be worth much more than book value, and other assets, such as inventory, may be worth much less than book value. Book value of equity is calculated by subtracting total liabilities and goodwill from a company's total assets.

Book value is roughly designed to give investors an idea of what a company would be worth if all its assets were *liquidated* (sold off). That's one reason why goodwill is excluded from book value, because goodwill is an intangible asset and can't be easily sold separately. Some investors look for undervalued companies by looking for where stock prices are below a company's book value.

Locating pitfalls and opportunities

When individuals meet a financial planner, one of the first things they do is create a *net worth statement.* The net worth statement outlines all the assets owned and all the liabilities owed by the individual. At just a glance, the financial planner can create a set of priorities for the person to achieve. Similarly, an investment banker can get a quick opinion on a company's opportunities and deficiencies by looking at the balance sheet, including

- **Opportunity to increase leverage:** One of the top tricks of investment banks is helping companies sell debt securities to increase their level of leverage. By deploying more debt, depending on where interest rates are, companies can push their profitability up and appease and please stock holders. When a company uses debt to boost profit, that in turn increases the return on equity invested in the business.

Increased debt can work both ways for a company. Investors may be pleased by the increased returns by using debt, but the change also increases risk. Greater leverage can be dangerous if a company's cash flow falls and the interest payments turn onerous. That's why leverage is often referred to as a "double-edged sword."

- **Finding uses for cash:** A big pile of cash sitting on the balance sheet attracts the attention of investment bankers and makes them salivate like one of Pavlov's dogs. Especially when interest rates are low, as they were during much of the early 2000s, having cash sitting idly by can have a high *opportunity cost,* meaning companies are missing out on better returns elsewhere. Investment bankers will approach cash-rich companies for possible uses of that cash, including mergers and acquisitions (M&A) activity.

Statement of Cash Flows

Most individual investors dwell on the income statement and, to a lesser degree, the balance sheet. Investors are keenly tuned into how much a company is earning (so they can look for potential stock price growth) and how much cash a company has (eyeing fat dividends).

But investment bankers know the power of a third, often overlooked financial statement: the *statement of cash flows*. The statement of cash flows is the place where the company tells investors where the dollars are coming and going in the business.

Cash flow is very different from net income. A company may book a sale as revenue, but that cash isn't received yet. The statement of cash flow concerns itself with cold, hard dollars that find their way into the company.

Seeing why the cash flow statement is so important in deal making

Cash is king in investment banking. Make no mistake about it: The ability of a company to take on more debt or even do a deal often hinges on the business's cash generation characteristics. Companies with large and stable cash flows are often candidates for investment banking techniques, as the manager of the business attempts to extract greater profit from the company using financial tools.

And keep in mind that although the income statement is important in investment banking analysis, it's largely a tool designed by accountants. Net income is generated when companies follow a set of rules that accountants say determines the profitability of a firm. The statement of cash flows, on the other hand, is much less subjective. When a company hauls in or spends a dollar, there's no questioning it. A dollar is a dollar. You can spend dollars — you can't spend profits!

Investment bankers often focus on the statement of cash flow because it's seen as being a bit more pure and less tainted by accounting nuances and gimmicks than other financial statements, especially the income statement.

Understanding the key parts of the document

Follow the money! That's the advice often given to detectives and investigators. And the same can be said to investment bankers. Tracing the movement of cash through a company can tell the investment banker a great deal about the company and its economic feasibility. The cash flow statement is a powerful document that shows investment bankers how the business is a cash-using (or cash-burning) machine. This section gives investment bankers a quick run through the parts of the cash flow worth paying the most attention to.

The statement of cash flows is broken into three distinct areas. Each areas reveals specific information about the type of cash flow.

Cash flows provided from (used by) operating activities

If you want to know how much cash it brought from the business itself, this section is the one for you. Here, you find how much of the company's profit came from conducting business in cash.

Calculating cash flows provided from operating activities starts with net income, taken right from the income statement. Uses of cash are then deducted from net income, and sources of cash are added back. The most important adjustments to cash flow in the eyes of investment bankers include

- ✔ **Adding back depreciation and amortization:** Net income takes a big hit from an expense that doesn't cost the company a bit of cash: depreciation. Accountants require companies to deduct from their reported profit the estimated monetary value of wear and tear on equipment. But that wear and tear may never actually cost real cash. Depreciation is added back to net income to come up with net cash flow from operations.

- ✔ **Stock-based compensation:** A big part of a company's overhead is the money paid to executives. But much of the payment to CEOs and the other executives at the top of the firm is never paid in cash, but in stock-based rewards. Because this pay isn't in cash, it's added back to net income.

- ✔ **Change in accounts receivable:** When a company sells goods and services, it often doesn't collect right away. That sale may be good enough to count as net income, but it's not enough for cash flow from operations. Accounts receivables are subtracted from net income as a result.

Cash flows provided from (used by) investing activities

You have to use cash to make cash. Companies can often borrow money to make improvements to their facilities, but many times a company taps its cash hoard to add capacity, expand facilities, or build new computer systems.

The starting point for calculating cash flows provided from investing activities is cash flows provided from operating activities (from the preceding section). From there, a number of adjustments are made to show investors how much cash is used or generated not just from the company's operations, but also its investments. Sources of cash are added back, while uses of cash are subtracted, as follows:

- ✔ **Capital additions:** Periodically, the time comes for companies to put money into assets to make them better or make them last longer. These investments are called *capital additions*. When such improvements to assets are made using cash, the amount must be subtracted from cash flow.

✔ **Proceeds from sales of property, plant, and equipment:** Companies sometimes find that they're sitting on assets they don't need or want anymore. When these assets are sold, they're a boost to cash. In this section, investors adjust their cash flow to reflect the influx of cash from divestitures.

✔ **Business acquisitions:** Companies buy other companies for a variety of reasons (see Chapter 4). Whatever the reason for the deal, if the buyout is done using cash, that must be reflected as a use of cash in the cash flow statement.

Cash flows provided from (used by) financing activities

Even the simplest companies typically use cash that's brought in from outside investors or lenders. Even a 5-year-old opening her first lemonade stand likely got started using a loan to buy lemons and sugar from her parents.

This section of the cash flow statement attempts to help investors see the inputs and outflows of different forms of financing, be it from debt or stock. Digging into this area of the cash flow statement gives investment bankers a clear view of where the company is getting and using cash to pay for its operations. This section includes the following:

✔ **Increases in debt:** When companies borrow, it's an addition to cash from financing and added to cash flow. Investment bankers can keep an eye on whether companies have been adding to debt if they see increases on this line item in the statement of cash flows.

Companies often distinguish when they add short-term versus long-term debt. Often, when companies restructure, they try to exchange costly debt that matures in a few years, called *short-term debt,* with longer-term debt that matures in five or more years. This common maneuver, which often taps the resources of investment bankers, is designed to save on current interest expense.

✔ **Repayment of long-term debt:** When companies pay down debt, they're using cash. This can be a good move for companies looking to reduce their debt and interest expense.

✔ **Cash dividends paid:** Increasingly, investors have urged companies to use their excess cash to pay a periodic cash payment, or *dividend.* Dividends can be suspended by companies if they hit hard times (unlike interest payments that must be made), but they're still significant uses of cash.

Calculating free cash flow

As you can see, the statement of cash flow is a very comprehensive financial statement. Literally, every dollar flowing in and out of the company is counted and classified into the proper category.

But investment bankers often mix and match items from the three sections of the cash flow statement to get numbers that are most telling for them. One of the best examples of this kind of adjustment is *free cash flow* (FCF). Free cash flow measures the company's cash flow power from its core operations, after making the necessary improvements to its assets to keep the business running smoothly. *Remember:* A company that doesn't invest in keeping up its plant and equipment isn't going to be in business for the long-term.

Free cash flow isn't provided to you on the statement of cash flows, so if you want to analyze it, you'll have to calculate it. Here's how to calculate free cash flow:

1. **Start with net cash flows provided from operating activities.**

   On the statement of cash flows, the last item in the section, cash flows provided from operating activities is *net cash flows from operating activities.* This number is net income adjusted for all the uses and sources of cash from the company's normal operations.

2. **Subtract capital additions from net cash from operating activities.**

   You'll find capital additions from the cash flows provided by investing activities section of the cash flow statement.

3. **Analyze the findings.**

   The free cash flow number gives investment bankers a good look at how much cash the company needs to keep running on an ongoing basis. It's a good idea to do the same calculation for past periods, too, to see if the company's cash flow usage is rising or falling over time.

If a company's free cash flow is negative, alarm bells should go off in your head. Negative free cash flow means the business, as it currently stands, is not economically feasible over the long term. Many Internet companies in the late 1990s and early 2000s, were propped up with easy cash financing from IPOs. But when those firms' cash hoards disappeared, most of the companies did, too, and along with them the value of investor's stakes in those firms.

Proxy Statements

The three primary financial statements are the income statement, balance sheet, and the statement of cash flows. These three documents, when looked at together, give investment bankers an excellent view of the profitability, financial resources, and cash-generating characteristics of any firm.

But there's another document, which isn't technically a financial statement, that's very valuable to investment bankers as well. This document, called the *proxy statement* (sometimes known by its formal name, DEF 14A), is a bonanza for anyone looking to learn more about the company.

There's much more to the proxy statement than we have room for in this section. Our goal here is to help you identify the parts of the document of most interest to investment banking.

Learning about the key players in a deal

Real-estate brokers know that the biggest part of doing a real-estate deal is getting to know the people involved. It's exactly the same when looking to broker deals with companies. Personalities, egos, and relationships play a huge part in just about every deal investment bankers do, including helping along mergers, divestitures, and IPOs.

Because personalities are so important, investment bankers must take the time to get to know the people running the company. An excellent place to get started is the proxy statement, which spells out details about the people of power in a company.

A few of the details about people in a deal you can uncover from the proxy include

- **Biographies of the top management:** The CEO, chief financial officer (CFO), and chief operating officer (COO) are the primary points of contact for investment bankers approaching a company. The proxy statement provides complete biographies of these top players. You'll find details including age, educational background, and tenure at the company. This information can be a good starting point to get to know the players.

- **Clues on relationships the top management has at other companies:** Most proxy statements divulge some of the personal contacts of the top management, information that can be extremely valuable for investment bankers who know where to look. For instance, the proxy breaks out all the other companies the executive works with, usually as a member of the board of directors. You can be sure the management team member knows these other directors well, which is a way to start the networking process.

✔ **Details about the board of directors:** Some CEOs like to act like they own the place, but that's usually not the case. Typically, with most large companies, which are largely owned by public shareholders, the management team answers to the *board of directors* (a body of professionals hired by the shareholders to oversee the company's management team). The proxy spells out who these people are and describes their backgrounds — again, very useful information to the investment banker.

Investment bankers pay close attention to the board members who are part of the finance and risk management committees of a company. These subgroups of the board of directors are responsible for overseeing many of the activities that interest investment bankers the most, including decisions to invest in new facilities or divesting assets.

Identifying the management team's incentives

The biggest reason for diving in to the proxy statement and looking at the way the executives are paid isn't to get paycheck envy (although that may be a side-effect of doing so — during 2012, for instance, the median total compensation paid to CEOs of companies in the Standard & Poor's 500 was $9.7 million, up 8 percent from 2011, according to a *USA Today* analysis). The reason investment bankers pay such close attention to the way CEOs are paid is to understand what makes them tick, financially.

A deal may make perfect sense based on what the financial statements say, but investment bankers may hit resistance if the deal somehow works against a manager's personal interests. As Nobel laureate Milton Friedman said, "It is a law of economics that people respond to incentives. That's just how it is, no way around it."

For instance, an empirical look at the financial statements may make a great case for divesting a business unit. The business may be a total loser, generating low returns relative to the enormous investments needed to keep the business humming. A sale may bring cash into the company that could be paid as a dividend or plowed into another area of the business that's more profitable.

But an examination of the CEO's pay structure may explain why there's resistance to the deal. For instance, if the CEO's bonus is based in part on the company's total revenue hitting a certain size, a divestiture would likely reduce revenue and, in turn, reduce the CEO's bonus.

There are cases when the company's management may welcome a deal. It's pretty typical for the employment contracts of top executives to come with lucrative bonuses when a company is bought out, called *golden parachutes*. These deals can be worth hundreds of millions of dollars.

Analyzing management pay packages

It's important to understand that the management of companies are hired hands. The CEO and the rest of the management team are employed by the shareholders of the company to run it in the best way to generate returns for the stakeholders. But the CEO isn't running the company for fun — he expects to get paid (and paid handsomely) for his time and effort.

Before an investment banker even thinks about approaching a CEO to discuss a deal, it's imperative to understand the size and nature of the CEO's pay. And that's very possible using the proxy.

You can spend quite a bit of time analyzing the proxy, looking for all the ways the management is paid. The best way to see, quickly, how much CEOs are paid is to head to the summary compensation table in the proxy statement. The key portions of a manager's pay breaks down as follows:

- ✔ **Salary:** This is the annual base pay received by the executive. Typically, the salary received is a relatively small portion of the total pay package. Due to various tax rules, companies try to keep the salary below $1 million.

- ✔ **Bonuses:** Many executives are eligible for added cash payments if they meet certain predetermined performance goals. These bonuses can be quite hefty when executives accomplish the tasks.

- ✔ **Stock awards:** Increasingly, more executives are being granted *restricted stock,* which are special buckets of company stock that are locked until the executives meet certain preset guidelines for performance.

- ✔ **Stock options:** Stock options in this context are contracts that give the executives the right, but not the obligation, to buy company stock at a preset value sometime in the future. Stock options can become extremely lucrative when a company's stock rises. Stock options have been losing popularity versus stock awards for CEO pay because there's a concern that they encourage managers to do anything possible just to push up the stock price in the short term — because the stock options only have value if the price of the shares rises over time. The options are priced using a complex mathematical formula that estimates what the options were worth the day they were given to the executive, or the *grant-date value.*

✔ **All other compensation:** Ever wonder how the other half lives? In this part of the proxy, you get to find out. In this section, the companies spell out all the perks they give CEOs, including the use of the company jet, country club memberships, and private security. These perks, although relatively small in terms of absolute dollars, can be a big deal to executives because they're some of the sweet part of success.

✔ **Total:** All the executives' forms of pay are summed up here and put into the grand total.

Chapter 8

Perfecting the Financial Ratios for Investment Banking

. . . .

In This Chapter

▶ Finding out how investment bankers use ratios to glean insights from financial statements

▶ Uncovering how much companies are worth using valuation ratios

▶ Seeing how financially well positioned a company is with liquidity ratios

▶ Stacking up companies against each other using profitability ratios

▶ Detecting how well management uses shareholder money with efficiency ratios

▶ Tracking how quickly a company drives its bottom line with growth-rate analysis

. . . .

*I*f you're like most people, many ratios in your life provide insights about your daily routine. Your car's miles-per-gallon is a ratio that tells you how efficient your car uses energy. And your effective tax rate indicates how much of your paycheck winds up in Uncle Sam's hands.

Investment bankers, too, make extensive use of ratios to glean insights about companies and industries. Ratios are almost entirely calculated by extracting different pieces of data from the financial statements and comparing them with each other across time and with similar companies. It's the process of comparing financial data that provides keys to insightful analysis.

In this chapter, we show you how investment bankers tear apart the financial statements and apply ratio analysis to see what's really going on. You find out how richly a company's stock is prized by investors using *valuation multiples*. You see which companies may need a big-time infusion of cash to stay afloat using the *liquidity multiples*. You see how to size up a company's money-making potential using *profitability ratios*. You also understand how well the management team is putting shareholders' money to work using the *efficiency ratios*. Plus, understanding a company's growth prospects is also a use of ratio analysis.

The financial statements are useful, but ratio analysis makes them invaluable. In this chapter, you find out how to get ratios to work for you.

Valuation Multiples: Assessing How Much the Company Is Worth

The top question investors ask is how much a company is worth. Putting a price tag on a company using its financial statements is a full-time occupation of many of the world's most-famous investors. But as is often the case for investment bankers, what's even more important than what a company is actually worth is how much other investors *say* it's worth. The famous economist John Maynard Keynes made the analogy to picking the winner of a beauty contest. The goal isn't to identify the most beautiful woman, but to identify the woman the most people think is the most beautiful. Alas, the market is a fickle judge of beauty.

Many of the financial products and offerings investment bankers sell are based on the *market valuation* of a company, or the price investors place on an entire firm. Market valuation can rise and fall over the years as investors' attitudes about a company ebbs and flows. And it's exactly these changes in investors' appetites for a company and its securities that investment bankers must closely monitor. Timing can be critical when selling investment securities, and investment bankers want to sell when the demand for the securities is strong.

Valuation multiples can be invaluable tools in helping investment bankers gauge when demand for a company's stock or debt may be strong. Watching the trend in these ratios can help make an offering more successful for the sellers of the securities, the company.

Investors' favorite valuation tool: P/E ratio

If there's a famous valuation ratio, it's the *price-to-earnings* or P/E ratio. Even regular individual investors are often familiar with P/E ratios, and they use them as a guide to indicate when a stock is richly valued or arguably under-valued. The P/E ratio at its essence is a simple division problem:

$$P/E \text{ Ratio} = \frac{\text{Stock Price}}{\text{Earnings per Share}}$$

The P/E ratio tells investment bankers how much investors are willing to pay for a claim to a dollar of a company's earnings. The higher the P/E ratio, the more richly valued a company and its stock are.

At its heart, the P/E ratio is simple, but it can quickly get complicated as you dig deeper. The numerator of the ratio, the stock price, is something everyone can agree on. Investment bankers can obtain the stock price from any quote service. But the denominator, a company's earnings, is subject to debate. Individual investors often look at *forward P/E ratios,* which are the stock price divided by how much the company is *expected* to earn over the next year. But investment bankers tend to look at things a bit differently.

Investment bankers often want to look at P/E in a purer form that's based on hard numbers from the financial statements. For that reason, it's common for investment bankers to zero in on P/E based on historical earnings minus any extraordinary items. That means investment bankers divide the stock's current price by a company's diluted earnings per share excluding one-time items (such as restructurings, divestitures, and another non-recurring items). A company's diluted earnings per share excluding one-time items is often calculated as follows:

Diluted Earnings per Share Excluding One-Time Items = (Total Revenue – Cost of Revenue – Operating Expenses + Interest Expense – Income Tax Expense – Preferred Dividend + Unusual Items) ÷ Diluted Shares Outstanding

A company's diluted shares outstanding is a tally of all the shares there might be of a stock in the wild if all claims to the company were converted — including executives' stock option grants, outstanding warrants, and convertible bonds converted into common stock. The diluted shares outstanding can be obtained directly from a company's balance sheet.

Going old school with price-to-book

Price-to-earnings is a popular measure, but an imperfect one. The P/E ratio can tell investment bankers what investors are willing to pay for a dollar of earnings. A company's earnings, while important, are just one dimension of its value. Another measure, one that's closely watched by investors who are looking for bargains and investment bankers alike, is book value.

Book value is the corporate equivalent of a person's net worth. Investment bankers often focus on tangible book value, because it strips out assets that may be hard to accurately value or quickly sell. A company's tangible book value is its tangible assets minus its liabilities. The *price-to-book ratio* is the company's stock price divided by book value. The ratio tells investment bankers how much investors are paying for every dollar the company would raise if it were, in theory, liquidated and book value could be realized for the assets and liabilities.

In some situations, the price-to-book is preferable to P/E:

- ✔ **When dealing with a young company:** When companies are just starting out, they may have diminutive levels of earnings or even losses. In cases like these, the P/E ratio may be ridiculously high or not even meaningful.

- ✔ **When a cyclical company is in a downturn:** Earnings of some companies rise and fall by large degrees along with the ups and downs of the economy. During periods of economic decline, a company's P/E may look artificially high if the stock price hasn't fallen by as much as earnings. This can give a misleading impression of valuation.

- ✔ **When dealing with a capital-intensive business:** In some industries, massive investments in plant, property, and equipment are required. These firms may make enormous investments that are more significant to the value of the company.

Putting a price on profitability

Even if you're not an investment banker, you probably have heard of P/E ratios and price-to-book. Investment bankers are drawn to strange-sounding words and acronyms, especially to get a better handle on valuation. *Enterprise value to EBITDA* is certainly a ratio that's a bit off the beaten path. But it's designed to give investment bankers a more accurate read on how richly the market values a company by making a number of arcane, but reasonable adjustments. These adjustments can give investment bankers a way to compare how richly different companies are valued, even if these companies are carrying different amounts of debt. The enterprise value/EBITDA ratio is often used along with the P/E by investment bankers to see how pricey a company is.

Market value is certainly the most common way for investors to gauge how much a company is worth. *Market value* is the company's stock price multiplied by its number of shares outstanding.

But market value, while objective, has its shortcomings when it comes to measuring the value of a company. A company's market value is a reflection of the value of the company's stock. Stock investors, in theory, give a company's value a haircut to reflect the debt the company is carrying. This valuation haircut makes total sense for stock investors, but not so much for investment bankers who need to know how much the entire company, not just its stock, is worth.

Famous fan of book value: Warren Buffett

Book value may seem like an arcane concept, but it has many loyal followers. One of the best-known advocates of the utility of book value is famed investor Warren Buffett. Buffett even tells his Berkshire Hathaway investors that book value is one of the most useful (and simple) ways to measure the performance of the company against the broad stock market.

Every year, investors jump on the release of Berkshire Hathaway's annual report. The sage advice and clever turns of phrase are definitely part of the appeal of the lengthy document. But at the very top of the annual report, presented on the very first page, is a year-by-year list of

the company's book value per share. The rise or fall in Berkshire's book value per share is compared with the change in value of the Standard & Poor's 500 market index including dividends. When Berkshire's book value rises by more than the S&P 500, Buffett considers that to be a year the company executed well.

No financial measure is perfect. Buffett himself points to some of the shortcomings to the statistics in his owner's manual to Berkshire Hathaway shareholders. Still, the fact that Buffett pays such close attention to book value highlights how important the measure is, despite the flaws.

To make the market value statistic fit their needs, investment bankers often use *enterprise value,* which is the market value of a company with its net debt added back.

$$\text{Enterprise Value} = \text{Market Value} - \text{Cash and Short-Term Investments} + \text{Total Debt}$$

You're now halfway to understanding the enterprise-value to EBITDA ratio.

Another acronym you're practically guaranteed to hear if you hang out with investment bankers long enough is *EBITDA.* EBITDA is short for *earnings before interest, taxes, depreciation, and amortization.* The EBITDA measure is investment bankers' answer to the widely accepted but flawed measure of corporate earnings called *net income.* EBITDA involves a series of adjustments to net income to get to a measure of profitability that's not distorted by accounting or financial maneuvers.

EBITDA is calculated as follows:

$$\text{EBITDA} = \text{Net Income} + \text{Tax} + \text{Interest} + \text{Depreciation and Amortization}$$

Now that you're a master of enterprise value and EBITDA, the trick is to bring them together. Dividing enterprise value by EBITDA tells investment bankers the total value placed on a dollar of the company's earnings adjusted items that don't cost cash, like depreciation and amortization.

Since we're already talking about EBITDA, it seems only natural to discuss its close cousin, *EBIT.* EBIT is — you guessed it — earnings before interest and taxes. EBIT is a way to look at a company's profit that makes it a bit easier to compare with different companies. The measure adjusts a company's profit, adding back interest expenses and taxes, to get at a company's core, or *operating profit.* EBIT is calculated as follows:

$$\text{EBIT} = \text{Revenue} - \text{Cost of Goods Sold} - \text{Operating Expenses} - \text{Depreciation} - \text{Amortization}$$

Some investment bankers loosely interchange EBITDA with cash flow from operations, but that's not completely accurate. EBITDA and cash flow from operations involve different calculations. (If you want to understand what cash flow from operations is, there's a full explanation in Chapter 7.)

Liquidity Multiples: Checking Companies' Staying Power

No matter what kind of shape a company is in, investment bankers can usually find a financial product to offer the management. Investment bankers are a particularly creative and innovative bunch. When a company is growing and in need of cash to expand or grow, the investment bankers' ability to sell securities is very valuable.

But when a company is running into trouble, and needs creative ways to stay afloat, the investment banker is again tapped to help line up investors willing to inject much needed cash into the company.

Investment bankers can use liquidity ratios in a number of ways to gauge what kind of financial shape a company is in or to tailor the products and services pitched to the company. Here are some ways an investment banker might use the liquidity ratios to understand a company's health:

- ✔ **To size up how much of a company's financial resources are tied up in debt:** Companies can raise money in a variety of ways, with offering stock and selling debt being among the most common. The financial ratios help investment bankers see how reliant companies are on debt financing versus equity, or stock, financing. Here's where the *debt-to-equity ratio* comes in handy.

- ✔ **To determine whether a company can keep its head above water financially:** Many companies can afford all their bills, including those from their investment bankers, as long as the business is humming along. But it's important for investment bankers to understand what would happen if the business suffered a hiccup. Would the company's stumble be enough to make it unable to pay its upcoming bills? The *quick ratio* was designed to handle this question.

✔ **To see how much of a bite borrowing takes from profits:** A company can turbo-charge its profits by using all sorts of borrowed money. But the question is whether the business is able to justify that level of borrowing or leverage. Additionally, investment bankers need to know how much larger a company's profit is than interest payments, which is measured by the *interest coverage ratio*.

Deciphering debt to equity

Companies usually have a number of ways to raise money. And choosing between their chief options — issuing debt or stock — can have a profound influence on the company. For instance, companies that load up on debt can give their profit a real jolt when things go well because they're able to invest the money into moneymaking assets. But debt comes with a cost (interest), and if the cost of borrowing outstrips the returns, the company is actually destroying value.

Investment bankers, too, must understand the mix of a company's financing sources to tailor the products they sell. For instance, if a company is already getting a big portion of its financing from debt, then it may be a tough sell to talk the company into another debt offering.

Calculating a company's debt-to-equity ratio is pretty straightforward. It's simply the company's total liabilities divided by shareholder's equity. Both of these items are readily available from a company's balance sheet, as described in more detail in Chapter 7.

Interpreting debt-to-equity ratios is a bit of art mixed with a dash of science. The higher the debt-to-equity ratio is, the greater proportion of a company's finances comes from debt.

It's true that the higher the ratio, the more the company relies on debt financing. Some industries are more stable, though, and can comfortably handle more debt than others can. Industries that require large investment in equipment and those with stable cash flow — like electric utilities — tend to handle higher debt-to-equity ratios than those with less investment required, like software firms. It's important to consider debt-to-equity along with interest coverage, which you'll read about shortly. You can see how widely debt-to-equity ratios can vary by different industries in Table 8-1.

Table 8-1	Debt-to-Equity Ratios by Industry
Industry	*Debt-to-Equity Ratio*
Oil and gas refining and marketing	27%
Industrial conglomerates	103%
Technology software	8%
Health care	10.2

Source: Thomson-Reuters

Getting up to speed with the quick ratio

Quick! Could you pay off your bills if your income suddenly went to zero? It's a harrowing thought, but that's the kind of thinking investment bankers must sometimes apply to companies. Knowing how to stress-test a company and knowing what would result if the unexpected happened is what the quick ratio does. The higher the quick ratio, the more the company has in *liquid assets* (assets that can readily been turned into cash) that could be used to pay upcoming bills. The ratio is calculated as follows:

$$\text{Quick Ratio} = \frac{\text{Total Cash and Short-Term Investments} + \text{Receivable}}{\text{Total Current Liabilities}}$$

Notice that the quick ratio excludes inventory. While inventory is an asset that can be sold, it often takes time to sell and the amount received can be unpredictable, so it's excluded from the quick ratio.

Interpreting interest coverage

There are several places where more coverage is better, and that certainly goes for Speedo bathing suits. More coverage is also good for companies when it comes to making interest payments.

When companies take on debt, they're assuming liability for the resulting interest and principal payments. These payments aren't negotiable and companies don't have the right to pay them when they feel like it. Interest is due and must be paid or bad things happen, including wiping out the common shareholders if things degenerate enough. The city of Detroit discovered that in mid-2013.

Investment bankers must understand not only how much debt a company has relative to stock, using the debt-to-equity ratio described earlier, but also how onerous the interest payments are with respect to operating earnings. Interest coverage is a catchall term for a number of ratios designed to help investment bankers measure the significance of interest payments.

With investment bankers, a top interest coverage ratio is EBIT/interest expense, which is calculated by dividing a company's earnings before interest and taxes by the interest expense. The higher a company's interest coverage ratio, the more it's able to afford its interest payments.

We describe EBIT more fully in the "Putting a price on profitability" section, earlier in this chapter. Interest expense comes right off the income statement, as described in Chapter 7.

Profitability Ratios: Seeing How a Company's Bottom Line Measures Up

Beginners in investment banking commonly refer to a company as having "high margins." That kind of clichéd talk may sound impressive in a locker room, but it sounds quite naïve in a boardroom.

As more experienced investment banking professionals know, the term *profit margin* doesn't really mean much. *Profit margin* is a catchall term that describes a number of financial ratios that are designed to help put a company's profitability into perspective. The key ways to measure margins include gross margin, income from continuing operations margin and net margin.

Ratios to measure a company's profitability stem from the same financial document: the income statement. The income statement is a powerful financial statement that lists all the company's main forms of income and expenses. Investment bankers can glean many insights just by scanning this document.

But the income statement gets even more interesting after its data is applied to ratios. Financial ratios just put different parts of the income statement into perspective to provide additional insights not seen by looking at absolute numbers.

There are countless ways for investment bankers to slice and dice the financial statements, and there are countless financial ratios. But in this section, we fill you in on several of the ratios that matter most or that come up most frequently in investment banking transactions.

Why gross margin isn't so gross after all

If you knew a company turned a gross profit of $3 billion, that piece of information by itself wouldn't tell you much. If you read Chapter 7, you know that *gross profit* is what's left of revenue after paying direct costs. But $3 billion in isolation isn't very telling. Enter gross margin. Gross margin is a relatively simple calculation that tells investment bankers a great deal about the business.

A company's *gross margin* is gross profit divided by total revenue. The product tells you how much of every $1 in revenue the company keeps after paying direct costs. In essence, this is the money that's left and can be used to pay overhead and provide a return to shareholders.

Investment bankers can use gross margin as a way to see how profitable a company is before the distortion of *overhead costs,* which are often more controllable than direct costs. Like most ratios, though, the gross margin number itself is most meaningful in comparison with other companies and other industries, as you can read about in Chapter 9.

Income from continuing operations: Looking at profit with a keen eye

A company's gross margin may tell you how a company is doing managing its revenue and raw materials costs, but there's much more to running a business profitably.

Investment bankers pay attention to *income from continuing operations margin* as a way to see what proportion of revenue the company is able to hang onto after paying all its costs, including overhead, before the distortion of interest expenses and other peripheral costs. The ratio disregards unusual or one-time items that don't have anything to do with the ongoing functioning of the business, such as asset sales or restructuring charges.

Income from continuing operations margin is calculated as follows:

> Income from Continuing Operations Margin = (Total Revenue – Cost of Revenue – Operating Expenses + Net Interest Expense + Unusual Items – Income Tax Expense) ÷ Total Revenue

The result will be a percentage that tells you how much of every dollar the company keeps from revenue after paying all the ongoing costs of doing business.

Keying into profits with net margin

Net income isn't perfect. After all, net income is a financial measure created by accountants for everyone, not a tool designed for investment banking professionals. Even so, and despite the criticism mounted on net income, it's still a basis of accounting that all companies must follow. The uniformity of net income makes it a valuable tool, if anything, to compare disparate companies with each other.

Another beauty of net margin, despite its shortcomings, is that it's easy to calculate. Net income is provided by companies on their income statements. Calculating net margin is just a matter of:

$$\text{Net Margin} = \frac{\text{Net Income}}{\text{Total Revenue}}$$

This calculation of net margin gives you a percentage that tells you how much of every dollar a company earns after paying *all* its expenses, at least following the sometimes convoluted rules of accountants.

Net margin is another example of a profitability margin that can vary wildly depending on the industry the company is in. Investment bankers must take the time to carefully compare a company's net margin with peers before drawing significant conclusions from it. You can get a good feel for how net margins can vary by industry in Table 8-2. Again, industry analysis is so important to investment banking that you can dig into the topic with more detail in Chapter 9.

Table 8-2	Net Margin by Industry
Industry	*Net Margin (Five-Year Average)*
Energy	12.7%
Technology	11.8%
Healthcare	11.4%
Industrials	9.7%

Source: Thomson-Reuters

Efficiency Ratios: Knowing How Well the Company Is Using Investors' Money

O.P.P. may be best known as being "other people's property," or even the 1991 hit rap song from Naughty by Nature. But it's an apt description of the way companies are structured and financed.

Most large public companies are not owned by the CEO or the management team. Large public companies are run using other people's property, specifically stock and bonds.

But investors don't entrust money to management lightly and they're not doing it for fun. Investors are looking to get a return on their invested capital and pay close attention to whether management is delivering adequate returns.

Efficiency ratios can be a very useful way for investors to monitor whether a company's management team is putting money entrusted to it to good use. CEOs like to talk a big game and say they're positioning the company well for the future. But the efficiency ratios cut beyond the hot air, something investment bankers must be well prepared to address. Efficiency ratios not only show if the management is a proper steward to the financial resources entrusted to them, but by how much.

Efficiency ratios are examples of how insights can be gleaned by comparing data from two separate financial statements: the income statement and the balance sheet. Such cross-financial statement analysis can be very insightful when putting a company's profit into context.

The primary efficiency ratios of most importance to investment bankers include

- ✔ **Return on assets:** Is that fancy factory the company borrowed money to buy really paying off for investors? Find out using return on assets. Return on assets tells the investment banker how much of a profit is being driven from the company's fixed investments, such as plant, property, and equipment.

- ✔ **Return on capital:** Companies may sell stock and they may issue debt. Raising money puts cash into the hands of the management team, which then, presumably, invests that cash in projects that generate returns. But are the returns the management is getting enough to justify the cost of the money they raised? That's the question investment bankers can answer using return on capital.

> ✔ **Return on equity:** If there's anyone who focuses on what kind of return they're getting, it's the shareholders. After all, the bondholders know what they're getting. As long as the company stays in business, and pays its debts, bondholders can collect both the *coupon rate* (the interest rate the borrower agreed to pay during the life of the loan) paid on the bonds the company issued and get the principal amount of the loan back. But stockholders don't receive a payment as certain or concrete as an interest payment. That's where return on equity comes in. This handy ratio can tell stock investors what kind of return the company is generating on the money entrusted to it.

Finding out about return on assets

When investors buy stock or debt issued by a company, they're taking a leap of faith. The assumption is that the company is going to use the money to buy assets that can be used to drive higher profits, which can be paid to shareholders. But the type of assets bought can have a big influence on the returns shareholders ultimately get.

Let's say a company needs to buy a fleet of cars for salespeople to deliver product. That's reasonable. The company could do the prudent thing and buy moderately priced Ford vans. But a company may instead decide that it would be a heck of a lot more fun if the salespeople were cruising around in brand-new Ferrari sports cars. True, that would be more fun, but it would wreak havoc on the company's return on assets (ROA).

Poor investments that don't deliver the return are what investment bankers are looking for with the ROA calculation. The measure is calculated as:

$$\text{Return on Assets} = \frac{\text{Net Income}}{\text{Average Total Assets}}$$

You already know how to get the company's net income, to plug into the numerator. To get the denominator, the average total assets, you'll have do to a bit of work. Add the value of the company's assets at the end of the period you're analyzing to the value of the assets at the beginning of the period and divide by 2.

Investment bankers know that the higher the ROA, the better the company is harvesting profit from the assets it has acquired and deployed. Imagine that the company with the fleet of vehicles hauls in $10 million in net income. Now, the company using the low-cost Ford vehicles has assets of $100 million. That company's ROA is 10 percent. But if the company instead opts for the Ferrari fleet, and has assets of $500 million, suddenly the ROA drops to a paltry 2 percent.

ROA can vary greatly based on the industry that the company is in. (Sense a theme here?) And for that reason, investment bankers pay close attention to industry analysis with ROA. But even so, investment bankers can use this ratio to pinpoint companies that are finding intelligent ways to extract profit from their assets, especially by comparing ROA from year to year.

Digging into return on capital

Return on capital (ROC) is an extremely important financial ratio to investment bankers. It shows investors how much of a profit the company is hauling in from the level of capital — both debt and equity — plowed into the company. Again, if a company has access to boundless capital, it wouldn't be surprising that the company would generate lofty returns. ROC is a ratio that attempts to quantify how skilled the management is at putting the money — both debt and equity — entrusted to it to work.

Calculating ROC takes a bit of work. The formula, in a simplified form, looks like this:

$$\text{Return on Capital} = \frac{\text{Tax-Adjusted EBIT}}{\text{Average Capital Invested in Company}}$$

Looks easy, right? The trouble is, it takes a couple of additional steps to derive the numerator, tax-adjusted EBIT, as well as the denominator, average capital invested in the company.

First, to get tax-adjusted EBIT, there is a shortcut: You'll start with EBIT (see "Putting a price on profitability," earlier in this chapter). You could go to all sorts of trouble adjusting EBIT for taxes, but a simple workaround used by many investment bankers is to simply multiply EBIT by 0.625. This will take EBIT down by the appropriate corporate tax rate of 37.5 percent.

Now, it's time to get average capital invested in the company. Average capital invested in the company is a tally of all the debt and equity invested in the company. Because it's an average, it's generally advisable to take the capital invested in the company during the most recent 12-month period, add the capital invested in the company during the previous 12-month period, and then divide the sum by 2.

If your head is spinning on this one, don't fret. Table 8-3 has all the information you'd need to calculate Hershey's return on capital.

Table 8-3	Calculating Hershey's Return on Capital	
Financial Measure	**2012 ($ millions)**	**2011 ($ millions)**
EBIT	1,208.32	Not needed for calculation
Total equity	1036.75	857.32
Minority interest (debt)	11.62	23.63
Short-term borrowings (debt)	118.16	42.08
Current portion of long-term debt	257.73	97.59
Long-term debt	1,530.97	1,748.50
Total capital	2,955.24	2,769.12

Source: S&P Capital IQ

In Table 8-3, believe it or not, you have more than enough to calculate return on capital. Using the formula from earlier, you calculate return on capital as follows:

$$\text{Return on Capital} = \frac{\text{Tax-Adjusted EBIT}}{\text{Average Capital Invested in Company}}$$

$$= \frac{\$1,208.32 \times 0.625}{\left(\dfrac{\$2,955.24 + \$2,769.12}{2}\right)}$$

$$= 26.39$$

This tells you that Hershey generated a 26.4 percent return from the assets invested in it. Not too shabby.

As is the case with most of the financial ratios, the real analysis by investment bankers is done by comparing the ROC from a prior period — say, 2011 in this example — or against the ROC of another company in the industry. It's also important to note that most of the systems that investment bankers use — such as Bloomberg, S&P Capital IQ, and Thomson-Reuters — can calculate ROC.

Uncovering company secrets with return on equity

Stockholders think bond investors are a boring lot. And bond investors think that stock investors are wild-eyed dreamers with no respect for the dangers of investment risks. Given the often acrimonious relationship between stock investors and bond investors, it's not surprising they would keep their interests separated in the financial ratios.

Stock investors don't get too concerned about whether bond investors are getting their due, as long as they're getting theirs. The return on equity (ROE) ratio is a way to see how well management is making use of the money invested in the business by the shareholders. Return on equity is calculated using data obtained from both the income statement and the balance sheet, as follows:

$$\text{Return on Equity} = \frac{\text{Income from Continuing Operations}}{\text{Total Equity}}$$

If you can't recall how income from continuing operations is calculated, flip back to "Income from continuing operations: Looking at profit with a keen eye," earlier in this chapter.

Calculating a company's growth rate

Investment bankers know full well that financial statements are largely a look back at a company's past. A company's most recent balance sheet, for instance, tells you what the company owned and owed at the point in time at which the statement was produced. The criticism of financial statements is that they're ancient history by the time they're released in this world of hyperactive trading.

Just looking at static financial statements can be a bit limited when it comes to seeing financial trends. Using trends, an investment banker may be able to intelligently speculate in which direction a company may be headed. Think of financial trends as the investment banker's crystal ball. The crystal ball may be a bit cloudy, but it does provide a sense of the trends.

Companies often omit growth rates from their financial statements, leaving it up to investment bankers to calculate growth rates on their own. Companies, however, in their 10-K filings often provide several years of financial results that investors can use to calculate simple growth rates. Here's a basic guide to calculating a growth rate:

$$\text{Growth Rate (for a Period)} = \frac{\text{Latest Number} - \text{Previous Number}}{\text{Previous Number}}$$

This formula can be applied to just about any two numbers you'll find on the financial statements to spot trends. In Table 8-4, you see an example of calculating growth rates for various measures of Hershey.

Table 8-4	Hershey's Growth Trends		
Financial Measure	*2012 ($ millions)*	*2011 ($ millions)*	*Growth Rate*
Revenue	$6,644.3	$6,080.8	9.3%
Cost of goods sold	$3,784.4	$3,548.9	6.6%
Selling, marketing, and administrative costs	$1,703.8	$1,477.9	15.3%
Interest expense	$95.6	$92.2	3.7%
Net income	$660.9	$629.0	5.1%

Looking at Hershey's growth rates gives investment bankers an entirely different perspective on the company's financials. With Hershey, you can see that the company is finding ways to drive nearly double-digit percentage revenue growth from the chocolate business. The company is also keeping a good relative control on its raw materials costs, shown by the modest 6.6 percent increase in cost of goods sold.

But the growth analysis of Hershey pinpoints a potentially troubling 15.3 percent increase in selling, marketing, and administrative costs, or so-called "overhead." This piece of information can drive the investment banker back to the 10-K to get more answers.

It turns out that Hershey's overhead costs jumped in 2012 due to higher promotion costs, employee-related costs, incentive pay, and costs connected with its acquisition of Brookside Foods, a Canadian maker of chocolate-covered fruit-juice pieces.

This is critical information for investment bankers to know. Bankers must be sensitive to the fact that Hershey management is certainly eyeing the rising overhead costs before approaching it with a deal, especially another merger opportunity.

Chapter 9

Sizing Up the Industry

In This Chapter

▶ Creating a comparison set of peers for industry analysis

▶ Seeing how companies differ from one another in key areas

▶ Comparing and contrasting companies' growth and other metrics

▶ Measuring differences of companies' profitability and valuation

▶ Understanding why investment banking requires knowledge of the complete industry

*T*he theory of relativity is a mind-blowing concept from Albert Einstein that says, among other things, that space and time are best understood in context to each other. The importance of comparison isn't just heady science.

Consider what happens in a classroom. If a student gets an A on a paper, she may be overjoyed until she finds out that all the other students got A's, too. Her A isn't as meaningful when, in context, it's not all that unusual. The dreaded "bell curve" is a way to separate the average students from the truly exceptional ones.

The importance of comparison doesn't stop in the classroom. Even the super-rich understand this principle. What's the fun of having a 50-foot yacht when someone else at the country club has a 100-foot one?

The same theory of relativity applies to investment banking, especially when it comes to studying the financial statements and financial ratios. As you see in Chapter 8, although many insights can be gleaned from the financial statements, much of the deeper analysis requires putting the data into context. And the best way to really size up a company's financials is to compare them against similar companies.

Industry analysis is the technique investment bankers use to put financials and financial ratios into perspective. In this chapter, you learn the tricks of the investment banking trade when it comes to sizing up companies' financial results to get deep insights into companies and the industries they operate in.

Performing an Industry Analysis

It's not enough for investment bankers to dive into the financials of the company they're interested in. Sure, digging into that one company's financial statements and ratios is a critical first step to understanding its profitability, efficiency, and valuation.

But imagine you've created a beautiful spreadsheet that crunches down the company's gross profit margin, return on assets, and price-to-book. Now what? Those numbers are helpful when compared with previous years at the company, but in isolation there's only so much investment bankers can glean from them.

Investment bankers know that understanding a company and its financial situation requires an industry analysis. Taking a broader look at a company's performance shows investment bankers where a company is especially weak or strong, giving clues of what financial overhauls or tweaks might be needed.

Understanding why industry analysis is important

"It's all relative," is a common cliché but one that's especially true when it comes to financial analysis. Financial ratios can vary wildly based on the industry a company is in.

Don't make the folly of making judgments about a company based on its absolute financial ratios. Just about every type of financial ratio is highly dependent on the characteristics of the industry the company is in. Not taking the time to compare the ratios to the industry will likely lead to faulty or biased conclusions.

Investment bankers can use industry analysis to help them in several key areas, including the following:

- ✔ **Pinpointing unusual areas of the business or anomalies:** Some of the most telling aspects of a company's financials are those areas that are outliers. Finding a company where debt loads are unusually low versus the industry or where growth is sluggish can be a way to identify investment banking products that may apply to that company.

- ✔ **Finding areas in which the competition is taking the lead:** CEOs and company management are acutely aware of what the competition is doing. If another company in the industry is posting monster revenue growth, you can be sure the CEO is wondering how to get a piece of that action. It may be a new hit product that has been a success with consumers or a new part of the world where demand is untapped.

✔ **Identifying areas management is keyed in on:** CEOs are constantly looking around to see how their peers are doing. That's especially true with CEO pay, where companies actually examine the paychecks of CEOs, and use that as a way to know how much to pay their CEO. But the same goes for most of the items on the financial statements. If a company, for instance, isn't boosting revenue as quickly as others in the industry, you can be sure the CEO is trying to find out why. Investment bankers may be called on to help the company tap that source of growth.

Creating a comparison universe

Before you can start doing some serious analysis of the industry, you have to define what the industry is and who the big players in it are. The first part of an investment banker's industry analysis is to define which companies are to be included in the universe.

Picking the correct companies to include in the *comparison universe* is important since the mix can have a big sway on the conclusions reached. Putting companies into categories used to be more difficult, but the development of classification systems and the decreased role of hard-to-classify conglomerates has made the job much easier.

Conglomerates are large and widely diversified companies that oversee a collection of somewhat unrelated businesses. Conglomerates were very popular in the 1960s, because low interest rates allowed companies to scoop up businesses using borrowed money. Conglomerates were a way for investors to diversify their portfolios, before the creation of index mutual funds, which spread investors' risks over dozens of stocks. But since the 1960s, conglomerates fell out of favor, with General Electric and Warren Buffett's Berkshire Hathaway being two of the most famous survivors.

There are several ways that investment bankers are able to generate their universes to compare with. Building the list takes quite a bit of research and may require you to consider different companies, and perhaps toss them out of the universe if you decide they're not applicable.

Digging into the Global Industry Classification Standard

Finding all the players in an industry may seem overwhelming, but much of the work may be done for you.

There's a massive industry organization system called the *Global Industry Classification Standard* (GICS), which groups companies much like zoologists have a way of organizing similar animals. Just as animals are placed into a genus and species, companies are put into *sectors* and *industry groups*. GICS was developed by investment professional firms Morgan Stanley Capital International (MSCI) and Standard & Poor's to assist in the analysis of companies. In other words, all their work makes your job a bit easier. You can take a look at the entire GICS structure at www.msci.com/products/ indices/sector/gics/gics_structure.html.

Individual investors often confuse *sectors* and *industry groups*, but they're actually quite different ways to look at groups of companies. *Sectors* are broad categories that roll up a number of relevant industry groups. *Industry groups* can be then further sliced into individual industries.

There are ten sectors, or main groupings that categorize all the major areas of businesses. Those ten sectors are then broken down into 26 industry groups. And those 26 industry groups break down into 70 industries.

It may help to see a summarized version of the breakdown of sectors and industry groups, as in Table 9-1.

Table 9-1	The Ten Sectors	
Sector	*Select Industry Groups*	*Select Industries*
Energy	Energy	Energy Equipment and Services Oil, Gas, and Consumable Fuels
Materials	Materials	Chemicals Construction Materials Containers and Packaging
Industrials	Capital Goods	Aerospace and Defense Building Products
	Commercial and Professional Services	Professional services
	Transportation	Airlines Road and Rail
Consumer Discretionary	Automobiles and Components	Auto Components Automobiles

Sector	*Select Industry Groups*	*Select Industries*
	Consumer Durables and Apparel	Household Durables Leisure Equipment
	Retailing	Distributors Internet and Catalog Retailers
Consumer Staples	Food, Beverage, and Tobacco	Beverages Food Products
	Household and Personal Products	Personal Products
Healthcare	Healthcare Equipment and Services	Healthcare Equipment and Supplies
	Pharmaceuticals, Biotechnology, and Life Sciences	Biotechnology Life Sciences and Services
Financials	Banks	Commercial Banks Thrifts and Mortgage Finance
	Diversified Financials	Diversified Financial Services Consumer Finance Capital Markets
Information Technology	Software and Services	Internet Software and Services IT Services
	Technology Hardware and Equipment	Communications Equipment Computers and Peripherals
Telecommunication Services	Telecommunication Services	Diversified Telecommunication Services Wireless Telecommunication Services
Utilities	Utilities	Electric Utilities Gas Utilities Water Utilities

Source: MSCI, S&P Capital IQ

Here's an example: Let's say you wanted to look into the investment banking industry. (Imagine that, given the book you're reading right now!) It turns out that the Investment Banking and Brokerage sub-industry is a member of the Capital Markets industry. The Capital Markets industry is a part of the Diversified Financials industry group, which is part of the Financials sector.

When you figure out which sector and industry group the company you're studying belongs in, you can get a good start on your industry universe. For instance, imagine that you're preparing an analysis of tech giant IBM. You may be tempted to compare it with other tech giants Microsoft and Apple. And it's true, IBM is part of the Information Technology sector, as are Microsoft and Apple. But IBM is in the Software and Services industry group and the IT Consulting industry. IBM gets most of its revenue from consulting, not from selling hardware or operating systems. IBM's peers in the IT Consulting industry includes firms like Accenture, Cognizant Technology, and Teradata.

Seeing who companies say their rivals are

If anyone knows who a company's competitors are, it's the company's management team. Companies in the same industry are intensely competitive with one another. And you can be sure they know which companies are trying to steal business from them.

For a variety of reasons, companies don't like to talk publicly about their competitors very often. But investment bankers paying close attention to the regulatory filings will see that, from time to time, companies may name firms they consider to be competitive, at least with part of their business. These lists of competitors may be named in the company's 10-K or 10-Q. Another treasure trove of competitive information comes when a company in the industry files to sell shares to the public in an initial public offering (IPO). In the IPO *prospectus* (a document that a company selling securities provides to interested investors that describe the investment), the company's investment bankers are required to disclose a list of all the companies that are considered competitive.

IBM, for instance, gives great detail about its competitors for each of its major business units in its regulatory filings. IBM lists Accenture, Amazon. com, Computer Sciences, Fujitsu, and Hewlett-Packard as rivals to its Global Services consulting business. IBM lists computer service firm CA Technologies, Microsoft, and Oracle as competitors in its Software unit. Big Blue, IBM, even lists General Electric as a rival for its lending unit, called Global Financing.

Checking out the peers from which boards of directors set CEO pay

If there's one area in which CEOs don't want to slip behind their competition, it's their own pay. Each year, companies' boards of directors determine how much to pay the CEO and other top management. It's a much-watched process that many investors pay attention to. But more important to investment bankers than the amount being doled out to the CEO is the process used to determine the pay. Companies pay close attention to the other companies in the industry, and in the process, they do much of the industry analysis for investment bankers.

Whether CEOs make too much or not enough is beyond the scope of this book. But for investment bankers, the part of the proxy statement that shows the universe of companies with which a company compares CEO pay is priceless.

Adjusting the industry comparison universe

At this point, you've discovered how to take a good first crack at creating an industry comparison universe. Creating the initial list using the GICS or even the list of competitors from the company's CEO compensation list is a great starting point. You can even combine these approaches to come up with a master list.

But depending on the analysis you plan to do, you'll need to winnow the list down a bit. There are times when certain companies may technically be rivals, but in reality, the companies aren't really comparable. You'll want to toss these outlier companies out of your industry comparison universe. A company may not be an appropriate peer for investment banking analysis when that company is

- ✔ **Not a pure-play competitor:** There may be times when a company's biggest competitor is actually a unit embedded inside a larger firm. When this happens, comparing a company against another company that gets most of its business from an unrelated area can be inappropriate.

- ✔ **At a different point in its lifecycle:** Investors pay particular attention to the size of companies they're comparing against. Some financials can be highly dependent on the size or market share of a company. For instance, it would be a bit outlandish to compare the revenue growth of a large company with a dominant market share with a company that just started.

- ✔ **Being propped up by artificial means:** Periodically, a company in the industry may not really be operating on its own two feet. Companies that emerge from bankruptcy protection may have their debt wiped out, making their liquidity ratios not all that applicable. A company may get a bailout from the government or private investors, which can also skew its numbers. We're looking at you AIG and GM.

Unearthing Company Trends and Common sizing the Financial Statements

Astrologers know there's only so much you can learn by gazing at just one star in a telescope. Part of the true mystery of the heavens is answered by knowing how the stars have changed over time, as well as how they behave in relation to each other.

Studying companies may not be as galactic as star gazing, but insightful investment bankers know that it also requires putting financial results into context. Investment bankers traditionally look to put financial statements into perspective by

- ✔ **Looking at trend data:** A single year of data only tells you so much. You can look up on the income statement that a company reported net income of $10 million. So what? What's even more important is how much the company made the *previous* year. If the company reported net income of $5 million the previous year, it just doubled its profit. But if net income was $100 million the year before, the company is regressing.

- ✔ **Common sizing the balance sheet:** *Common sizing* is a technique used by investment bankers to put line items on the financial statements into relationship of the total. It's appropriate to put a company's individual assets into perspective, for instance, as a percentage of the company's total assets. Common sizing data can be very valuable when compared to the numbers from rival firms.

- ✔ **Common sizing the income statement:** There's no reason for the balance sheet to have all the fun with common sizing. The technique can also be applied to the income statement, which compares expenses and profit to total revenue. The real magic of common sizing the income statement, though, comes from comparing one company's numbers to the numbers of others in the industry.

Comparing growth rates

Serious investment bankers don't just look at one year's financial statements. For in-depth analysis of financials, investment bankers rely on several years of financial data, which are the raw ingredients of *trend analysis,* in which analysts try to see whether key indicators of the company's performance are on the upswing or headed downward. And to take this trend data to the next level, investment bankers are looking for ways to compare with related companies' trends as well.

There's a magical formula you need whenever calculating the change in one number from another. This calculation will be the way that all the percentage changes you read about in this chapter are devised. Here's the way to remember it:

Percentage Change = ([New Number − Old Number] ÷ Old Number) × 100

Let's use a basic example: Imagine a corn plant was 10 inches tall before a farmer poured a bucket of fertilizer on it. After two weeks, the plant grew to be 18 inches tall. Here's how much the plant grew:

Percentage Change = ([18 − 10] ÷ 10) × 100 = 80%

This formula is critical when measuring trends.

Looking at an example: Dell

Instead of stepping you through the theoretical ways that trend analysis may aid the investment banker, it's prudent to take a real example. Perhaps you recall that, in 2013, Michael Dell expressed interest in taking his computer company, Dell Computer, private in a leveraged buyout. News reports indicated that Dell's revenue growth was slowing relative to the industry and that being private would allow the company to make investments needed to remain competitive. (Investment in new equipment and expansion is called *capital expenditures.*)

An investment banker would use trend data to quantify this financial story. The first step would be to get Dell's revenue and capital expenses for several years, both of which are available from Dell's income statement and statement of cash flow from the company's latest 10-K filing. If you need a refresher course on how to access the 10-K, flip back to Chapter 6. To save you time, Table 9-2 is a presentation of several years of Dell's revenue and capital spending.

Table 9-2	Dell's Revenue and Capital Spending		
	Fiscal 2013 ($ millions)	Fiscal 2012 ($ millions)	Fiscal 2011 ($ millions)
Revenue	56,940	62,071	61,494
Capital expenditures	513	675	444

Source: Dell 10-K filing for fiscal 2013, ending February 1, 2013

Interpreting the results

Table 9-2 looks pretty, but at its face, you can't glean much trend information until you convert the absolute numbers into percentage changes. And when you do the math, you generate a table like the one in Table 9-3.

Table 9-3	Dell's Revenue and Capital-Spending Trends	
	Fiscal 2013 (% change)	*Fiscal 2012 (% change)*
Revenue	−8.3	0.9
Capital expenditures	−24	52

Now the Dell story becomes crystal clear and quantified. Revenue did fall off 8.3 percent in fiscal 2013, certainly not a positive development. But even more alarmingly, the company cut back its capital expenditures by 24 percent. That's a disturbing trend because technology companies rely on innovation and new products for revenue growth in future years. At this point, investment bankers can begin to see the problem that Dell is trying to address.

Measuring trends next to industry

Before investment bankers can jump to any conclusions about what they've seen in the trends, it's important to measure those trends against other companies. After all, maybe Dell's 8.3 percent decline in revenue is actually less severe than that reported by other tech companies. And perhaps, the rest of the industry is cutting back in capital spending, so a 24 percent reduction isn't all that unusual. Knowing this would put the trend data in a much different light.

Using the techniques from earlier in this chapter, you prepare an industry comparison list. Using the list of peers from the computer hardware industry, you create a chart showing the revenue and capital expenditures trends at the rivals, which looks like Table 9-4.

Table 9-4	Computer Hardware Trends	
	Revenue Change Comparable 2013 Period (% change)	*Capital Expenditures Change in Comparable 2013 Period (% change)*
Apple	18.8	89.3
Hewlett-Packard	−5.0	−23.1
NCR	7.7	44.4

Source: Company filings (Apple 12-month period ended March 2013; Hewlett-Packard 12-month period ended January 31, 2013; NCR 12-month period ended March 2013)

Sizing up Dell's results, it's clear the company is in danger of falling behind the investments being made by other computer hardware companies, Apple and NCR. But it's interesting to note that Dell's closest direct rival, Hewlett-Packard, is similarly pulling back on its capital expenditures in light of declining revenue. Investment bankers can use this industry analysis to draw deeper conclusions.

There's no rule that says the companies have to end their fiscal years on December 31. Sometimes companies in the same industry are on different reporting calendars, meaning they report quarters ending in slightly different months, as is the case with Dell and most of its peers. This is just a limitation of reporting that investment bankers must use judgment to work through.

Comparing leverage

The balance sheet is where companies list out all the assets it owns and the liabilities it owes. Examining the balance sheet by itself can be a valuable exercise. One of the best uses of the balance sheet is finding out how much debt a company has, or how *leveraged* a company is. Leverage can magnify profits during the good times but spell major financial troubles if the company slows down or if interest rates rise.

The true power of the balance sheet, though, shines through when using the financial statement to compare the financial resources of a company with that of its peers. But here's the problem: How do you compare the assets and liabilities of different companies that may be in the same industry but are of dramatically different sizes? If a company has a total load of debt of $1.9 billion, is that high, low, or average compared with the industry?

The tool to adjust for companies having different scales is called *common sizing*. Common sizing is a financial technique in which all the aspects of financial statements are put in relation to the total. When common sizing the balance sheet, investment bankers divide all the assets and liabilities by the total assets. This exercise of common sizing puts the numbers into perspective and makes them truly comparable with the industry.

Using a real example, it's easier to see how common sizing works. Hershey, the giant food company, showed a breakdown of its liabilities (refer to Table 7-1). That table showed that in 2012, the food company's short-term debt is equal to 2.5 percent of its total assets, the current portion of the company's long-term debt is equal to 5.4 percent of total assets, and long-term debt has reached 32.2 percent of assets. That information is very useful to the investment banker because it shows the company is largely counting on debt that doesn't come due in more than a year. (Keep in mind that while short-term debt, the current portion of long-term debt, and long-term debt are among Hershey's biggest liabilities, there are others, so the percentages don't add to 100 percent.)

But the investment banker may want to take things a step further by common sizing the balance sheets of rivals, creating a table like the one shown in Table 9-5.

Table 9-5	Comparing Balance Sheets		
Competitor	*Short-Term Debt as % of Total Assets*	*Current Portion of Long-Term Debt as % of Total Assets*	*Long-Term Debt as % of Total Assets*
Mondelez	0.4	4.8	20.6
General Mills	8.5	3.6	24.3
Hershey	2.5	5.4	32.2

Source: S&P Capital IQ, based on packaged foods and meats industry as of December 2012 for Mondelez, November 2012 for General Mills

The common sizing industry analysis shows the investment banker that Hershey has more of its liabilities held in the form of long-term debt, giving the company more flexibility in the short term than its peers.

Comparing various profit margins

Comparisons are also important to investment bankers trying to gauge how profitable companies are. And again, common sizing is a tool that investment bankers can use to rank and compare a company's profit-producing power.

When common sizing the income statement, you're putting all the company's expenses into perspective by comparing them to the company's revenue. This technique, done by dividing all the elements of the income statement by the company's revenue, gives you a quick way to see how the company's profit margins compare with other companies'.

To show the power of common sizing with the income statement, you can try it out using the airline industry. The airline industry is known for its often tight profit margins and cutthroat competition. To dig deeper, you can common size the income statement of Delta Air Lines and then see how that matches up to the industry. Notice how after Delta's income statement is common sized in Table 9-6, you get a keen look into the company's profitability and where its biggest expenses lie.

Table 9-6	Common Sizing Delta's 2012 Income Statement	
Income Statement Item	*Absolute 2012 Amount ($ millions)*	*Common Sized (% of revenue)*
Total revenue	36,670	100
Cost of goods sold	29.323	80
Gross profit	7,347	20
Selling, general, and administrative expenses	1,590	4.3
Operating income	2,600	7.1
Net income	1,009	2.8

Source: Delta Air Lines, S&P Capital IQ

The common sizing analysis of Delta Airlines confirms that the airline is definitely a relative low net margin business. The company earned just 2.8¢ of every dollar of revenue in 2012 as net income. A vast majority of the company's revenue is chewed up by the company's cost of goods sold, which includes jet fuel.

But to understand how Delta stacks up, it's important to common size the income statements of its rivals, to create a chart like the one in Table 9-7.

Table 9-7	Common sizing Delta's Rivals		
	Gross Profit % of 2012 revenue	*Operating Income % of 2012 Revenue*	*Net Income % of 2012 Revenue*
United Continental	24.0	3.7	−1.9
Southwest Airlines	21.6	4.7	2.5
Delta Air Lines	20.0	7.1	2.8

Source: S&P Capital IQ

The common sizing analysis of the companies in the airlines industry definitely shows how the industry has little control over its direct costs, such as jet fuel. The gross profit as a percentage of revenue is pretty consistent in the low to mid 20 percent range. Where the airlines have the most power to control costs is in overhead costs. This information is helpful for investment bankers because they may look for financial products to help airlines boost their profitability.

Seeing How a Company Stacks Up: Comparing the Key Ratios

How do investment bankers know if the annual bonus they got was big? There's an old saw on Wall Street that says you got a good bonus as long as it's bigger than the one the person sitting next to you got.

That's a flippant way to look at pay, but that way of thinking spans beyond the cubicles in the investment bank's high-rise to the way that companies' financials are analyzed. Companies' financial results, especially when synthesized and looked at as financial ratios, can't be fully understood in isolation. Investment bankers must compare companies' financial ratios with the financial ratios at other firms in the industry. Such comparisons give investment bankers deeper insights into how a company is performing outside the ups and downs of the industry.

Sizing up valuation

Valuation (the process of putting a price tag on a company) is one area where most investors appreciate the value of comparison. In Chapter 8, we fill you in on the value of financial valuation ratios, including the price-to-earnings (P/E) ratio and the enterprise value–to–EBITDA (EV/EBITDA) ratio.

Flip back to Chapter 8 if you need a refresher on what ratios measure and how to calculate them.

P/E

The P/E ratio tells you how much investors are paying for a claim to $1 of a company's earnings. When it comes to valuation ratios, the P/E is certainly one of the most famous because many people use it as a benchmark to tell them if a stock is relatively cheap or expensive.

The trouble is, though, that the P/E doesn't tell you much by itself. The ratio is most valuable when compared to that of similar companies or even the entire stock market. Keep in mind, too, that P/E ratios rise and fall as stock prices fluctuate and earnings change.

There are several different ways to calculate a P/E, as shown in Chapter 8, so you'll want to use the same method for all the companies in your universe. It's best to compare a company's P/E to that of its peers, but it can also be interesting to look at how a company's P/E compares to the market over different points in time. You can see the trailing P/E of the Standard & Poor's 500 over different times in history in Table 9-8 for a comparison.

Table 9-8	S&P 500's P/E through Time
Date	*Operating P/E (Trailing)*
December 31, 2012	14.7
December 31, 2011	13.0
December 31, 2010	15.0
December 31, 2000	23.5
December 31, 1990	14.6

Source: S&P Dow Jones Indices

EV/EBITDA

The P/E is a helpful benchmark of company's value in large part due to simplicity. If you have access to a computer and financial websites, you can get a company's P/E pretty quickly. But investment bankers usually dig deeper, using EV/EBITDA, where EV is enterprise value and EBITDA is earnings before interest, taxes, depreciation, and amortization. You can read more about what these measures are and what they tell you in Chapter 8.

But for now, know that EV/EBITDA is best appreciated when used to look at a valuation of a company compared with its peers. Calculating EV/EBITDA requires a calculation using data, pulled from the financial statements, like what you see in Table 9-9.

Table 9-9	Calculating EV/EBITDA for Hershey in 2012
Data Point	*Financial Statement Line Item ($ millions)*
Market value	16,119.64
Cash and short-term investments	466.2
Total debt and minority interest	2,007.01
Total revenue	6,644.25
Cost of goods sold	3,743.89
Selling, general, and administrative (SG&A)	1,692.05
Depreciation and amortization	194.74

Source: S&P Capital IQ as of December 31, 2012

The first task for the investment banker is to calculate enterprise value. Using the formula in Chapter 8, you know the following:

Enterprise Value = Market Value – Cash and Short-Term Investments + Total Debt and Minority Interest

Referring to Table 9-9, you can find all the data you need to plug into the formula to find:

Enterprise Value = $16,119.64 – $466.2 + 2,007.01 = $17,661 million

Take a deep breath. You're halfway there. Now it's time to calculate EBITDA. The formulas for EBITDA is as follows:

EBITDA = Total Revenue – Cost of Goods Sold – Selling, General, and Administrative + Depreciation and Amortization

Again, inputting the data from Table 9-9, you find:

EBITDA = $6,644.25 – 3,743.89 – 1,692.05 + 194.74 = $1,403.05 million

Last, you divide enterprise value by EBITDA to find that Hershey had an EV/EBITDA ratio as of December 31, 2012, of 12.6.

But what does that mean? To find out, you perform the same calculation with other firms in the packaged foods and meats industry and you find something like you see in Table 9-10.

Table 9-10	Comparing EV/EBITDA
Competitor	*EV/EBITDA*
Mondelez	7.9
General Mills	10.2

Source: S&P Capital IQ as of Dec. 31, 2012

Comparing Hershey's EV/EBITDA to select peers in its industry shows that investors are willing to pay a greater premium for shares of Hershey. This is important information for the investment bankers to consider when evaluating options for perhaps issuing stock or conducting a merger.

For this example, just two competitors are looked at. In a real-world analysis, you'd want to create a larger universe of competitors.

There are some online services, like Thomson-Reuters, that will help you take an average of the entire industry (more on that in Chapter 21).

Comparing total debt-to-equity

Managing a company's mix of debt and equity financing is a big part of what investment bankers do for their clients. Learning to size up a company's total debt-to-equity ratio is a key part of understanding its *capital structure* (the mix of the sources of funds a company uses to operate itself). Chapter 8 shows how to calculate and analyze debt-to-equity ratios. But it's important, too, to see how the debt-to-equity ratio can vary greatly among companies, as you can see in Table 9-11.

Table 9-11	Comparing Total Debt-to-Equity
Company	*Total Debt-to-Equity in 2012*
Hershey	181.9%
Mondelez	77.8%
General Mills	95.2%

Source: S&P Capital IQ, data for December 31, 2012, except through February 2013 for General Mills due to fiscal year

Investment bankers can see, at a quick glance, that Hershey is much more dependent on debt than its peers, relative to equity financing. It's a reminder that Hershey will be more interested in investment banking products that may help it manage its leverage.

Sizing up companies on their efficiency

Efficiency ratios help investors, and investment bankers, see how well management is handling the cash entrusted to it by its investors and bond-holders. For this reason, efficiency ratios, such as return on equity can be somewhat of a report card to judge management. You can find out everything there is to know about return on equity (ROE) in Chapter 14.

But just remember that before being critical of management, using ROE, you have to put this ratio into context. Some industries generate higher returns than others and some businesses require larger investments in plants and equipment. It's natural for some industries to have higher returns on equity.

Industry ratios

If you notice anything in reading this chapter, it's that there's practically no end to the ways investment bankers can study and pick apart a company. You can dig deep into the financial statements and off-the-shelf financial ratios like P/E and EV/EBITDA.

But investment bankers with deep industry insights often follow financial measures that are more closely tied to the specific industry. Many industries have key benchmarks that are particularly useful to them.

Chapter 10

Understanding Stocks and Focusing on Past Transactions

Much of what investment bankers do is based on complex mathematical formulas, ratio analysis, and forecasting. In other words, investment bankers are pros at making educated guesses about all things financial, ranging from what companies are worth to how much an asset should sell for.

The ability to formulate reasonable hypotheses is a key aspect of investment banking. After all, investment bankers are often in the situation of having to sell investment products that have never been sold before and, thus, are difficult to value based on history.

But even though financial history rarely repeats itself exactly, there's no question that it often rhymes. Savvy investment bankers know that one of the best ways to gauge what something may be worth is seeing how similar assets are valued on the open market.

This chapter explains what stock, often called *equity,* is and why the value on the market may not be equal to the value investment banker's measure on their spreadsheets. You see how securities markets are created to determine price for various assets. Market prices, even if the investment banker disagrees with them, are important to investment bankers' work. You also find out how to look up past transactions, a key way investment bankers see what the market prices for assets have been. You also see how to not just look at market prices but use those prices in a way to improve your understanding of the assets and the values they may garner.

Introducing Stock

DIS. IBM. MSFT. FB. These are the *stock ticker symbols* of some of the most recognizable American companies, Walt Disney, International Business Machines, Microsoft, and Facebook, respectively. These unique stock symbols are typed into computer trading systems and punched into investment bankers' computer systems to get up-to-date stock prices and trading volumes. Investment bankers are so used to chattering about companies like symbols, almost like chess pieces on a game board, that the idea of what the stock represents can lose its meaning.

But what is a share of stock? What does a share of stock represent? In its simplest form, common stock is a financial security that gives its owner a claim to a prorated portion of the company's earnings. Stock, often referred to as *equity* by investment bankers, is an ownership stake in a company.

The owners of stock, called *stockholders* or *shareholders,* have dibs on a proportionate part of a company's earnings. The number of shares of stock owned indicates how much of the company the shareholder owns. For instance, imagine a company has carved itself into 223.7 million pieces, or *shares.* Those are the number of shares the company has *outstanding,* as is the case with Hershey as of 2013.

You can always look up how many shares a company has outstanding on the balance sheet. Most investing websites and investment banking services also provide a listing of the company's shares outstanding.

Stock values can also be helpful to an investment banker measuring the *market value,* or total value investors are putting on a company, also known as *market capitalization.* You just need to know:

Market Value = Number of Shares Outstanding × Current Per-Share Stock Price

Using Hershey as an example, imagine the stock is trading for $86.66 a share. Because you know the company has 223.7 million shares outstanding, you know that stock investors are valuing the entire company at $19.4 billion. Now, that's a whole lot of chocolate.

Characteristics of stock

Stock investors are typically seen as being among the daredevils of the investment world. Stocks are generally high-risk, high-return types of investments. Stocks typically generate some of the highest returns of any major investment (see Chapter 4). Stocks typically deliver returns to investors in the form of

✔ **Dividends:** Companies, if they choose, may make periodic (usually quarterly) cash payments to the shareholders of record. These payments, typically made from cash generated by the business, can be an important part of the total return investors receive by holding a stock. Companies may also choose to make large one-time dividend payments. Dividends can be a very significant part of a company's *total return* to investors (see Table 10-1).

Investors typically look at dividends in terms of a *dividend yield.* The dividend yield puts the dividend in relation to the stock price, by dividing the annual dividend by the stock price to arrive at a percentage return. For instance, if a stock that is trading for $50 a share pays an annual $1-per-share dividend, the dividend yield is 0.02, or 2 percent of the share price.

✔ **Stock price appreciation:** After companies first sell shares to the public, the investors who buy those shares are free to buy and sell at will in the *secondary market.* Investors are constantly buying and selling the shares based on what they think the future of the company will be. The price investors are willing to pay for the share ebbs and flows as new information comes into the market and future prospects for the firm rise and fall.

✔ **Special business transactions:** Although not nearly as common as dividends and stock price appreciation, some companies may look to special transactions to unlock value. One of the most common events, and one that involves investment bankers, are spinoffs. Spinoffs occur when companies break out a part of their business and set it up as a separate company, often with its own stock.

Table 10-1	Where Stock Investors Get Return on S&P 500		
Year Ending	*Total Return Change*	*Stock-Price Appreciation*	*Dividend Yield*
December 31, 2012	16.0%	13.4%	2.6%
December 30, 2011	2.1%	0.0%	2.1%
December 29, 2000	−9.1%	−10.1%	1.0%
December 31, 1995	37.6%	34.1%	3.5%
December 31, 1990	−3.1%	−6.6%	3.5%

Source: S&P Dow Jones Indices

Stock sounds pretty ideal so far, with the dividends and the chance at stock price appreciation. But there are some pretty grave downsides to equity that are the constant boogeyman for stockholders to think about, including the following:

✔ **Dividends can be suspended or canceled at any time.** Unlike interest payments on bonds, which must be paid by companies, dividends can be halted or cut at any time. And cutting dividends is a constant danger when times get tough. During the financial crisis that erupted in 2007, most large banks cut their dividends to a penny a share or eliminated them completely.

✔ **Stocks can go down, too.** Stocks aren't for the weak of heart. They can fall or even plummet during times of economic uncertainty or crisis. Sometimes stock declines can be complete, resulting in a total loss for investors. Complete losses on stock investments were commonplace for many dot-com investors in the 1999–2000 time period.

✔ **Stocks investors' claims to assets are inferior.** If things go really wrong at a company, stockholders are last in line at the asset buffet. If a company sells itself off, or liquidates, the assets generated are first paid to the employees and short-term creditors and then to the bondholders. When things go really bad, when companies enter bankruptcy protection for instance, it's pretty typical for stockholders to wind up with nothing and the bondholders to end up as the new owners of the company.

Types of stock

Stock comes in all shapes and sizes. Companies and their investment bankers have great latitude in deciding what rights they bestow on the ownership they sell to shareholders. Stock offerings can be customized in various ways, but typically there are three main types of stock to be aware of:

✔ **Common stock:** If you buy 100 shares of Walt Disney stock, you're most likely buying the common stock. The shares of common stock are the typical shares being sold by the company. Common stock, at most companies, accounts for a vast majority of the shares outstanding.

✔ **Preferred stock:** Sometimes to encourage investors to become owners of a company, there's a bit more inducing required. *Preferred stock* is a unique type of stock that attempts to give shareholders a more bond-like experience. Preferred stock typically pays a higher dividend yield than what's being paid on the common shares. That's attractive to investors who may normally steer clear of stock and instead go for bonds. Preferred stock dividends, though, can be halted like common stock. But if a company halts preferred stock dividends, shareholders must be made whole with the lapsed dividends before there can be a dividend paid on common shares. Preferred stock can also be *callable,* meaning the company can at any time buy the shares from investors at a pre–agreed-upon price. But, don't get seduced by the name — preferred stock really isn't better for investors if the company is wildly successful. Preferred stockholders don't share in the upside like common stockholders do.

✔ **Stock options:** Options are financial instruments that give their owners the right, but not the obligation, to buy or sell a stock at a pre-set price sometime in the future. Options can be used by speculators who want to bet that a stock price will rise or fall in the future. Options come in different varieties, including *puts,* which give owners the right to sell, and *calls,* which give the right to buy. Options can also be granted to company executives as a form of incentive pay. *Warrants* are types of long-term options that are issued by the company itself, rather than standard options that are issued by exchanges like the Chicago Board Options Exchange. Options are complex tools; you can read more about them in *Stock Options For Dummies,* by Alan R. Simon (Wiley).

Understanding stock pricing

Stock trading is part of the financial services offered by some of the largest investment banking firms. But trading is also a matter for investment bankers to be aware of because it can affect the perception of what assets are worth. Investment bankers may dutifully calculate what they think an investment is truly worth, using prudent financial analysis. But all that goes out the window when investors and markets value the asset entirely differently.

The value of assets, especially shares of a company, is determined by the active market bringing together willing buyers and sellers. This process creates a price at which sellers are willing to part with the asset and buyers are willing to pay for that same asset. Knowing the market price of an asset is very valuable, especially when the market price is different from the value that the investment bankers' models say.

When the value being placed on companies varies wildly from what investment bankers think companies are worth, it can be a huge opportunity. During the dot-com boom of the late 1990s and 2000, investors were willing to pay astronomical sums for Internet companies that often didn't have earnings much less revenue. Investment bankers' models would have shown that these companies were long on promise, but short on real value. Nonetheless, investment bankers made fortunes preparing these companies to sell stock to the public that had a voracious appetite to own a piece of what they thought was the future. The curious thing is that these investors were correct in a sense — the Internet was an innovation that transformed our lives and the way we do business. However, many of the Internet companies simply weren't good investments. Even to this day, some observers of the initial public offering (IPO) market believe the market will never be as active as it was during the Internet boom.

Finding Past Transactions

Don't expect to get a phone call when a big investor is going to buy or sell a particular stock. Although that knowledge would be helpful, so you could update your company valuation, that's not how the world works.

Most trading activity is done in private using the buying and selling facilities of stock market exchanges including the NYSE and NASDAQ. There are some exceptions when investors are significant enough that they do have to report their trades (see Chapter 6). But they only have to report these trades with a significant time lag.

But don't let the fact most investors don't have to tell you what they're doing discourage you from digging into past transactions. Investment bankers who know where to look can easily find out how investors are valuing various assets.

Tracking the stock market

The investment banker's best friend in tracking the value of companies is the stock market. Usually starting after a company sells stock to the public in an IPO, those shares are free to trade as investors buy and sell. Those transactions, conducted on an exchange with *publicly traded securities,* are recorded and posted for all to see.

Investors are well trained to find stock prices, and they can do that easily using most well-known financial websites, including a few you can read about in Chapter 21. Investors can view stock charts, to see graphically how stock prices have changed over time, or download tables of historical stock prices into their spreadsheets for further analysis.

Studying private deals

Just to make things more difficult, not all companies have publicly traded stock. *Privately held companies* (those that are closely held by private investors and that don't have shares of stock trading on an exchange) are much more difficult to track. Some private companies may have shares of stock, usually held by early employees or investors, but these shares can't be traded as freely as can shares of publicly traded companies.

Looking up historical transaction data on private companies is much more tricky, and sometimes it isn't even possible. That means that analyzing private transaction deals also requires a bit of estimation and approximation, with techniques such as the following:

- ✔ **Comparing with public companies:** Even if a company isn't publicly traded, you can sometimes triangulate its value using valuation techniques. Databases such as those from Dun & Bradstreet, Bloomberg, and S&P Capital IQ may often provide limited financial statements for private companies. Sometimes, though you can't get the profit reported by private companies, there are decent estimates of its revenue. You may be able to extrapolate the value of the private company by applying the industry's valuation, such as by using price-to-revenue or price-to-book multiples.

- ✔ **Checking to see if debt is sold:** Just because a company doesn't have stock that's publicly traded doesn't mean there isn't any market pricing available. Many large private companies may have debt outstanding. Investors can buy and sell a company's debt obligations and investors can look up the prices of the debt to get an idea of how creditworthy the company is considered. Another bonus: Even private companies must provide financial statements on the Securities and Exchange Commission's EDGAR system if they have sold debt to the public.

- ✔ **Finding rounds of venture capital raised:** Even private companies may disclose when they've lined up significant amounts of money in a round of financing with investors, such as venture capital firms. Twitter disclosed it was planning to raise $100 million in funds on November 17, 2010, well before the company even thought about an IPO.

- ✔ **Looking for transactions with public companies:** Private sales aren't so private when they're done by publicly traded companies. When a company makes a significant buy or sell of interests in another company, that transaction may need to be disclosed. For instance, investment bankers took note of the 8-K filing by advertising firm Interpublic Group on November 20, 2012. That filing disclosed that the company sold its remaining stake in Facebook for $95 million. Similarly, companies may disclose when they buy or sell their interests in private companies, giving a rare glimpse at their market value.

- ✔ **Checking pre-IPO marketplaces:** The wait for a company to sell shares in an IPO can be a long one for early employees. Employees, who may have been granted shares as part of joining the company, may be eager to sell so they can buy those Ferraris they've been pining for. Not long ago, these investors would just have to wait for the IPO. But the introduction of new marketplaces for investors to sell their shares in a company that hasn't gone public yet are springing up. Two of the emerging pre-IPO marketplaces are SecondMarket (`www.secondmarket.com`) and SharesPost (`www.sharespost.com`). Both are websites that allow holders of shares of private companies to sell those shares to *accredited investors* (those deemed to be sophisticated or wealthy enough to handle the risks).

Companies that sell stock to the general public must typically follow all the rules of IPOs. The most important rule that affects companies looking to go public is the requirement to *register* securities with the SEC. Companies and their investment bankers must follow strict disclosure and filing guidelines to meet securities registration rules.

There are exceptions to the rule that calls for public securities to be registered, though. For instance, a company may sell shares to investors who are accredited. Accredited investors are those considered to know the risks of buying unregistered securities. Typically accredited investors are large banks, investment companies, and insurance companies. But accredited investors may also be charitable organizations or companies with assets of more than $5 million, according to SEC rules. Individuals must meet pretty high bars to be considered accredited, including a net worth of more than $1 million (excluding a primary residence) or annual income of more than $200,000.

Looking at pre-IPO marketplaces

The pre-IPO marketplaces have morphed from obscure websites to useful guides for investment bankers interested in private companies. These sites aggregate the shares private investors are looking to sell in companies that are privately held. The systems then pair up willing buyers for the shares and facilitate the transaction. Transactions are then compiled allowing members of the pre-IPO marketplaces to see what kinds of valuations the companies have.

Both SecondMarket and SharesPost are only available to members. Once you register to sign up, if you're an accredited investor, you can view some of the shares and companies that are available on the site.

Pre-IPO marketplaces help illuminate the long-dark area of private companies. They're a breakthrough in creating a somewhat orderly market for an area of securities that was long orphaned. But don't make the mistake of thinking that the prices on pre-IPO marketplaces are indications of what companies are truly worth once they do go public. A classic example was Facebook. On private marketplaces, the company commanded a value, when extrapolated, of $100 billion. But just a year after the company conducted its IPO in May 2012, the market value of the company on the NASDAQ fell to roughly $60 billion. Pre-IPO marketplaces can cause market values to appear distorted because they lack the *liquidity,* or deep pool of buyers and sellers, which can unrealistically distort the price.

Examining buyouts

Buyouts can be precious pieces of information for investment bankers trying to see what different companies, especially smaller, private ones, are worth.

If a buyout is large enough, the buying company will put out an 8-K regulatory filing alerting its investors of the size and value of the deal. Not all these mergers and buyouts pan out for the acquiring companies, but they can give investment bankers comparable transactions to analyze.

Consider an example. Cisco Systems, a large computer networking gear maker, is known for being a big acquirer of small companies. By monitoring deals made by Cisco, investors can see what networking companies are going for on the market. During the first part of 2013, for instance, Cisco either outright bought or made private placement investments in 11 different companies. *Private placements* are significant investments in a company that comes short of buying the whole thing. Because private placements are offered to a select group of large investors, these offerings don't need to be registered with the SEC.

Analyzing Past Transactions

When you understand how to track past transactions and how investors place their bets on securities and investments, patterns begin to emerge. By examining the stock prices of publicly traded companies, as well as smaller, privately held competitors, you can see how much demand there is for securities in the industry. Knowing what investors will pay for securities, and how easy it will be to sell them, is a critical aspect of investment bankers' jobs.

Knowing what the market will bear

As is the case with everything from ice cream cones to baseball tickets, the price of a stock hinges on the balance of supply and demand. When companies sell stock for the first time, those shares eventually need to find their way into the hands of investors willing to hold them.

The supply of stock is somewhat stable. Companies can increase the number of shares by selling stock in a *follow-on offering,* which is an additional sale of stock following the IPO. Conversely, companies can reduce the number of shares outstanding with *stock buybacks.* In a stock buyback, companies use their excess cash reserves to buy stock in the open market.

Investors have grown increasingly skeptical of the value of stock buybacks. Fans of buybacks point out companies may buy back their stock to boost their much-watched earnings per share. How? When the company's profit, or *net income,* is divided by a smaller number of shares, then earnings per share rises. *Earnings per share* is net income divided by the number of shares outstanding. If the number of shares outstanding falls, earnings per share rises. But critics point out that some companies routinely buy back stock when it's expensive, a bad timing decision. Critics say that, in many cases, shareholders would've been better off just getting a dividend than they are when the company buys its own shares.

The supply of stock may be relatively stable, but demand for the shares is anything but. Investors, traders, and speculators crowd into the stock market and buy and sell shares of companies the same way 10-year-olds trade Skylanders figures. The process pushes the stock price up and down, causing buyers to constantly examine their financial models to decide if the stock is attractively priced or is too expensive.

Knowing when the market is distorted

Examining stock prices and other market prices is valuable, because the data is based on actual dollars and shares trading hands. But investment bankers need to be aware of the fact that oftentimes stock prices don't exactly reflect reality.

Sometimes even sophisticated investors get so enamored with a stock, an industry, or the entire market that they chase the stock to astronomical heights. Investment bankers need to be aware of periods of temporary insanity in the markets — they need to be the sober parties even when there's a stock mania brewing. The market is usually effective pricing stocks over the long run. But investment bankers may get a tip that market prices aren't reflecting reality when

✔ **Valuations get stretched.** Valuation ratios, such as the P/E and price-to-book can be a reality check for investors during times of market insanity. When investment bankers see the P/Es of certain stocks or industries blow away historical averages, it can be a clue that something strange is afoot.

Stocks can be overvalued or undervalued for a very long time. Just because a stock has an elevated P/E doesn't guarantee that the P/E will revert to the mean anytime soon. But an elevated P/E is a sign that investment bankers need to pay attention to.

✔ **Insiders start selling their stock.** There are two types of activities often referred to as *insider trading:* the legal kind and the illegal kind. It's illegal for insiders of companies, such as employees, to use *material and nonpublic information* to trade for personal gain.

But there's a legal type of insider trading, which is simply when company executives buy or sell shares of the company's stock. When CEOs buy company stock, some investors see it as a sign the stock is under-valued. Similarly, when investors see lots of insiders dumping stock, that's a sign the stock may be overvalued.

Investment bankers know insiders must reveal their trades in regulatory filings called the *Form 4*. You can access Form 4 documents from the SEC's website (www.sec.gov).

Sometimes, insider moves can be very prescient. For instance, an early investor in Facebook and board member, Peter Thiel, filed a Form 4 on May 22, 2012. In this filing, Thiel disclosed he was selling more than 10 million shares of Facebook stock at $37.58. Talk about perfect timing. Facebook's shares began to decline in September 2012, hitting a low of $17.55. But other times, CEOs just sell to raise money to buy a house or put their kids through college. They also may be selling to diversify their portfolios as they typically have a lot of eggs in the company basket. (They're people too, you know.) These types of insider stock sales aren't very indicative of the future direction of the stock.

✔ **Stocks start gaining in parabolic moves higher.** Sometimes the public gets so enamored with a company's stock or an entire industry that the price gets pushed to ridiculous heights. Armed with tools such as discounted cash flow analysis (see Chapter 12), investment bankers can dispassionately estimate how much a stock is worth based on certain assumptions, and realize when market values are much higher.

Some investors push shares of popular stocks well above the actual value of the company. Apple was a classic example. In 2012, the stock was one of the most popular in many investors' portfolios. But reality soon caught up, and the stock fell about 50 percent, to below $400 a share.

Tabulating key ratios for past deals

Looking up past stock transactions may be like a bit like financial sleuthing. You may have to dig into somewhat obscure financial documents to look up past transactions. If you're lucky, and the company is public, you can just punch the stock's symbol into a computer and get the prices and historical quotes.

But obtaining the past transaction data, the number of shares bought or sold, and when they were bought or sold is just part of the puzzle. To complete the historical transaction analysis, investment bankers must combine their knowledge of the company's outstanding stock to put some real numbers behind the market's moods.

When companies are invested in, or bought out completely, that presents a whole new opportunity for investment bankers to apply their ratio analysis skills. Investors can look at past transactions to give them a rundown of the company's valuation.

Take a recent example of leading U.S. pork producer, Smithfield, which in 2013 received a $4.7 billion cash buyout offer from Chinese conglomerate Shuanghui International. The amount paid for the stock is the *implied equity value*. Specially, Shuanghui was paying $34 a share for each of Smithfield's 139 million shares outstanding.

The deal, finalized in 2013, gives a fascinating glimpse into how to put a price tag on a past transaction. Digging further into the ratios and terms of the deal reveals much more to investors. First of all, as part of the deal, Shuanghui also agreed to assume Smithfield's significant liabilities, including debt, amounting to $2.2 billion. At the same time, though, Shuanghui would pick up the company's $310 million in cash. Adding the cash buyout and assumed liabilities to the $4.7 billion cash buyout offer, but subtracting Smithfield's cash, gives the company an *implied enterprise value* of $7.0 billion.

The implied enterprise value of a proposed transaction can be tricky. Just remember that the cash buyout price for the stock is just part of the deal. The buyer is also on the hook for the liabilities and debt, which adds to the price tag. But the buyer also gets the company's cash pile, which in effect reduces the cost of the deal. Think of it this way. It's like selling your house for $30,000, but the buyer takes on your mortgage of $200,000. The enterprise value of the value is $230,000. The formula for enterprise value is:

$$\text{Implied Enterprise Value} = \text{Implied Equity Value} + \text{Assumed Liabilities} - \text{Cash}$$

After you measure the deal's implied enterprise value, you can really put the deal through the ratio wringer. Investment bankers particularly like to see what the buyer is paying for the company's earnings before interest, taxes, depreciation, and amortization (EBITDA). You can calculate this by dividing the implied enterprise value by EBITDA. This calculation gives you a ratio that you can use to compare with the industry to see how the buyer fared.

Likewise, you can calculate the deal's implied equity value divided by net income, which can be compared to other companies' price-to-earnings ratios. And don't forget implied equity value to book value, which can be compared with other companies' price-to-book ratios. These ratios typically state how many times value is to the underlying financial measures. For instance, if a company's implied enterprise value is $9.20 and the EBITDA is $1, that means implied enterprise value is 9.2 times, or 9.2x, EBITDA. The analysis looks much like what you see in Table 10-2.

Table 10-2	Breaking Down Smithfield's Buyout Ratios
Ratio	*Value*
Implied enterprise value/EBITDA	9.2x
Implied equity value/net income	25.7x
Implied equity value/book value	1.5x

Source: S&P Capital IQ

The transaction ratios above can then be compared against those of other deals to gauge what kind of deal the buyer has negotiated. For instance, another big meatpacking deal occurred in December 2011 when Leucadia National bought National Beef Packing for $1.4 billion. But that deal was valued at 4.8x enterprise value to EBITDA, well below the 9.2x paid for Smithfield, says S&P Capital IQ.

When past transactions reveal insanity

One of the classic examples of when the stock market went cuckoo over a stock came in one of the most cuckoo years on Wall Street, the year 2000. In March of that year, 3Com, a network equipment maker, announced that it planned to *spin off*, or create a separate public company, its Palm unit. Palm was one of the pioneering makers of handheld computers.

There's where transaction analysis comes in handy. As part of the spinoff of Palm, 3Com announced it would spin off the rest of the company by the end of 2000. For every share of 3Com they owned, 3Com shareholders would get 1.5 shares of Palm. Logic would tell you that shares of 3Com should have been 1.5 times higher than of Palm, assuming the rest of 3Com had no value, given the terms of the Palm spinoff offer.

Yet, here's the strange part: The frenzy over shares of Palm, a hot company at the time, caused the Palm shares to soar to $95.06 apiece during the first day of trading for the Palm IPO. Mathematics would dictate, then, that shares of 3Com should trade for $145. But instead, shares of 3Com dropped to $81.81 on the first day of trading for Palm. This disconnect showed that naïve investors were bidding up shares of Palm to ridiculous levels and not paying attention to the terms of the deal, according to research by Owen Lamont and Richard Thaler of the University of Chicago Graduate School of Business. And get this: Shares of Palm ultimately lost 90 percent of their value in the year following their IPO.

Understanding the pitfalls

Past financial transactions may seem like they're etched in stone. Real deals by actual buyers and sellers involve investors trading money for securities, and are not the output of some theoretical mathematical model. But investment bankers must remember that past transactions, though very telling of where the market was then, aren't always indicative of how the market will value things now or what they will be worth in a few months.

Sometimes it can be tempting to assume that if another company sold for $1 million, for instance, a company that's four times bigger would be worth $4 million. But that kind of thinking has some serious shortcomings due to pitfalls in historical price analysis, such as the following:

- ✔ **Liquidity distortions:** One of the most common mistakes made when analyzing past data is extrapolation. Investors often falsely figure that if 10 percent of a company sold for $1 million, the whole company is worth $10 million. But reality isn't that simple. Keep in mind that when just 10 percent of the company was sold, the shares were scarcer and buyers had to compete more vigorously for those shares. But try unloading the other 90 percent of the stock, and the market gets awash in shares, and the price may come down.

- ✔ **Big fish problem:** When a small company has an interesting technology or product, there's often no shortage of larger companies with the financial wherewithal to buy that company. And it's not all that uncommon for big companies to have bidding wars with each other for smaller companies with promising products. But when a small company commands a massive valuation, don't make the mistake of carrying that valuation multiple to other, larger companies in the industry. Several companies may be able to afford to buy SoftLayer Technologies for $2 billion, as International Business Machines did in June 2013. But there aren't many companies that can afford to buy IBM, so IBM doesn't necessarily command that same valuation multiple.

- ✔ **Lack of information:** Investment bankers willing and able to do some digging can usually find some details on the valuation of companies that were bought out or invested in. And there's a plethora of information available on companies that sell shares to the public in IPOs. These companies produce *prospectuses* (see Chapter 3), which contain piles of data that can be analyzed.

But investment bankers must appreciate the fact that many deals fly under the financial radar. When private companies buy other private companies, for instance, those deals are difficult to get details on. Even public companies don't have to give much in the form of details on deals that are considered to be small. Missing the complete story on past transactions limits the value of this type of analysis a bit.

Chapter 11

Applying Investment Banking to Fixed Income

Typically, investment bankers talk about buying up a company's stock to acquire a company. With their investment banking gurus at their side, convincing them that the shares are undervalued, financial tycoons often target a company's stock to buy up.

But behind the scenes, companies often have outstanding debt. The holders of this debt, called *bondholders,* need to be dealt with, too, when a company is bought, restructured, or otherwise put through the financial engineering machine.

Bondholders usually sit quietly in the background, silently accepting their interest payments from the company. But they tend to raise their voices during times of major financial upheaval at companies.

The concerns of bondholders are voiced loud and clear when a company that's the target for acquisition has issued bonds as well as stock. The bondholders are a constituency that a company has to deal with. And when a company hits hard times and can no longer keep up with interest payments, the bondholders more often than not find themselves in the pole position, because their claims to the company outrank the stockholders' claims.

Bondholders may be behind the scenes, but savvy investment bankers know they're a group of investors not to be trifled with. And that's where this chapter comes in. Here, we fill you in on what bonds are and the different varieties they come in. Then we explain where bondholders fall in the hierarchy of who gets paid when. We tell you how bond prices are calculated. And we close the chapter with a brief discussion of when companies opt for issuing bonds instead of stocks.

Introducing Bonds

A *bond* is a financial security recognizing that an investor is loaning money to a corporation. In essence, it's an IOU. In return for the bondholder's money, the corporation is obligated to make periodic interest payments to the bondholder and to repay the loan when the term of the loan ends. The basic terms of the bond include the bond's *maturity* (the original length of the loan), the *coupon rate of interest* (the rate of interest on the bond), and the *denomination* of the bond (the amount of the loan).

All the basic terms of the bond are detailed in the *bond indenture,* which is a legal document that lays out all the rights of the bondholder and the obligations of the issuer. The terms of a bond issue represent a compromise between the interests of the firm and the interests of the bond investor — each of them gives up something in order to get something in return.

The firm wants to pay the lowest interest rate possible and have the most business flexibility. On the other hand, the investor wants the highest interest rate possible and to limit the firm from certain actions (such as taking on further burdensome debt, thus weakening the existing bondholders' positions and lowering the probability that they'll receive the promised interest and principal payments).

The bond indenture often contains a description of *restrictive covenants* (terms of the bond indenture that limit the behavior of issuers). Typically, covenants place limitations on the ability of the firm to take on additional debt unless certain tests are satisfied. For example, debt may be limited by covenant to 50 percent of *total capitalization* (the sum of debt and equity). Unfortunately, bond indentures are written in legalese and are typically incomprehensible to the average investor.

Just as currency comes in different amounts, or *denominations,* so do bonds. The denomination of a bond is the amount that's being borrowed. The denominations of corporate bonds are generally $1,000 or $5,000, and the typical bond pays interest *semiannually* (every six months).

Leveraging your way to the top

In the context of corporations, borrowing is often referred to as *leverage.* This term comes from physics and the concept of a lever — when a lever is placed in the right spot, it enables you to lift a very heavy object with very little effort. In the corporate setting, a firm can borrow money and magnify a smaller equity stake into larger gains if the firm is successful. In essence, if the company can earn a higher rate on the money than it pays out, leverage works.

Remember: Leverage is a double-edged sword. If a firm earns *less* on the borrowed funds than it

pays to the bondholders, the value of the equity actually declines, and the result of leverage is negative. You may have seen how leverage can work in the residential real estate market — you put up a little equity (in the form of the purchase price of your house), and if the market cooperates, that equity grows. Unfortunately, many people learned that leverage can be negative as a result of the recent real estate bubble — they owe more on their mortgages than their homes are worth. Leverage is great . . . until it isn't.

Technically, a bond issue from a large corporation may be for hundreds of millions of dollars, but it's divided into smaller chunks so that individual investors can afford to purchase the bonds and so that investors can diversify across companies and lower the risk of their holdings.

Unlike stocks, the holder of a bond has no ownership interest in the corporation. A bondholder can only receive what is promised — nothing more. That's why bonds are often referred to as *fixed-income securities.* If everything goes as planned, a bondholder knows exactly what she'll receive and the return she'll earn if she holds the bond to maturity. If you bought a bond of a wildly successful company — like Microsoft or Apple — and you held it to maturity, the best you could hope for is to receive the promised interest payments and the full return of the principal amount. Contrast that experience with a stockholder of one of these corporations, who would've seen his initial investment grow exponentially in value.

So, why are bonds bought and sold? Well, corporations issue bonds so that they can obtain the money to build or renovate facilities, purchase new equipment, or, in the case of leveraged buyouts, even purchase other companies — in essence, to grow the business. Issuing bonds is a way of raising money (or *capital*) — an alternative to selling stock in the company. (For more on stocks, see Chapter 10.)

As for why people buy bonds, an old saying in the financial markets applies: "You can either eat well or sleep well." Investing in bonds may allow investors to sleep well because, typically, bond returns are much more stable than stock returns. However, over the long term, investing in stocks provides investors with higher returns, allowing them to eat better than bondholders.

"No pain, no gain" applies in the investment banking world as much as in the gym. Investors take on pain (or risk) in exchange for gain (or return). Typically, the more risk (or volatility) that investors accept, the more they may expect in return.

Returns are easy to measure. It's simply the appreciation in the value of the investment plus any interest or dividends paid. Risk is trickier to measure. Academics typically look at *standard deviation,* a statistical measure that quantifies how much an asset swings in price. Table 11-1 shows you how much higher stock returns have been than bond returns. The Return column shows how much the investors earned; the Standard Deviation of Return column shows how much the asset class, on average, changed in price during a given year.

Table 11-1	Statistics for Various Asset Classes Based on Annual Returns (1926–2011)	
Asset Class	*Return*	*Standard Deviation of Return*
Large stocks	11.77%	20.30%
Small stocks	16.51%	32.51%
Long-term corporate bonds	6.36%	8.35%
Long-term government bonds	6.14%	9.78%
Intermediate-term government bonds	5.54%	5.67%
Treasury bills	3.62%	3.10%

Source: Ibbotson SBBI 2012 Classic Yearbook: Market Results for Stocks, Bonds, Bills, and Inflation, 1926–2011 (Ibbotson Associates)

Identifying the Various Types of Bonds

The kind of bond we describe in the preceding section is a *plain-vanilla bond* — the simplest type of corporate bond. Nothing against vanilla — it's fine for ice cream — but as you may suspect, the bond market is not limited to plain-vanilla bonds. Investment bankers are an innovative and enterprising lot, and they've developed many bond variations. We describe the most prominent bond varieties in this section.

Convertible bonds

A *convertible bond* is just like a plain-vanilla bond, except the bondholder has the right to exchange the bond for a fixed number of shares of stock in the firm. The bondholder gets to decide whether to convert the bond into stock. As you may suspect, in exchange for receiving this valuable option — and it can be quite valuable — the bondholder agrees to receive lower interest payments than he would have in the absence of the option.

If the firm is successful and the stock price rises, the option to convert to common stock becomes more valuable, and the market price of the convertible bond will rise dramatically. Firms issuing corporate bonds hope that they're eventually converted because that means the corporation was successful and the stock price rose.

Callable bonds

A *callable bond* gives the issuer — the corporation — the right to pay the bondholder back earlier than the full term of the bond. In essence, the debt is cancelled and the bondholder receives back her principal — and generally a bit more than the principal amount, because most callable bonds have a *call premium* (the difference between the amount the investor receives if the bond is called and the principal amount of the bond). In this case, the corporation (not the investor) has the option, so callable bonds are issued with higher interest rates than non-callable bonds. Corporations call bonds when doing so is to their advantage — specifically, when interest rates in the market haven fallen since the issue of the bonds and they can re-issue debt at a lower interest rate.

Puttable bonds

A *puttable bond* gives the investor the right to demand early repayment of the principal, effectively canceling the loan. Because the investor has the right, the interest rates on puttable bonds are lower than those on plain-vanilla bonds from the same issuer. Investors only demand early repayment when interest rates in the market rise and they can find better deals (higher interest rates) on current bond issues.

Floating-rate bonds

The terms *fixed income* and *bond* are often used interchangeably. However, there is an entire class of bonds whose holders don't really receive a fixed income at all, because the interest payments change with reference to other interest rates or even to the price of a commodity. An example of a *floating-rate bond* (also known as an *adjustable-rate bond*) is one that changes in relationship to a benchmark such as the six-month Treasury rate. The bond contract states whether the rate can reset several times a year or annually. If rates rise in the market, the holder of a floating-rate bond will receive higher interest payments, and the corporation's borrowing costs will increase.

Zero-coupon bonds

Some corporations issue *zero-coupon bonds,* which have no periodic interest payments. All the cash return from these bonds comes at maturity. They're issued at a pure discount. The big disadvantage of zero-coupon bonds is that the holder must pay annual taxes on the imputed interest on the bonds.

Knowing Their Place: The Position of Bondholders

The *capital structure* of a firm describes who has supplied the funds to the firm and where those suppliers stand in seniority in terms of being paid back. A company's capital structure is a breakdown of where the money used by the company has come from, be it stockholders or bondholders.

If a firm gets into financial difficulty and the assets have to be liquidated, bondholders are in line to be paid before any money accrues to stockholders. This is an enormous advantage. How well bondholders are protected is related not only to the value of the assets but also to how much of the capital was supplied by bondholders versus stockholders. The larger the proportion of equity in the capital structure, the larger the *equity cushion* (safety net) for bondholders. A company that has 20 percent debt and 80 percent equity has a much greater equity cushion than one that has 80 percent debt and 20 percent equity.

Not all bonds are created equal. Any investor must know exactly where in that proverbial line she stands. How close you are to the front of the line determines the probability that you'll be repaid.

Some bonds are *secured* (backed by certain assets of the borrower). In the case of default, the secured bondholder can force the sale of the pledged assets in order to satisfy her claims. These bonds are also referred to as *mortgage bonds.*

What happens to bondholders in mergers and acquisitions

Let's say you're a bondholder of a company that's been affected by a merger or acquisition (whether your company was the one that bought another company or was bought). How are you affected? Unfortunately, there is no one consistent answer to that question. Sometimes the bondholders are positively affected; other times, their position is greatly weakened.

The key motivation behind any merger is the concept of *synergy* — the two companies combined are worth more than the two companies operating separately. In essence, 1 + 1 = 3. Theoretically, if true synergies can be realized, and if the bondholders' position in line either remains the same or is enhanced, bondholders should welcome the merger or acquisition.

But getting a deal to work out is much more difficult than investment bankers and CEOs like to admit. If a great deal of new debt is issued to fund the merger or acquisition, for instance, then some of the existing bondholders may find themselves in a weakened position and see the value of their bonds decline.

The mantra of corporate management is to "maximize shareholder value" — after all, the shareholders own the company. But who's looking out for the bondholder and ensuring that his needs are being addressed? Really the only line of defense for bondholders is what is spelled out in the indenture. A *bond trustee* is responsible for enforcing the provisions of the indenture.

With respect to mergers and acquisitions, several types of covenants safeguard the interests of bondholders and protect against actions that could enrich shareholders at the expense of bondholders. The goal of bond covenants is to place some restrictions upon management to limit risk-taking behavior to an appropriate level. In the absence of these types of restrictions, you would see management taking on higher levels of debt and engaging in riskier strategies that have large payoffs if successful. After all, management compensation is often tied to the value of the equity through stock options and other incentive plans. The idea of increasing leverage is akin to the old line "Heads, I win; tails, you lose." In this context, management and shareholders are the "I" and bondholders are the "you." Betting with other people's money is good work if you can get it. Common covenants include the following:

- **Debt covenant:** A debt covenant limits the amount of additional borrowings of the bond issuer. These limits are generally some multiple of earnings before interest, taxes, depreciation, and amortization (EBITDA).

- **Mergers covenant:** A mergers covenant is designed to ensure that the bond debt and the assets that support the debt remain with the same organization. If the issuer of the bond merges with another company, then the bond obligation must remain with the merged company.

- **Change-of-control covenant:** The change-of-control covenant is quite powerful and allows the bondholder to put the bonds back (sell back to the corporation) at a premium to principal amount of the bond if a qualified change-of-control event occurs. Common change-of-control events include the sale of substantially all assets, the acquisition of more than 50 percent of the issuer's common stock by a third party, a merger with another company, and a liquidation of the company. This covenant effectively safeguards the bondholder against a firm taking on substantial leverage (as in a leveraged buyout) and weakening the bondholders' positions.

Only after the secured bondholders have been paid are the *debenture holders* (the bondholders who hold debt that is *not* backed or secured by specific assets of the company) eligible to be paid. Debenture holders are often referred to as *unsecured creditors*. There are even differences in seniority between debenture holders — not all debenture holders have the same place in line for receiving payment if the company runs into trouble because there are senior and junior debenture holders. Last in the bond line are the junior debenture holders. They're paid only if all the other more senior bondholders' possessive claims are satisfied. As with most lines for scarce resources — whether Justin Bieber tickets or the latest iPhone – the further back you stand in the line, the greater the probability that you'll walk away empty-handed.

Understanding Bond Pricing

Overall, valuing bonds is a much easier task than valuing stocks because the expected cash flows are contractually specified (at least for plain-vanilla bonds). In this section, we walk you through how bonds are priced.

Introducing the concept of present value

Valuing bonds relies on the basic principle of *present value* (a dollar to be received today is worth more than a dollar to be received tomorrow or at some point in the future). The rationale is that a dollar received today can be invested to earn interest and will be worth more at a later date.

It may seem like a great deal of math is required to value bonds — and it is — but the mathematical proficiency needed is around a junior-high level, so don't be intimidated by it!

The present value of an amount to be received one year (or one period) in the future is

$$\text{Present Value} = \frac{\text{Future Value}}{(1+r)}$$

where *r* is the appropriate interest rate or discount rate (more about that in a bit).

So, the present value of a dollar to be received a year from today if the appropriate interest rate is 6 percent is:

$$\text{Present Value} = \frac{\$1.00}{(1+0.06)} = \frac{\$1.00}{(1.06)} = \$0.9434$$

In other words, a rational investor shouldn't care whether she receives $0.9434 today or $1.00 a year from now. The difference between the two amounts — $0.0566 — represents the interest she could earn on the $0.9434 at the rate of 6 percent. This simple idea is the basis for all discounted cash-flow models in finance and investments.

Extending this idea beyond a year, the present value of a dollar to be received in *two* years is

$$\text{Present Value} = \frac{\text{Future Value}_2}{(1+r)^2}$$

The subscript 2 after Future Value indicates that the amount is to be received two periods (or two years) from today, and the superscript 2 after $(1 + r)$ indicates that interest on that amount could be earned for two periods (or two years) if it was received today instead of in two years.

So, the present value of a dollar to be received in two years if the appropriate interest rate is 6 percent is

$$\text{Present Value} = \frac{\text{Future Value}_2}{(1+r)^2} = \frac{\$1.00}{(1+0.06)^2} = \frac{\$1.00}{(1.06)^2} = \$0.8900$$

In other words, a rational investor shouldn't care whether he receives $0.8900 today or $1.00 two years from now. The difference between the two amounts — $0.1100 — represents the interest he could earn on the $0.8900 at the rate of 6 percent compounded for two years. Compounding refers to the ability to reinvest the interest earned in year 1 and earn interest in year 2 on both the original amount and the year 1 interest.

Extrapolating this idea, the present value of an amount to be received at any point n in the future is simply

$$\text{Present Value} = \frac{\text{Future Value}_n}{(1+r)^n}$$

So, the present value of a dollar to be received in ten years if the appropriate interest rate is 6 percent is

$$\text{Present Value} = \frac{\text{Future Value}_{10}}{(1+r)^{10}} = \frac{\$1.00}{(1+0.06)^{10}} = \frac{\$1.00}{(1.06)^{10}} = \$0.5584$$

Again, a rational investor shouldn't care whether she receives $0.5584 today or $1.00 in ten years. The difference between the two amounts — $0.4416 — represents the interest she could earn on the $0.5584 at the rate of 6 percent compounded annually.

By the way, this is an illustration of compound interest, a concept that none other than Albert Einstein called the eighth wonder of the world.

Adding dollars at different points in time: A-Rod isn't making as much as he thinks he is

After you've computed the present values of different cash flows to be received in the future, you can add them together because they're expressed in terms of today's dollars. But adding dollars at different points in time is a mistake — even though they're expressed in dollars, they aren't in the same units. You should only add dollars to be received at different points in time after you've put them all in terms of present value.

Financial journalists often add dollars incorrectly when reporting the value of some huge sports contracts. For example, *The New York Times* reported in 2007 that New York Yankee Alex Rodriguez had signed a ten-year contract worth $275 million dollars. Assuming that the contract made equal payments of $27.5 million per year over the ten years of the contract, even at a relatively low discount rate (say, 5 percent), the contract in present value terms would be worth $212.35 million — still mind boggling, but a far cry from the more sensational $275 million value reported by the press.

The idea that you shouldn't add dollars to be received at different points in time is best illustrated by the concept of a *perpetuity* (a type of bond that pays the holder annual payments forever). Examples of perpetual bonds are consols issued by the British government. The value of any perpetual bond is certainly not infinity — although the payment stream continues forever — but it's simply the annual payment stream divided by the appropriate discount rate:

$$\text{Value}_{\text{Perpetuity}} = \frac{\text{Annual Cash Flow}}{r}$$

So, if a perpetual bond pays the holder $25 per year, and the appropriate discount rate is 8 percent, the value of the bond is

$$\text{Value} = \frac{\$25}{0.08} = \$312.50$$

A far cry from infinity.

Relating yield to maturity and price

What we describe in the preceding section is literally all the math you need to know to value a plain-vanilla bond, because the cash flows are all specified. For example, suppose we have a five-year annual-pay bond with a principal value of $1,000. Assume that the bond pays interest of $40 annually and that the appropriate discount rate for the bond is 6 percent. The value of the bond is

$$\text{Present Value} = \frac{\$40}{1.06} + \frac{\$40}{\left(1.06\right)^2} + \frac{\$40}{\left(1.06\right)^3} + \frac{\$40}{\left(1.06\right)^4} + \frac{\$1,040}{\left(1.06\right)^5} = \$915.75$$

The discount rate used to value a bond is what is known as the *yield to maturity* on that bond. In other words, the discount rate that equates the value of the future cash flows to the price is the yield to maturity on the bond. In the preceding example, if an investor bought the bond today for $915.75 and held it to maturity, he would earn exactly 6 percent on that investment.

This bond is said to be selling at a *discount* from par or principal value of $1,000, because the stated interest rate on the bond (known as the *coupon rate*) of 4 percent is less than the yield to maturity of 6 percent. Alternatively, if the coupon rate on the bond is greater than the yield to maturity, the mathematics show that the bond would be selling for more than the principal or par value and would be selling for a premium. For example, if the same bond had a yield to maturity of 3 percent, it would be selling for $1,046.39 — a premium of $46.39 to par value. Finally, if the bond were selling at a yield to maturity of 4 percent, it would be selling for exactly $1,000 and would be said to be selling at par.

There is an inverse relationship between market interest rates and bond prices: As interest rates in the market rise, the prices of bonds fall. Alternatively, as interest rates in the market fall, the prices of bonds rise. Corporate bonds are issued at or near par value, so when you see a bond selling at a discount, you can infer that since the time that the bond was issued, market interest rates have fallen. Conversely, if a bond is selling at a premium to par value, that bond was issued in a higher interest rate environment.

What determines the yield to maturity?

The general level of market interest rates isn't all that goes into determining the yield to maturity of a bond. The yield on a bond is made up of two major components:

✔ The yield on a similar default-free bond

✔ A premium above the yield on a default-free bond to compensate for the specific credit risks of the bond issue

In the United States, the yield on U.S. Treasury securities are considered the benchmark yields because they're considered default-free, are the most liquid securities traded, and are not callable.

Playing the spread: How different factors affect bond prices

Credit risk on a bond is related to the risk that an issuer may default on interest payments or repayment of the principal. Of course, if a bond defaults, that doesn't meant that the investor will lose her entire investment in the bond. Investors in bonds that default typically recover some significant portion of their investment. Suffice it to say, bonds with higher default risk sell at higher yields to maturity.

Credit spreads are defined as the risk premium over similar-maturity Treasury securities. Credit spreads are a mathematical way to measure how much more yield investors get on one bond than another. Credit spreads are critical for investors to make sure they're being compensated enough for the extra risk they're taking on a bond with more potential problems. For instance, if ten-year Treasury bonds are yielding 3 percent, and a particular corporate issuer is yielding 5 percent, then the credit spread is 2 percent, or 200 basis points. (A *basis point* is defined as one-hundredth of a percentage point.)

Credit spreads tend to widen during economic downturns as investors become concerned that corporate profits and cash flows will decline and negatively impact the ability of firms to service their debt. So, during recessions, credit spreads tend to widen on virtually all corporate issues and the prices of bonds decline overall. Conversely, during economic recoveries and booms, credit spreads tend to narrow as investors become more optimistic about firm cash flows.

The combination of these different factors determines the specific yield to maturity for a bond issue. Both economic-wide (macro) and firm-specific (micro) factors affect the yield to maturity on bond issues and, thus, the value of bonds.

Considering bond sensitivity to changes in interest rates

All bonds are sensitive to changes in the general level of market interest rates, but the sensitivity varies from bond to bond. The interest rate sensitivity of a bond varies inversely with the coupon rate and directly with its term to maturity. Analysts have developed a measure of interest rate sensitivity called *duration* that takes into account both the coupon rate and term to maturity factors.

The coupon rate effect

Bonds with higher coupon rates are less sensitive to changes in interest rates than bonds with lower coupon rates. For example, we can contrast the interest rate sensitivity of a five-year zero-coupon bond with an initial yield to maturity of 5 percent, with that of a five-year 5 percent coupon bond with an initial yield to maturity of 5 percent (assuming that the bond pays interest annually).

The five-year zero-coupon bond selling to yield 5 percent to maturity will be priced at

$$\text{Price}_{zero} = \frac{\$1,000}{(1.05)^5} = \$783.53$$

The price of the five-year, 5 percent coupon bond selling to yield 5 percent will be $1,000 because the yield to maturity and the coupon rate are identical.

Now, assume that yields in the marketplace rise by 100 basis points due to general economic uncertainty and that the bonds both sell at a yield to maturity of 6 percent. The new price of the zero-coupon bond will be

$$\text{Price}_{zero} = \frac{\$1,000}{(1.06)^5} = \$747.26$$

With this increase in interest rates of 100 basis points, the price of the zero-coupon bond fell by 4.63 percent.

If the yield to maturity rises to 6 percent, the price of the 5 percent coupon bond is

$$\text{Price} = \frac{\$50}{1.06} + \frac{\$50}{(1.06)^2} + \frac{\$50}{(1.06)^3} + \frac{\$50}{(1.06)^4} + \frac{\$1,050}{(1.06)^5} = \$957.87$$

With this increase in interest rates of 100 basis points, the price of the 5 percent coupon bond fell by 4.21 percent. Thus, the lower coupon bond is more sensitive to changes in interest rates than the higher coupon bond. If interest rates rise, you would rather be holding higher coupon bonds than lower coupon bonds.

The term to maturity effect

Bonds with longer terms to maturity are more sensitive to changes in interest rates than bonds with shorter terms to maturity. To illustrate this point, contrast the price change of similar zero-coupon bonds, one with 5 years to maturity and one with 30 years to maturity, when yields go from 5 percent to 6 percent.

As shown in the preceding section, the market price of a five-year zero-coupon bond falls from $783.53 to $747.26, a decrease in price of 4.63 percent when the yield to maturity on the bond rises from 5 percent to 6 percent.

Contrast that with the change in price on a 30-year zero-coupon bond when the yield to maturity on the bond rises from 5 percent to 6 percent. At a yield of 5 percent, the price of the bond is

$$\text{Price} = \frac{\$1,000}{(1.05)^{30}} = \$231.37$$

At a yield of 6 percent, the price of the bond is

$$\text{Price} = \frac{\$1,000}{(1.06)^{30}} = \$174.11$$

When yields rise from 5 percent to 6 percent, the price of the 30-year zero-coupon bond falls by 24.75 percent. Suffice it to say, you'd rather be holding shorter-term bonds than longer-term bonds if interest rates rise.

Duration

The two preceding sections show that price volatility of a bond varies inversely with its coupon rate and directly with its term to maturity. *Duration* is a combined measure of interest rate sensitivity that takes into account both of these properties.

Duration is one tool investment bankers use to determine how risky a bond investment is. It's defined as the time-weighted term to maturity of a bond in which the cash flows are weighted according to when they're received in a present value sense.

When you compute the duration for a bond, the unit of measurement is in years. You calculate duration simply by finding the present value of each cash flow as a percentage of the price of the bond and multiplying that value by the year in which the cash flow is received. The sum of those values is the time-weighted term to maturity of the bond and represents the duration of the bond.

Table 11-2 calculates the duration for a ten-year, 5 percent coupon bond with a 7 percent yield to maturity (assuming annual interest payments). This bond has a duration of 7.94 years. It will show interest rate sensitivity that is identical to a zero-coupon bond with 7.94 years to maturity.

Table 11-2	The Duration of a 5 Percent Coupon, Ten-Year Bond with a Yield to Maturity of 7 Percent			
Year	Cash Flow	Present Value of Cash Flow at 7%	Present Value as a Percent of Price	Year x Present Value as a Percent of Price
1	$50	$46.73	0.0544	0.0544
2	$50	$43.67	0.0508	0.1016
3	$50	$40.81	0.0475	0.1425
4	$50	$38.14	0.0444	0.1776
5	$50	$35.65	0.0415	0.2075
6	$50	$33.32	0.0388	0.2328
7	$50	$31.14	0.0362	0.2534
8	$50	$29.10	0.0339	0.2712
9	$50	$27.20	0.0316	0.2844
10	$1050	$533.77	0.6210	6.2100
Total		**$859.53**		**7.9354**

Duration has many useful properties. One is that you can compute the duration of a fixed-income portfolio simply by computing a weighted average (weighted by value) of the bonds in the portfolio. In that way, an investor can determine the interest rate sensitivity of his fixed-income portfolio and can estimate how much the portfolio will change in value given a change in market interest rates.

Portfolio managers often adjust the duration of their portfolios by buying and selling bonds in anticipation of interest rate changes. For example, if you thought interest rates were going to decline (and bond values would rise), you would want to lengthen the duration of your portfolio. Conversely, if you thought interest rates were going to rise, you would want to shorten the duration of your portfolio.

Tracking the Bond Market

The evening news typically tells viewers how the Dow Jones Industrials or S&P 500 stock indexes performed that day, but results in the bond market generally aren't reported by the popular media. There isn't the equivalent of a widely followed bond market index to the two popular equity indexes. So, bond investors typically consider the U.S. Treasury yield curve the appropriate bond market benchmark and monitor changes to the yield curve to gauge the bond market and interest rates.

The U.S. Treasury yield curve is simply a graph showing the relationship between yield on a U.S. Treasury security in relation to the maturity of the instrument. U.S. Treasury securities are used because they're always issued by the same entity — the U.S. Treasury — and they have no default risk. So, they give an idea of what investors demand for the pure time value of money.

Most often, the yield curve is upward sloping (like the one in Figure 11-1). In other words, longer-maturity (longer-duration) Treasury bonds have a higher yield to maturity than shorter-maturity Treasury bonds. This makes intuitive sense: A longer time period generally has greater risks, just because there's more time for unexpected things to happen.

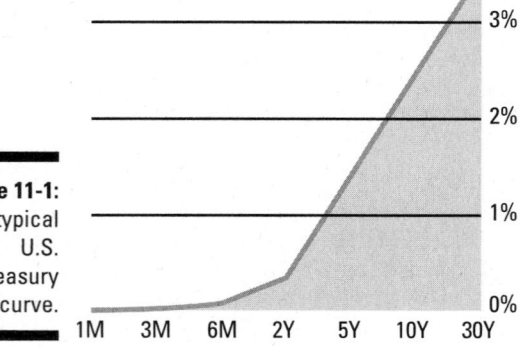

Figure 11-1: A typical U.S. Treasury yield curve.

Most lenders prefer to lend short term, and most borrowers prefer to borrow long term. To induce lenders to lend long term, lenders must be offered a time premium.

Sometimes, however, the yield curve can become flat or even inverted. A flat yield curve is one in which all yields are very close to one another. An inverted yield curve happens when shorter-term yields are actually higher than longer-term yields. Many people believe that a flat or inverted yield curve is a precursor to an economic recession or slowdown. Lenders are willing to accept a lower long-term yield to lock in the current returns, while borrowers are willing to pay higher rates in the short term because they believe they'll be able to get more favorable long-term rates in the future.

Investors typically look at the very short end of the yield curve (the 90-day Treasury bill rate), the middle of the yield curve (the 10-year Treasury bond rate) and the long end (the 30-year Treasury bond rate) to get a handle on the bond market. When people in the investment management industry ask how the bond market did, the answer typically involves detailing what happened to both the 90-day Treasury bill and the 30-year Treasury bond.

Finding bond pricing data

Several free sources of bond pricing data are available. One of the best sources is the website for the Financial Industry Regulatory Authority (FINRA). On FINRA's website (`http://cxa.gtm.idmanagedsolutions.com/finra/bondcenter/default.aspx`), you can find a depiction of the current U.S. Treasury yield curve and look up quotes for specific bonds, whether they be corporate, Treasury, or bonds issued by other entities.

Another source of bond pricing data is the public website for Bloomberg (`www.bloomberg.com/markets/rates-bonds`). The public Bloomberg site is limited to providing you information on the yield curve (you can't look up quotes for specific bonds), but at a glance you can see the yield curve for the U.K. and Japan, as well as for the United States. In addition, the Bloomberg site provides a graphic that compares the current yield curve to the yield curve that existed one month and one year ago.

One caution concerning bond pricing data: U.S. Treasury securities are among the most actively traded and liquid securities in the world. So, the quotes are both current and accurately portray what a current buyer or seller would pay or receive. Most corporate bonds aren't very liquid, and recent transaction prices may not indicate what a current buyer or seller would pay or receive for the instrument.

Debt or Equity: How a Company Chooses

Both debt and equity are issued by companies who need funds to expand their operations. The factors that management considers are numerous, but the goal is always to raise capital in a cost-efficient manner. Just as an investor wants to buy undervalued assets and sell overvalued assets, companies choose between debt and equity based on the relative cost of the capital source.

If a firm's management believes that interest rates are low and likely to rise in the future, they often choose to issue long-term debt at a fixed rate. If interest rates do indeed rise, the market value of the debt will decline. Because that debt is a liability of the firm and the liability declines in value, the firm wins. A prime example of this was in May 2013 when Warren Buffett's Berkshire Hathaway issued $1 billion in corporate debt. The Oracle of Omaha was on record as saying that he believed that interest rates were historically low and would increase in the future. Issuing debt was a way of selling what he believed was an overvalued asset. (We wonder who feels confident buying these bonds — betting against Mr. Buffett has been a losing proposition for several decades.)

If a firm's management believes that interest rates are high and are likely to decline in the future, they'll choose to issue shorter-term debt, callable debt, or perhaps debt with a floating interest rate. That way, they aren't locked into paying a high interest rate for an extended period of time, and they have the flexibility to refinance when rates fall.

Companies generally don't like to issue equity if they believe that their stock is undervalued. This form of financing is expensive and dilutes the ownership of the current stockholders.

If the equity is undervalued but debt financing appears to be expensive, companies may choose to issue convertible bonds. That way, if the value of the equity rises, the bondholders will convert and extinguish the debt. In addition, the conversion price is generally set at a substantial premium above the market price of the equity at the time the bond is issued. If things work out the way the firm would like, the value of the stock will rise, bond-holders will convert, and the firm will have effectively issued stock at a price that is above what it could have received in a straight equity offering.

Companies can also increase their leverage without issuing debt. They can buy back (or repurchase) company stock in the open market, thereby increasing their debt-to-equity ratio. A firm will buy back stock when it has excess cash and the management believes that the market undervalues that stock. Stock buybacks tend to bolster the stock price of the firm, because the percentage of the company that any individual stockholder owns effectively increases after a buyback. Buybacks are often preferred to cash dividends, because only the shareholders who want to sell the stock back will incur a tax liability.

Part III

Taking Investment Banking to the Next Level

Courtesy of S&P Capital IQ

Dig into the discounted cash flow analysis in a free article at `http://www.dummies.com/extras/investmentbanking`.

In this part . . .

✔ Perform a discounted cash flow analysis to put a price tag on a company.

✔ Find out how to calculate weighted average cost of capital so you can understand thresholds that define a successful deal.

✔ Discover how leveraged buyouts work in order to appreciate the allure of debt to pay for deals.

✔ See how return on equity is used as a tool by investment bankers so you can see how financial measures can help measure the effectiveness of a company's management team.

Chapter 12

Doing a Discounted Free Cash Flow Analysis

*T*he real meat and potatoes of investment banking involves developing and applying financial models. And financial models aren't plastic pieces you glue together with pungent-smelling glue. Financial models are built by running numbers to demonstrate the best ways to improve the efficiencies, net incomes, and valuations of businesses.

Investment bankers earn their big paychecks by showing CEOs, boards, and management teams that by issuing or buying back certain securities they've already sold, going public or going private, purchasing companies or spinning off divisions, and making other changes in the way the firm operates, the value of the firm can be increased. Sell-side investment banking analysts earn their keep by identifying undervalued companies for clients to buy stock of, or by identifying overvalued companies their clients should sell. Investment banking is a very bottom-line oriented industry, and financial models are the foundation — the raw materials of the investment banking process.

Financial models are typically developed and manipulated by young 20-something investment banking associates who join investment banking firms after studying these standard models in elite business schools. Junior analysts often command six-figure salaries immediately upon graduation from business school, and they typically work long hours honing their skills by preparing financial models and presentations for more senior investment bankers to pitch to clients and potential clients.

The financial value and longevity of any firm rests upon its ability to generate positive cash flow. It's just like a working household, where the cash coming in must exceed the cash going out in order for the family to be able to stay afloat financially in the long term. Financial models are built on the premise that the value of any firm is simply the *present value* of all future cash flows. (For more detail about present value refer to Chapter 11.) Unlike other assets, such as sports cars, jewelry, boats, and homes, holders of financial assets don't draw psychic income by owning a flashy physical asset that they can show off to friends and make their neighbors jealous. Financial assets like stocks and bonds are generally valued in a very unromantic and unemotional fashion. As Joe Friday said, "Just the facts, ma'am."

This chapter presents the primary financial model that investment bankers employ: the *discounted free cash flow model*. At its core, the discounted free cash flow model is pretty simple, and you can get a solid handle on this model and its variations in the pages that follow.

Don't be too concerned about the math. If you can add, subtract, multiply and divide, you can follow the presentation and understand the basics of the model. Of course, the model can certainly get more complicated as it's refined and modified by investment bankers.

Chapter 20 details ten ways to improve these models. But first, the basics.

Gearing Up for Discounted Free Cash Flow

The basic discounted free cash flow model requires the analyst to complete two basic tasks: First, the analyst must estimate future cash flows to the firm. After creating the cash flow estimate, the analyst must forecast the appropriate *discount rate* (an interest rate that is used to put a future cash sum into today's dollars; see Chapter 11) to apply to those cash flows.

The value of any financial asset can be determined by the following basic formula:

$$\text{Value} = \frac{CF_1}{(1+r)^1} + \frac{CF_2}{(1+r)^2} + \ldots + \frac{CF_n}{(1+r)^n} + \ldots$$

where CF_n is cash flow at time n and r is the appropriate discount rate.

Don't let the scary appearance of the formula rattle you. It's just the mathematical way to state that the value of any asset is simply the present value of all future cash flows that the owner of that asset is entitled to. So, as we show in Chapter 11, the value of a bond is simply the present value of all the interest payments and the return of principal value that the bondholder receives. Likewise, the value of a share of stock is equal to the present value of all the future dividend payments that the stockholder receives. (See the "Valuing a Share of Stock" section at the end of this chapter for more information.)

The value of an entire corporation is determined via a model that estimates free cash flows to the firm and discounts them back to the present via a discount rate called the *weighted average cost of capital* (WACC; see "Calculating the Weighted Average Cost of Capital," later in this chapter).

Free cash flow (FCF) is not a formal accounting concept like gross margin or net income, so it's sometimes defined somewhat differently by different people. In its most basic form, free cash flow is the amount of cash flow from operations (CFO) remaining after paying for any needed capital expenditures. CFO is simply the cash flow generated by normal business operations and doesn't include items that may be one time in nature — such as the sale of a building or even the sale of an entire division. Capital expenditures are investments that a company must make to replace assets that are worn out and need replacing or expenditures made in new assets to fuel future growth. In addition, since FCF is cash flow available to all capital suppliers (including bondholders), interest expense needs to be added back (net of taxes) in computing FCF. The net of taxes aspect refers to the fact that interest on debt payments are tax deductible. So, FCF is computed as follows:

$$\text{FCF} = \text{CFO} + \text{Interest Expense} (1 - \text{Tax Rate}) - \text{Capital Expenditures}$$

The discounted free cash flow model states that the value of the firm is equal to the value of all future free cash flows to the firm discounted at the WACC:

$$\text{Firm Value} = \frac{\text{FCF}_1}{(1+\text{WACC})^1} + \frac{\text{FCF}_2}{(1+\text{WACC})^2} + \ldots + \frac{\text{FCF}_n}{(1+\text{WACC})^n} + \ldots$$

One thing that may trouble you when looking at the formula is that it has an infinite number of terms. Don't despair. As you'll see, by making a simple assumption or two, the formula breaks down into a finite and very manageable number of terms.

Computing free cash flow

Virtually all investment bankers begin their analysis with the most recent period of performance of the company in question. Suppose we wanted to determine the free cash flow for IBM for the most recent year. We can go to the Securities and Exchange Commission's online EDGAR system and get the latest 10-K filing for IBM (Chapter 6 gives detailed instructions on using EDGAR).

For this example, the following values are provided for IBM for the year ended December 31, 2012 (amounts are in millions of dollars):

Income Statement Item	Amount (In Millions of Dollars)
Cash flow from operations	$19,586
Payments for property, plant, and equipment	($4,082)
Proceeds from disposition of property, plant, and equipment	$410
Investments and business acquisitions (net)	($3,123)

From supplemental disclosures on EDGAR, we find that IBM paid $1.022 million of interest to debt holders in 2012 and had an effective tax rate of 24 percent.

From this information, we compute free cash flow to the firm as follows:

1. **Add the cash flow from operations to the after-tax interest**.

   The cash flow from operations is $19,586. The after-tax interest is $1,022 \times (1 - 0.24) = \$776.72$, which we'll round up to $777. So, $19,586 + $777 = $20,363.

2. **Subtract the payments for property, plant, and equipment**.

   Payments for property, tax, and equipment total $4,082. So, $20,363 − $4,082 = $16,281.

3. **Add the proceeds from disposition of property, plant, and equipment**.

   The proceeds from disposition of property, plant, and equipment total $410. So, $16,281 + $410 = $16,691.

4. **Subtract the investments and business acquisitions (net)**.

   Investments and business acquisitions (net) total $3,123. So, $16,691 − $3,123 = $13,568.

So, the current free cash flow to the firm for IBM is $13,568 million, or more clearly stated, $13.6 billion. Wow, that's a lot of zeros.

Forecasting free cash flow

Determining free cash flow for any past year isn't difficult and most analysts would, in fact, agree on its calculation. You simply take historical values and plug and chug into the formulas and — *voilà!* — you have a value for free cash flow. But valuation models aren't based upon the past; they're based upon expected future cash flows.

The basic models and tools used by analysts are the same, but the application of those tools and models — the assumptions made — can differ dramatically. That's why two analysts can examine the same company, use the same valuation models, and arrive at wildly different valuations. One analyst can believe that a stock is significantly undervalued, and the other can believe that the same stock is wildly overvalued.

The basic models they're applying are the same, and the historical data they're reviewing is the same. The difference involves the assumptions about the future that they make. As Shakespeare wrote, "Therein lies the rub." That's why financial analysis is part science and part art.

To forecast free cash flow, analysts must forecast cash flow from operations. Cash flow from operations is simply:

Cash Flow from Operations = Earnings before Interest and Taxes + Depreciation − Taxes

Now, this is starting to sound complicated, but to get to earnings before interest and taxes, analysts must forecast sales and how much it cost to produce and sell those products. In essence, analysts must forecast the entire income statement of the firm for the foreseeable future.

The typical income statement of a manufacturing firm looks something like this:

Sales

Less: Cost of sales

Gross Profit

Less: Selling, General and Administrative Expenses

Earnings Before Interest and Taxes

Less: Interest

Earnings Before Taxes

Less: Taxes

Net Income

Spreadsheet analysis

The spreadsheet is the analyst's best friend, because the typical method of forecasting involves plugging in the current year's values for the income statement and making assumptions about the growth rate of each of the items and the relationships among them — and, importantly, how those relationships may change because of something the firm (at the urging of its investment banker, of course) may do.

For example, analysts may forecast that sales will grow at 8 percent for the first three years, 6 percent for the next three years, and 4 percent thereafter. How do they make these assumptions? They look at the overall economic outlook, the competitive industry landscape, and the position of the company's products within that industry.

The procedures used to develop forecasts and the analysis may be very detailed and painstaking, but the bottom line is that they're forecasting the future, and that's fraught with error.

Likewise analysts will make assumptions about the growth rate of selling, as well as general and administrative expenses. By setting up the analysis in a spreadsheet, the analyst can change the assumptions and see how that affects earnings before interest and taxes. Then, of course, depreciation and taxes must be forecast to arrive at cash flow from operations.

Calculating the Weighted Average Cost of Capital

The *weighted average cost of capital* (WACC) is a very important input into the discounted cash flow models. It's defined as the average rate of return of a company's suppliers of capital, and it's the rate at which the future cash flows of the firm are discounted back to a present value for valuation purposes. All else equal, the higher the WACC, the lower the value of the firm. That's because the cost of capital is higher for riskier firms.

IBM can access capital much more inexpensively than can an unproven, startup firm. And investing in IBM is much less risky than investing in an unproven startup firm. One thing that market participants agree on is that to induce investors to make riskier investments, they must expect higher returns.

The formula for WACC is simple: It's a weighted average. The individual component costs of the different types of capital (stocks and bonds) are weighted by the percentage of stocks and bonds in the *capital structure* (how the firm is financed — the percentage of financing that has come from stock and the percentage that has come from bonds). So, the WACC formula is simply

$$WACC = \frac{D}{D+E}r_d + \frac{E}{D+E}r_e$$

where D is the value of debt, E is the value of equity, r_d is the required return on debt, and r_e is the required return on equity.

So, if we have a company that is financed with one-third debt and two-thirds equity, and the after-tax required return on debt is 5 percent, and the required return on equity is 10 percent, the WACC for the firm is:

$$WACC = \frac{1}{3}(5\%) + \frac{2}{3}(10\%) = 8.34\%$$

When we apply the discounted cash flow models for this firm, we would discount all the future cash flows at an 8.34 percent annual rate.

One of the first variations that you see in determining the WACC is that some investment banking analysts use current market value weights when calculating the WACC, while other analysts use target weights. *Current market value weights* are simply the current weights observed in the capital structure. *Target weights*, on the other hand, incorporate the analyst's expectations about the capital structure he believes the company will likely use over the foreseeable future. In the previous example, the analyst may believe the company will issue more bonds than stock in the future, and a capital structure of one-half debt and one-half equity may be more likely.

Understanding why the weighted average cost of capital is so important

Because WACC is an estimate of the cost of funding for a firm, the concept of WACC is critically important for the internal operations and planning of the firm. If the firm's managers — often with the help of their investment bankers — can identify opportunities to invest in projects or ideas that return more than the cost of capital, the value of the firm will increase. This is how wealth is created.

Profitable projects or ideas could be a new product line, expansion of a current product line into a new market, the acquisition of a product line from a competitor, or even the acquisition of a competitor. If a firm can acquire funds at a cost of 8 percent and earn 12 percent on those funds, the value of the firm will increase, and the stockholders (and management and the investment bankers) will be very happy.

The WACC is often considered a hurdle rate, and any potential investment that the firm is contemplating must promise a return that is greater than the WACC. However, there is one caveat: When firms compare returns from potential investments to the WACC, the implicit assumption being made is that the potential investment has the same risk as the current firm as a whole. That isn't a bad place to start, but firm analysts and investment banking analysts need to adjust the WACC for project risk if the project is considerably more risky or less risky than the firm as a whole.

Adjusting WACC for a project's risk works both ways. If a firm is manufacturing a product and can reduce its costs by acquiring a more efficient production machine that already exists, then that project isn't very risky. Most analysts would agree that the cash flows from this project could be reasonably discounted at a much lower rate than the firm's WACC because the risk implicit in this project is very low. Conversely, a firm may be considering selling an entirely new product line in a brand-new market. You could reasonably argue that the cash flows from this project should be discounted at a rate higher than the WACC because of the higher risk level.

Measuring the cost of debt and equity

To determine the WACC, an analyst must first estimate the individual component costs of capital — the cost of debt and the cost of equity. As you see in this section, the cost of debt capital is very straightforward — there is little controversy on how it's estimated and there are few alternatives. The cost of equity, on the other hand, can be estimated using several different methods, which may produce widely different cost estimates. Again, this is where the art of investment banking deviates a bit from the science.

Cost of debt capital

To estimate the cost of debt capital for a firm with publicly traded bonds, the investment banking analyst has to look no further than the bond market to determine at what yield to maturity the firm's bonds are selling for in the marketplace. (For more on yield to maturity, see Chapter 11.)

Companies usually have more than one outstanding bond issue, so analysts will calculate an average bond yield — using market value weights. This average yield to maturity of all the outstanding debt of the firm is that firm's before-tax cost of debt.

But there's one more step. Because the Internal Revenue Service allows companies to deduct interest costs before arriving at net income that is subject to taxation, the true after-tax cost of debt is considerably lower than the before-tax cost of debt. In fact, it's adjusted for the firm's corporate tax rate. Thus, the formula for after-tax cost of debt is as follows:

After-Tax Cost of Debt = Before-Tax Cost of Debt × (1 – Tax Rate)

If the average yield to maturity on a company's bonds is 8 percent and the company's tax rate is 30 percent, the firm's after tax cost of debt is as follows:

After-Tax Cost of Debt = 8% × (1 – 0.3) = 5.6%

Cost of equity capital

One of the most difficult and controversial aspects of completing a discounted cash flow analysis is determining the appropriate required rate of return (or cost) on equity. The relationship between risk and required return is perhaps the most basic in investments.

Riskier assets should provide higher returns in the long run to compensate investors for assuming that risk. There is an old saying in investments: You can eat well or you can sleep well. This refers to the fact that if you take more risk, your returns are likely to be higher. However, in the short run, the volatility of those riskier investments may cause you to lose sleep at night.

In general, stocks are riskier than bonds, so stockholders should expect to earn higher returns than bondholders over the long run — and they do. Table 11-1 in Chapter 11 shows that over the long run, stocks return significantly higher returns than bonds and small stocks return significantly higher returns than large stocks. We refer to the expected return of one asset class over another as a *risk premium*. But how do we determine the theoretically correct required rate of return for a specific company's equity?

Few analysts would disagree about the methodology to estimate the cost of debt capital, but there is no one universally accepted method for estimating the cost of equity capital. So, different analysts will come up with widely different estimates of a firm's cost of equity capital. All methods, however, start out with a fundamental premise — they start out with a risk-free rate and add a premium or series of premiums for the risk that the equity holder is bearing. And all analysts agree that the cost of equity capital is higher than the cost of debt capital.

Two of the more popular methods for determining the cost of equity capital are the *build-up method* and the *capital asset pricing model* (CAPM). The build-up method is generally used for smaller, privately held firms, while the CAPM is more appropriate for large, publicly traded firms. The CAPM occupies a prominent place in investment banking and is discussed in the following section. Here, we focus on the build-up method.

The build-up method simply starts with the current risk-free rate (usually estimated as the yield on long-term U.S. Treasury securities) and adds various premiums for different sources of risk inherent in equity securities. Both the number of premiums and the values for each of the categories will vary from analyst to analyst, but a typical build-up method will add premiums for the following categories:

- **Market risk premium:** This is the additional return that is required for an investor to purchase an average stock rather than simply invest and earn the risk-free rate by buying government securities. The equity risk premium is generally considered for the market as a whole and often is thought of as the premium applying to large capitalization stocks (like the Standard & Poor's 500).

  The equity risk premium is most often determined by using historical data. For example, Table 11-1 shows that large stocks have returned a premium of 5.63 percent annually over the return for long-term government bonds for the time period from 1926 through 2011.

  Some analysts chose not to use historical equity risk premiums and instead simply plug in a forward-looking forecast that they believe is more applicable to the current investing environment. To that point, many investment professionals believe that the equity risk premium is smaller today than it has been historically. More on this in the following section.

- **Size premium:** Small stocks are generally considered riskier than large stocks for many reasons. Over time, small stocks have earned higher returns than large stocks. From Table 11-1, you can see that small stocks returned a premium of 4.74 percent over large stocks from 1926 through 2011.

- **Idiosyncratic premium:** This is a catch-all category where the analyst can apply her own judgment to adjust the cost of equity for a myriad of factors. Perhaps the analyst feels that the firm will be subject to significant litigation risks in the future or is in an industry that may be negatively influenced by future government policy changes.

So, assuming that current yields on long-term government bonds (the risk free rate) was 3.2 percent, for a hypothetical small company with an idiosyncratic premium of 2 percent, using historical values for the premiums, the build-up method would estimate the cost of equity capital at:

$$\text{Cost of Equity} = \text{Risk-Free Rate} + \text{Market Risk Premium} + \text{Size Premium} + \text{Idiosyncratic Premium}$$

$$\text{Cost of Equity} = 3.2\% + 5.63\% + 4.74\% + 2\% = 15.57\%$$

Unlike the cost of debt, the IRS does not provide a tax break for payments to equity holders. So, the after-tax cost of equity is the same as the before-tax cost of equity.

You can look up the current risk-free rate by checking online systems, such as Bloomberg, S&P Capital IQ, or public financial news websites for the yield on the benchmark ten-year U.S. Treasury.

Understanding the capital asset pricing model

The CAPM is a financial model that was developed in 1964 by Nobel Prize winner and Stanford finance professor William Sharpe. It transformed the way that financial professionals think about risk and return.

Sharpe built on earlier work by Nobel laureate Harry Markowitz who first advanced the notion that the risk of an asset should be measured not in isolation, but with respect to that asset being added to a portfolio or collection of assets. In other words, an asset may look very risky if just examined by itself, but the real measure of risk should be how it adds to or reduces the risk of an already existing portfolio — because most people hold a portfolio of assets and not simply a single asset.

Beta is the measure of risk

The intuition behind the CAPM is that you measure an asset's risk relative to the average risk of the market. For simplicity's sake, most analysts define the market as the most widely followed market indices — typically, a large-cap index such as the S&P 500 Index.

The measure of risk for the CAPM is called *beta* (β). An asset's beta is calculated by determining, on average, if an asset is more or less volatile than the market as a whole.

By definition, the market has a beta equal to 1.0. If an asset is less volatile than the market, it will have a beta lower than 1.0. If an asset is more volatile than the market, it will have a beta greater than 1.0.

The good news is that you don't need to compute betas. Many financial websites compute betas for you, and you can simply look them up. For instance, Yahoo! Finance (`http://finance.yahoo.com`), Thomson Reuters (`www.reuters.com`), and MSN Money (`http://money.msn.com`) report betas for securities. Betas are estimates calculated over different time periods and in relation to different indices, so you'll find that the betas reported by different providers will vary. You'll also find that the beta for a particular security will vary over time.

Table 12-1 provides a listing of betas for several Dow Jones Industrial Average components as of July 16, 2013. You'll see that according to the beta measure,

Alcoa is much more risky — when added to a portfolio — than the market, while Johnson & Johnson is much less risky than the market. American Express, on the other hand, has a risk nearly identical to the market.

Table 12-1	Betas for Stocks as of July 16, 2013
Stock	*Beta*
Alcoa	1.94
American Express	0.99
General Electric	1.32
IBM	0.73
Johnson & Johnson	0.40

Source: Yahoo! Finance

Applying the CAPM

All you need to know to estimate the required rate of return on equity (r_e) according to the CAPM are the following three inputs:

- **Risk-free rate of return:** This is generally the current yield on 90-day Treasury bills issued by the U.S. government, but some analysts use a longer-term (10-year or 30-year U.S. government bond rate). You can look up this rate on any number of financial websites including Yahoo! Finance and Bloomberg (www.bloomberg.com). On July 16, 2013, the return on 90-day Treasury bills was 0.03 percent — a historically low yield!

- **Market risk premium:** The market risk premium is simply defined as the expected return on stocks minus the return on U.S. Treasury bills. It is, in effect, the premium an investor earns for investing in the market versus simply investing in Treasury bills. This is where the art of investment banking comes in. There is no one source to look up what the market risk premium is, so the analyst must estimate it. One method is to look at history and see what it has averaged over a long period of time. Using the data in Table 11-1, the market risk premium from 1926 through 2011 is 8.15 percent — computed as the difference between the return on large stocks (11.77 percent) and the return on Treasury bills (3.62 percent).

- **Beta:** As noted earlier, you can look up a stock's beta on a number of financial websites.

The first two inputs — the risk-free rate of return and the market risk premium — are the same for all stocks. So, according to the CAPM, the only variable that changes when we examine different stocks is beta.

The formula for computing the required rate of return on equity according to the CAPM is:

$$r_e = r_f + \beta \times (\text{Market Risk Premium})$$

where r_f is the risk-free rate and β is, well, beta.

To compute the required rate of return on General Electric equity, we simply plug the values into the equation:

$$R_e = 0.03 + (1.32 \times 8.15) = 10.79\%$$

So, the appropriate required return on equity capital for General Electric stock, according to the CAPM, is 10.79 percent.

The same calculation for IBM results in a much lower required rate of return on equity capital of 5.98 percent. Because IBM is considered much less risky than General Electric, investors will require a lower expected rate of return to invest in it.

Postscript on CAPM

One of the great debates in academic financial circles involves how well CAPM works — that is, how well it explains the long-term relationship between risk and return for stocks over time. More data-based studies — academics refer to them as *empirical studies* — have been done critiquing the CAPM than on virtually any other topic in finance over the past half-century. At best, the evidence on the veracity of CAPM is mixed. Suffice it to say that the relationship between risk and return isn't as simple or as reliable as the CAPM hypothesizes. The evidence is not consistent with a simple straight-line (or linear) relationship between risk (beta) and return over either long-term or short-term time periods. In fact, over some time periods, lower-beta stocks have outperformed higher-beta stocks — and, stocks in general have underperformed government bonds.

One of the key insights to the CAPM is that the only risk that investors are compensated for — and the only risk that they should be concerned with — is the systematic risk of the firm relative to the broad market. All other risks can be diversified away by holding a well-diversified portfolio of many securities. The intuition behind the model is terrific and has caused investors and investment bankers to look at risk differently. Similar to Churchill's view that "democracy is the worst form of government except all the others that have been tried," although it is by no means a bulletproof theory, the CAPM is the best theory to explain the risk/return relationship that the greatest financial minds have been able to devise.

So, what does the analyst take from this? CAPM is a terrific starting point to determine the cost of equity capital, but most analysts understand that it isn't a perfect depiction of reality and adjust their estimates of the cost of equity accordingly.

Going for Terminal Value

Up to this point, we've presented the basic valuation model and have discussed how to estimate the different components of the model — the free cash flows and the weighted average cost of capital. In this section, we put it all together and show you how investment bankers arrive at the value of a company.

As we show earlier in this chapter, the discounted free cash flow model states that the value of the firm is equal to the value of all future free cash flows to the firm discounted at the WACC:

$$\text{Firm Value} = \frac{\text{FCF}_1}{(1+\text{WACC})^1} + \frac{\text{FCF}_2}{(1+\text{WACC})^2} + \ldots + \frac{\text{FCF}_n}{(1+\text{WACC})^n} + \ldots$$

It may seem like an impossibility to apply a valuation model that has an infinite number of terms. But, depending upon the simplifying assumptions the analyst makes about the growth of free cash flows, the model is actually quite workable. In this section, we look at three variations: the no-growth case, the constant growth case, and the two-stage growth case.

Knowing the perpetuity growth formula

The simplest application of the formula for firm value is that case in which the free cash flows are assumed to be constant through the foreseeable future. This may be the case for very mature firms that aren't expected to change or evolve much in the future. In this case, the formula for firm value reduces to the following:

$$\text{Firm Value} = \frac{\text{FCF}}{\text{WACC}}$$

That's it! A formula with a seemingly infinite number of terms reduces to dividing two numbers. You simply take the estimate of FCF and divide by your estimate of WACC. For example, if a firm with a WACC of 10 percent had free cash flow of $400 million annually, and that was expected to remain the same for the foreseeable future, the estimate of firm value would be:

$$\text{Firm Value} = \frac{\$400 \text{ million}}{0.10} = \$4 \text{ billion}$$

Thus, a fair value for this entire firm — including both the debt and the equity — would be $4 billion. If all the debt and equity could be acquired for less than $4 billion, it would be a good investment if the assumptions embedded in the analysis prove to be sound.

Applying the constant growth formula

It is a rare case that free cash flows to the firm would remain constant for the foreseeable future. Cash flows are expected to grow over time for most firms. Does that mean that our valuation model gets a lot more complicated? The answer, thankfully, is no. In fact, the model is quite simple if we can assume a constant growth rate in free cash flow for the foreseeable future. This is likely for firms that have been established for quite some time, but are still very much in the growth stage and won't be in the mature, no-growth stage for quite some time.

In the case of constant growth of free cash flow, an estimate of firm value is the following:

$$\text{Firm Value} = \frac{\text{FCF}_0 \times (1+g)}{\text{WACC} - g}$$

where FCF_0 is free cash flow for the current year, g is the growth rate expected in free cash flow, and WACC is the estimate of the weighted average cost of capital.

So, for our hypothetical firm with current free cash flow of $400 million and a WACC of 10 percent, if we assume that free cash flows are going to grow at 5 percent for the foreseeable future, firm value is estimated to be:

$$\text{Firm Value} = \frac{\text{FCF}_0 \times (1+g)}{\text{WACC} - g} = \frac{\$400 \text{ million} \times (1.05)}{(0.10 - 0.05)} = \$8.4 \text{ billion}$$

Note, that in this case, the value of the firm is more than double the value in the no-growth situation. This shows that compound growth is a wonderful concept. That is why none other than Albert Einstein said that "Compound interest is the eighth wonder of the world." The same concept applies with compound growth of free cash flows.

Applying the two-stage growth model

What if we want to value a firm that has free cash flows that are expected to grow in the future but are not expected to grow at that same rate forever? For instance, suppose that our firm with current free cash flow of $400 million is expected to grow at a robust 20 percent for the next two years and then grow at a more pedestrian 5 percent rate thereafter. How do we value the firm?

The answer is that we determine the present value of the free cash flows from the firm during the abnormal growth period and then add to that the present value of the free cash flows to the firm when the constant growth rate begins:

Firm Value = PV of FCF during Non-Constant Growth + PV of FCF during Normal Growth

In our case, the free cash flows during the non-constant growth period will be:

Year one = $400 million × (1.20) = $480 million

Year two = $480 million × (1.20) = $576 million

So, the PV of the free cash flows during the non-constant growth period is:

$$\text{PV during Non-Constant Growth} = \frac{\$480 \text{ million}}{(1.10)} + \frac{\$576 \text{ million}}{(1.10)^2} = \$912 \text{ million}$$

Now, we need to find the present value of the free cash flows during the constant growth period. Two years from now, the firm is expected to have free cash flows of $576 million and those free cash flows are expected to grow at a constant rate of 5 percent. Because we can apply the constant growth formula, in two years, the firm will have an expected value of:

$$\text{Firm Value in Two Years} = \frac{\$576 \text{ million} \times (1.05)}{0.10 - 0.05} = \$12.096 \text{ billion}$$

But, remember, this is a value in two years, so to put it in terms of a present value, we have to discount that amount back to the present:

$$\text{Present Value} = \frac{FV_2}{(1 + \text{WACC})^2} = \frac{\$12.096 \text{ billion}}{(1.10)^2} = \$9.997 \text{ billion}$$

So, to complete the analysis, the firm value is:

Firm Value = $912 million + $9.997 billion = $10.909 billion

Note that in this example, the firm value is $2.5 billion more than in the constant growth case. Again, this shows the power of compound growth, why investors are enamored with growth companies, and why firms and investment bankers are so interested in identifying ways for firms to grow.

This example assumes one non-constant growth period, but it can certainly be modified to encompass as many different non-constant growth periods as the analyst can imagine.

Stress-testing the results

Firm values are very sensitive to the major inputs to the valuation process — the estimates for growth in free cash flow and the estimate of the WACC. Even small modifications in these estimates can have a significant impact on firm value.

Investment bankers should stress-test their results to examine the impact of their major assumptions on firm value. *Stress testing*, or using a combination of hypothetical values interpreted with human judgment, gives investment bankers an idea of how confident they should be in their valuations. To illustrate, we'll assume the constant growth model, with a current free cash flow estimate of $400 million. Table 12-2 shows how much the firm value changes by changing either the WACC or the growth rate of free cash flow, or both.

Table 12-2		Firm Value (in Billions) for Various WACCs and Growth Rates				
				WACC		
		8%	9%	10%	11%	12%
	7%	$42.8	$21.4	$14.3	$10.7	$8.6
	6%	$21.2	$14.1	$10.6	$8.5	$7.1
Growth Rates	5%	$14.0	$10.5	$8.4	$7.0	$6.0
	4%	$10.4	$8.3	$6.9	$5.9	$5.2
	3%	$8.2	$6.9	$5.9	$5.2	$4.6

As you can see, a relatively tight range of both WACC and growth estimates provides widely diverging firm values. For example, when you assume a constant WACC of 10 percent, firm value ranges from a low of $5.9 billion to a high of $14.3 billion when you change the constant growth estimate from 3 percent to 7 percent. Likewise, if you assume a constant growth rate of 5 percent, firm value ranges from a low of $6 billion to a high of $14 billion when you change the WACC estimate from a high of 12 percent to a low of 8 percent.

Relatively small changes in the input assumptions matter a great deal. This is precisely why investment banking analysts will differ in their opinions on whether a firm is undervalued or overvalued. If you're wondering why some analysts believe a firm is an attractive candidate for acquisitions and others don't, you need to look no further than the assumptions they employ in their analyses. To paraphrase James Carville, "It's the assumptions, stupid!"

Valuing a Share of Stock

As you've seen throughout this chapter, investment banking analysts use variations of the free cash flow model to value entire firms. These models are the basis for suggesting potential actions — like mergers and acquisitions and stock repurchases — to increase the value of the firm. However, another very common variation of these discounted cash flow models involves valuing the common stock of a firm and forms the basis for making buy and sell recommendations to clients.

Similar to valuing an entire firm, the value of a share of stock should be equal to the cash flows received by the owner of that stock. The ultimate owner of a share of stock receives dividends from the firm and that's it. Sure, most investors buy stock because they believe it'll go up in value and they'll be able to sell it for more than they bought it for, but the only cash flow received by the owner of a share of stock is dividends. So, the value of a share of stock is equal to the present value of all expected dividends from owing that share of stock.

The discount rate used to discount those cash flows to a present value is the required return on equity discussed earlier and is most often computed by using the CAPM. The equation for the value of a share of stock is:

$$\text{Share Value} = \frac{D_1}{(1+r_e)^1} + \frac{D_2}{(1+r_e)^2} + \ldots + \frac{D_n}{(1+r_e)^n} + \ldots$$

where D_n is the dividend at year n and r_e is the required return on equity.

Once again, it appears that we have a daunting task, because we have to solve an equation with an infinite number of terms. But, as before, if we make the simplifying assumption that dividends are going to grow at a constant rate forever, the formula reduces to a very simple form:

$$\text{Share Value} = \frac{D_0 \times (1+g)}{r_e - g}$$

So, to value a share of stock assuming a constant growth rate in dividends, all we need to do is look up the current annual dividend, and come up with estimates of that growth rate and an estimated required return on equity.

We can use publicly available data to apply this formula and value a share of stock of Occidental Petroleum (ticker symbol: OXY). According to Thomson Reuters, the consensus estimate long-term earnings growth rate for Occidental Petroleum of the analysts who cover the stock is 5.38 percent. We can use this earnings growth rate as a proxy for dividend growth because, in the long run, the two growth rates tend to be very similar for established firms. Occidental Petroleum's beta as computed by Thomson Reuters is 1.22. So, to value a share of OXY stock, we simply need to compute the required return on equity for OXY. Using the CAPM, as shown earlier in this chapter, OXY's required return on equity is:

$$\text{Required Return on OXY Stock} = r_f + \beta(\text{Market Risk Premium}) = 0.03 + 1.22 \times (8.15) = 9.97\%$$

Therefore, the value of a share of OXY stock is estimated to be:

$$\text{Share Value} = \frac{D_0 \times (1+g)}{r_e - g} = \frac{\$2.56 \times (1.0538)}{0.0997 - 0.0538} = \$58.77$$

According to this simple analysis, a share of OXY stock would be worth $58.77. At the time of the writing of this book, a share was selling for nearly $90 per share, so our analysis would imply that the shares are overvalued by a substantial amount — approximately $30 per share. Does this mean we should all run out and sell our shares of OXY and perhaps even short-sell the shares? The answer is no. We would need to more carefully evaluate our assumptions and determine how realistic these inputs are.

For example, the consensus growth estimate provided by Thomson Reuters has a very small sample size of only four analysts. In fact, one analyst estimated the growth rate to be 8 percent. With an 8 percent growth rate and a required rate of return of 9.97 percent, the shares would be estimated to be worth over $140 each. Another analyst estimated the growth rate to be a paltry 2.6 percent. This would imply a value of $35.64. This simple analysis illustrates why some investors are buying OXY at the market clearing price and other investors are selling the stock at that same price. They have different expectations for future cash flows from the firm.

Chapter 13

Structuring a Leveraged Buyout

. . . .

In This Chapter

▶ Seeing how leveraged buyouts are structured

▶ Distinguishing between the different forms of debt in a leveraged buyout

▶ Understanding seniority and maturity concepts in leveraged buyout deals

▶ Constructing a leveraged buyout model from start to finish

. . . .

*I*nvestment bankers earn their keep by helping client firms make fundamental changes in their structures and operations. Advising firms on the process of structuring leveraged buyouts (LBOs) is an important tool in the investment banker's toolbox.

Leveraged buyouts are deals in which a buyer borrows money (usually a large sum) and uses that money to purchase a target. LBOs are favorite tools by investment bankers and other financial wizards because the returns can be enormous. When you buy another company using borrowed money, the income generated relative to the amount of cash you put at risk can be very large.

Investment bankers also love LBOs because they're tricky deals with lots of moving parts. Companies that want to do LBOs may not have the expertise in all the areas needed to pull off a successful LBO, ranging from borrowing money, lining up investors, measuring a company's cash flow and convincing the target company to sell. Investment bankers have the expertise in many of those areas to help (and, of course, charge fees along the way).

You can discover what LBOs are for and how investment banking plays a big role in them in Chapter 5. We dive deeper into LBOs in this chapter, filling you in on some of the nuances that make them so lucrative. You discover how different types of debt can be used in LBOs to make them be successful. You see how debt can be structured in different ways to make LBOs pay off. Finally, you get a front-row seat to how investment bankers put LBOs together.

Seeing How Leveraged Buyouts Are Structured

As the name suggests, the structure of an LBO is predicated on debt, debt, and more debt. The primary reason for all this debt is that the interest payments on debt are tax-deductible expenses and reduce a company's tax bill, while dividend payments to shareholders are not tax-deductible payments. If the reconstituted firm can use the debt wisely, it can create a lot of value for its *equity holders* (the investors who put their money into a deal, which will be combined with borrowed money to buy the target), and the *private equity sponsor* (the company that accumulates investment dollars from investors to be used to buy out firms) can earn a very healthy rate of return on its *invested capital* (the total amount of debt and equity plowed into the buyout price of the deal).

The types of financing

LBOs are structured using several different types of financing, including bank debt (both revolving and traditional debt), junk bonds, mezzanine financing, and good old-fashioned equity. We cover all these forms of financing in this section.

Bank debt

LBOs are generally financed with two different kinds of bank debt: revolving credit and traditional term loans. Nearly all LBOs will contain both kinds of bank debt in the firm after it has been recapitalized, or injected with the investment dollars of the equity investors and the debt borrowed from lenders.

Revolving credit

Revolving credit for a firm functions just like a credit card for an individual. Credit cards for consumers are not meant to buy large-ticket items, like houses, but to be a way to pay for day-to-day costs and repaid quickly, like at the end of the month. Similarly, a company's revolving credit is not to be a permanent source of funds — to purchase assets such as plant and equipment — but is a source of funds for temporary working capital needs. One common use for revolving credit is to purchase inventories or raw materials. The revolving credit line is accessed when the funds are needed and then is paid down when cash is available.

Unlike credit card debt for individuals, revolving credit is the cheapest form of capital for a firm and is usually issued at a floating rate, such as the prime rate plus a certain percentage or LIBOR (the London Interbank Offered Rate) plus a certain percentage. The prime rate is the rate that commercial banks charge their very best customers. LIBOR is the average interest rate estimated by leading banks in London that these banks would be charged if they borrowed from other banks.

The revolving credit rate will change with changes in the reference or benchmark interest rate, either the prime rate or LIBOR. The perceived riskiness of the borrower determines what kind of a percentage will be added to the benchmark rates. Strong credit risks will be able to borrow funds at the benchmark rates or slightly above them, while weaker credit risks — including most LBOs — will pay a much higher premium above the benchmark rates.

Traditional term loans

Most traditional term loans are similar to loans many of us have on our cars and homes. If you own a house, you probably borrowed from a bank or mortgage lender with the agreement that you'd pay the money back in a set number of years. Similarly with traditional term loans, money is loaned to the company for a specific time period — the *term* — and the loan is paid back over the term of the loan in equal payments on a periodic basis (generally quarterly).

The payments throughout the life of the loan are the same size, and a portion of each payment represents interest on the loan plus a repayment of principal. The process whereby a term loan is paid down via equal payments is called *amortization*. Early payments on an amortized loan have a higher portion that represents interest. As the amount of the loan gets paid down, the portion representing interest declines and the portion representing principal increases.

Some term loans, however, are structured differently and may require the firm to pay only interest on the loan during the term of the loan and pay the principal back in the form of a large payment — a *bullet payment* — at the end of the term.

Loans that amortize are less risky than loans with a large payment at the end of the term, so amortizing loans will carry a lower interest rate than loans that don't amortize. Companies like to issue loans with bullet payments because it reduces the amount of cash necessary to make the required debt payments — cash that can be used for other purposes. In the case of LBOs, this other purpose is likely to pay down other forms of debt.

Bank term loans often carry various restrictive *covenants* (contractual terms that limit the actions of the firm; see Chapter 11). Covenants are intended to increase the probability that the bank loans will be paid back in full. Typical covenants restrict the ability of the firm to make additional acquisitions, to take on debt beyond a certain level, and to make dividend payments to shareholders. The whole idea behind covenants is to preserve cash flow so that the bank will be paid back. But covenants restrict the options available to management and can inhibit the ability of the firm to pursue some profitable strategies.

Junk bonds

LBOs became extremely popular in the 1980s, and this popularity was driven by the development of the junk bond market. As the name screams out, *junk bonds* are bonds of lesser quality than the typical class of bonds that investors like to invest in, referred to as *investment-grade bonds*.

The difference between junk bonds and investment-grade bonds simply has to do with the perceived quality of the issuer, measured in part by the bonds' ratings. Bond rating agencies — such as Standard & Poor's, Moody's Investors Service, and Fitch Ratings — assign ratings to bonds just like teachers assign letter grades to students. Bond ratings range from AAA (the highest rating) down to C and D, which refer to bonds that are already in default on some of their payments.

There is rampant grade inflation with bond ratings, just as there is grade inflation in colleges and universities. A letter grade of C is not "average" in either context. Investment grade bonds have ratings that are BBB– or higher by Standard & Poor's and Baa3 or higher by Moody's. Junk bonds are those bonds that are below investment grade. So, a bond is either considered investment grade or junk. It seems that both bonds and college students all exist in Lake Wobegon, where everyone is above average.

The purpose of bond ratings is to provide investors with an idea of the creditworthiness, or the risk of the bond. *Creditworthiness* refers to how likely the lender is to receive his promised interest and principal payments. Like teachers' grades, bond ratings are driven by both quantitative and qualitative considerations. Also, like teachers' grades, bond ratings are extremely important. For instance, some institutional investors are only allowed to invest in investment-grade bonds and are prohibited from investing in junk bonds. In fact, if they hold a bond that is *downgraded* (or the rating is lowered) from investment grade to below investment grade or junk status, they have to sell that bond from their holdings, even if it's at a sizeable loss.

Just as many people feel teachers often are wrong with the grades they assign to students, credit agencies can be way off on their ratings. The recent financial crisis witnessed many investment-grade securities — many even rated AAA — failing and bondholders left with investments that were worth fractions of what they paid for them. Many investors learned the hard way that bond ratings are only one bit of information and they shouldn't substitute bond ratings for careful due diligence on behalf of the investor.

Although some individual investors invest in junk bonds, the market is dominated by large institutional investors such as mutual funds, foundations, and endowments. The analytical sophistication necessary to successfully identify junk bond investments is beyond the expertise of most individual investors. However, individual investors often invest in the junk bond markets through high-yield bond funds. They let the experts pick junk bonds and invest in a diversified portfolio of them.

The history of the junk bond: When junk became "golden"

Prior to the 1980s, most junk bonds were considered investment grade when they were originally issued. That is, these bonds were considered much more creditworthy when they were originally issued, but the issuing companies' fortunes weren't as bright as the bond rating agencies had originally thought. Rating agencies periodically reassess the ratings on bonds and will raise or lower ratings according to new information or changes in market conditions. The language of investment is really colorful and descriptive. Bonds that have been reduced from investment grade to junk status are referred to as *fallen angels*.

What changed in the 1980s was that many LBOs were financed with *original-issue junk bonds* — that is, bonds that were issued at below investment-grade status. The original-issue junk bond market was the brainchild of Michael Milken from Drexel Burnham Lambert, a firm that at one time controlled roughly two-thirds of the junk bond market and revolutionized it. The popularization of the original-issue junk bond market was the rocket fuel that the LBO market needed to grow and prosper. But, like all rockets, they eventually run out of fuel and fall back to earth. The same happened in the late 1980s in the junk bond market as a combination of events — including weakness in the economy as well as Milken and Drexel Burnham Lambert being charged with insider trading and market manipulation — led to the return to earth of the junk bond market.

Now, why on earth would anyone invest in something labeled as "junk"? Wouldn't we all want to invest in securities that are investment grade? It all has to do with the risk and return tradeoff. In financial markets, for investors to consistently earn higher returns, they generally have to invest in higher-risk investments. Junk bonds are also known by another term: *high-yield bonds.* The return (or yield to maturity; see Chapter 11) on junk bonds is higher than the yield on investment grade bonds. In fact, the expected return on bonds is closely related to the bond rating — the higher the bond rating, the lower the yield to maturity. Thus, investors are attracted to junk bonds because of the expectation of higher returns.

Junk bonds become particularly attractive when yields in the bond market, in general, are low. Many investors have a specific yield target and must buy lower and lower rated bonds to earn that yield when market interest rates are particularly low. Junk bonds also become attractive when investors' aversion to risk decreases. For instance, as the financial crisis is further and further in the rearview mirror of many investors, they become much more willing to invest in riskier and riskier securities. This is the situation that exists in the bond market as of the writing of this book in late 2013.

The junk bond market is generally only accessible to those LBOs that are fairly large in scope — that is, companies with market capitalizations in the high hundreds of millions of dollars or over a billion dollars. Smaller LBOs tend to be financed with mezzanine debt, described in the next section.

Mezzanine debt

Just like the mezzanine level of a theater is between the main floor and the balcony, mezzanine debt is a form of financing that is between traditional debt and equity. In fact, mezzanine debt has attributes of both debt and equity and is often referred to as a hybrid form of financing. It's very popular with LBOs that are in the middle-capitalization range (below $1 billion) — restructurings that are too small to have access to the junk bond market.

Mezzanine debt is typically structured as intermediate term debt — perhaps three to five years. Mezzanine debt usually has an *equity kicker* or *equity sweetener*. What this means is that the bonds will come with warrants attached in order to make them more attractive to the purchaser. A *warrant* is simply the right to buy a specific number of shares of the company's stock at a predetermined price for a specified period of time. For example, a warrant may be issued that allows the holder to buy a share of stock in a company over the next three years at a price of $10 per share.

Warrants are usually *underwater* when they're issued, meaning that the current stock price is below the predetermined price (known as the *exercise price*). For instance, in our example, the current stock price might be $7 per share, and the exercise price of the warrants is $10 per share. It would not pay the holder to exercise their warrant and buy the stock today for $10, because they can purchase the shares without using the warrant for $7. But what happens if the company is very successful and the stock price rises dramatically? The warrants will become extremely valuable. Let's say our company's stock price rises from $7 to $21 in three years. The holder of the warrant would have the right to buy a share of stock that is worth $21 at a price of $10 — these warrants are very valuable because they're $11 *in-the-money* (the stock price is above the exercise price). In our example, what this implies is that, upon exercise, the warrant holder will realize a gain of $11.

Warrants give the bondholder a great deal of upside potential and allow the bondholder to participate like a stockholder in the event that the company is successful. The other advantage to warrants is that the holder has the right to either exercise the warrants (and buy the stock) or sell the warrants to someone else. Either way, the warrant holder can realize the value of the warrants. The warrants are also *detachable,* meaning the holder can sell the warrants and still retain the debt.

As you can see, mezzanine debt really does represent a middle ground between debt and equity. It has the characteristics of traditional debt, because the holders of mezzanine debt receive periodic interest payments. Yet, it has the characteristics of stock, because the holders of mezzanine debt can participate in the growth in the value of the firm through exercising their warrants and becoming stockholders.

The benefit to the company of issuing mezzanine debt with warrants attached is that they can issue that debt at a much lower interest rate than other debt that didn't have warrants attached. Investors in mezzanine debt may be looking for annual returns in the 20 percent range. The bonds may be issued with an interest of only 8 percent. The other 12 percent return may come in the form of the value of the warrants. This type of financing also preserves precious cash flow for the firm. If the firm can limit the amount of cash that needs to be spent to make the interest and principal payments on the debt, it will help the cash flow of the firm. If the firm really wants to preserve cash, it will issue debt at a lower interest rate and attach more warrants. The more warrants attached to the debt, all else equal, the lower the interest rate that investors will be willing to accept on the debt.

Typical investors in mezzanine debt are large institutional investors such as insurance companies, commercial banks, mezzanine debt funds, and other private equity firms. But unlike investing in the equity of a typical LBO, this form of investment is *passive,* because the private equity firms buying mezzanine debt don't take a management role in the restructuring of the company or in its operations going forward.

Mezzanine financing has some unique characteristics, including the following:

- ✔ **How it's negotiated:** Unlike junk bonds, the terms of mezzanine financing are generally negotiated between the issuing firm and the purchasers.

- ✔ **The difficulty of selling:** Mezzanine debt is more difficult to sell than some other types of debt. It's much less marketable than junk bonds, and it's generally held to maturity by the entity originally acquiring the debt. If mezzanine debt is sold, it's done in a private negotiation and typically involves price concessions on behalf of the seller.

- ✔ **The connection with the LBO sponsor:** A portion of the mezzanine financing is typically provided by the same private equity company sponsoring the LBO.

✔ **Lower rights:** Similar to junk bonds, mezzanine debt has lower seniority than traditional bank debt. In terms of claims to the assets of the firm, the holders of mezzanine debt stand in the claims line behind banks providing financing but in front of equity holders. Thus, the claims of mezzanine debt holders are subordinated (or below) the claims of other, more traditional debt holders. Mezzanine debt holders truly do have seats in the mezzanine of the theater of claims.

Equity

At the bottom of the capital structure, under this large mound of debt, are the equity holders (or stockholders). These individuals own the company and are entitled to the returns of the company only after all the debt holders' claims have been satisfied in full. Typically, the majority of the equity is held by the *private equity partnership* — the firm that sponsored the LBO and put the deal together. A minority portion of the equity may be held by the management of the firm in an effort to properly incentivize the management to do what's in the best interest of the equity holders, because they're equity holders.

Expected returns to equity holders in LBO transactions are quite high — higher than all debt holders to compensate equity holders for their place in the claims line. In the theater of claims, equity holders have seats high in the balcony.

LBO equity is typically held by private equity firms — both by the limited partners and the general partners. The typical investors in private equity partnerships are the usual *institutional investors* — pension funds, endowments, insurance companies, and funds of funds. But, limited partnership shares are also held by wealthy and ultra-high-net worth individual investors. Because the risk of equity in LBO deals is quite high, these investors typically diversify their investments by purchasing stakes in many LBO deals.

Understanding seniority and maturity

Seniority and maturity are extremely important concepts when it comes to the suppliers of capital in an LBO. *Seniority* is where the provider of funds stands in the line of priority with regards to being paid (see Chapter 11). Like any line — well, other than the line to be drafted into the military — you want to be close to the front of the line. And in terms of supplying capital to LBOs, that principle is no different.

There is a direct relationship between the expected return to a specific form of capital with respect to seniority. The more senior the claim of the form of financing, the lower the expected return. That is why, for instance, revolving bank debt has the lowest expected return of all the types of financing and why equity has the highest expected return. Revolving bank debt is the least risky form of financing to the LBO — that is, it has the highest likelihood of being paid back (revolving credit providers are at the very front of the line). On the other hand, equity is the riskiest form of financing. Equity holders are only entitled to returns after all other claims have been satisfied — they're at the back of the line. There is certainly no guarantee that the firm will be successful and that anything will be left over for the equity holders after all the debt holders' claims have been satisfied. In fact, it's possible that all the debt holders can receive what they were promised, yet the firm doesn't generate sufficient cash flow for anything to be left over for equity holders.

Another critical aspect of understanding the way debt comes into play with LBOs is maturity. Maturity refers to when the debt comes due and needs to be paid back. As was indicated earlier, a revolving credit line never matures, but it's expected that it will be periodically paid down. That is, the amount of revolving credit will vary across time for the typical firm.

Term loans issued in LBO transactions typically have maturities between four and eight years. Junk bonds issued to fund LBO transactions typically have maturities that are longer than term loans but shorter than investment-grade bonds. At the time of issue, original-issue junk bonds typically have maturities between five and ten years. This contrasts with investment-grade bonds that are typically issued with much longer maturities — up to 30 years. Equity has no maturity and is, in essence, a perpetual claim.

Now, just because a particular form of debt has a specific maturity does not mean that the debt will be in existence until the maturity date. For instance, much like mortgage loans for individuals, term loans typically have no *prepayment penalties* — the company can retire the debt before maturity without incurring a penalty. On the other hand, junk bonds typically don't allow the company to pay them off early. That is definitely an advantage for junk bond holders, because issuers generally want to pay off debt early only if the cost of debt (the interest rate) has gone down. Akin to the situation with an individual and a home mortgage, refinancing filings generally take place when interest rates have fallen and the individual can obtain a less expensive mortgage.

Building a Leveraged Buyout Model

The entire point of the LBO is to construct the investment so that the equity holders earn large returns on their investments by using high levels of debt to leverage (or magnify) these returns. In essence, the equity holders are using "other peoples' money" to increase their returns.

This story of leverage should sound familiar, because it's used in any number of contexts in the world of finance — both in corporate and personal finance. Leverage is great when it works, because it amplifies the returns that an investor can earn. It seems we've all heard from the braggart who bought his house with 5 percent down, effectively being leveraged 19 to 1. When the price of the house doubled, his return was tremendous. But leverage also can amplify losses, and the experience of the recent financial crisis reinforced this notion in a very painful way for many homeowners who purchased homes, only to find that a scant few months or years later the home was worth substantially less than the mortgage they owed.

Investment bankers build LBO models based upon pro forma cash flow statements. *Pro forma* simply means "for the sake of form" and refers to cash flow statements that are projected to be realized if things go as expected. These should not be best-case scenarios — if everything goes perfectly. Instead, they should represent models that project cash flows if things go as they likely will. As emphasized throughout this book, conservatism in projecting cash flows is a terrific quality for an investment banker and leads to more satisfied clients and investors. But, too often, investment bankers get overly zealous with their projections and make unrealistic assumptions that are likely to lead to disappointing results.

Creating a pro forma model

The first step in an LBO analysis is to project the cash flows of the firm over the expected time frame of the LBO — generally six to eight years. The specific cash flow definition generally used in the LBO market is *earnings before interest, taxes, depreciation, and amortization* (EBITDA).

Akin to real estate agents looking at the prices that comparable homes have sold for in the area to set an asking price for a home just being listed, investment bankers will look at comparable LBOs that have recently been transacted in the marketplace to determine the debt levels that the market will likely support to fund the LBO. These debt levels are generally referred to as multiples of EBITDA. For instance, the likely level of total debt may be four times EBITDA or six times EBITDA. The level of debt that the market will likely support for an LBO is a function of both the risk of the particular LBO and current market conditions.

Risk of the LBO

LBOs are high-risk, high-return operations. Investors too often fixate on the enormous returns they might enjoy if everything works out according to plan. But in business, things don't always work the way they're supposed to.

The risk of an LBO refers to the variability or volatility of the EBITDA projections and how likely they are to be reached. The less variability in the EBITDA projections — that is, the more certain the analyst is that there won't be negative surprises in EBITDA in the foreseeable future — the higher the multiples of EBITDA that the LBO will support. That is why simple businesses with stable cash flows (such as firms that produce consumer staples like food) are the best targets for LBOs, because their cash flows are more stable and less vulnerable to surprises due to downturns in the economy or technological innovations.

Market conditions

Some markets are simply better for LBOs than others. When credit conditions are loose and the risk appetite of market participants is strong, the multiples of EBITDA that an LBO will support expand and it's an opportune time for private equity sponsors to participate in the LBO market. Investment bankers often refer to these kinds of markets as "easy money" periods. Alternatively, when credit conditions tighten and the risk appetite of market participants is weak, it's a poor time for private equity sponsors to participate in the LBO market.

In the wake of the recent financial crisis of 2008 and 2009, the LBO market basically disappeared for a period of time due to "tight money" and the freezing of the credit markets. Firms that had LBOs planned around the time of the outbreak of the credit crisis had to cancel their plans because credit was simply not available.

Market conditions can make a huge difference in the level of debt that an LBO deal will support. For example, according to S&P Capital IQ, during the fourth quarter of 2009, the average leverage of large corporate LBOs was slightly less than four times EBITDA. In the third quarter of 2012, the average leverage of LBOs expanded to nearly six times EBITDA. Over less than a three-year time period, the amount of debt supported by large corporate LBOs had expanded by nearly 50 percent! Now, remember, these numbers are averages. Some deals command much higher multiples based upon the specific circumstances of the firm. However, timing related to market conditions is extremely important when considering an LBO.

As you may expect, there is a direct relationship between how attractive the market values LBOs and the volume of LBOs that are brought to market. Given poor market conditions, the volume of LBOs fell substantially in 2009, because the terms of LBOs were simply not attractive. Volume has picked up as the multiples of EBITDA have increased, but LBO volume as of this writing (in late 2013) still had not returned to the pre–financial crisis levels of 2006 and 2007.

Deciding on methods of financing

When constructing an LBO deal, analysts will consider market conditions to determine just how much debt they think the market will support. Investment bankers want to construct a deal that maximizes the amount of debt capital and minimizes the amount of equity capital, while still putting together a package that will ensure the long-term success of the firm. After all, if the firm can't generate sufficient cash flow and survive over the long run, the equity holders will lose because their positions will ultimately be worthless.

Let's assume that market conditions are fairly good and will support a total debt to EBITDA multiple of six times. Let's also assume that our cracker-jack investment banking analysts have crunched the numbers and that the EBITDA level of our target firm is $300 million annually. This means that the total debt supported by the market for our hypothetical deal is likely to be in the range of $1.8 billion.

But the deal isn't going to be financed solely with debt. Analysts will also look to comparable deals for some gauge as to how much equity cushion other comparable deals are commanding. In poorer markets, when investors are more risk averse, the amount of equity required to successfully undertake LBOs expands. Conversely, in strong markets when investors' risk appetites inflate, the amount of equity required for LBOs decreases. For the sake of our hypothetical LBO, let's assume that the amount of equity provided in similar LBOs is 1.5 times EBITDA, or $450 million. Thus, the financing for our LBO will consist of $1.8 billion in total debt and $450 million in equity, for a total capitalization of $2.25 billion. The purchase price of this LBO is effectively 7.5 times EBITDA.

Now, it's very likely that the debt that is issued in this LBO will be of different varieties. A typical LBO structure may have 50 percent to 60 percent of the debt consisting of term bank loans and a revolving credit commitment and the other 40 percent to 50 percent consisting of mezzanine debt (because this hypothetical transaction would be awfully small for the junk bond market).

Thus, our LBO capital structure might look like the following:

Revolving credit agreement (LIBOR plus 2%)	$100 million
Five-year term loan at 8%	$900 million
Mezzanine debt	$800 million
Equity	$450 million
Total	$2.25 billion

Seeing how the results work out

So, what does $2.25 billion buy you? Well, in our example, it buys you an income stream of $300 million annually in EBITDA. That is, the LBO sponsor paid a total of $2.25 billion for the cash flows of the target firm that are estimated to be $300 million annually. Now, we've really simplified things here by assuming that EBITDA stays constant for the foreseeable future at

$300 million, but in all likelihood, that number will expand over time. Let's assume that over the next five years our firm is able to completely pay down the five-year term loan from cash flow. And that is generally what happens in LBOs — in the first few years nearly all the cash flows are used to pay down the debt. Given our assumptions, how much will our equity holders have earned on their investment?

Conservatively assuming that five years from now the firm will still sell at an EBITDA multiple of 7.5 times — and this is likely to have expanded because the firm has become less leveraged and the cash flows should be more stable — the total firm will still be valued at $2.25 billion. However, the debt will have been reduced by $900 million, and the equity will have increased in value by $900 million (because we're assuming that the value of our firm has remained at a constant 7.5 times EBITDA). *Remember:* In an LBO, the cash flows from operations — particularly in the early years — are primarily used to pay down the debt. So, equity holders will have invested $450 million in the firm, and in five years that investment will be $1.35 billion, or a gain of $900 million. The *internal rate of return* (discussed in Chapter 5) on this investment is 24.5 percent, not a bad return on capital. This internal rate of return is the interest rate that equates a present value of $450 million to a future value in five years of $1.35 billion. Again, this is a very, very conservative simplification because it assumes that EBITDA remains constant at $300 million annually when in all likelihood it will have increased during that time period.

The importance of taxes in a leveraged buyout

The basis of all LBO transactions is quite simple. If, after taxes, the private equity sponsor can earn more on borrowed funds than those borrowed funds cost them, it pays to use leverage. If that isn't the case, then leverage doesn't pay. But the key point to remember is that the tax code encourages lending as interest payments are tax deductible. If a firm is in a marginal corporate tax bracket of 35 percent, the effective after-tax cost of debt with an 8 percent interest rate is not 8 percent. Instead, it's 8 percent × (1 – 0.35) = 5.2 percent. So, Uncle Sam encourages firms to borrow rather than to raise equity.

What can go right and what can go wrong

Our example is very simplistic, but a couple of very significant developments can take place to make our LBO much more attractive. An LBO is a moving target — the company that's refinanced is changing, morphing, and hopefully growing. There are a few considerations investment bankers must consider when thinking about what can go right with an LBO, including the following:

✓ **EBITDA can improve.** EBITDA is likely not to remain constant, but to grow over time. As EBITDA grows, assuming the multiple of EBITDA at which the firm sells for stays the same, the value of the firm will not remain constant, but will also grow.

✓ **Refinancing can make the deal more attractive.** The firm may find that it's actually able to refinance some of its debt at a lower interest rate.

✓ **Valuations on deals can be more positive.** The multiple at which our firm may sell for can also expand. Given market conditions and the fact that our firm is less debt laden, that same cash flow stream may command a larger multiple than 7.5 times in five years. Suppose our cash flow stream commands a multiple of 10 times and we're able to completely pay down our term loan of $900 million. Now, we have equity worth $2.1 billion. This represents an internal rate of return of 36.1 percent annually.

Circumstances can go against an LBO, too, and spell trouble for a deal. Some potential problem spots for LBOs include the following:

✓ **Returns end up being subpar.** The LBO may not realize the rate of return that investment bankers project on their pro forma statements. Cash flows can, of course, fall short of projections, and we may not reach the levels of EBITDA forecast by overly optimistic analysts who want to see an LBO deal completed.

✓ **The economic climate may turn hostile.** Economic conditions can change, and market interest rates may rise, making it more difficult, if not impossible, to refinance debt at lower rates.

✓ **Investors can sour on LBOs.** What may prove to be most damaging is that investors in general may become more risk averse, shunning LBO deals, and the multiple of EBITDA at which the firm sells may decline. For instance, in our example, if the EBITDA multiple in five years is 5.5 instead of 7.5, the equity holders' internal rate of return on the LBO will be 10.8 percent — less than half the rate of return that we believed we would earn.

Chapter 14

Determining the Strength of a Company's Return on Equity

*H*ow do investment bankers, investors, and management judge how well a company is performing? For most publicly traded companies, the obvious answer would be how well the stock is doing. The bottom-line test of performance is often whether the value of the stock has risen or fallen in recent times and how the stock has performed relative to other publicly traded stocks in the company's industry or the broad stock market. But how should we judge the performance of privately held companies? What metrics do investment bankers look for when evaluating private companies and determining the feasibility of bringing such companies public via an initial public offering?

Investment bankers look to the numbers to see how a firm is performing relative to itself over time (in terms of a trend analysis) and against other companies. Generally this analysis is done by examining ratios calculated from financial statements like the balance sheet and income statement. As you saw in Chapter 8, there are a multitude of categories of ratios that investment banking analysts as well as investors can focus on:

✔ **Activity ratios:** These ratios evaluate how efficiently the company is operating the business and focus on such functions as inventory and accounts receivable management, as well as what level of sales the firm achieves from its asset base.

✔ **Liquidity ratios** evaluate the company's ability to meet short-term obligations such as paying suppliers, bondholders, and landlords.

✔ **Solvency ratios** are the complement to liquidity ratios and measure the firm's ability to meet long-term obligations to bondholders, lessors, and other long-term creditors.

✔ **Cash flow ratios** evaluate the company's ability to generate a sufficient level of cash flow to pay creditors and fund future growth.

✔ **Price multiples** evaluate the price of the company relative to fundamentals such as earnings, sales, cash flow, or book value.

✔ **Profitability ratios** evaluate the ability of the company to generate profits relative to revenue, invested assets, and owners' equity.

Chapter 8 describes several profitability ratios including return on assets, return on capital, and return on equity. But in this chapter, you find out how to go beyond the fundamental ratio. In this chapter, you discover return on equity (ROE) and see why it's generally considered to be the most important metric for management, investors, and investment bankers. The chapter also explains why not all ROEs are created equal. That, in fact, two companies can have identical ROEs and one company can be in a much better financial position than the other company. With ROE, it isn't just the bottom-line number that counts; it's how the firm gets there.

Understanding the Importance of Return on Equity

The goal of most businesses in a capitalistic system is to make money for their owners because it's their money — they provide risky capital. Owners commit money to a company with the expectation that the company will put that money to productive use and that the owner will be handsomely rewarded for this commitment of funds by providing him with a return.

In fact, for years, business students have learned that the overriding goal of the corporation is to maximize shareholder wealth as measured by stock price. Financial markets not only reward individuals that productively use capital but also help to allocate capital to those businesses that consistently earn solid returns on the capital employed. But what are the primary drivers associated with rising stock prices and happy investors?

What return on equity shows

Investment bankers earn their paychecks by helping managers determine which actions are likely to result in an increase in shareholder wealth. But even if you can't take actions that directly result in an increase in shareholder wealth, you *can* take actions that, over the long term, are highly correlated with rising stock prices. The surest way to achieve that goal is by helping a company increase its return on equity.

As the name suggests, return on equity measures how well the company is producing a return on the money supplied by stockholders — the ultimate owners of the company. It's computed as:

$$\text{Return on Equity} = \frac{\text{Net Income}}{\text{Shareholders' Equity}}$$

Return on equity is also important because it dictates how quickly a firm is able to grow internally — that is, by reinvesting earnings. When a company earns money, it can do two things with that money:

- ✔ Reinvest the money in the firm.
- ✔ Pay out the earnings as dividends to investors.

Typically, firms retain some of the earnings in the firm and pay some out as dividends. One of the key items investment bankers must estimate is the long-term growth rate in the earnings of a company:

$$\text{Long-Term Growth Rate in Earnings} = \text{Return on Equity} \times (1 - \text{Dividend Payout Rate})$$

The dividend payout rate is simply what percentage of net income the company pays out in dividends. For example, if a company earns $100 million and pays $25 million out in dividends, the dividend payout rate for that company is 25 percent. If that same company could average a return on equity of 20 percent, then its long-term growth rate in earnings would be

$$\text{Long-Term Growth Rate in Earnings} = 20\% \times (1 - 0.25) = 15\%$$

There is a direct trade-off between dividends and future growth. The higher the dividend payout rate, the lower the future growth. Essentially, investors can receive their return now in the form of higher current dividends or later in the form of higher earnings and, hopefully, a higher stock valuation.

Some companies pay out a relatively large portion of their earnings in the form of current dividends, while others choose not to pay any dividends and, instead, reinvest all their earnings in the company to provide for future growth. Investors know this and companies generally develop dividend payout policies that attract certain types of investors. For example, many public utilities have very high dividend payout rates and are preferred by people who want to supplement their current income with dividend income.

Other more growth-oriented companies may have very low or no dividend payouts. Warren Buffett's Berkshire Hathaway, for example, has never paid a dividend. And the shareholders of Berkshire Hathaway are quite pleased that the firm hasn't paid dividends, because the firm has averaged a 19.7 percent compound annual return over 45 years from 1968 through 2012. Just $1 invested in Berkshire Hathaway in 1968 would've grown to over $3,267 by the end of 2012!

Later in this chapter, we explain how to closely examine the profitability of the Coca-Cola Company and break down the profitability of Coca-Cola into its component parts. But, as a preview, take a look at Table 14-1 and see how consistently high Coca-Cola's return on equity has been over the past ten years.

Table 14-1	Return on Equity for Coca-Cola
Year	*Return on Equity*
2012	27.4%
2011	27.1%
2010	37.8%
2009	27.5%
2008	28.4%
2007	27.5%
2006	30.8%
2005	29.6%
2004	30.3%
2003	30.8%

Both the level of ROE and the consistency of ROE indicate that the Coca-Cola Company has a terrific business model and is incredibly well managed. These kinds of results are what firms strive to provide for shareholders.

Pros and cons of return on equity versus other profitability measures

Return on equity isn't the only profitability measure that investment banking analysts pay attention to, although it is arguably the most important one. Several other measures deserve consideration, and we calculate them in this section, explaining how they work for one of the most popular companies with investors and the general public, the Coca-Cola Company (ticker symbol: KO).

You probably already know Coca-Cola is a ubiquitous brand around the world. In fact, none other than Warren Buffett himself has indicated he thinks that it's the best brand in the world. A measure of the strength of Coke's brand is that there are Coca-Cola stores online, in New York City, and in Las Vegas. When people will pay you to advertise their brand, you know you have a strong franchise.

Table 14-2 presents abbreviated financial statements (income statement and balance sheet) from the Coca-Cola Company for the years 2010, 2011, and 2012.

Table 14-2   Financial Statements for the Coca-Cola Company (in Millions of Dollars)

Abbreviated Income Statement	2012	2011	2010
Sales	48,017	46,542	35,119
Cost of Goods Sold	(19,053)	(18,215)	(12,693)
Gross Profit	28,964	28.327	22,426
Selling, General, and Administrative Expenses	(18,185)	(18,154)	(14,013)
Earnings Before Interest and Taxes	10,779	10,173	8,413
Interest Income	471	483	317
Interest Expense	(397)	(417)	(733)
Equity Income	819	690	1025
Other Income	137	529	5185
Earnings Before Taxes	11,809	11,458	14,207
Taxes	2,723	2,812	2,370
Net Income	9,086	8,648	11,837

(continued)

Table 14-2 *(continued)*

Abbreviated Income Statement	2012	2011	2010
Abbreviated Balance Sheet	2012	2011	2010
Current Assets	30,328	25,497	21,579
Long-Term Assets	55,846	54,477	51,342
Total Assets	86,174	79,974	72,921
Current Liabilities	27,821	24,283	18,508
Long-Term Debt	14,736	13,656	14,041
Other Liabilities	10,449	10.114	9,055
Total Equity	33,168	31,921	31,317
Total Liabilities and Equity	86,174	79,974	72,921

Source: EDGAR

The other profitability measures that investment bankers consider are gross profit margin, operating profit margin, and net profit margin. In the following sections, we compute each of these measures for year 2012 and explain the significance.

Gross profit margin

Gross profit equals sales minus the cost of goods sold. Coca-Cola's gross profit margin for 2012 is computed as follows:

$$\text{Gross Profit Margin} = \frac{\text{Gross Profit}}{\text{Sales}} = \frac{\$28,964}{\$48,017} = 0.603 = 60.3\%$$

This profitability measure shows the basic cost structure of the firm and, like many calculated measures, is very industry specific. The beverage industry is characterized by very wide margins. The actual cost to produce and bottle the product is fairly low. The real significant costs come in advertising and building the brand.

Over the last three years, Coca-Cola has been able to maintain a fairly stable gross profit margin — the margins were 60.9 percent and 63.9 percent in years 2011 and 2010, respectively.

 It's not enough to just eyeball one year's gross profit margin and think that tells you much. One thing investment bankers would key their eye on with the Coca-Cola example is the fact that the trend in the ratio is down slightly. Further erosion in gross profit margin over the next couple years may be cause for concern.

Operating profit margin

Operating profit (also known as *earnings before interest and taxes*) is gross profit minus sales, general, and administrative expenses (SG&A). Coca-Cola's operating profit margin for 2012 is computed as follows:

$$\text{Operating Profit Margin} = \frac{\text{EBIT}}{\text{Sales}} = \frac{\$10,779}{\$48,017} = 0.224 = 22.4\%$$

This profitability measure tells you what percentage of sales is left over after paying all costs prior to paying the suppliers of capital (stockholders and bondholders) and Uncle Sam (taxes). This gives the analyst an idea of what's left (on a percentage basis) to pay taxes and the suppliers of capital. An eroding operating profit margin would be cause for concern.

Over the last three years, Coca-Cola has been able to maintain a very stable operating profit margin — the margins were 21.9 percent and 24.0 percent in years 2011 and 2010, respectively. This would indicate to the analyst that over the last three years, Coca-Cola has experienced very little business risk.

Net profit margin

Net profit margin is defined as bottom line net income (after taxes and interest expense have been paid) divided by sales. Coca-Cola's net profit margin for 2012 is computed as follows:

$$\text{Net Profit Margin} = \frac{\text{Net Income}}{\text{Sales}} = \frac{\$9,086}{\$48,017} = 0.189 = 18.9\%$$

Simply put, net profit margin measures how much of every dollar of sales the company is able to keep as earnings. Over the last three years, Coca-Cola has had very enviable net profit margins — the margins were 18.6 percent and 33.7 percent in 2011 and 2010, respectively. Now, you may think that analysts would be concerned that net profit margin declined considerably from 2010 to 2011. However, when you dig deeper, you see that this was the result of a one-time, extraordinary gain from the acquisition of Coca-Cola Enterprises North American business operations. A net profit margin in the neighborhood of 19 percent is more consistent with the history of the company.

How return on equity can help guide an investment banking deal

Companies looking to expand and grow often look to acquire other companies to fuel that growth. And one of the most attractive elements of any acquisition target is its ability to generate a high return on equity. So, investment bankers will scour the markets looking for firms that are able to provide high returns to shareholders and hope that deals can be structured so that those firms can be purchased at an attractive price.

It isn't simply the final return on equity number that matters most to a savvy investment banker. Instead, how a company achieves that return on equity is crucial to determining whether a company is an attractive acquisition target. Is the high return the result of borrowing a lot of money — does leverage fuel the return? Is the return the result of high profit margins, or does it result from modest profit margins and high turnover? These questions are the kind that investment bankers must provide answers to when pitching potential deals to company management. DuPont analysis is a well-established and widely used tool to provide systematic answers to these questions.

Using a DuPont Analysis

In golf, an old adage says, "We aren't painting pictures, we're writing numbers." What this means is that, on a given hole, it doesn't matter how a certain score is achieved — what matters is the number that a golfer ultimately writes on his scorecard. One golfer could have hit a couple of awful shots on a hole, ended up in a bunker or two, but managed to escape the hole with a par because of one miracle shot. His playing partner could've hit all very solid shots and ended up making the same score. Yet, for that hole, the two competitors were equal.

Obviously, over the long haul, the chances for success are dramatically different for those two competitors if their play on that hole was indicative of their overall play.

The same is true for companies and the evaluation and comparison of their respective ROEs. For companies, as we explain in this section, what matters isn't just the number they write on their scorecard (their financial statements), but how they get to that number. In other words, not all ROEs are created equal, and that's what DuPont analysis is designed to highlight.

The humble beginnings of the DuPont analysis

You can thank a financial analyst for the wonders of the DuPont analysis. What has come to be known as the DuPont model of financial analysis was developed in 1914 by engineer F. Donaldson Brown at the DuPont chemical company. Shortly after Brown joined the firm, DuPont bought a large share of General Motors, and he was charged with changing the business operations of GM to make it more profitable and increase the value of DuPont's holding in GM. Essentially, Brown served the function of a sort of internal investment banker, and he sought to highlight the acquisition's strength and weaknesses. Brown was quite successful in this task, turning GM into a profitable enterprise. The model he developed was adopted throughout much of corporate America. It has become a staple of investment bankers and has been taught for decades in introductory and advanced financial analysis courses in business schools throughout the world.

Essentially, the DuPont model breaks down return on equity into its component parts and helps provide the analyst with a road map on what the company is doing right and where improvement is possible and perhaps warranted. The results of the DuPont analysis can be compared for the same firm across time via a trend analysis or can be compared to other companies in a cross-sectional analysis.

The three-factor DuPont method

There are two formulations of the DuPont method — the three-factor method and the five-factor method. The three-factor method shows that return on equity is a function of the product of three different ratios:

- ✔ Net profit margin
- ✔ Total asset turnover
- ✔ Leverage

A higher ROE can be achieved by an increase in any of the three ratios.

We cover net profit margin earlier in this chapter. *Total asset turnover* is defined as sales divided by total assets and is calculated for Coca-Cola in 2012 as follows:

$$\text{Total Asset Turnover} = \frac{\text{Sales}}{\text{Total Assets}} = \frac{\$48,017}{\$86,174} = 0.557 \text{ times}$$

Total asset turnover provides an indication of the effectiveness of the firm's use of its asset base. All else equal, a higher total asset turnover is better than a lower one. Total asset turnover is a metric that varies by industry. Total asset turnover at Coca-Cola for the years 2011 and 2010 was 0.583 and 0.482, respectively.

One of the easiest (and also one of the riskiest) ways that a firm can increase its ROE is to borrow more money. This practice is known as *leverage,* and just as in the physical sciences where a strategically placed lever can allow some-one to move a large object with a little bit of force, strategically borrowing money can allow a firm to magnify returns. In fact, leverage works when you can make more money on the borrowed money than it costs you. Of course, leverage is often referred to as a double-edged sword because leverage can magnify losses when you make less money (or you lose money) on borrowed funds than they cost you. Many people learned about leverage the hard way with residential real estate in the recent financial crisis.

The leverage ratio is defined as total assets divided by stockholders' equity. So, a firm with no borrowed funds would have a leverage ratio of 1.0. The leverage ratio for Coca-Cola for the year 2012 is as follows:

$$\text{Leverage Ratio} = \frac{\text{Total Assets}}{\text{Stockholders' Equity}} = \frac{\$86,174}{\$33,168} = 2.598$$

This leverage ratio indicates that a substantial portion — over 50 percent — was being supplied by borrowing funds (both short term and long term) for the year 2012. The leverage ratios were 2.328 and 2.505 for years 2010 and 2011, respectively. The leverage ratio is expanding slightly. All this debt may seem very risky, but for a firm with very little underlying business risk, like Coca-Cola, it's a prudent strategy.

Putting it all together

As we mention earlier, a firm's ROE is the function of the product of three different ratios. For the year 2012 for Coca-Cola, the DuPont analysis is as follows:

$$\text{Return on Equity} = \text{Net Profit} \times \text{Asset Turnover} \times \text{Leverage}$$
$$= \frac{\text{Net Income}}{\text{Sales}} \times \frac{\text{Sales}}{\text{Assets}} \times \frac{\text{Assets}}{\text{Equity}}$$
$$= \frac{\$9,086}{\$48,017} \times \frac{\$48,017}{\$86,174} \times \frac{\$86,174}{\$33,168}$$
$$= 0.189 \times 0.557 \times 2.598$$
$$= 0.274 = 27.4\%$$

This type of breakdown provides an investment banker with a great deal of insight on how a firm may go about improving its return on equity. In the case of Coca-Cola, it's hard to imagine that there is much room for improvement, but one area may be in total asset turnover. Of course, Coca-Cola could increase its total asset turnover simply by slashing the prices of its products. However, that would lower its net profit margin. The key for Coca-Cola is to strike a balance between selling more product and not eroding its net profit margin.

The five-factor DuPont method

A further refinement of the three-factor DuPont model is achieved by breaking down net profit margin into its three components:

- Operating profit margin
- The effect of non-operating items
- The tax effect

Through this analysis, the investment banker can get a better idea on how that net profit margin is being generated and see if there are any troubling trends. We explain each of these three components in the following sections.

Operating profit margin

We introduce operating profit margin earlier in this chapter. It's defined as earnings before interest and taxes divided by sales; for Coca-Cola in 2012, it was 22.4 percent. This is the percentage the company earns on sales before paying Uncle Sam and the suppliers of capital. The key here is that it involves income from operations — what the company is in the business of doing (in the case of Coca-Cola, making and selling beverages). It does not include extraordinary items (such as selling a plant or spinning off a division) or take into account the payment or receipt of interest payments or the paying of taxes.

Effect of non-operating items

Oftentimes, companies have significant non-operating items that affect profitability. The effect of non-operating items takes into account everything in the income statement between its operating income (EBIT) and its earnings before taxes (EBT). For Coca-Cola, from Table 14-2, you can see that these non-operating items include interest income, interest expense, equity income, and other income.

Coca-Cola both receives and pays interest. But that isn't their main business. Coca-Cola's main business is bottling and selling beverages. Segmenting these sources of income and expenses allows the analyst to isolate the effects of the main business.

Likewise, Coca-Cola has equity income (income that the company receives from investments in other businesses) and other income (one-time extraordinary items). When evaluating the profitability of the main business of Coca-Cola, these items should not be included.

The effect of non-operating items is simply reflected in the five-factor DuPont analysis as EBT divided by EBIT. For the year 2012, for Coca-Cola, this calculation is as follows:

$$\text{Effect of Non-Operating Items} = \frac{\text{EBT}}{\text{EBIT}} = \frac{\$11,809}{\$10,779} = 1.096$$

If a company has more non-operating expenses than non-operating sources of income, this ratio is less than 1.0. If, like Coca-Cola, the company has more non-operating sources of income than expenses, this ratio is greater than 1.0.

In 2010, 2011, and 2012, this ratio varied dramatically for Coca-Cola. In 2010, the ratio was 1.689; in 2011, it was 1.126. The dramatic increase in 2010 was due to the one-time, extraordinary gain from the acquisition of Coca-Cola Enterprises North American business operations that we mention earlier. The point to be made here is that the five-factor DuPont analysis draws the analyst's attention to that occurrence.

Tax effect

The last ratio included in the five-factor DuPont model is the tax effect. Essentially, this tells the analyst what percentage of EBIT the company is able to keep to be able to provide a return to the suppliers of capital. This ratio is simply 1 minus the company's realized tax rate. For 2012, this ratio for Coca-Cola is computed as follows:

$$\text{Tax Effect} = 1 - \left(\frac{\text{Taxes}}{\text{EBT}} \right) = 1 - \left(\frac{\$2,723}{\$11,809} \right) = 1 - 0.231 = 0.769$$

This ratio indicates that Coca-Cola paid an average tax rate on earnings of 23.1 percent, and the firm was able to keep 76.9 percent of earnings. The ratios for 2010 and 2011 were 0.833 and 0.755, respectively. Once again, the ratio for 2010 was skewed by the extraordinary item.

Putting it all together

The five-factor DuPont model breaks down return on equity into the five components described earlier. For Coca-Cola for the year 2012, the five factor DuPont model is as follows:

Return on Equity = Operating Profit Margin × Effect of Non-Operating Items
$$\times \text{Tax Effect} \times \text{Turnover} \times \text{Leverage}$$
$$= \frac{\text{EBIT}}{\text{Sales}} \times \frac{\text{EBT}}{\text{EBIT}} \times \left[1 - \left(\frac{\text{Taxes}}{\text{EBT}}\right)\right] \times \frac{\text{Sales}}{\text{Assets}} \times \frac{\text{Assets}}{\text{Equity}}$$
$$= 0.224 \times 1.096 \times 0.769 \times 0.557 \times 2.598$$
$$= 0.274 = 27.4\%$$

This analysis provides the analyst with more detail and more insight as to how Coca-Cola is generating its remarkable return on equity.

Interpreting the Results

Up to now, we've looked only at Coca-Cola and compared how ROE and the components in ROE for both the three- and five-factor models have trended over the past few years. One of the most illuminating aspects of DuPont analysis is to compare a company to the industry it operates in and to its chief competitors.

Cola wars

You've likely heard about the blindfolded taste tests that ask consumers to compare the taste of Coke and Pepsi to each other. Financial analysts can do a variation of the taste test to see which company "tastes" better to investors.

The data in Table 14-3 allows the analyst to perform a three-factor DuPont analysis on Pepsico and compare the results to that of the Coca-Cola Company.

Table 14-3 **Financial Data for Pepsico and Coca-Cola (in Millions of Dollars)**

	2012		2011		2010	
	Pepsico	Coca-Cola	Pepsico	Coca-Cola	Pepsico	Coca-Cola
Sales	65,492	48,017	66,504	46,542	57,838	35,119
Net Income	6,178	9,086	6,443	8,648	6,320	11,837
Total Assets	74,638	86,174	72,882	79,794	68,153	72,921
Stockholders' Equity	22,417	33,168	20,704	31,921	21,273	31,317

Source: EDGAR

The first thing to notice is that Coca-Cola and Pepsico are of comparable size when looking at sales, total assets, and stockholders' equity. Investment bankers are very careful not to use companies that are of dramatically different size when doing cross-sectional comparisons. A multi-billion-dollar global firm should not be compared to a smaller, regional firm even if they're in the same fundamental industry.

Table 14-4 presents a three-factor DuPont analysis of Pepsico and the Coca-Cola Company for the years 2010 through 2012.

Table 14-4   Three-Factor DuPont Analysis for Pepsico and the Coca-Cola Company

	2012		2011		2010	
	Pepsico	Coca-Cola	Pepsico	Coca-Cola	Pepsico	Coca-Cola
Return on Equity	27.5%	27.4%	31.1%	27.1%	29.7%	37.8%
Net Profit Margin	9.4%	18.9%	9.7%	18.6%	10.9%	33.7%
Asset Turnover	0.877	0.557	1.096	0.582	1.178	0.482
Leverage	3.330	2.598	3.520	2.505	3.204	2.328

What the numbers mean

The Coca-Cola Company and Pepsico are two remarkably well-run firms in a business that is really pretty simple and doesn't rely on sophisticated technologies. In fact, these two beverage giants have become the dominant global players in an industry that has very small barriers to entry. They've both built remarkable global brands. In fact, Interbrand — a global brand consultancy firm — has ranked Coca-Cola the number-one brand in the world and has ranked Pepsi 22nd.

The return on equity — the return that both companies have earned on shareholder equity — is quite high and consistent over the time period studied. Any investor would have been thrilled to have their money providing these kinds of returns over the past three years.

A close perusal of the three-factor DuPont model shows that the firms get to their near identical ROEs in very different ways. Pepsico's net profit margin is roughly half that of Coca-Cola, while its total asset turnover is substantially higher. Additionally, Pepsico is a much more highly leveraged firm than Coca-Cola is.

Looking past the numbers for insight

The case of the cola wars provides a prime example of Warren Buffett's quote on investing: "There's more than one way to get to heaven." What Buffett meant by this was that good investment results can be achieved using various methods. Coca-Cola has a business model that relies on a higher net profit margin, lower turnover and lower leverage than Pepsico. The good news for Coca-Cola is that the firm could conceivably take on more debt in its capital structure to magnify returns in the future. Pepsico has less room to take on more debt.

Likewise, Coca-Cola has very wide net profit margins and would likely be able to prosper during a protracted price war in the beverage industry. Pepsico's net profit margin is already fairly thin, and it doesn't have as great a margin of safety in this area as Coca-Cola does.

Where Pepsico shines is in its ability to generate a given level of sales per dollar of assets. The area that Coca-Cola could conceivably improve upon is generating more dollars of sales on its asset base.

But how does the market view Coca-Cola and Pepsico? One way of answering this question is to see what multiple of current earnings these firms are selling for in the market. As of August 2012, Coca-Cola was selling at nearly 21 times earnings and Pepsico was selling at slightly under 20 times earnings. Both companies were selling at a premium to the market, because the Dow Jones Industrial Average was selling at around 17 times earnings. The fact that the market is ascribing a premium to the earnings of both firms shows that these are very well-run companies with terrific future prospects.

Telling companies how to react to the numbers

Coca-Cola and Pepsico aren't attractive takeover candidates. They're simply too big, and the market has already recognized the value in these firms. However, going through the DuPont analysis of both firms is instructive when thinking about ways that investment bankers can counsel companies to make them better acquisition candidates.

Companies must focus on providing an attractive return on equity. This is the most important metric for companies looking to be acquired by other firms or looking to go public themselves. Investors focus on ROE, so firm managements must focus on ROE.

Also, companies must realize that even though the bottom-line ROE number is extremely important, it's equally important that number be realized in an attractive manner. In other words, investors and potential buyers aren't fooled by high ROEs that are achieved merely by high degrees of leverage. In fact, the most attractive firms are those with solid ROEs that also have unused borrowing capacity — firms that can be "leveraged up" to realize even higher ROEs.

Part IV
Applying Investment Banking

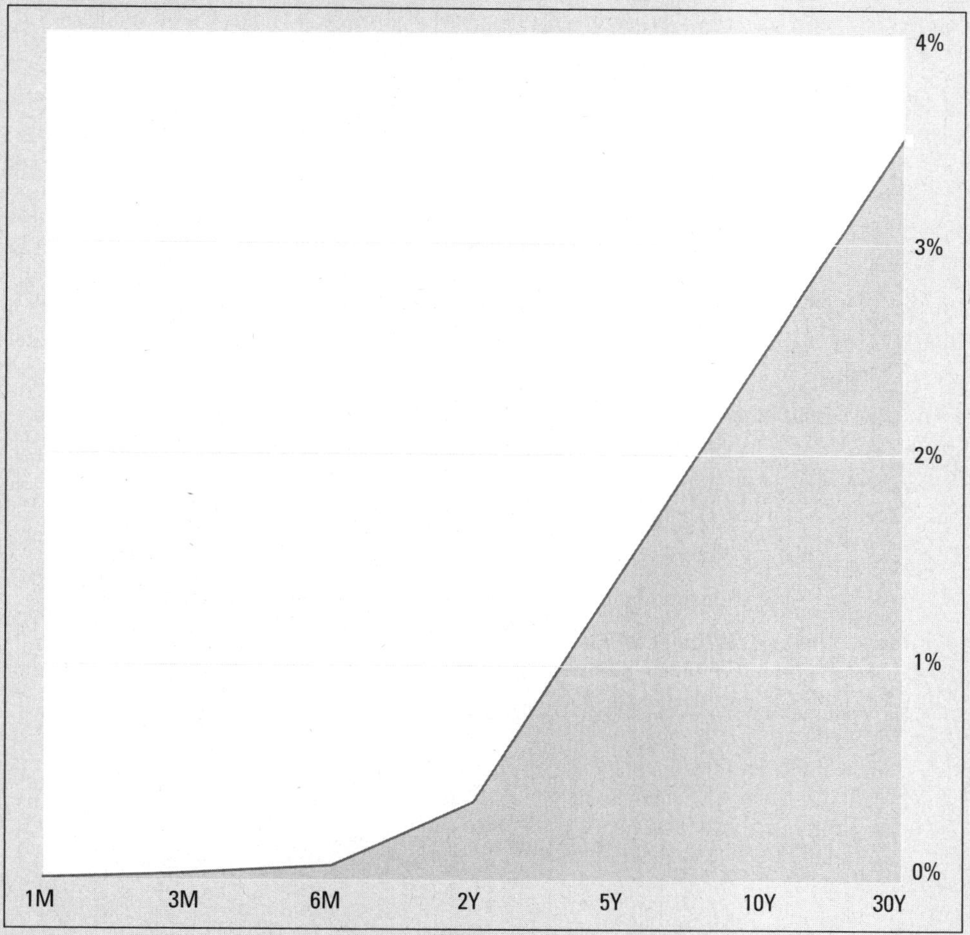

In this part . . .

✔ Understand what rules and stipulations guide what can and cannot be done in the world of investment banking so you don't risk breaking the rules and getting into big trouble.

✔ Explore the financials more deeply so you can confidently tear about a company's financials and understand what makes the company tick.

✔ See how money is managed so you can appreciate the flow of capital through the financial system and see the role investment bankers can play.

✔ Cut your teeth on a case study in order to apply all the things that are explained in this book and be ready for real-life investment banking.

Chapter 15

Knowing the Rules

Some people would say investment banking is a highly regulated industry, while others would contend that it isn't regulated nearly enough and more government oversight is warranted. The recent financial crisis of 2007 and 2008 has refocused debate on the role of regulation and the perceived failure of oversight to prevent the near meltdown of the financial system and subsequent global recession. Trying to strike the proper balance between free market forces and the protection of investors is a difficult task that lawmakers have wrestled with through time. In this chapter, we will fill you in on the current state of financial regulation and how we got to where we are.

The History of Regulation of Investment Banking

As is the case with most industries, the regulation of the investment banking industry has evolved through time. Unlike most fields, however, major changes in legislation have come in clusters and have been precipitated by seminal crises in the markets.

The goals of investment banking regulation

According to the primary U.S. regulator, the Securities and Exchange Commission (SEC), "The mission of the U.S. Securities and Exchange Commission is to protect investors; maintain fair, orderly, and efficient markets; and facilitate capital formation." The SEC attempts to accomplish this by requiring full disclosure of all relevant information related to specific securities and financial advisors. The goal is not to prevent losses by investors, but to allow investors to make informed investment decisions by requiring the disclosure of audited financial and other information.

The concept of a level playing field is central to the regulation of capital markets, thus several aspects of regulation relate to the dissemination of investment information — providing for fair and equal access to investment opportunities across investors. If investors believe that the markets aren't a fair game — that, for instance, the markets are skewed to the advantage of large institutions and major investors — investors won't trust them or participate in them, and an inefficient allocation of resources across the economy and stunted economic growth will result. Regulation should provide investors with a sense of trust in the markets.

Why the rules of today are the result of days past

American historian James A. Field, Jr., a professor at Swarthmore College, was quoted as saying that "It is proverbial that generals always prepare for the last war." The same can be said of regulators with respect to the investment banking industry. Sweeping regulatory changes generally come out of market crises, and the recent past is certainly no different. The two biggest crisis periods of the last 100 years — the market crash of 1929 (and subsequent Great Depression) and the financial crisis that began in 2007 — both resulted in major legislation affecting the financial markets. To say that financial regulation is reactive rather than proactive is a gross understatement. Regulators, it seems, have looked to prevent the last crisis instead of trying to avoid the next one.

How regulations have shaped the investment banking industry

To understand today's securities regulation, you need to know how it developed. Rules passed decades ago are still binding today. The history of regulation of the investment banking industry begins during the Great

Depression with the passage of the Glass-Steagall Act of 1933. The main purpose of this act was to separate *investment banking* activities (primarily securities underwriting and trading) from *commercial banking* activities (taking deposits and making loans). This was done because many people felt that commercial bank participation in the stock market was too risky an endeavor and that depositors' funds shouldn't be used to speculate in the stock market (sound familiar?). It was widely believed that the combination of commercial and investment banking activities within the same firms contributed to the crash of 1929 and the subsequent Great Depression.

The year 1933 also witnessed another seminal regulatory act with the Security Act of 1933, which guides the industry's behavior to this day. The main purpose of this act was to regulate the *primary securities market* — that is, the new issue or IPO market. This piece of legislation required that firms issuing securities must fully disclose all material information concerning the new issue. It also required that investment banking firms provide investors with a *prospectus* (a formal legal document that contains all relevant information — including audited financial statements and other disclosures) on all new issues.

The very next year witnessed the passage of the Securities Exchange Act of 1934. The primary purpose of this act was to regulate the *secondary market* (the market where already existing securities are traded). The main points of this act involved setting margin requirements, audit requirements, registration requirements for stocks listed on exchanges, and disclosure requirements. The act also created the SEC as the primary enforcement agency for securities laws.

The final two pieces of major legislation that had its genesis in the stock market crash of 1929 were the Investment Advisors Act of 1940 and the Investment Company Act of 1940. The Investment Advisors Act and subsequent amendments provided that investment advisors with a minimum asset size under management must register with the SEC. It also provided guidelines regarding the fees and commissions they may collect and detailed the liability of advisors. The Investment Company Act of 1940 detailed requirements for mutual funds (both open- and closed-end) and exchange traded funds (ETFs).

It was near the turn of the century before the next major regulatory change took place. The history of legislation doesn't simply involve putting more rules on the books — for the investment banking industry, the next big development was the repeal of the Glass-Steagall Act in 1999. The rationale for allowing institutions to engage in both commercial and investment banking activities was to make the large U.S. institutions more competitive on a global basis. Hindsight is, of course, 20/20, but even the staunchest supporters of this repeal would have to believe that it contributed to the severity of the financial crisis that began in 2007. It brought into the common vernacular the concept of financial institutions that are "too big to fail." That is, allowing firms that are so interconnected to fail would prove disastrous to the overall financial markets and, as a result, prove devastating to the economy.

The Ins and Outs of Modern Investment Banking Rules

Investment banks are governed by a myriad of complex legislation that is enforced by several government agencies and self-regulatory organizations, most notably the SEC, the Financial Industry Regulatory Authority (FINRA), and the various securities exchanges including the New York Stock Exchange (NYSE) and the Commodities Futures Trading Commission (CFTC), among others. One of the problems with regulating the financial markets has been a difficulty in coordination by the various regulators.

The types of rules imposed on investment banking

Investment banks are subject to many rules that govern their activities, but the primary focus of regulation is on information flow — ensuring that all investors have equal access to information and one group is not disadvantaged relative to another.

Illegal insider trading

Under certain limitations, insiders are allowed to trade in the securities of the firm that they're involved in. The SEC defines *illegal insider trading* as "buying or selling a security, in breach of a fiduciary duty or other relationship of trust and confidence, while in possession of material, nonpublic information about the security." Information is *material* if its disclosure would likely have an impact on the price of a security; that is, if investors would want to know the information before making an investment decision. Information is *nonpublic* if the investing public has not been made aware of it. For instance, potential mergers and acquisitions, unreleased company earnings numbers, upcoming changes in management, and any regulatory approval or rejection of a patent would all be considered material information.

In addition to trading for one's own benefit, it is illegal to pass along that information to others who trade on it. Investment bankers have access to much more and better information than the typical investor. In order to maintain a level playing field for all investors, those individuals in possession of inside information are strictly prohibited from trading on that information unless and until it is released to the public through proper channels like a press release or required filings.

A recent focus of the SEC on insider trading has been on so-called *expert network firms*. These firms often access the knowledge of company insiders and pass along specialized information to hedge funds and other institutional investors. Although it is certainly legal to consult experts including company insiders on developments that affect the company, if the information obtained is not public, it cannot be traded upon.

There are instances, however, where individuals break these rules and have been brought to justice. For instance, in a high-profile case in 2012, former Goldman Sachs board member Rajat Gupta was convicted of leaking confidential information from Goldman Sachs board meetings to Galleon hedge fund tycoon Raj Rajaratnam. Gupta was fined $5 million and sentenced to two years in prison.

Market manipulation

Market manipulation occurs when market participants conspire to distort prices and trading volumes in order to mislead the markets. A classic example of market manipulation is a *pump-and-dump strategy* in which a firm or individual acquires a position in a company, releases positive (and often false or very misleading) information about that company, and then dumps the stock at a profit when the price increases. Pump-and-dump occurrences tend to be concentrated in the micro-cap or penny stock market — markets for small, thinly traded stocks — because these markets are much easier to manipulate.

The traditional image of pump-and-dump purveyors was that of the so-called *boiler room* where individuals would cold-call unsuspecting investors and promote a specific stock or stocks. The advent of the Internet and social media made it much easier to accomplish a pump-and-dump strategy. All it takes is a few strategically placed comments or false rumors to get gullible investors to fall prey to unscrupulous operators. One of the most famous pump-and-dump cases involved 15-year-old high school student Jonathan Lebed, who made hundreds of thousands of dollars by posting on Internet message boards and using social media to promote stocks that he owned. Lebed eventually settled with the SEC and paid a fine of nearly $300,000 but was allowed to keep some of the profit from the strategy.

Market manipulation can also be done by people who take a short position in a security — that is, bet on the stock price falling by short-selling or buying *put options* — and then denigrate the stock by spreading (often false and misleading) information. Once the stock price falls, these "stock bashers" close out their positions at a profit. Although it certainly isn't illegal for market participants to point out the weaknesses of particular stocks, it is illegal to spread false and misleading rumors. As you may suspect, cases of stock bashing are very difficult to prove.

Not all market manipulation is meant to distort prices in the market. Another form of market manipulation is *churning,* in which market makers collude to make it appear that the buying and selling in a security is much more active than it actually is. A *market maker* is a firm that is a dealer in a particular security, standing ready to buy and sell, hoping to profit on the bid-ask spread, which is the difference between the quoted buy price and sell price.

For instance, a market maker may quote a buy price of $20.25 per share and be willing to sell the security for $20.50 per share. A successful market maker doesn't care as much if the price of the securities that it makes a market in rises. The market maker is concerned with the ability to match buyers and sellers and profit on the spread between the prices. Investors prefer to invest in securities that have a deep and liquid market and often look to the volume of shares traded in a day or a week as an indication of how deep the market is. Market-making firms could manipulate volume by simultaneously buying and selling the stock or colluding with others to do so.

Information flow

Because information is the lifeblood of the investment banking industry, regulations govern what information is required and how that information is released. The information that is required is explained in Chapter 6. How information is released is an area that can be characterized as in flux due to the changing ways in which individuals communicate.

One prominent regulatory change adopted by the SEC in 2000 targeted companies and their disclosure of information — a regulation that had a large impact on the investment banking profession. Regulation Fair Disclosure (Reg FD) requires that companies disclose material information to investors at the same time.

Before the adoption of Reg FD, companies often practiced *selective disclosure* — alerting professional analysts covering the company to developments prior to disseminating the information to the larger public. Oftentimes, these disclosures took place on quarterly conference calls between the company and firm analysts. Because information is the valuable commodity in the investment business, providing information to one group prior to more widespread dissemination was viewed as creating an un-level playing field. Essentially, the firms receiving selective disclosure could front-run the other firms, trading first on that information.

Reg FD has taken an interesting turn in the era of social media. The case that really brought attention to this issue was that of Netflix CEO Reed Hastings, who posted on his Facebook page in July 2012 that Netflix monthly viewing hours had exceeded one billion for the first time. Netflix did not simultaneously release the information in the more standard press release or Form 8-K filing. Despite the page having over 200,000 followers, including analysts and reporters, the SEC originally charged Hastings with a violation of Reg FD. The SEC has subsequently changed its stance and said that companies can use social media to disseminate information if certain requirements are met. It doesn't strain credulity to believe that many more people saw the Facebook posting than would have seen the standard disclosure. Welcome to the 21st century!

How investment banking rules changed after the financial crisis

Securities laws continue to evolve, and investment bankers need to keep up. In July 2010, President Obama signed into law the omnibus Dodd–Frank legislation. At the time of this writing, the law is still morphing and has expanded to a mind-numbing 9,000-plus pages in length, affecting nearly every aspect of the financial markets. It continues to be subject to intense lobbying efforts by the investment banking industry and will undoubtedly be in flux for years to come.

The ultimate outcomes of many aspects of the law are unknown, but for investment banks some of the most important provisions and proposed provisions of the legislation include the following:

- **Increased transparency in the derivatives markets:** Many firms, including investment banks, take huge positions in the derivatives markets. A *derivative* security — like an *option* or *swap* — is simply a security whose value depends on (is derived) by the value of another security. For instance, the value of a *call option* or *put option* on a share of stock depends upon the price of that share of stock. The problem with many complex derivatives — like credit default swaps (for more on derivatives and credit default swaps see Chapter 16) — are that these holdings are both difficult to value and difficult to find information on. The problem is that many of the transactions in the derivatives market do not take place on organized exchanges where prices and volume levels are disclosed, but they take place over the counter or in private negotiations between the buyer and seller. Thus, there is limited transparency in these markets concerning both the pricing and the volume of the positions. The failure of Lehman Brothers and the dire financial situation faced by American International Group (AIG) was largely attributed to positions each firm had in derivatives security markets, particularly in credit default swaps.

- **Increased capital requirements:** One of the most important provisions of the Dodd–Frank legislation involves increasing the capital (or equity) requirements of banks, effectively lowering the amount of leverage (borrowing) that investment banks can utilize in their operations. Many investment banking firms got into trouble during the crisis — and ultimately were bailed out by taxpayers — because these firms were so highly indebted that when some of their proprietary trading bets went against them, the losses were magnified and they didn't have the funds available to absorb the losses. By increasing the amount of firm equity relative to borrowing of investment banks, the intention of the legislation is to create a more stable and secure banking system.

✔ **Limitations of proprietary trading:** This area is still under intense negotiation and review, but one of the most contentious areas of the Dodd–Frank legislation involves limitations on proprietary trading by investment banking firms. The so-called Volcker Rule (named after former Federal Reserve Chairman Paul Volcker) would restrict banking firms from making speculative investments on their own account, only allowing them to trade on behalf of customers. The investment banking industry is fighting this provision because proprietary trading has traditionally been a profit center for investment banks. Investment banks won't give up this revenue stream without a fight.

✔ **More intense scrutiny and reform of the credit-rating agencies:** Credit-rating agencies such as Moody's, Standard & Poor's, and Fitch Ratings provide ratings on a variety of financial securities — from government bonds to corporate bonds and mortgage-backed securities. These ratings are meant to provide investors with a sense of the likelihood that an issuer will default on a particular security. Rating agencies played a central role in the recent financial crisis, as many securities — particularly mortgage-backed securities — that had been given very high or the highest credit quality ratings defaulted as homeowners defaulted on their residential mortgages. Investment banks are major users of the services of these rating agencies, because it's much easier to sell highly rated securities to investors because the buyers believe them to be relatively safe. Investment banking firms are the lifeblood of these rating agencies, because investment banks pay the rating agencies to rate the securities.

There is an obvious conflict of interest with issuer-paid ratings — investment banks want high ratings for the securities they're putting together, and rating agencies want the continued business of these investment banks. High ratings make both parties happy but can mislead investors who rely on these ratings as part of their investment decision-making process. The Dodd–Frank legislation provides for increased scrutiny of credit-rating agencies.

✔ **Risk retention of asset-backed securities:** One of the most criticized practices of some investment banking firms that came out of the recent financial crisis was that firms put together securities (primarily mortgage-backed securities) of questionable quality and sold them to clients. In fact, what has been dubbed "the greatest trade ever" was when hedge-fund manager John Paulson effectively short-sold the U.S. housing market through a series of trades that several investment banks helped him engineer. Clients of the investment banking firm were on the other side of these trades. The Dodd–Frank legislation addresses this issue by mandating that a firm that puts these securities together retain at least 5 percent of the credit risk of those assets. In other words, investment banks are required to have some "skin in the game," and if the value of these securities goes south, the investment banking firm will suffer similarly to the client who purchased the assets.

✔ **Executive compensation:** One of the raging debates in business today involves the level of executive compensation, particularly within the financial services industry. Many people were outraged with the salary and bonus packages provided to executives from firms in the financial services arena that received government bailouts. Although not placing any dollar restrictions on salary and bonuses of executives, the Dodd–Frank legislation requires that companies must include a resolution in their proxy statements approving the compensation of top executives. It also requires that firms disclose certain statistics regarding executive pay, for instance, the ratio of CEO pay to median employee compensation. Requiring more disclosure will increase the scrutiny on executive pay packages.

The Rules on Analysts

The game has changed dramatically for Wall Street analysts over the past 15 years. Many of the changes were brought about as the result of abuses triggered by conflicts of interest described in this section. The problems were exacerbated as the compensation of analysts soared and the financial rewards for bending and breaking the rules were astronomical.

Why rules were needed

Investors and potential investors look to security analysts to provide them with professional, unbiased opinions on the investment potential of a stock. After all, the analyst is assumed to have the knowledge and skills to investigate and form a recommendation — generally "buy," "sell," or "hold" — on a stock's future potential. Many analysts are highly trained individuals who went to the top business schools and were taught various state-of-the-art valuation techniques. Professional certifications (such as the Chartered Financial Analyst [CFA] designation) train analysts on the ins and outs of analyzing companies, and these qualifications signal to investors that these individuals have the skill set to provide sound advice.

Given all this training, what could possibly go wrong? Why around the turn of the recent century did stock analysts earn reputations that rivaled used-car salesmen? It all centered on behavior that resulted from conflicts of interest that were inherent in the role of analyst at investment banking firms, and led to changes in regulation meant to curb abuses and mitigate these conflicts.

During the time of the Internet boom, many analysts — like Jack Grubman, Mary Meeker, and Henry Blodget — became media darlings and commanded multimillion-dollar annual compensation packages. A positive report on a company, or an upgrade of the company's stock to a "buy" or a "strong buy" by one of these rock-star analysts, could result in significant increases in the price of that company's stock. Although few and far between (more about that later), a negative report or the downgrade of a company's stock to a "sell" recommendation or even from a "sell" to a "hold" could result in the price plunging as investors sell their holdings.

The not-so-delicate balancing act analysts play

Stock analysts are employed by investment banking firms that do more than simply issue buy, sell, and hold recommendations on individual stocks to investors. Investment banking firms are paid to bring companies public by underwriting IPOs. These firms advise corporate client firms on strategies to increase firm value such as during mergers and acquisitions or in leveraged buyouts. Investment banking firms also invest their own money in the markets in proprietary trading activities.

Without clients, investment banking firms wouldn't exist. Like any company in any industry, the lifeblood of an investment banking firm are clients or customers. Customers want to be happy and investment banking firms want them to be happy. What makes investment banking customers really happy is when their company stock price increases. Stock prices generally don't rise when analysts issue negative or neutral recommendations on stocks. Perhaps that explains why analysts are overwhelmingly bullish, and the ratio of buy to sell recommendations by Wall Street firms is typically in the area of 10-to-1. By the way, this isn't an issue that is isolated to U.S. markets. In the Chinese and Korean markets, buy-sell recommendation ratios can approach 20-to-1. In fact, rather than issue a negative recommendation, it's common for some investment banking firms to simply drop coverage of a firm.

Corporate firms want a relationship with an investment banking firm that will continue to increase demand for the company's stock even well after the IPO. Corporations are less likely to maintain a relationship with an investment banking firm that doesn't provide favorable coverage on its stock. Thus, there is pressure on analysts to issue favorable recommendations on the firms with which they have investment banking relationships. Perhaps this explains why, for instance, Henry Blodget allegedly referred to Internet search company InfoSpace as a "piece of junk" and a "powder keg" in internal e-mails, while simultaneously recommending the stock to investors.

Providing advice to both the corporation and investors in that corporation would appear to represent a conflict of interest. This has led many critics of investment banking firms to wonder if it's really possible for these firms to effectively serve two masters — the corporations and the investors. This is the tightrope that the investment banking firm attempts to navigate.

As we note earlier, a change in analyst recommendation — particularly from a prominent analyst — from a "hold" to a "buy" or from a "buy" to a "hold," for instance, can lead to dramatic stock price changes following the release of the recommendation. A pending recommendation change is valuable information that is coveted by market participants. Investment banking firms engage in proprietary trading using their own funds and have large clients who would benefit from advance notice of any recommendation changes. Suffice it to say, the investment banking side of the business is very interested in developments from analysts.

If the conflict of interests outlined here weren't enough, there may be other incentives that have driven analysts to make certain recommendations on stocks that are not driven by the fundamentals of the company. In a widely reported scandal, Salomon Smith Barney telecommunications analyst Jack Grubman raised his rating on AT&T from a "neutral" to a "buy" rating in 1999. Grubman later admitted in an internal e-mail that his decision was motivated, at least in part, by a desire to get his children placed in an exclusive NYC preschool program. Conflicts, it seems, like ice cream, come in a variety of flavors.

What disclosure and compliance are required

The result of the conflicts outlined earlier and the belief that analysts don't always operate independently but can be influenced by factors other than the desire to make an objective determination of an investment's prospects, resulted in a call for increased regulation of the analyst profession. Former Supreme Court Justice Louis Brandeis once said, "Sunlight is said to be the best of disinfectants; electric light the most effective policeman." In the spirit of Brandeis, a series of regulatory changes — including both disclosure of conflicts of interests and prohibitions of actions — has transformed the analyst profession.

As an indication of the seriousness of the problem, in April 2003, ten of the largest investment banks agreed to pay a pretty steep price — $1.4 billion in total — and were forced to abide by a series of regulations governing their behavior.

There is recognition by the regulatory authorities and the industry that while not all these conflicts of interest can be completely eliminated via stricter regulations, they need to be properly disclosed. The following represents a synopsis of the major changes to regulations and required disclosures governing analysts:

- ✔ **A prohibition on analysts receiving compensation for investment banking activities:** Analyst compensation cannot be tied directly to a specific investment banking activity. Going even further, if any part of the compensation of analysts is tied to general investment banking activity at the firm, that must be disclosed in the firm's research report. The intent is to tie an analyst's compensation solely to the quality of his research and not to how much investment banking business may result from continuing coverage.

- ✔ **A prohibition on promises of favorable research:** Investment banking firms cannot promise a favorable research rating or a specific price target to secure investment banking business. Firms are also prohibited from issuing a report on a company within 40 days after an IPO.

- ✔ **A prohibition on analysts being involved in soliciting investment banking business:** Prior to the change in regulations, star analysts often accompanied investment bankers on their recruiting trips when seeking new or maintaining existing investment banking clients.

- ✔ **A prohibition on influence by investment bankers:** Analysts are prohibited from being supervised by the investment banking departments of their firms. In addition, analysts cannot discuss research reports with investment bankers prior to distribution.

- ✔ **A requirement to certify analyst reports:** Specifically, Regulation Analyst Certfication (Reg AC) requires analysts to certify that their views accurately reflect their beliefs about the future performance of the subject company. This is similar to the requirement that CEOs and CFOs certify the accuracy of their financial statements.

- ✔ **A requirement to disclose firm compensation:** Investment banks issuing research reports must disclose in the report if they managed or co-managed a public offering or received any compensation for investment banking services in the past year. Such a disclosure signals to investors that the firm may have a vested interested in the performance of the company.

- ✔ **A requirement to disclose holdings or investment banking ties during public appearances:** How often have you wondered if the analysts appearing on TV touting a stock hold positions in that stock? Analysts must now disclose if they or their firms have a position in the stock or if the company is an investment-banking client. This helps the viewer form her own opinion about the validity of the recommendation.

✔ **A requirement to disclose financial interests on reports:** On research reports, analysts must disclose if they own shares of the companies.

✔ **A requirement to disclose what the firm's ratings mean:** Firms must fully explain — in plain English — what any ratings terms like *buy, sell,* or *hold* mean. Firms must also disclose the percentage of the ratings that they have in each category, and also disclose the percentage of investment banking clients that they have in each category.

✔ **Limitations of personal trading by analysts:** Analysts are investors too. But, they aren't allowed to trade on the companies they follow during blackout periods. Specifically, analysts can't trade for 30 days before and 5 days after they issue a research report. They're also prohibited from trading against their most recent recommendation. That is, an analyst cannot issue a "buy" recommendation, watch the stock run up, and then, once the blackout period is over, sell her holdings in the stock.

Why Simply Making Rules Isn't Enough

If all these rules are in place, why do crooks like Bernie Madoff and others get away with bilking millions and billions of dollars from investors? How does such a highly regulated industry have systemic problems such as those exemplified by the concept of "too big to fail"? Besides having the proper laws on the books, two elements are necessary to achieve successful regulation of the financial markets:

✔ **The ability to regulate:** The ability to regulate refers to having properly trained regulators in place.

✔ **The will to regulate:** The will to regulate refers to putting appropriate regulations on the books and providing the funding to those regulators to enforce the regulations. In the most recent financial crisis, the SEC and other financial regulators didn't have either the appropriate regulations or the proper funding.

By now, most people have heard the story that Harry Markopolos, a forensic accountant and financial professional, provided a detailed document to the SEC showing that Bernie Madoff was running a multibillion-dollar Ponzi scheme. Markopolos figured this out when he tried to devise a strategy that would compete with Madoff and couldn't replicate Madoff's consistently good results. Yet, it took many years before Madoff was investigated and eventually indicted. SEC executives and investigators were brought before Congress and chastised for being asleep at the wheel. Yet, much of the blame can be laid at the feet of Congress for providing inadequate funding to the SEC — a circumstance that led to underqualified and overworked investigators.

The typical background of an SEC employee involves legal training, not financial training. The SEC is charged with policing an industry that has increased exponentially in complexity in recent years with the advent of collateralized debt obligations, credit default swaps, and other financial instruments that are the result of the efforts of some of the brightest and most creative minds in the investment banking industry.

The best and the brightest in the field — including master's and PhD graduates from the top business schools — work for investment banking firms and hedge funds and command multimillion-dollar pay packages. The average SEC employee, not trained in finance but in the law, makes a fraction of that. As an aside, there is a revolving door at the SEC between the agency and the industry that it regulates. Specifically, many SEC employees leave the agency and are hired by investment banking firms who pay them multiples of their SEC salaries to help them navigate the regulatory landscape.

In 2012, the SEC budget was $1.3 billion, which sounds like a lot of money until you realize that it's responsible for ensuring the proper functioning of U.S. financial markets worth at least $19 trillion. To put this in perspective, the SEC budget is equal to approximately $1 for every $14,329 that it is charged with protecting. Another way to look at the size of the SEC budget in relation to the financial markets is that, in 2011, three individuals — Ray Dalio of Bridgewater Associates, Carl Icahn of Icahn Capital Management, and James Simons of Renaissance Technologies — each earned more in one year from operating in the financial markets than the entire SEC budget. Suffice it to say, the investing public can't expect a filet-mignon regulator on a macaroni-and-cheese budget.

Chapter 16

Seeing How Some Companies Lie, Cheat, and Steal Their Way to the Top

In This Chapter

▶ Understanding how companies can manipulate accounting numbers

▶ Seeing how investment bankers can identify accounting problems

▶ Identifying potential accounting red flags

▶ Understanding the importance of accounting assumptions

▶ Developing a skeptical nature

*T*he lifeblood of investment banking is the analysis of financial statements like the ones we introduce in Chapter 7 (for example, the income statement, balance sheet, statement of cash flows, and proxy statement). Even though each of these statements is prepared using the same rules — generally accepted accounting principles (GAAP) — and the financial statements are audited by independent accounting firms, like Alice in Wonderland, things aren't always as they seem. A successful investment banker is part financial analyst and part detective. An inquisitive and skeptical nature is essential.

One of the fastest-growing fields related to the accounting profession is *forensic accounting,* which uses accounting, auditing, and investigative skills to essentially get behind a company's financial statements and explain what's really going on — what's behind the numbers. Investment bankers need to draw on the principles of forensic accounting when counseling companies, preparing them to go public, and advising them on mergers-and-acquisitions (M&A) activity.

This chapter shows you some of the most common creative accounting methods that some companies employ to fool both investment bankers and investors into believing they're performing better than they actually are. Of course, the primary motivation to mislead the markets is that executive compensation is tied to firm performance. Relatively minor improvements in earnings per share and stock price can mean added millions of dollars for executives of large, publicly held corporations.

There are tremendous temptations to represent a firm's results in the most favorable light. Investment banking analysts and investors alike should do as Deep Throat advised Woodward and Bernstein to do: "Follow the money." In this chapter, we provide examples from well-known and highly visible firms to illustrate the various methods that executives can use to mislead people. The financial improprieties commonly used by firms generally fall into one of the following categories:

- ✔ **Overstating revenue:** To make earnings appear greater than they actually are, some firms use accounting manipulations to overstate revenues.

- ✔ **Understating expenses:** To make the bottom line appear more attractive, some companies understate expenses occurred in a given period either by ignoring them or by moving them into a future year.

- ✔ **Overstating the financial position:** Some firms use unrealistic assumptions or outright accounting tricks to bolster the value of assets or understate the value of liabilities in order to make the firm's financial statements appear stronger than they really are.

In the pages that follow, we provide real-world examples of each of these accounting games. In several cases, the featured firm wasn't simply engaged in *one* of these misleading practices, but was involved in multiple scams. Astute investment bankers need to be vigilant in order to identify these behaviors before they or their clients incur losses from investing in these firms.

Did You Really Sell That? When Companies Aggressively Report Revenue

It would seem pretty straightforward to identify when a sale has been made. When you have a yard sale and get rid of an old box of baseball cards or the fondue set your crazy uncle gave you as a wedding present, you likely consider the sale consummated when the buyer hands you the cash and walks off with your unwanted items.

In the corporate world, however, things aren't as simple as transactions in yard sales. What if someone comes to your yard sale and promises to pay you tomorrow for your items? What if you send your items to someone who has simply expressed an interest in buying them? What if you send your items to someone who says he'll try to sell them for you? Have the items truly been sold? Some corporate executives have stretched the limits of credulity in booking sales.

Don't let the sun go down on me

To understand how companies cook the books, you need to understand why they do it in the first place. And there are few better examples of why cheating is so tempting than with the career of Al Dunlap, a CEO who garnered a reputation as a successful, yet ruthless turnaround specialist.

Dunlap earned the colorful nickname "Chainsaw Al" while at Scott Paper by firing thousands of employees, closing plants, and cutting costs to the bone. After downsizing Scott Paper and making it more attractive to suitors, he engineered the 1995 sale of the firm to Kimberly-Clark and personally parachuted off with a lucrative cash payout of over $100 million.

Sunbeam — maker of grills, blenders, bread makers, coffee makers, microwave ovens, and many other consumer products — hired Dunlap shortly after he left Scott Paper, and it appeared that his methods were very successful in turning Sunbeam around. Shortly after Dunlap assumed control, Sunbeam went on a buying spree, acquiring several well-known brands; the stock price soared. In 1996, when he took the company over, it had reported negative net income and in 1997 it reported large positive net income — an impressive turn of events. Dunlap's reputation was burnished, and he was lauded as a hero. Or was he?

A careful examination of the numbers reveals that while revenue increased by a robust 19 percent in 1997, inventories and accounts receivable both increased at a much higher rate — 59 percent for inventories and 38 percent for accounts receivable. This situation is certainly not ideal, and it would raise red flags for any forensic accountant worth her salt. Mounting inventories meant warehouses were filling up with unsold goods. Rising accounts receivables meant the company was accumulating IOUs from customers. Ideally, both receivables and inventory would grow no more than the increase in revenues. Not seeing those things move in lockstep raised suspicions of mismanagement, accounting games, or outright fraud. In Sunbeam's case, it was allegedly a little bit of all three.

What was going on at Sunbeam reveals the key to why companies cheat with their numbers in the first place: The company was recognizing sales on products at the time of simply shipping an invoice — but not the product — to customers (the retailers) in a practice known as *bill and hold*. As an example, Sunbeam was invoicing hardware stores for outdoor gas grills in the fourth quarter of the year, and holding that inventory in Sunbeam's warehouses, knowing full well that the grills weren't even going to be shipped to the retailers and put out for sale until the spring. Yet, Sunbeam was counting those grills as sold when they were sitting in their own warehouses! In fact, Sunbeam was offering incentives for retailers to agree to this practice — a practice that is pejoratively referred to as *channel stuffing*.

Typically, businesses produce inventories, sell them to firms on credit (resulting in an account receivable), and finally collect on that account receivable by getting the cash. If a firm is growing, all those accounting line items should be growing by approximately the same rate. If inventories and accounts receivable are growing faster than revenue, then either customers are paying awfully slowly or inventory is piling up — both developments that signal problems.

Sunbeam overstated revenue by aggressively booking sales. Reported net income did increase in 1997, but cash flow was decidedly negative — the grills were sitting in Sunbeam's warehouse and not generating cash. An examination of Sunbeam's statement of cash flow revealed that Sunbeam had positive net income in 1997, yet actually had negative cash flow. This was exactly the *opposite* situation as occurred in 1996, when the firm had negative net income but positive cash flow. This turn of events was alarming. As any businessman knows, you can't pay bills with inventory — you can only pay bills with cash.

Dunlap was fired in 1998, and the Securities and Exchange Commission (SEC) investigated and determined that, for 1997, at least $60 million of Sunbeam's reported $189 million in earnings from continuing operations before income taxes came from accounting fraud. The SEC issued a consent judgment against Dunlap, and he was permanently barred from serving as an officer or director of a public company. Sunbeam declared bankruptcy in 2001 and emerged from bankruptcy in 2002 as American Household, Inc., a privately held company. In 2009, *Condé Nast Portfolio* named Dunlap the sixth worst CEO of all time. Just imagine: There are five CEOs worse than he was!

The truth?

The vast majority of the accounting scandals reported in the popular press involve U.S.-based companies. Lest you believe that accounting irregularities are confined to U.S. borders, the case of the Indian technology service provider and back-office accounting firm Satyam will show that these improprieties are clearly not just a U.S. phenomenon. In fact, some pundits have dubbed Satyam "India's Enron" — a moniker no firm covets. Ironically, *Satyam* means "the truth" in the ancient Indian language Sanskrit. So, how did the truth become synonymous with fraud?

Satyam was founded by Ramalinga Raju with a handful of employees in 1987. As outsourcing to India became popular, Satyam rode the wave and grew to be one of the largest and most celebrated firms in India. It employed more than 50,000 people and was listed on both the New York Stock Exchange and Bombay Stock Exchange. At its peak, the market capitalization of Satyam was over $9 billion, and the firm, as well as Raju, enjoyed a sterling reputation as one of India's business titans.

The high-flying firm came crashing down when it was found to have allegedly falsified revenue, income, and the level of interest-bearing deposits over an extended six-year period from 2003 to 2008. Skeptical investment banking analysts could've examined the reported numbers and clearly seen that something was rotten in the state of Denmark — or in this case, in the city of Hyderabad, India.

Just like the case of Sunbeam (see the preceding section), Satyam's revenues were growing rapidly — in this case, despite the slowing of the world economy due to the financial crisis that began in 2007. Specifically, revenues in 2008 were reported to have risen by an astonishing 46 percent. That would certainly be a good thing if the growth were real. The problem is that accompanying this shocking revenue growth, three accounts receivable items on the balance sheet — short-term trade receivables, long-term trade receivables, and unbilled revenue — were all growing at a pace much higher than revenue.

If the company is doing an adequate job of collecting from customers, receivables should grow no faster than revenues. In fact, ideally the growth rate in receivables would be less than revenue growth as companies improve their collection cycle.

The rapid growth of the receivables and unbilled revenue accounts certainly indicated a problem. At best, it said that Satyam was doing a poor job of collecting its receivables; at worst, fraud was highly likely. However, the most unusual item on the balance sheet was an amount that was reported separate from cash — investments in bank deposits. It's quite unusual that this would be broken out from cash, and it's an indication that perhaps the auditors were provided with different documentation for these accounts than they normally see for cash. Suffice it to say, there certainly must have been a reason this amount was treated separately. The increase in the receivables accounts plus the odd cash-like account amounted to nearly $375 million. According to the SEC lawsuit on this matter, Satyam allegedly overstated revenue by over $430 million in 2008. This overstatement of revenue resulted in an overstatement of assets and provided the warning signs that "the truth" was far from it.

U.S. President James Garfield (or maybe it was Mark Twain) once said, "The truth will set you free, but first it will make you miserable." This is an accurate depiction of the unraveling of the Satyam scandal. In a letter to the board of directors of Satyam in early 2009, Raju confessed to this elaborate accounting scam and admitted that he falsified accounts and dramatically inflated the financial position of Satyam. The firm was eventually sold via a public auction process, and Raju was disgraced.

Lucy, You Got Some 'Splainin' to Do: When Companies Understate Their Expenses

One of the most basic principles of accounting is the *matching principle*. GAAP are based on the premise that a company should match expenses incurred to produce revenues with revenues in order to accurately report a company's profitability during a specific time period.

In addition to overstating revenues, companies that understate expenses appear more profitable than they actually are. Firms may defer expenses from the current period to future periods in order to understate expenses and make the current period look better. The most common example of this is extending the depreciation period for assets beyond that which is reasonable.

What a waste

The waste disposal business is commonly portrayed in movies and TV series as being corrupt and controlled by organized crime. One of the biggest accounting scandals was allegedly perpetrated not by members of the Soprano family, but by the NYSE-listed firm Waste Management. The details of this scandal may be less salacious than typically portrayed in mob movies — nobody got "whacked" — but the ramifications of the scandal were far reaching and so economically significant than the Soprano family would've been proud of the turmoil that it caused.

At the most basic level, garbage disposal is a fairly simple business, one that doesn't appear on the surface to be particularly ripe for abuse. Firms in this business collect and dispose of rubbish. Among other assets, Waste Management owns garbage trucks and landfills. However, in the late 1990s, profits were allegedly inflated to the tune of $1.7 billion by some fairly unsophisticated accounting machinations that went undetected by corporate auditors who were asleep at the switch. So, how did the executives at Waste Management pull off a multi-billion-dollar fraud?

Garbage trucks are assets the value of which is used up, or *depreciated*, over time. Companies must estimate the useful lives of their depreciable assets and take annual charges to recognize that those values have declined. If a garbage truck costs $100,000 and can be expected to be used for ten years and have no residual or salvage value, then the firm is required to take a depreciation charge of $10,000 per year to account for the decline in value of the truck. This isn't a cash expense and doesn't require any outlay of funds, but the charge will reduce net income before taxes by $10,000. If a company wanted to make net income appear better in the current year, it could depreciate the truck over a longer period — say, 20 years — and the reduction in net income before taxes would be only $5,000. This is exactly what Waste Management did. It simply extended the assumed useful lives of certain assets to an unsupported age.

As if that weren't enough, Waste Management also failed to account for some other expenses that are common in the waste-disposal business. A landfill is an asset of a waste-disposal company. But, as the landfill gets increasingly filled with garbage, the value of the landfill declines. In addition to overstating the useful lives of its garbage trucks, Waste Management also failed to account for the fact that its landfills were filling up. It should've been taking charges against the value of the landfills. Those charges would've reduced net income and made the firm appear less profitable.

Astute investment bankers should examine the assumed depreciable lives of the firm's significant assets to understand if the firm is making conservative or aggressive accounting assumptions — or, if it's just making plain unrealistic and fraudulent assumptions.

The SEC investigated Waste Management, and the firm principals agreed to a settlement that involved multiple millions of dollars in payments and banned the executives from serving as officers or directors of any public company. The firm's auditing firm, Arthur Andersen, was also fined by the SEC for being complicit in the fraud.

Crazy like a fox

Crazy Eddie was a U.S. retailer of electronic goods. The firm was founded in 1971 by CEO Eddie Antar and primarily operated in the New York City area. Many people remember the firm because of its unusual radio and television commercials telling consumers, "Crazy Eddie, his prices are insane!" The firm became part of the popular culture, and the commercials were even parodied in a *Seinfeld* episode. The company went public in 1984, and the stock price increased rapidly from its IPO price of $8 to over $75 per share by 1986. Crazy Eddie was getting rich, and his shareholders were thrilled.

Things changed dramatically in just a few years. By 1989, the firm was in bankruptcy, and Antar fled the country. He was later caught and sentenced to eight years in prison. So, what happened and what were the clues that analysts could've used to determine that Eddie was not only crazy but also perpetrating a fraud?

The accounting game that Antar was playing involved understating the cost of goods sold — the cost of the stereos and eight-track players that the firm was selling — thus, overstating his profits. In fact, Crazy Eddie overstated inventory by $65 million — more than the cumulative profits since the company went public — in order to report higher profits, please his shareholders, and line his own pockets. The overstatement of earnings resulted in an overstatement of owners' equity. The accounting equation balanced because inventory was also overstated, and no one was the wiser.

But, the overstatement of inventory was so dramatic that it should've drawn the attention of even the most inexperienced junior investment banking analyst. One of the most common ratios utilized by analysts is *days inventory outstanding,* which helps determine how efficient a firm is in managing its inventory of goods for sale. It simply measures the average number of days a company holds its inventory before selling it. An examination of Crazy Eddie's days inventory outstanding shows that it nearly doubled from 80 days to over 146 days from 1984 to 1987. The increasing number of days worth of inventory on hand is indicative of a significant problem — either problems selling inventory or an overstatement. In this case, it was an overstatement.

Missed It by That Much: When Companies Overstate Their Financial Position

The two previous accounting tricks — overstating revenue and understating expenses — are both involved primarily with the income statement providing a misleading representation of net income. Firms also have been known to do things to overstate the value of their assets or understate the value of their liabilities, making their balance sheets appear stronger than they actually are.

Those pesky pensions: The epidemic of firms understating pension liabilities

One of the biggest crises facing many city and state governments is the future pension and health benefit obligations of workers. Quite simply, these governmental entities have promised more future benefits than they likely will be able to deliver. And these benefits to retired (and soon to be retired) schoolteachers, firemen, policemen, and other government employees are staggering in relation to the budgets of these government entities.

The pension epidemic is not limited to governmental entities. Many U.S. corporations have also promised participants in defined *benefit* pension plans more than the companies will likely be able to deliver or are planning for. For clarification, a defined benefit pension plan promises the recipient a certain pre-specified benefit upon retirement. In a defined *contribution* pension plan, the amount of the employer's contribution is specified, but the future benefits are not.

Simply put, in a defined *benefit* plan the employer bears the risk that the investments set aside in the plan will be enough to cover the obligation. Any shortfall must be made up by the corporation. On the other hand, in a defined *contribution* plan, the employee bears the risk of underperformance and may find she doesn't have enough money to fund her retirement and may face the prospect of subsisting on macaroni and cheese and Ramen noodles into her golden years.

Accounting for both the pension assets and pension liabilities require several assumptions to be made. These estimates require the work of *actuaries* (business professionals who deal with the financial impacts of risk and uncertainty). (There is no truth to the rumor that actuaries are people who really wanted to be accountants but didn't have the personality for it.) Total employer contributions to a defined benefit plan are very complex to determine because they depend upon a myriad of factors, including the length of time retirees will, on average, live. The assets of a defined benefit plan are held in a pool, rather than in individual accounts for each employee. Once established, employers must continue to fund the plans, even if the company has no profits or loses money in a given year. Because the employer makes a specific promise to pay a certain sum in the future, the employer assumes the risk of fluctuations in the value of the investment pool.

As you might suspect, when assumptions must be made, there are opportunities for unscrupulous, opportunistic or just plain overly optimistic executives to game the system to their advantage. With respect to defined contribution pension plans, one must look no further than the assumed rate of *return on pension assets* to determine if the firm is being conservative or aggressive in its accounting assumptions. Higher assumed rates of return are aggressive in that there is less margin of error or safety cushion built in to absorb potential investment underperformance. In the long run, if the actual investment rate of return is lower than the assumed rate of return, the company is required to make up the shortfall.

In the short run — and remember, much of managements' incentive compensation is related to current earnings — assuming a higher rate of return on assets will allow the firm to make lower pension contributions and will increase reported firm earnings per share. If a firm assumes an 8 percent rate of return on pension assets, it will make lower current contributions into the pension fund than if it assumes a 7 percent rate of return. We won't get into the nitty-gritty of how these assumptions are determined and how much latitude is given to the firm under GAAP, but suffice it to say, some firms are more realistic than others in projecting both future pension liabilities and the size of the pension fund asset pool that will be used to extinguish those liabilities.

Historically, the common rule of thumb for most pension plans is to have about 60 percent of assets invested in stocks and the remaining 40 percent of assets invested in bonds. If yields in the bond market are around 2 percent (which they were in mid-2013) and if 40 percent of the pension portfolio was invested in bonds, to earn an assumed rate of return of 8 percent on the entire portfolio, stocks would have to provide an average annual return of 12 percent. Now, a 12 percent average rate of return on stocks is not out of the realm of possibility given history, but it is certainly an aggressive assumption and looks pretty dicey given the state of financial markets today.

The expected (or assumed) rate of return on defined benefit pension plans is found in the notes to financial statements in the annual reports and 10-Ks companies prepare for distribution to investors. Table 16-1 provides a sample of the expected rate of return on defined benefit pension plans for several of the largest companies listed on the New York Stock Exchange. You can see how dramatically different the assumptions are. And keep in mind that a difference in the assumed rate by just a few basis points can mean a difference of many millions of dollars. Note that Johnson & Johnson uses much more aggressive return assumptions than American Express. Is there any reason to believe that Johnson & Johnson will earn a much higher return on investments than American Express will?

Table 16-1	Assumed Rates of Return on Pension Plan Assets			
Year	*American Express*	*Alcoa*	*General Electric*	*Johnson & Johnson*
2010	6.9%	8.75%	8.0%	8.68%
2011	6.9%	8.50%	8.0%	8.62%
2012	6.7%	8.50%	8.0%	8.45%

The assumed rates of return on pension assets give you a clue about how conservative or aggressive the firm is being in the current year, because this assumption affects current period earnings and the income statement. Another assumption that must be made with respect to defined benefit pension plans is the discount rate used to determine the total pension liability.

The *net pension liability* (total pension liability less accumulated plan assets) appears as a liability on the balance sheet. The higher the discount rate being assumed to discount future pension liabilities, the lower the value of pension liabilities will appear on the balance sheet. So, if a firm wants to make its financial position appear stronger, it will assume a higher discount rate to apply to pension liabilities. Firms cannot simply pull these assumptions out of thin air. The discount rate should reflect economic realities — specifically, if interest rates in the government bond market are low and expected to remain low, it's difficult to justify a high discount rate.

In Table 16-2, you can see how the four firms we profile in Table 16-1 differ with respect to the discount rates they apply to pension liabilities. A pattern is emerging. Johnson & Johnson had the most aggressive assumptions with respect to assumed rates of return on pension assets and also has the most aggressive assumptions with respect to discount rates used to determine pension liabilities. Taken together, and when compared to other very large corporations, Johnson & Johnson appears to be toward the more aggressive end of determining both current pension costs and long-term pension liabilities. From this brief analysis, you can't conclude that the management of Johnson & Johnson is understating the firm's current pension costs and long-term pension liabilities, but it does warrant a closer look by analysts and is something to closely monitor moving forward.

Table 16-2   Discount Rates Used to Determine Pension Liabilities

Year	American Express	Alcoa	General Electric	Johnson & Johnson
2010	5.3%	5.75%	5.28%	5.71%
2011	4.7%	4.90%	4.21%	5.13%
2012	3.8%	4.15%	3.96%	4.25%

How extensive is the problem of underfunded pension plans largely due to unrealistic return assumptions? According to the actuarial firm Milliman, in mid-2013, total pension deficits in the 100 largest corporate defined benefit pension plans was around $226 billion, and the average plan was considered 86 percent funded. Further evidence from *The New York Times* reported that of the 500 companies in the S&P 500 Index, 338 have defined benefit pension plans and only 18 are fully funded.

Investment bankers need to look at the assumed rates of return on pension assets to get an accurate picture of the true financial health of the firm. In particular, they should be on the lookout for companies that raise their assumed rates of return on pension assets when conditions in the financial markets don't warrant such an increase. That's a red flag for future shortfalls, and it may signal other potential accounting manipulations.

As reported by Andy Kessler in *The Wall Street Journal,* this is precisely what General Motors did in the early 1990s. The company found that its pension shortfall had risen from $14 billion in 1992 to over $22 billion in 1993. So, it needed to put more money in the pension fund, right? Its investment bankers suggested a different path — that the firm raise its assumed rate of return on assets and invest a greater proportion of its pension fund in alternative assets (see Chapter 17) with higher rates of return. That way, the shortfall would disappear. So, with the stroke of a pen, GM's financial position improved. If only it were that easy. This situation portended things to come for the once proud carmaker.

We are the world

The telecommunications firm WorldCom was one of the darlings of Wall Street at the end of the 20th century. It had grown from a relatively obscure firm based in Hattiesburg, Mississippi, to one of the largest corporations in the world. Its longtime eccentric CEO, Bernie Ebbers, was consistently praised as being an innovator and one of the most influential leaders in business. Ebbers was a billionaire and lived the high life, owning several estates and other businesses across the country.

WorldCom was on the recommended lists of many Wall Street firms and was widely held by many money managers. When the alleged accounting fraud was uncovered and the house of cards folded, WorldCom filed for bankruptcy in 2002, in what at the time was the largest corporate bankruptcy ever. Ebbers was sentenced to 25 years in prison for fraud, conspiracy, and filing false documents with regulators. His infamy was cemented when CNBC named him the fifth worst CEO of all time. What happened and why were so many investment bankers, analysts, and fund managers duped by Ebbers and his accounting chicanery?

WorldCom had a number of accounting improprieties (too numerous to describe, including making personal loans to Ebbers to fund his margin calls on WorldCom stock), but the fraud that was the ultimate undoing of the firm was largely based upon a very simple notion: Expenditures were classified as long-term investments and capitalized instead of simply being charged to the current period as the routine expenses that they were. Specifically, the firm took normal expenses (in this case, *line costs,* the fees paid to other telecommunications companies for the use of their lines and satellites) and recorded them as increases in assets (property, plant, and equipment) rather than expenses. To unsuspecting investors and analysts, it appeared that the company was growing its asset base by investing in long-term assets that would be productively used for many years to produce revenue. Instead, WorldCom was simply paying "rent" for the use of the lines and satellites of other firms. The analogy to personal finance was that WorldCom was renting an apartment but booking the rent payments as equity in the apartment.

What clues did investment banking analysts miss that would've alerted them to questionable accounting practices and make them doubt the veracity of the financial results? One of the simple tools that many analysts use to discern trends in a firm is *common size analysis* of both the income statement and balance sheet. This technique involves taking an income statement and showing every line item as a percent of revenue and taking the balance sheet and showing every line item as a percent of assets. That way, analysts can look at common size statements across time to identify trends — both positive and negative in the different line items and asset classes. The goal of common size analysis is to identify what's changing and what may warrant more scrutiny.

A common size analysis of WorldCom's income statements across time shows that line costs as a percentage of revenue was steadily declining over time — falling from around 55 percent in 1996 to around 40 percent in 2001. At the same time, property, plant, and equipment as a percentage of assets had risen from roughly 20 percent in 1996 to over 45 percent in 2001. Couple that with the fact that WorldCom's chief competitors had line costs as a percentage of revenues that were fairly constant throughout the same period, at around 50 percent and, in retrospect, it's easy to see the game that the company was playing.

The message of the WorldCom debacle is that simple tools and a skeptical nature can lead the investment banker to the heart of the matter. Yet the scam wasn't uncovered until many investors had lost a great deal of money, investment banks had lost some reputational capital, and auditors had come under fire.

Keeping Investors Off-Balance

You would think that by looking at a company's balance sheet, you would get an accurate picture of all the firm's assets and liabilities and, as a result, you'd have a good idea of how financially strong the company is. Unfortunately, that isn't always the case. Firms often use accounting machinations to remove some liability items from the balance sheet — by using off–balance sheet financing or creating off–balance sheet entities — in order to make the firm appear stronger. (It's ironic that these transactions are called "off–balance sheet," because often both the intent and the result is to keep investors off balance. We'll be here all night!)

The use of off–balance sheet financing and the creation of off–balance sheet entities is not in and of itself nefarious. In theory, their creation and use makes perfect sense. However, like virtually any tool, if used improperly, they can be misleading and potentially destructive. The creation of off–balance sheet entities and the removal of liabilities from the balance sheets of many companies was a major contributing factor to the recent financial crisis and resulted in a tightening of accounting rules regarding these transactions.

What's an example of off–balance sheet financing? Companies often choose to rent rather than buy capital assets such as equipment or trucks. This is done through an *operating lease,* and the company is allowed to record only the rental payments, and not the whole cost of the asset on its financial statements as a liability. By keeping both this asset and debt off the balance sheet, the company looks more attractive — it seemingly has more debt capacity — and serves to understate the true indebtedness of the firm.

The following case studies present examples of the use of off–balance sheet items and describe some clues to alert investment banking analysts to potential problems.

Enron's special purpose

Enron was one of the largest financial scandals in history, and the name is truly synonymous with corporate greed and mistrust. The fall of the firm had significant ramifications on the accounting industry: Its auditor, the venerable firm Arthur Andersen, was dissolved as a result of its involvement with Enron. Investors lost billions of dollars, and employees lost jobs and retirement savings, largely due to some sophisticated accounting tricks. The scandal also led Congress to pass the watershed Sarbanes–Oxley Act, which enhanced corporate governance standards and increased reporting requirements for firms.

Enron was a Houston-based energy and commodities corporation that, like WorldCom, was a Wall Street favorite and appeared on many investment firms' buy lists. Enron began as a relatively simple natural gas company and evolved into an extremely complex firm that had holdings in, among other assets, pipelines and power plants, and placed huge bets in energy markets. The firm was lauded as being innovative right up until the time that the fraud was uncovered. In fact, *Fortune* magazine named Enron the most innovative company for six consecutive years. Unfortunately, it was the accountants and financial managers at Enron who were really innovative.

An operating lease is a relatively simple example of off–balance sheet financing, but the creation of special-purpose entities (also known as special-purpose vehicles) is a more complex version of off–balance sheet financing and one that played a role in many high-profile accounting scandals. A *special-purpose entity* (SPE) is most often a subsidiary company that, from a legal standpoint, has its own assets and liabilities. It's created by the firm by transferring assets to the special-purpose vehicle to carry out a defined purpose, activity, or series of transactions. The usual purpose is to finance certain assets or services. For example, an oil drilling company may set up an SPE to finance specific oil exploration projects. In effect, the SPEs have no purpose other than the transactions for which they are created. The legal form for these entities may be a limited partnership, a limited liability company, a trust, or a corporation.

Enron grew at a remarkable pace — from 1996 to 2000, revenues increased by more than 750 percent — and much of the growth centered around and was fueled by the creation and use of SPEs in a complex and dizzying array of transactions. In Enron's case, the typical SPE was created to fund a specific project, like a pipeline, and keep the debt off the balance sheet. When the pipeline was transferred to the SPE, Enron would book the projected profits from the pipeline on its books, even if the pipeline wasn't yet operational. Enron was engaged in hundreds of these types of partnerships.

 So, how could an investment banker have figured out that Enron was a financial accident waiting to happen? A major clue appears in the notes to the financial statements. Analysts often find the most interesting information not in the financial statements themselves, but in the *notes* to the financial statements. The 2000 Enron Annual Report (the last Enron Annual Report produced before the company imploded) reported nine unconsolidated equity affiliates to the tune of $5.3 billion in the footnotes — which should've alerted readers to potential problems. If a company owns more than 50 percent of a company, it must be consolidated on the parent company's balance sheet, but if a company owns less than 50 percent, it typically stays off the balance sheet as an unconsolidated affiliate. In the case of Enron, the majority of these affiliates were listed as being 50 percent owned by Enron — just below the level that would've required consolidation. (Accounting rules have now been changed, restricting companies from keeping many SPEs off their balance sheets.)

But the real clue is in the note about *related-party transactions*. A related-party transaction is simply a business deal between two parties that are joined by a special relationship prior to the deal. There are many related-party transactions common to businesses that are wholly appropriate and innocent enough — for example, a company may hire the CEO's brother-in-law to cater a corporate event. But the notes to the financial statements show that Enron was *gorging* on related-party transactions, and the related parties were the senior executives at Enron. In essence, Enron was partnering with itself. If this doesn't scream conflict of interest, we don't know what does. These arrangements allowed the firm to conceal and perpetuate the massive fraud. The following paragraph appears in the 2000 Enron Annual Report:

> In 2000 and 1999, Enron entered into transactions with limited partnerships (the Related Party) whose general partner's managing member is a senior officer of Enron. The limited partners of the Related Party are unrelated to Enron. Management believes that the terms of the transactions with the Related Party were reasonable compared to those which could have been negotiated with unrelated third parties.

Even in the convoluted legal language in which it was presented, the skeptical analyst should've smelled a rat. And some analysts did. In a *Fortune* magazine article in March 2001, Bethany McLean questioned the firm's valuation (at 55 times earnings) and business model, stating that what it does is "mind-numbingly complex." So, why were so many investors and analysts bullish on Enron? The truth is likely that Enron's stock performance had been spectacular, and much like in the Bernie Madoff case, analysts and investors simply wanted to ride the wave and not question a good thing.

Another explanation is that many analysts didn't want to admit that they didn't really understand Enron's business model. The description that Enron itself provided in the 2000 Annual Report is several pages long and virtually unintelligible. If you can't describe what a firm does in a paragraph or two, warning lights should flash. One credit-rating agency analyst, in reference to Enron's business model, was quoted as saying, "If you figure it out, let me know." When professional analysts admit they can't understand a company, it's time to abandon ship — especially when those analysts are charged with rating the creditworthiness of those firms.

A mountain of a scandal

In Greek mythology, Mount Olympus was the home of the 12 gods of the ancient Greek world. The majestic Mount Olympus is one of the largest mountains in Europe, and its namesake — the Olympus Corporation — spawned a global accounting scandal of mountainous proportions.

The Olympus Corporation is a Japanese-based manufacturer of precision machinery and optical equipment — most notably cameras — and has a long and distinguished history. Founded in 1919, shares of Olympus traded on the Tokyo Stock Exchange, and American depository receipts (ADRs) of Olympus traded on the New York Stock Exchange. An ADR is a certificate issued by a U.S. bank that entitles the holder to a certain number of shares of a foreign stock. It makes it easy for U.S. investors to invest in foreign-based companies. So, the Olympus scandal affected investors in both Japan and the United States.

In late 2011, it was discovered that Olympus had engaged in a series of complex maneuvers to allegedly keep a significant loss and, hence, a major liability off its financial statements since about 1990, making its financial position look better than it was for many years. It's estimated that the loss was slightly less than 100 billion Japanese yen in 1990. For many years, Olympus kept the loss off its own books by transferring financial assets that had declined in value to a series of companies that were not consolidated into Olympus's balance sheet. Like Enron, Olympus made use of SPEs. The loss was transferred by having these SPEs purchase the financial assets from Olympus at their accounting-book value rather than their lower fair-market value. The funds used by these other entities came from bank borrowing conveniently arranged by Olympus. What this meant was that Olympus didn't report any gain or loss on the sale.

This may have continued without being uncovered, but in the late 1990s the accounting rules changed — largely as a result of other Japanese accounting scandals — such that Olympus now had to consolidate these outside entities on the corporate balance sheet. To keep the ruse going, Olympus had to allegedly devise a scheme to avoid recognizing the losses. Olympus management engineered a plan to purchase these entities back at a price much greater than their true value and recorded the excess of the purchase price over the fair value as goodwill. At the same time, Olympus overpaid for other acquisitions, apparently paying high "fees" that could be used to further obscure the losses. As an example, Olympus acquired the Cyrus Group in a $2.2 billion deal in 2008. In conjunction with this deal, Olympus paid the highest M&A fee ever — a staggering $687 million.

So, effectively Olympus kept liabilities and losses off its books for many years (understating liabilities and overstating owner's equity) and booked assets as goodwill to make the books balance. The jig was up when Olympus had to finally recognize a loss. But it didn't give up without one last-gasp effort — it tried to label the loss as simply an impairment loss related to the numerous acquisitions.

The unique aspect of the Olympus case is that it went on for such an extended period of time. In the interim, there were many warning signs at Olympus that investment bankers chose to ignore. Certainly, the large amounts of goodwill on the balance sheet and the staggering M&A payment fee should've given even casual observers pause.

Swap meet

Everyone understands the concept of a trade or a swap. Youngsters trade baseball cards on the playground, and many economies are based on barter transactions in which goods or services or traded. In principle, *credit default swaps* are fairly simple transactions that are a type of insurance policy. The purchaser of a credit default swaps pays a premium for protection against an adverse outcome — the default of a particular financial instrument. So, if that's all they are, how did credit default swaps contribute so much to the financial crisis, and why has Warren Buffett referred to these derivative instruments as "weapons of mass destruction"?

Derivatives are simply securities whose value depend or are derived by the value of another asset. A call option on a share of stock is dependent upon the value of the share of stock.

When you think of an insurance policy, you think of being compensated for the potential destruction or loss of value of an asset that you own. For instance, when you purchase insurance on your car, you're protecting your-self financially in case something happens to your car — like it's stolen and destroyed or is damaged in an accident. Credit default swaps work like insur-ance policies. Let's say you own some bonds issued by the government of France. You can purchase a credit default swap and, in return for premium payments, you'll be paid off if the government of France defaults on those bonds.

However, there is one big difference: In the car and homeowner insurance markets you can only buy insurance on your own car or your own house. You can't buy insurance on your neighbor's car or your brother-in-law's house. The purchase of insurance is a means to hedge your exposure to adverse events — to reduce your risk. Credit default swaps, on the other hand, can be purchased (and sold) by any entity, whether it has a position in the underly-ing asset or not. In this way, credit default swaps can be used to speculate on events. For instance, if you think that the government of France may default on its bonds, you can purchase a credit default swap that pays you if that indeed happens.

Investment bankers are a very creative lot and have developed credit default swaps on just about any asset you can imagine, including sovereign debt, mortgage-backed securities, and corporate debt. Investors can take either bullish or bearish positions on the creditworthiness of entities by selling or buying credit default swaps. By the way, this is how renowned hedge-fund manager John Paulson made billions during the mortgage crisis — he bought credit default swaps on mortgage-backed securities, betting that a significant number of mortgage holders would default on their obligations. When that happened, his insurance paid off handsomely.

Now, the interesting thing about derivative markets is that they are a *zero-sum game*. The party that was on the correct side of the contract wins, and the party on the other side of the contract loses an equal amount. If I buy a credit default swap and the underlying asset doesn't default, I lose an amount equal to the premiums that I agreed to pay. The seller of the credit default swap pockets those premiums. If I buy a credit default swap and the asset defaults, I'm paid the difference of the expected value of the asset and what its liquidation value is. The potential losses of buyers of credit default swaps are limited to the premiums they pay, while the potential losses of sellers of credit default swaps can be virtually unlimited.

In the financial crisis that began in 2007, the big winners were those individuals and firms who bet against the mortgage market by purchasing credit default swaps on mortgage-backed securities. The big losers were those firms such as Deutsche Bank, Lehman, and American International Group (AIG) and clients of those firms who sold those same credit default swaps.

Selling credit default swaps is tremendously alluring for companies. The premiums they receive are immediately booked as revenue and increase the firm's earnings in the short run, while the potential negative ramifications are generally far out in the future. Plus, many people at these firms that sold credit default swaps thought there was no way these securities would ever default. Some individuals at AIG thought of this as "free money" — they collected the premiums and never thought they'd have to pay out on defaults.

The lesson to be gleaned from this experience is that investment bankers should carefully examine the disclosures that firms make with respect to selling credit default swaps. If a firm has sold credit default swaps, it potentially has large negative exposures. If the firm, on the other hand, has purchased credit default swaps, its potential losses are limited to the amount invested. Details on credit default swaps are included in the footnotes of the annual report and Form 10K.

As an interesting aside, Buffett sold some credit default swaps on municipal bonds before the beginning of the financial crisis. They may be weapons of mass destruction, but if the Oracle of Omaha sees a profit opportunity, he has shown that he will act upon it.

What Should an Investment Banker Do?

The case studies in this chapter should serve as cautionary tales to encourage investment bankers to perform due diligence on the companies they're working with. There are often time pressures to complete analyses and make decisions, and mistakes are most often made under duress. In addition to looking for the specific accounting manipulations presented in these case studies, investment bankers should heed a few timeworn axioms:

- **Trust but verify.** Just because an accounting firm has signed off on the financial statements, it doesn't mean that these statements accurately reflect the realities of the business or that the financial statements were constructed with conservative accounting assumptions in mind.

- **If it looks too good to be true, it probably is.** Exceptional financial performance is to be applauded, but an investment banker should figure out why a particular firm is outperforming other firms in its industry, or is thriving despite a lackluster economy. The corporate world is highly competitive, and a firm whose performance is truly a positive outlier is rare. Make sure that the performance of the firm is truly exceptional and not the result of "exceptional" accounting.

- **Don't invest in anything you don't understand.** One of the most basic tenets of investing is to understand what you're investing in. The world's greatest investor, Warren Buffett, has stayed away from technology companies because he says he doesn't understand them. Sometimes it's difficult to admit that you don't understand something, but many investment bankers would be well served to emulate Mr. Buffett and realize when they're outside their circle of competence. It isn't how big your circle of competence is, but how well you define and operate within the perimeter.

Chapter 17

Understanding Alternative Investments and Asset Management

*I*f you're like most people, when you hear the term *investments,* you immediately think of stocks and bonds. Stocks and bonds are the vanilla and chocolate of the investing world. There is nothing wrong with vanilla and chocolate — they're quite tasty. But just as ice cream lovers often want to satiate their palates with more exotic flavors, investors are increasingly looking to expand their holdings into assets beyond stocks and bonds. The broad class of assets outside traditional stocks and bonds is referred to as *alternative investments,* and it's rapidly gaining in popularity with both institutional and individual investors. Investment bankers are increasingly also putting together deals and offering funds in the alternative asset arena.

Knowing Your Alternatives

Alternative investments are any investments outside of stocks and bonds. Anything from real estate to precious metals, commodities, and even bottles of vintage wine are types of alternative investments that are increasingly attracting the attention of many institutional and well-heeled individual investors.

Alternative investments are often attractive from both a risk perspective and a return perspective. From a risk standpoint, alternative investments are viewed as good diversification vehicles because their returns are often not closely related to the returns from stocks and bonds. In other words, when stocks and bonds are performing poorly, precious metals like gold may perform better. Alternative investments are also attractive from solely a return standpoint, because the returns from asset classes such as venture capital and hedge funds can be greater than returns from the more traditional asset classes.

We cover four of the more popular types of alternative investments — hedge funds, venture capital, commodities, and real estate — in this section.

Hedge funds

If there were ever a contest for the most misleading naming convention, the term *hedge fund* would be a winner. The term *hedge* is defined as "a means of protection or defense." The act of hedging in finance involves risk reduction or protection against adverse outcomes. Companies producing goods or providing services that rely on certain commodities will hedge against price increases on those commodities by contracting in the futures markets to purchase inputs well in advance of production. For example, airlines will often hedge against rising jet fuel prices by contracting in advance to purchase oil in the *futures markets* (markets that allow investors and traders to bet on the price of commodities months or years from now). If fuel prices go up, the airline is unaffected because the cost has been agreed to in advance. This allows airlines to better manage costs, plan, and reduce risk.

So, a hedge fund must be some sort of vehicle that allows investors to reduce risk, right? Not hardly. A hedge fund is simply a professionally managed pool of money that is largely unregulated and can only be accessed by sophisticated (accredited) investors (see the nearby sidebar).

Whoever came up with the name *hedge fund* was a pure marketing genius, because the goal of most hedge funds is not to reduce or limit risk, but to seek high returns by taking positions in a wide variety of asset classes. Hedge funds typically take positions in complex derivative securities and strategies involving derivatives securities and often leverage highly concentrated positions.

There are a wide variety of hedge funds that pursue many distinctly different investment strategies and styles. Although some people refer to hedge funds as an asset class, they're more accurately defined by their strategies. The most common types of hedge-fund strategies include the following:

- ✔ **Long-only:** These funds are most like stock mutual funds. They buy stocks they believe are going to go up in value.

- ✔ **Equity long-short:** In these funds, managers purchase the securities of stocks they expect to go up in value while short-selling stocks they expect to fall in value. Often, these types of funds choose to specialize in particular sectors or geographical regions of the stock markets.

Sophisticated = someone who makes bank

So, is a sophisticated investor someone who eats Grey Poupon mustard and is an expert in Impressionist art? The term doesn't refer to the level of culture or gravitas of the individual. Instead, the federal securities laws define a sophisticated investor as an individual who has a net worth (excluding his or her home) of $1 million or who has earned more than $200,000 per year in each of the last two years. In essence, the securities laws attempt to limit hedge-fund investing to people of means who can afford to bear risk, because hedge funds are largely unregulated. Institutional investors like foundations or endowments are also considered sophisticated investors.

✔ **Event-driven funds:** These funds invest in securities of corporations involved in special situations such as bankruptcy, spinoffs, mergers and acquisitions, and other restructuring events. As an example, these funds buy or sell the stocks and bonds of firms involved in mergers and acquisitions — betting that some securities are overvalued while others are undervalued.

✔ **Relative value and arbitrage funds:** These funds seek to identify securities and positions that have the same risk and return characteristics and purchase the underpriced securities and sell the overpriced securities. One of the most common types of relative value funds is *convertible arbitrage,* which typically purchase convertible bonds and sell the common stock of the issuer.

✔ **Global macro funds:** These funds have the broadest investment style of all hedge-fund categories. They have no limitations on the asset classes, security types, or geographical locations of investments. They invest in whatever investments strike the fancy of the asset manager. They often take highly leveraged and large positions.

✔ **Fund of funds:** A fund of funds invests in many different hedge funds. This strategy can help reduce the risk of a single manager achieving poor performance or running off with investors' funds, because the investor's holdings are spread across many different hedge-fund managers. Although this sounds like a very prudent and risk-averse strategy, the downside is that it introduces another layer of fees — those of the manager of the fund of funds.

Managers of hedge funds are the new titans of business — the Rockefellers and Mellons of the 21st century. These new-age billionaires include John Paulson, Stephen Cohen, and James Simons, men who have amassed fortunes by achieving investment returns that often exceed market averages by wide margins.

Successful hedge funds get the headlines, but there are some major risks to investors. First of all, not all hedge funds do well, in fact, most do not. And if a hedge fund is on a hot streak, the managers know it and demand to be paid accordingly. Running a hedge fund is a lucrative business — fees paid to managers are typically 2 percent of assets under management annually, as well as a cumulative payout of 20 percent of the profits of the fund. This fee structure is often referred to as "two and twenty" and means that considering these fees, hedge-fund managers must really bring home the bacon to earn their keep. And some certainly do. For instance, James Simons' Medallion Fund at Renaissance Technologies has returned an average annual compound return in excess of 35 percent since it was established in 1988. (Before you go running out and try to invest some money in Medallion, realize that the fund has been closed to new investors for many years.)

Venture capital

Venture capital is money provided to startup companies and young firms that don't yet have a track record that would allow them to tap the more traditional sources of funds, such as bank loans or initial public offerings (IPOs). Anyone who has watched the reality TV show *Shark Tank* is getting a glimpse into the world of venture capital financing.

Essentially, venture capital is the place where the entrepreneur with a great idea and a solid business plan gets seed capital or working capital from sophisticated investors who are looking for the next big thing like Microsoft or Cisco Systems — two companies that were financed by venture capital investment.

Venture capital firms are generally structured as partnerships. The limited partners are the investors and provide the capital. The general partner manages the investments — essentially figuring out which companies to invest in.

Unlike traditional stocks and bonds, investment in venture capital is very *illiquid* — the commitment of funds is generally for a fairly long time period (generally five to ten years) and cannot be readily bought and sold. In contrast to investing in traditional stocks and bonds, venture capitalists typically take a very large ownership position in a company and play an active role by providing management expertise and closely monitoring the company's progress.

The fee structure in venture capital is similar to that in the hedge fund industry. The two and twenty compensation scheme described in the preceding section is standard fare in the venture capital world. So, for the investment in a venture capital fund to prove to be profitable, the underlying investments must collectively perform at a high level to provide both the return to the investor and cover the management fees.

Venture capital investing is a risky endeavor — the average investment proves to be unprofitable. Most young firms simply don't make it and only a select few make it big. So, successful venture capital investing is a numbers game. To justify the risks taken, the returns expected by investors are much larger than those on traditional investments that involve less risk of failure. Many venture capital investors target returns of over 30 percent per year. To hit such a lofty target and to mitigate their risk, venture capital funds often invest in a large number of young firms. If a venture capital investor provides financing to ten firms and only one of them is successful — but that one is wildly successful — the investment can be a major success.

Success for the individual firm that receives venture capital financing — and for the venture capitalist that provided the financing — is realized when the firm goes public via an IPO or is sold to another company for a huge price. That's the ultimate dream of both the entrepreneur and the venture capitalist.

Commodities

The commodities asset class includes a wide variety of goods, ranging from agricultural commodities (such as corn, soybeans, and cattle) to precious metals (like gold, silver, and platinum). While assets such as stocks, bonds, and real estate are purchased for the expected stream of revenues that will come from owning the assets, commodities don't provide such cash flows and are purchased and sold on the basis of their consumption and speculative values.

Many firms buy and sell commodities in order to hedge their natural positions in commodities — airlines buy oil in the futures markets and farmers sell wheat in the futures markets. However, many investors buy and sell commodities as investments — in effect, speculating on future prices. One of the attractions to commodities as an asset class is that commodity prices and stock and bond prices generally don't move together. This quality helps to reduce risk of a portfolio that includes commodities along with stocks and bonds.

Investors can take positions in commodities either by purchasing the physical commodity — taking delivery of 5,000 bushels of corn or 1,000 barrels of crude oil — or by agreeing to buy or sell claims to these assets in the futures markets. Investors can buy or sell futures contracts based on many commodities, and these markets are global in nature. As you may suspect, transacting in the futures markets is the preferred method because these contracts are *liquid* (they can be readily bought and sold), and the investor doesn't have to find a place to store all that corn or crude oil.

Investors generally invest in commodities either passively or actively. Passive investment is often done by taking a position in a commodities index. A commodities index is much like a stock index, and the value of the index rises and falls as the value of the individual commodities rises and falls. One of the most popular ways to gain broad exposure to commodities is to purchase a futures contract on the Goldman Sachs Commodities Index.

Diversification 101

Diversification is one of the most fundamental tenets of investing. Simply put, diversification means not putting all your eggs in one basket. Most investors look to spread their holdings around to reduce the risk of owning a rotten egg. Investment bankers have a quantitative way to determine how much diversification can be achieved from combining different assets into a portfolio. The *correlation coefficient* between two assets measures how closely the prices of two assets have moved together in the past. If two assets move exactly together — that is, when one moves either up or down, the other moves up or down in lockstep in the same direction — the assets are perfectly positively correlated.

If two assets move exactly opposite to one another — when one moves either up or down, the other moves in lockstep in the opposite direction — the assets are perfectly *negatively* correlated. Most stocks are positively correlated with each other — that is, most stocks go up and down together. Correlation is why investing in commodities is so popular among many investors. The correlation coefficient between commodities and stocks and bonds tends to be pretty low.

If investors want to attempt to beat the market and earn rates of return that exceed that of a simple index of commodities, they may look to the services of a *commodity trading advisor* (CTA; a professional money manager who specializes in commodities and, for a fee, will provide individualized advice for investors) or may invest in *managed futures* (funds of futures contracts where the typical fees are similar to those in the hedge fund and venture capital industries — that is, two and twenty).

The greater fool theory says that the prices of some assets aren't determined because an investor thinks it's worth the price but because the investor thinks he can sell it to someone in the future at an even higher price — that is, sell it to a greater fool. The greater fool theory explains speculative bubbles through time from tulip mania in the Netherlands in the 1600s to the Internet bubble in 2000 and the residential real estate bubble of the last few years. Many people believe that the price of some commodities like gold are largely determined by the greater fool theory. Warren Buffett has made the point that if you put all the world's gold together, it would form a cube about 68 feet per side. For the value of that cube of gold, Buffett notes you could buy all the farmland in the United States and about 16 Exxon Mobils, and you'd have $1 trillion left over for walking-around money. What would you rather have?

Real estate

It's ironic that real estate is referred to as an alternative asset, given that home equity is often the single largest investment position that many investors in the United States hold. Generally, though, when investors refer to investing in real estate, they're considering any holdings beyond their personal residence.

Real estate has traditionally been very difficult to invest in for several reasons, chief among them illiquidity, large minimum investment, the unique nature of properties, and monitoring and upkeep required. Investment bankers are a very creative lot, and over the years, they've developed methods for investors to more easily access the real estate markets. The two major methods are through *real estate mortgage investment conduits* (REMICs) and *real estate investment trusts* (REITs).

REMICs purchase mortgages on both commercial and residential properties, place them in trust, and then issue interests in these mortgages to investors. Essentially, they allow investors to invest in a diversified portfolio of real estate mortgages. The securities issued by the REMIC are called *mortgage-backed securities* because the collateral or backing of the securities is the real estate that the mortgages were issued on. REMICs can be designed in many different ways, and some mortgage-backed securities are much riskier than others as investors found in the recent financial crisis.

REITs are publicly traded closed-end investment funds that invest in real estate directly or through mortgages on real estate. REITs trade just like shares of stock on major stock exchanges. Investment bankers have created three types of REITS:

- ✔ **Equity REITs:** Equity REITs purchase commercial, industrial, or residential real estate properties. Income is derived primarily from the rental on the properties, as well as from the sale of properties that have increased in value. Many equity REITs specialize in a particular market segment; some specialize in a particular geographic area.

- ✔ **Mortgage REITs:** Mortgage REITs invest in property mortgages. They may make original mortgage loans or purchase existing loans or mortgage-backed securities. The income is primarily from the interest that they earn on the mortgage loans.

- ✔ **Hybrid REITs:** Hybrid REITs invest both directly in property and in mortgages on properties.

Digging Into Asset Management

Many investment banking firms have robust asset management divisions that help clients manage their money. Investment banks typically offer financial advice, actively manage accounts, provide wealth management services, and offer financial counseling. The typical clients are institutional investors and high-net-worth and ultra-high-net-worth individuals. Investment banks typically offer proprietary products such as mutual funds to assist in this role.

Investment banks, particularly the large investment banks, want to be considered a one-stop shop for clients' financial needs. Asset management services are an important product and often a very profitable product line for these firms and one that increasingly attracts a great deal of attention.

Attracting investors to asset management

Investment banks often employ armies of analysts who follow the economy, firms, and industries. These analysts craft research reports and make recommendations regarding virtually everything from the direction of the stock or bond market, to the value of individual companies, or the attractiveness of investments in certain regions of the world or industries.

Analysts typically are assigned specialty areas — specific asset classes or industries — and produce research reports with buy, sell, or hold recommendations. These research reports are distributed to both buy- and sell-side clients. Investment banks compete on the basis of their research quality and eagerly await the rankings such as Institutional Investor's All-American Research Team and Zack's All-Star Analysts Ratings. Many analysts become stars themselves and command multi-million-dollar compensation packages. Internet analysts Jack Grubman, Henry Blodget, and Mary Meeker became famous (and later infamous) in the dot-com bubble in the mid to late '90s.

Be careful when listening to the recommendations of Wall Street analysts. Research analysts are presumably giving advice to investors on whether to buy or sell securities. But remember that they're working for the investment banking firms, which make huge amounts of money for selling securities. Both Grubman and Blodget are barred from being involved in the securities business for allegedly violating their duty to investors and placing their firms' interests over their own.

These analyst reports serve functions beyond simply helping clients make investment decisions. They assist traders of the firm's own proprietary accounts in making decisions, help the firm's sales force in suggesting new investment ideas to clients, as well as provide coverage to the companies whose securities the investment bank has assisted in recent IPOs.

Creating asset management tools

In Chapter 1, we explain that some investment banking firms actually make more money on asset management than on traditional investment banking functions. To become a full-service, one-stop shop for everything financial, investment banking firms have developed a plethora of asset management tools. We cover three of the most common — stock mutual funds, bond mutual funds, and exchange-traded funds — in this section.

Stock mutual funds

Most full-service investment banking firms offer their own mutual funds as an asset management tool to clients. A stock mutual fund is a professionally managed pool of money that simply takes clients' money and invests in a wide variety of companies. The big advantages of mutual funds are diversification (investors' funds are spread across many companies) and professional management. Investment banks earn management fees for managing mutual funds.

Mutual funds are also very liquid securities. *Open-end mutual funds* must stand willing to buy back their shares from their investors at the end of every business day at the net asset value computed that day. *Closed-end mutual funds,* on the other hand, trade in the *secondary market* (the active buying and selling of stocks on an exchange, such as the New York Stock Exchange) and may trade at a premium or discount to net asset value. The share value of a closed-end fund is determined by the interaction of buyers and sellers in the marketplace — by supply and demand — much like the value of a share of stock itself is determined.

The only limit to the variety of mutual funds is the creativity of investment bankers. Here are some of the most common types of stock mutual funds:

- ✔ **Sector or industry funds:** Invest in firms within a particular segment of the market such as healthcare or technology.
- ✔ **International funds:** Invest in stocks from around the world.
- ✔ **Emerging-market funds:** Invest in stocks from developing countries.
- ✔ **Country funds:** Confine investments to stock within a particular country.
- ✔ **Growth funds:** Invest in stocks forecast to have above-average growth prospects.
- ✔ **Value funds:** Invest in stocks that appear to be undervalued based upon fundamental investment metrics, such as price-to-earnings or price-to-book ratio (see Chapter 8 for more on these ratios).
- ✔ **Index funds:** Instead of being actively managed — that is, with professional managers making decisions on which stocks to buy and sell — the holdings simply mirror the composition of an index such as the S&P 500 or the Dow Jones Industrial Average.

- ✔ **Cap-based funds:** Limit their holdings to stocks within certain *market capitalization* (the value of the entire equity of the firm) ranges. Large-cap, mid-cap, and small-cap funds have become very popular for investors to focus on the market segment they desire.

Bond mutual funds

Bond mutual funds are structured in an identical fashion to stock mutual funds and are popular asset management vehicles created by investment banks. Bond mutual funds allow investors to diversify across many holdings — something difficult to achieve outside of bonds funds because bonds generally trade in larger denominations than stocks.

Here are the most common types of bond mutual funds:

- ✔ **Investment-grade funds:** Invest only in the debt of highly rated creditworthy companies.

- ✔ **High-yield funds:** Invest in the debt of below-investment-grade companies.

- ✔ **Municipal funds:** Invest in the debt issues of state, county, city, or other nongovernmental agencies.

- ✔ **International funds:** Invest in debt issues of companies and sovereign issuers outside the United States. A variety of international bond funds invest in the debt of emerging markets.

- ✔ **Treasury-Inflation Protected Securities (TIPS):** Bonds issued by the U.S. Treasury that pay a rate of interest that is adjusted on a semiannual basis with the rate of the Consumer Price Index (a measure of inflation).

Exchange-traded funds

An *exchange-traded fund* (ETF) is much like a mutual fund; it's invested in a diversified number of individual securities. However, unlike a mutual fund, an ETF actively trades on a stock exchange, much like stocks. Although mutual funds provide investors with liquidity on a daily basis, exchange-traded funds provide the investor with immediate liquidity.

Most ETFs are index funds, but since 2008 the Securities and Exchange Commission (SEC) has allowed the creation and marketing of actively managed ETFs. Investment bankers have created ETFs on stocks, bonds, and commodities.

The popularity of ETFs has increased dramatically in recent years. Some of the more popular ETFs are the sector SPDRs sponsored by State Street Global Advisors, which follow the sectors of the S&P Index. Another popular issue are the iShares ETFs sponsored by BlackRock, which track many country and industry indexes.

Managing Potential Conflicts with Clients

Given all the different functions of investment banking and all the various clients these firms serve, it is not surprising that the industry is rife with conflicts that need to be both managed and disclosed.

The investment banking industry has come under fire recently for behavior viewed as detrimental to market integrity. Investment banks have been accused of taking advantage of their unique position in the industry to manipulate markets and line their pockets. The result has been legislation designed to lessen this chance. (You can find more on legislation in Chapter 15.)

It's important that financial markets be viewed as a fair game. If individual investors feel that they're at a distinct disadvantage, they may withdraw from participation in the capital markets, and the flow of capital through the system will be reduced and capital formation will be less effective. These kinds of market frictions serve to stunt economic growth and reduce people's standards of living.

How asset management can cause conflicts

The lifeblood of investment banking is information. Managing who has that information, how that information is disseminated, and who can act upon that information is central to mitigating the conflicts of interest created from having an investment banking operation that serves so many masters. The following represents a sampling of the conflicts that exist in investment banking firms.

Let's put lipstick on this pig

One of the biggest potential areas of conflict involves investment banking firms that both provide investment banking services to a corporate client and have analysts producing research reports with buy or sell recommendations on that same stock. The potential conflict is obvious. Investment banks could offer favorable research coverage and in return expect the company's investment banking business. Companies, on the other hand, could penalize investment banks who have unfavorable research opinions by going to other firms for their investment banking business.

Mom likes me best

Investment banks often serve somewhat of a parental role for corporations. They don't want to appear to favor one client over another, just as parents try to treat all children equally. Investment banks often broker deals between companies and between clients.

Breaking down the Chinese Wall

One of the most famous episodes in Wall Street history that allegedly stepped over the line of conflict of interest involved the dot-com bubble in the late 1990s and early 2000s. Jack Grubman was a rock-star telecommunications analyst at Salomon Smith Barney who reportedly earned in excess of $25 million one year by issuing many favorable opinions on firms and fueling the rampant speculation in the markets that led to the eventual bursting of the bubble.

The problem was that his recommendations were fraught with conflicts and appear to be based upon more than simply the firms' investment prospects. One conflict was that Grubman was both making buy recommendations to investors and allegedly providing

investment banking advice to those same firms. These firms included some of the spectacular failures of the dot-com boom such as Global Crossing, WorldCom, and Qwest. In another instance, in some e-mails, Grubman admitted that he changed his hold recommendation on AT&T to a buy recommendation in order to get his kids into a highly competitive New York City preschool.

Blodget found himself in a similar bind with regulators. In 2003, the SEC charged Blodget with civil securities fraud for allegedly publishing misleading research reports while at Merrill Lynch. Blodget found himself banned from the securities industry and agreed to a fine of more than $2 million.

In one of the most infamous cases from the financial crisis, some pundits alleged that hedge-fund titan John Paulson's bet that the housing market would crash was arranged by investment banks that specifically created packages of mortgage-backed securities at the behest of Paulson. These securities were sold to clients of the investment banks so Paulson could wager against them. By the way, this seemingly clever strategy backfired on the investment banks because they ended up not being able to sell all the mortgage-backed securities. The result? When the real estate market tanked, the investment banks were left holding big losses.

The bottom line here is that it appears to be a major conflict of interest to create securities designed to make one client fabulously wealthy, while at the same time, lining up buyers for that same security. Can someone truly serve two masters?

Say it ain't so?

Investment banks manage money for client accounts, execute trades on behalf of clients, and trade using the firm's own capital — a practice known as *proprietary trading*. Information on order flow — the buy and sell orders in the pipeline both from firm clients and from funds managed by the investment bank on behalf of others — is extremely valuable information for anyone in the markets to have. For instance, if you know that there are a large number of shares of a certain stock to be liquidated for a major client, you have a pretty good idea that the stock is likely to go down in value in the near term. Likewise, if you know that a firm is a takeover target through your investment banking analysts, you know that, chances are, the stock price will advance when that information becomes public knowledge.

There is a temptation for investment bankers to take such privileged information about what clients are doing and trade on their own behalf prior to conducting trades on behalf of their clients. This is a practice known as *front running,* and it's both illegal and unethical.

How to eliminate and manage conflicts

We know that conflicts exist in investment banking, but how can they be eliminated or managed? The following are methods that investment banks use to both eliminate and manage conflicts.

Build a wall

For investment research to have any real value, it must be independent and objective. It must be based on the facts in evidence and not influenced by any relationships between the investment banking firm and the firm being researched. The best way to prevent information flow from the mergers and acquisitions and corporate finance personnel to the sales and traders at an investment bank is to erect a *Chinese wall* — the colloquial term for information and physical barriers implemented within a firm to separate and isolate people who make investment decisions from people who are privy to material nonpublic information that could influence those decisions.

A Chinese wall can refer to both informational and physical barriers. Investment banking firms often locate personnel with different functions on different floors or in other geographical locations. Also, information systems are designed to prevent unintended sharing of information between functional personnel.

Place restrictions

Firms often place restrictions on personal trading by employees and carefully monitor both proprietary trading and personal trading by employees. Firms often place companies on a restricted list when an investment banking firm has or may have material nonpublic information on companies.

Ensure compliance

Compliance has often been ridiculed as a necessary evil of investment firms, but that's changing. As the name suggests, the compliance function at investment banking firms is charged with the task of making sure the firm is not violating any laws in conducting business. At many firms, compliance is also responsible for ensuring that personnel are operating within the bounds of the firm's code of ethics.

All investment banking firms have compliance functions, but the emphasis some firms place on compliance and education regarding acceptable practices differs greatly. For compliance to truly matter at firms, the message must come from top management.

Disclose potential conflicts of interest

Disclosure is the best disinfectant. Federal securities laws require that investment banking firms disclose certain facts and relationships that could be (or could be interpreted as) potential conflicts of interest. These disclosures help clients and potential clients get the lay of the land and allow for more informed decisions.

Things that must be disclosed include, but aren't limited to, the following:

- **Conflicts:** Whether the investment banking firm is acting as a manager or co-manager of an impending underwriting for the company

- **Ownership:** Whether the investment banking firm owns more than one percent of the common stock of the company

- **Payments:** Whether the investment banking firm has received compensation for investment banking services from the company in the past 12 months

- **Market making:** Whether the investment banking firm makes a market in the securities or derivatives of the company

Establish a code of ethics

Codes of ethics are no panacea. Enron had a 64-page code of ethics that was distributed to all employees. Take the time to read it if you need a good laugh. Having said that, a robust code of ethics that is emphasized by top management sends a strong signal that the investment banking firm takes ethical behavior seriously.

Two nonprofit organizations of investment professionals — the CFA Institute (www.cfainstitute.org) and the Chartered Alternative Investment Analyst Association (CAIA; www.caia.org) — require their members to abide by a robust code of ethics. This gives clients and other investment professionals a strong signal about the ethical orientation of these professionals and the organization that employs them.

Chapter 18

Trying Your Hand at Investment Banking with a Case Study

*C*ongratulations! You're an investment banker. Well, at least you will be one in this chapter. After you read this chapter, you'll know how to piece together the complex framework of a merger or acquisition deal. You'll need to use your cunning, and things you've discovered in other chapters, to forge a mishmash of financial data into a cogent plan for a company looking to buy another one.

Investment bankers advise companies on ways to increase their value and ultimately the value of stock held by the owners of the firm. There are many different ways that companies can transform themselves and add value for stockholders. One of the most popular methods is to grow via acquisition.

This chapter walks you through a hypothetical case involving a company growing via acquisition of another firm and illustrates some of the quantitative and qualitative factors that investment bankers and company managements consider when making these transformative decisions.

Setting the Scene

In order to solve an M&A problem, you need a good grasp on who's doing the buying, who's doing the selling, and what the parties are hoping you, the investment banker, can help them accomplish.

The acquirer

Performance Ade is one of the leading firms in the sports energy drink industry. It has been in existence for ten years and has grown from a small venture capital–financed company into an international company with a globally recognized brand name. It's a stock market darling — it commands a high earnings multiple in the financial markets — and it's considered a growth company in the mature beverage industry. Although Performance Ade is very successful in the sports energy drink niche, company management and the board of directors want to expand into other segments of the beverage industry, particularly the soft drink segment. They're seeking to diversify in order to reduce their dependence upon the sports energy drink market and to capitalize on the existing Performance Ade brand and distribution channels.

Performance Ade produces a product that is viewed by the market as a high-quality product. The company has a high degree of marketing savvy and has positioned the Performance Ade drink as a premium product that captures a large portion of the high end of the market.

Performance Ade management is working with its investment bankers to determine how best to break into the more established (and much larger) soft drink industry. In consultation, company management and their investment bankers have determined that Performance Ade can either grow organically by developing its own products in the soft drink industry, or acquire another soft drink manufacturer to jumpstart this growth. Management is open to either alternative and is looking for counsel on which path to take.

The target

The company's investment bankers did a thorough industry analysis and came to the conclusion that the most likely company for potential acquisition was Yankee Beverages, a regional soft drink manufacturer in the Northeast. Yankee has been producing a product line of soft drinks that sell under both the Yankee name and various other private-label brands in stores throughout the region.

Yankee has been in business for nearly 85 years and, although the stock is publicly traded in the over-the-counter market, the company is still managed by members of the Gilmour family, who founded it. In fact, much of the stock is still held by members of the Gilmour family, and the family controls the majority of seats on the board of directors. The stock held outside the Gilmour family is thinly traded (there is not an active market for it) and is currently selling at a substantial discount to the typical firm in the industry (as measured by a price/earnings multiple).

The P/E ratio tells investment bankers how much investors are willing to pay for a claim to a dollar of a company's earnings. The higher the P/E ratio, the more richly valued a company and its stock are. For more on P/E ratios, see Chapter 8.

The revenues of Yankee Beverages have been fairly stable in recent years; unit sales have been flat and total revenues have been expanding at roughly the rate of inflation. The company hasn't actively been looking for ways to grow its product line, and in recent years, the free cash flow produced by the company has been used to virtually eliminate long-term debt and to provide robust dividend payments to the shareholders. The company has an extreme aversion to debt, because it barely survived the Great Depression, and debt financing is inconsistent with the very conservative philosophy of the Gilmour family. What little long-term debt there is left on the balance sheet is from a program from a few years ago in which Yankee modernized its plants, installing new state-of-the-art equipment.

The Gilmour family is in a transition phase with respect to involvement with Yankee. The grandchildren of the founder are all in their seventies, and their children and grandchildren show little interest in active involvement with the family business and are pursuing other interests.

Considering the Options

Performance Ade's management team may know a great deal about mixing and marketing tasty beverages to tempt consumers with. But when it comes to lining up money, running financial calculations and thinking through a make-or-break deal, that's where you come in as the investment banker. Having to weigh all the options may seem overwhelming, but it's a job you can easily handle if you break it into steps.

Identifying the options

Performance Ade wants to grow and diversify its revenue stream and can basically take one of two paths: It can develop its own products and brands or it can acquire another existing firm (or firms). Both of these alternatives have their advantages and disadvantages.

Growing organically — that is, building its own product line — is advantageous because management can build the firm in its own image. Building or buying a firm is analogous to the decision to build or buy a home. When deciding to build a home, you can build it exactly to your own specifications — you get the floor plan, the kitchen countertops, and the exact lighting fixtures that you want. When you buy a home, you oftentimes must compromise by accepting limitations such as outdated bathrooms or kitchens that are smaller than you would like.

The flip side is that when you're buying an existing home, you can generally occupy that home sooner than is possible in the typical construction scenario. In addition, you can often buy an existing home for less than it would cost you to build one. The same is true in the corporate world — some firms are selling for less than they're "worth" to someone who can do the investment banking equivalent of painting walls, replacing countertops, and landscaping.

The buy or build decision has many factors, but it often comes down to a matter of both price and *time to market* (how long it takes for the company to have products ready to sell). Many companies lean toward the acquisition route for growth because they're looking for immediate gratification. And why wouldn't they? Most investors are very impatient and want to see growth in earnings and share value.

Looking at financing

Though it's enormously successful, Performance Ade doesn't have a great deal of *free cash flow* (the amount of cash flow from operations [CFO] remaining after paying for any needed capital expenditures; see Chapter 12). It's a growing company and it has been using its prodigious cash flow to invest in more assets — particularly property, plant, and equipment — to support its robust sales growth. The firm does not pay a dividend to shareholders and has attracted an investor base that is growth oriented and not income oriented.

 Companies typically have a particular dividend policy and stick to it. This is what is known as the *clientele effect*. That is, investors often choose to invest in companies that have dividend payout policies consistent with their own goals and objectives. For instance, because retired individuals often need to supplement their income, they often have portfolios comprised of companies that pay out a large portion of earnings as dividends. Individuals who aren't looking to supplement current income, and are looking to minimize taxation, tend to invest in companies that don't pay dividends or may pay minimal dividends. Firms generally adopt a certain dividend strategy — either a high-payout or low-payout strategy — and stick to it. They don't want to alienate their dividend clientele.

Performance Ade, however, is in the unenviable position of needing to satisfy investors' ever-increasing growth expectations. The company has been able to grow largely through increasing its share of existing domestic markets and by expanding globally. However, it's becoming increasingly more difficult to capture market share because Performance Ade is already an industry leader in the niche market of sports energy drinks.

Performance Ade isn't saddled with a great deal of debt, because the firm was financed in its venture capital stage largely through convertible bonds that, as a result of the success of the company, have been converted into equity at the option of the original bondholders. This provides Performance Ade with a great deal of unused borrowing capacity, which is a terrific option for a firm to have. This is akin to an individual being virtually debt-free when seeking a mortgage loan, car loan, or money to fund a child's education. The less debt on an individual's balance sheet — or on a firm's balance sheet — the more willing lenders are to provide them with loans because the lenders have a large margin of safety.

Creating the Analysis

Stories are nice, but in the investment banking world, decisions come down to whether the numbers work out for both parties. That's why investment bankers sharpen their pencils — or, more accurately, fire up their laptops — and design financial models that allow both the acquired and target firms to win. These models are often iterative in nature and are constantly tweaked to provide each party with a winning hand. *Remember:* The goal should be to increase shareholder value — for the shareholders of both parties.

An analysis of the financial statements

We've talked about our two companies. Now let's take a look at their financial statements, and see if we can make a deal!

Note: These financial statements are being presented in terms of thousands of dollars. There is simply no reason to get bogged down with a bunch of extraneous zeros. Doing the analysis is easier with fewer zeros, and the implications are the same. So, other than any per-share information, all the numbers are presented in thousands of dollars.

Income statements

The income statements for the most recent year for Performance Ade and Yankee are presented in Table 18-1.

Table 18-1	Income Statements for 2012	
	Performance Ade	*Yankee*
Sales	$1,651,667	$710,000
Less: Cost of goods sold	$566,667	$359,000
Gross profit	$1,085,000	$351,000
Less: Selling, general, and administrative expenses	$600,000	$200,000
Operating income (EBIT)	$485,000	$151,000
Less: Interest expense	$50,000	$6,000
Earnings before taxes	$435,000	$145,000
Less: Taxes (30%)	$130,500	$45,000
Net income	$304,500	$100,000

As you can see, Performance Ade has over 2.3 times the sales volume that Yankee has, and over 3 times the net income. The key cost categories to compare are cost of goods sold and general, selling, and administrative expenses. For a beverage company, the largest elements of the cost of goods sold will be the ingredients such as sugar, labor costs, and depreciation on the machines used to produce the product. For a beverage company, the largest selling, general, and administrative expenses are those related to marketing and promotion.

Common size analysis is a tool used by investment bankers to compare two companies who may differ dramatically in size or structure. Investment bankers doing this analysis divide every category on the income statement by sales for that firm and allow you to see how the firms stack up in comparison to one another. (See Chapter 7 for a discussion of common size analysis.)

If you were to perform a common size analysis, you would find that Performance Ade has much larger general, selling, and administrative expenses than Yankee does, while Yankee has much larger cost of goods sold as a percentage of sales than Performance Ade does. This is consistent with the fact that Power Ade is a premium product, while Yankee doesn't produce premium products, operating on a more regional basis in the store brand or plain-label space. So, Performance Ade spends a greater percentage of revenues on advertising and promotion, while Yankee spends a higher percentage on the actual production of the product.

Balance sheets

The balance sheets for the most recent year for Performance Ade and Yankee are presented in Table 18-2.

Table 18-2	Balance Sheets	
Assets	**Performance Ade**	**Yankee**
Cash	$550,560	$200,200
Accounts receivable	$275,280	$205,000
Inventory	$206,460	$150,000
Property, plant, and equipment	$1,926,960	$757,000
Total assets	$2,959,260	$1,312,200
Liabilities and equity		
Accounts payable	$344,100	$212,200
Short-term debt	$619,380	$200,000
Long-term debt	$516,150	$110,000
Other liabilities	$344,100	$90,000
Equity	$1,135,530	$700,000
Total liabilities and equity	$2,959,260	$1,312,200

Akin to the common size analysis of the income statement, the analyst can perform a common size analysis of the balance sheet. However, instead of dividing all balance sheet amounts by sales or revenues, the analyst will divide them by total assets (or total liabilities and equity). Doing this shows that the asset bases of both firms are heavily weighted toward property, plant, and equipment. In the case of Performance Ade, this isn't surprising — it's a growing firm and it has been reinvesting all its earnings in expanding the business. In the case of a more established company like Yankee, it's a little surprising — however, remember that a few years ago Yankee renovated its plants and purchased state-of-the-art manufacturing equipment.

The accounts on the balance sheet are book values and may not have a close relationship to the actual value of the assets. Generally, cash, accounts receivable, and, to a lesser extent, inventory are carried on the balance sheet at values that are very close to actual market values. However, property, plant, and equipment may have a book value that is markedly different from the actual market value. For instance, a firm like Yankee may have real estate that is carried on the books at the acquisition value from over 85 years ago! Likewise, plant and equipment may have been written down from its purchase value due to depreciation deductions, but it may have a market value that is dramatically higher than the value on the books. Investment bankers need to assess market values in acquisition situations and not simply use book values as a proxy for market values.

Structuring a Deal

Buying a whole company isn't like walking into a store and buying a gallon of milk or a dozen donuts. In that case, you simply pay the price listed and you're the proud owner of breakfast. Firms looking to acquire other firms typically must pay a premium over the current stock price to be able to purchase enough shares to control the company. The amount over the current market price of the shares is called a *control premium* and is oftentimes over 20 percent of the current market value of the equity.

To illustrate, Table 18-3 contains some additional financial information concerning Performance Ade and Yankee.

Table 18-3	Additional Data	
	Performance Ade	**Yankee**
Stock price	$51	$84
Total shares	100,000	12,500
Earnings per share	$3.045	$8.00
Market value of equity	$5,100,000	$1,050,000
P/E ratio	16.7	10.5
Net income	$304,500	$100,000

As you can see, total market value of the equity of Yankee is $1,050,000, which is computed as the total number of shares outstanding of Yankee multiplied by the current price per share of $84. The first point of note is that the market value of equity of Yankee is higher than the book value of equity ($1,050,000 versus $700,000). This is fairly common, because the average market value–to–book value ratio for companies in the S&P 500 was near 2.5 at the time of the writing of this book. Performance Ade is currently selling at 4.5 times book value, largely reflecting the high growth expectations of investors and the strength of the Performance Ade brand.

To acquire Yankee, Performance Ade simply can't write a check for $1,050,000. Upon consultation with its investment bankers, Performance Ade management believes it can acquire Yankee for a 25 percent premium over market value. Thus, the cost to acquire Yankee is estimated to be $1,312,500.

Why would Performance Ade be willing to pay a 25 percent premium over the market value of Yankee's shares? After all, the shares are publicly traded and the market has determined that, in total, the shares are worth $1,050,000. The reason is that Performance Ade believes that there are some synergies that would result from a combination of the two companies — specifically, it believes that cost savings of $150,000 per year can be achieved from combining the two firms and reducing redundant costs. This is an immediate benefit. In addition, Performance Ade management believes it can take the Yankee brand, transform it, and achieve growth well in excess of the growth that Yankee has been able to accomplish on its own.

One of the biggest reasons to acquire another firm is that the acquiring firm can make more productive use of the assets and create more value than is currently being realized. Much like a baseball team that is a third baseman or shortstop away from being a contending firm, some companies are in a position to maximize the use of assets, while others are not.

Form of acquisition

Given the lack of debt in the capital structure of both Performance Ade and Yankee, issuing debt to purchase Yankee makes the most sense. Performance Ade has tremendous unused debt capacity and has a very steady revenue stream. The consistent and growing revenue stream and operating income provides creditors with the margin of safety they need in order to feel comfortable loaning Performance Ade the money at reasonable terms. In fact, with the help of their investment bankers, Performance Ade management has been able to secure bank financing at the rate of 8 percent in order to do the deal.

The shareholders of Yankee would also likely not be very interested in receiving stock of Performance Ade in lieu of cash. **Remember:** Yankee currently has a high dividend payout. Its shareholders would likely not want to receive stock of Performance Ade, a company that currently doesn't pay a dividend. So, Yankee shareholders would likely value the flexibility to reinvest their cash proceeds in a company with a high dividend payout. Now, these shareholders will incur tax consequences and be responsible for paying capital gains on their holdings, but the premium above market price will likely placate them.

Creating pro forma statements

What will the reorganized Performance Ade firm look like following the acquisition of Yankee? Investment bankers put together pro forma statements in order to model the new structure. The pro forma balance sheet is shown in Table 18-4.

Table 18-4	Performance Ade's Pro Forma Balance Sheet
Assets	*Amount*
Cash	$750,760
Accounts receivable	$480,280
Inventory	$356,460
Property, plant, and equipment	$2,683,960
Goodwill	$612,500
Total assets	$4,883,960
Liabilities and equity	
Accounts payable	$556,300
Short-term debt	$819,380
Long-term debt	$1,928,650
Other liabilities	$444,100
Equity	$1,135,530
Total liabilities and equity	$4,883,960

Notice that there is a new account on the balance sheet called goodwill. One way that goodwill comes into existence is when a company buys another company for more than the aggregate current value of that company's specifically identifiable assets (see Chapter 7). The accounting treatment for goodwill can become somewhat complicated, but the essence is in the case of Performance Ade purchasing Yankee, the total cost was $1,312,500. Performance Ade is buying the entire Yankee company with book value of equity of $700,000. Typically, the company must determine how much the assets listed on the balance sheet are currently worth, but let's assume here that the current book value of these assets approximates each of their market values. The difference between the purchase price and the net book value of equity of $612,500 is listed on the balance sheet as goodwill. As you can see, unlike inventories or property, plant, and equipment, goodwill is not a tangible asset. A company can't raise cash by selling its goodwill.

Most investors are less concerned with what the balance sheet will look like than the earning power of the reconstituted company. The pro forma income statement is shown in Table 18-5.

Table 18-5   Performance Ade's Pro Forma Income Statement

Income Statement Line Item	Amount
Sales	$2,361,667
Less: Cost of goods sold	$925,667
Gross profit	$1,436,000
Less: Selling, general, and administrative expenses	$650,000
Operating income (EBIT)	$786,000
Less: Interest expense	$161,000
Earnings before taxes	$625,000
Less: Taxes (30%)	$187,500
Net income	$437,500

As you can see, the newly constituted Performance Ade is more profitable and more highly leveraged than it was before it acquired Yankee. It's more profitable because its return on equity has gone from 26.1 percent ($304,500 ÷ $1,135,530) to a robust 38.5 percent ($437,500 ÷ $1,135,530). It's more highly leveraged because its total debt–to–total equity ratio has gone from 1.30 ($1,479,630 ÷ $1,135,530) to 2.81 ($3,192,130 ÷ $1,135,530). What this means is that the firm has been able to increase its profitability because it's earning more on its borrowed funds than those funds cost the firm.

But Performance Ade hasn't leveraged itself to a dangerous level. The pro forma times interest earned ratio (computed by dividing operating income by interest expense) is still a healthy 4.88 times. That gives lenders a fairly large margin of safety, especially given the stable revenues of the firm. It appears that the firm even has more unused debt capacity.

The new Performance Ade would also have higher earnings per share of $4.375 ($437,500 ÷ 100,000) than it did before the acquisition of $3.045 ($304,500 ÷ 100,000). This will generally be very well received by investors, because one of the most common valuation methods is to multiply earnings per share by a price/earnings multiple to obtain an estimate of firm value.

Before you assume the market will simply apply the same P/E multiple of 17 to the new Performance Ade that existed before the acquisition, a word of caution is in order. The financial markets are populated by some very sophisticated and knowledgeable investors and analysts. They'll recognize that the increase in earnings is the result of acquiring a lower-growth soft drink business by the higher-growth sports energy drink business. The P/E multiple applied by the market will likely be somewhere between the 10.5 applied to Yankee and the 17 applied to Performance Ade. The key will be how that market assesses the chances that Performance Ade will be able to successfully grow the revenues of Yankee beyond that under the current management.

Success or Failure

Like many things in business, the success or failure of any merger or acquisition often can't be determined immediately. Although the acquisition of Yankee by Performance Ade has made the shareholders of both companies better off in the short run, only time will tell if the Performance Ade will be able to integrate the operations of Yankee into one smooth operation and build long-term value. What can't often be predicted is the inability of different company cultures to integrate because, after all, companies are not simply comprised of inventories, buildings, and equipment — they involve people and personalities. Often, you can't determine if an acquisition was a good idea until many months or years after the event was announced. It's at that time when you can compare the pro forma financial statements prepared by investment bankers to the actual financial statements of the combined operation and determine if your investment bankers were more like fortune tellers or charlatans.

Part V
The Part of Tens

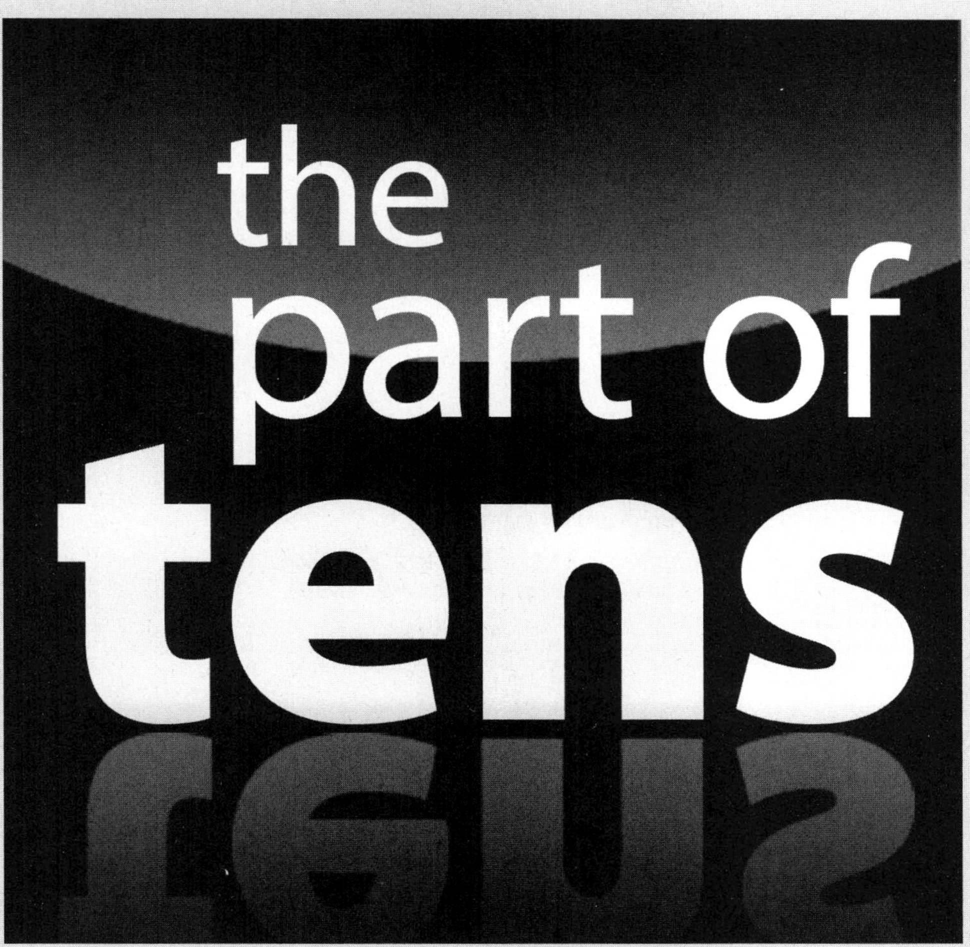

For ten ways investment banking touches Main Street, head to www.dummies.com/extras/investmentbanking.

In this part . . .

✔ Identify some of the great blowups in investment banking history so you can avoid being part of one in the future.

✔ Find out ways to make your discounted cash flow analysis even more accurate so that your analyses are more valuable in measuring the worth of a company.

✔ Pinpoint online resources so you can find additional information relevant to investment banking when needed.

Chapter 19

Ten of the Biggest Debacles in Investment Banking History

*I*nvestment bankers are supposed to be among the smartest people in the room. Many have trained at the top business schools, hired at high salaries, and live a life of great access to not only capital but knowledge.

But despite their collective brainpower, along with the talent and tools available to investment bankers, the industry has suffered some of the most egregious blunders ever witnessed in modern business. Because investment banking operations are so tightly woven with the financial system, even a minor misstep can have major ripple effects through the entire economy. A bad bet by an investment bank on an obscure financial instrument tied to home loans in Alabama can flow through the system and cause an investor in seemingly unrelated securities in California to lose money.

Such interconnectedness of investment banking with the rest of the economy is a big reason why it's so closely regulated and why the term *too big to fail* was coined. The importance of investment banking to our financial system and our economy as a whole is why investors need to not only remember some of the profession's darkest days, but learn from them as well.

The Dot-Com Boom and Bust

When it comes to the biggest black eyes ever suffered by the investment banking industry, the Internet stock bubble certainly makes the Hall of Shame as a first ballot inductee. During the late 1990s and in early 2000, demand for shares of Internet companies was raging. Investors, many of whom had never bought stocks before, saw the Internet as being the biggest engine of wealth creation since the Industrial Revolution. Investors didn't want to get left out, so they bought stock in virtually any firm with dot-com in the name.

The problem was many of the investors buying into these fledging companies, many of which didn't have any revenue — much less earnings — didn't understand what they were buying. Many investors simply didn't take the time to read the prospectuses and just piled in hoping to ride these stocks for short-term gains and then unload the shares to someone else. It truly was "the greater fool theory" in action.

Meanwhile, investment bankers were happy to keep shoveling out the Internet IPOs. Shares of companies with dot-com after their name dominated the IPO market. Many of these companies coming public had no business being public, because many of their operating models were flawed and wouldn't stand the test of time.

A vast majority of the Internet companies that went public during the late 1990s and 2000 crashed and burned in spectacular fashion. Perhaps the most dramatic way to see how much demand there was brewing for Internet stocks was by examining the massive first-day gains realized by these issues. The IPOs were priced and sold to the lucky investors at the offering price. But then, when the shares hit the stock market for the first time, investors poured in, sending the shares skyrocketing. You can see the biggest first-day run-ups in Internet IPOs in Table 19-1.

Table 19-1	Biggest First-Day Pops	
Date	*Stock*	*First-Day Gain*
December 9, 1999	VA Linux	697.5%
November 13, 1998	TheGlobe.com	606%
September 28, 1999	Foundry Networks	525%
February 11, 2000	Webmethods	507.5%
December 10, 1999	Free Markets	483.3%

Source: Jay Ritter, University of Florida (`http://bear.warrington.ufl.edu/ritter/Runup7513.pdf`)

Tainted Research Scandals

There was plenty of blame to go around for the Internet bubble of the late 1990s and 2000. Certainly, overenthusiastic and under-informed investors who piled into shares of untested and often unprofitable companies created a mania that ended very badly.

But the dot-com boom and bust also highlighted a problem with investment bankers' stock research teams. Investment bankers that provide research reports to clients are supposedly objective analysts who assess a company's prospects and advise clients on whether to buy the shares or avoid them.

It turns out, though, that in some cases the investment bankers' research divisions were doing more salesmanship than unbiased analysis. It was routine for the research arms of investment banking firms to provide glowing research on many of the same Internet companies that their firm was taking public. Outlandish price targets and earnings projections helped feed the Internet mania.

A series of investigations by the Securities and Exchange Commission (SEC) and other regulators found that securities analysts paid and encouraged investors to use their reports to help the investment bankers win lucrative investment banking business. These allegedly tainted reports lured in investors with trumped up research, just to line the pockets of the investment banks, regulators found.

And the penalties were severe, resulting in what's called the Global Analysis Research Settlements. Ten investment banks, including the giants at the time — Goldman Sachs, Merrill Lynch, and Morgan Stanley — were charged disgorgement and civil penalties of $875 million. Meanwhile, former investment bankers Jack Grubman and Henry Blodget agreed to pay $7.5 million and $2 million penalties, respectively, as part of the settlement and were both barred from working in investment banking again. Neither Grubman nor Blodget agreed or denied guilt.

Enron and the Accounting Scams

Accountants aren't known for being on the front pages. But accounting news dominated the front pages in 2001 and 2002 as bad bookkeeping and outright financial fraud were unearthed early in the decade. But investment banking got pulled down a notch, too.

Enron and WorldCom still rank among some of the biggest debacles in the financial world. These two companies ended up declaring some of the largest bankruptcy filings in U.S. history, as you can see in Table 19-2.

Table 19-2	Largest Publicly Traded Bankruptcy Filings	
Company	*Bankruptcy Date*	*Assets (millions)*
Lehman Brothers	September 15, 2008	$691,063
Washington Mutual	September 26, 2008	$327,913
WorldCom	July 21, 2002	$103,914
General Motors	June 1, 2009	$91,047
CIT Group	November 1, 2009	$80,448
Enron	December 2, 2001	$65,503

Source: BankruptcyData.com

It's hard to pinpoint the single source of blame for the accounting crises at Enron and WorldCom. But investment banking certainly played a role, especially in the Enron case. Part of Enron's downfall had to do with the company morphing from being a stable energy company to getting involved in riskier business activities, but without having the proper controls.

The Mortgage Debacle and Collapse of Lehman

Do you have a pulse? If the answer is yes, you had all it took to get a mortgage in 2006. Investment bankers, tired of the deal market for IPOs and stocks, saw the housing market getting red hot. Suddenly, investment bankers got very interested in real estate. The result was disastrous for the economy and the housing industry and proved fatal for some investment banking firms like Lehman Brothers.

The ultimate bankruptcy of Lehman (also appearing in the list of big companies filing for bankruptcy in Table 19-2) not only spooked the financial markets and helped spark the financial crisis of 2007, but killed off one of the oldest and most prestigious U.S. investment banks.

At the core of the issue was the explosion of subprime mortgage loans. In the old days, homebuyers would visit a local bank and get a loan. That bank would hold the loan and collect the interest on it. But investment banks revolutionized the mortgage business with securitization. The investment banks would make or buy mortgages and bundle them into securities that would be sold to outside investors looking for higher yields than were available for U.S. government bonds.

Lehman was especially aggressive in the area, and was focused on making loans to buyers with shakier credit, called *subprime loans.* Lehman would bundle these risky loans up and hope to sell them in a financial game of hot potato. The models used to value these securities had very many faulty assumptions — the most important assumption being that large numbers of borrowers would not default at once. But when the housing market stopped rising, the music stopped, many borrowers couldn't service their loans, and Lehman was left holding the bag.

The Flash Crash

May 6, 2010, was a regular trading day when all of a sudden crisis hit. In just a matter of minutes, the Dow Jones Industrial Average plunged a jaw-dropping 1,000 points, only to recover just as quickly. The markets were already jittery over the European debt crisis at the time, which was accompanied with civil unrest in Greece.

It took months before regulators could even begin to explain what happened to seriously rattle investors on the day of the Flash Crash. Some of the culprits included *high-frequency trades* (buys and sells entered, usually by computer programs, to take advantage of short-term swings). But the reasons for the crisis are debated even to this day.

The London Whale at JPMorgan and Barings Bank

Proprietary trading represents a significant source of revenue for most investment banks during most time periods. However, sometimes investment banks have losing streaks from proprietary trading, and it costs the firms. Large trading losses are embarrassing episodes for investment banks. After all, how can investment bankers say they're the smartest people in the room, and charge a fee to advise others on trading strategies if they lose money on their own trades? But in extreme cases, trading losses can even be so severe as to destroy a firm.

The so-called London Whale case at JPMorgan qualifies as an embarrassing episode. One of the firm's traders, Bruno Iksil with the cool nickname "London Whale," made a number of bad bets on *credit default swaps,* or financial instruments that allow investors to buy and sell risk. (For more on credit default swaps, see Chapter 16.) The bad bets resulted in JPMorgan having to report a loss of $2 billion at its original estimate, which got even bigger after all the trades were unwound. The bad moves also resulted in an investigation into the company's risk controls.

The trading losses at Barings Bank were much more severe, so severe, that they put an end to the storied banking firm that traced its roots to the mid-18th century. Barings fell apart again at the hands of a rogue trader by the name of Nick Leeson. Leeson was making aggressive bets on the speculative future market out of the bank's Singapore office.

Long-Term Capital Management

Investors have had their fair share of scares through the years. But when it comes to one of the biggest "uh-oh" moments, the collapse of asset management firm Long-Term Capital Management comes to mind.

Long-Term Capital Management was a hedge fund founded by John Meriwether, formerly a legendary bond trader at Salomon Brothers. The board of directors at Long-Term Capital Management was composed of some of the best and brightest minds in finance and included among its ranks Noble Prize winners in finance.

These high-powered financiers thought they'd found a way to outsmart the market. They used complicated trades that capitalized on differing prices of U.S., Japanese, and European bonds. The strategy relied on the relationships between the securities reverting to the mean and worked fantastically in the early years, and investors poured money into the firm.

But as quickly as things ramped up, they unraveled. Long-Term Capital Management took a hit during the 1997 East Asian Financial crisis, when many of its trades went against it. But the wheels came off in the 1998 Russian financial crisis, when the Russian government defaulted on bonds. The event sent investors scurrying to buy U.S. treasuries and dump Japanese and European bonds. That was something the Long-Term Capital Management team didn't foresee and their fancy models didn't anticipate. This resulted in the implosion of their trading system. As Long-Term Capital faced big losses, it was forced to sell its positions putting the market in a tough spot. Long-Term Capital was so interwoven in the financial system, and counted many investment banks as customers and counterparties, that its poor health was a threat to the system.

At one point, several massive investors including Warren Buffett offered to bail out the firm. But those efforts were declined. Things got so ugly that the federal government stepped in to organize a bailout including funds from many of the top investment banks.

Long-Term Capital Management offered an early glimpse at how interconnected the financial system is. Essentially, LTCM was the genesis of the concept of "too big to fail."

Bankruptcy in Jefferson County, Alabama

Municipal bonds, as described in Chapter 11, are supposed to be among the safest investments around. They're designed to be decent investments for widows and orphans. Very few municipal bonds have suffered a default.

But the muni bond market suffered a massive shock in November 2011, when Jefferson County, Alabama, filed for bankruptcy. It was one of the biggest ever municipal bankruptcy filings, involving debts of more than $3 billion.

The county's woes were connected to the construction of a sewer system that was supposed to cost about $300 million, according to the BBC. But it turns out the system ended up costing $3.1 billion due to construction problems and bum investment bets on bonds and derivatives. The SEC wound up charging J.P. Morgan Securities and two of its former directors of "an unlawful payment scheme" that allowed them to profit from Jefferson County's bond offerings.

Although municipal woes are extremely ugly, they're not unheard of. The idea that a county the size of Orange County, California, could file for bankruptcy protection was almost unimaginable until 1994. That year the county in Southern California went that way, creating a permanent stain on the once pristine world of municipal bonds. A series of bad bets on risky investment products called *derivatives* were largely to blame. Yet the prize, if you can call it that, for the biggest municipal bankruptcy occurred on July 18, 2013, with the city of Detroit. Detroit's bankruptcy filing was estimated to involve debt valued at upwards of $20 billion.

IPO Allocations with CSFB

When companies go public, it's an exciting time for the CEOs, management teams, and other employees. But it's also a big win for investment banks and their clients. Investment banks as part of the underwriting process will get shares of the IPO. And during heady times, these shares are like the Golden Tickets in Roald Dahl's classic book, *Charlie and the Chocolate Factory*. There have long been investigations into whether investment banks have used their shares of lucrative IPOs to curry favor with other executives to win additional investment banking business.

A landmark settlement in this area arose in January 2002, when the SEC filed charges against Credit Suisse First Boston for "abusive practices relating to the allocation of stock in 'hot' initial public offerings.'" The firm paid a $100 million resolution. Among the infractions, according to the SEC, CSFB "extracted" some of the profits its customers gained by quickly selling Internet IPOs like Gadzooks Networks and MP3.com. The SEC said that CSFB gave shares of hot IPOs to more than 100 of its customers, who returned 33 percent to 65 percent of their IPO profits to CSFB. "CSFB wrongfully obtained tens of millions of dollars in IPO profits through this improper conduct," the SEC found.

Bad Mergers and Acquisitions Like AOL Time Warner

Investment bankers love mergers and acquisitions (M&A). These deals generate huge fees for the investment bankers as companies buy and sell each other in an effort to create value for shareholders.

But while M&A are hugely profitable for investment bankers, and one of their top lines of business, the track record of M&A deals isn't all that great. Although difficult to quantify, there's no shortage of mergers that go wrong. When a company announces plans to buy another company, it will generally see immediate destruction of shareholder wealth and a reduction of its stock price.

Even today, the combination of AOL, the Internet content and access company, with media giant Time Warner is a poster child for M&A deals gone wrong. At the time of the deal, AOL was known as America Online. America Online paid an estimated $124 billion to buy Time Warner in the deal announced in 2000 just before the Internet bubble burst.

But the deal failed to produce any significant benefits for either firm. AOL, facing competition for access from telephone and cable companies, saw its cash cow of selling monthly access drop off. On May 28, 2009, Time Warner announced it would spin off AOL into a separate company on December 9, 2009, after failing to find another company to buy it. Time Warner's 95 percent stake in AOL was worth $6.3 billion based on estimates at the time. That marked a remarkable destruction in value from the price paid.

Chapter 20

Ten Ways to Improve a Discounted Cash Flow Analysis

*I*nvestment bankers spend a great deal of time constructing financial models on spreadsheets and manipulating them to arrive at values for companies, divisions, and potential projects. These models are often very complex and involve many assumptions and inputs. This chapter provides some ideas on how investment bankers can improve their analyses and deliver greater value to clients.

Financial Analysis Isn't Physics

In many disciplines mathematical calculations need to be carried out to several significant digits and the results applied to complex processes. For instance, when NASA is launching rockets to "infinity and beyond," calculations involving satellite orbits and descent angles need to be exact. Minor mistakes can be disastrous and result in aborted missions and losses of millions of dollars. Likewise, when engineers are building bridges and buildings, the calculations need to be quite precise. Given that physics and engineering are two of the more popular backgrounds for investment bankers, it isn't surprising that many young investment bankers bring that precise quality to the spreadsheets when building their financial models.

Should that sales growth rate be 7.65 percent or 7.6 percent? Should the after-tax cost of debt be 5.35 percent or 5.37 percent? These types of questions on inputs to the financial models are often agonized over, and models are revised with very minor changes. But financial analysis isn't physics. The goal of any financial model is to provide a very rough *estimate* of the value of a company, division, or potential project — not a precise value.

One of the biggest mistakes investment bankers make is to provide clients with an "illusion of precision." Determining that the value of a share of company stock is $95.47 or that the internal rate of return on a project is 22.47 percent gives the false impression that the calculations are exact and can be trusted. In reality, the final number is the result of many estimates on many different parameters.

Many very successful investors, including Warren Buffett, Benjamin Graham, and Seth Klarman, focus on a concept called *margin of safety*. This simple notion is that investors should not purchase a stock because they believe it is worth $95.37 a share and it's selling in the market for $91.25. Instead, investors should buy a stock with a market price of $91.25 a share that they believe is worth in excess of $140. In other words, many of the assumptions the investor made in computing his value may be overly optimistic, yet there is enough wiggle room that the investment will still make him money even if his optimistic projections don't pan out.

Show Your Sensitive Side

Manipulating financial models involves making numerous assumptions on many variables. Sales growth rates and gross margin percentages are just two of the multitude of parameters that investment bankers need to forecast when making their cash flow forecasts.

What investment bankers realize, however, is that not all values entered into financial formulas are created equally. Some inputted values have a much greater impact on bottom line estimates than others and it's incumbent upon investment bankers to realize which estimates are more critical than others. They'll then focus their efforts on making sure they spend more time on the more critical inputs than the less critical ones.

The way investment bankers can discover which inputs truly matter is to perform a *sensitivity analysis*. With a sensitivity analysis, the analyst will simply vary one input at a time and see how much the bottom line cash flow forecast is affected — for instance, changing the sales growth rate from 8 percent to 9 percent, or changing the gross margin percentage from 20 percent to 21 percent.

If changing the input has a negligible effect on the cash flow estimate, the analyst knows she doesn't need to expend a great deal of time and effort making sure she has the best possible estimate of that variable. However, if a small change in an input results in a large change in the cash flow estimate, that's a signal that the investment banker should invest a great deal of time and effort making sure that she can justify that particular input. Identification of the critical variables through sensitivity analysis will add a great deal of value to the process of estimating cash flows.

Monte Carlo Isn't Just for High Rollers

The advent of high-speed computers with large data storage ability has been a boon to investment bankers and their model making. Although any investment banking deal that is made will have only one ultimate outcome attached to it, technology allows investment bankers to develop financial models to provide a more complete analysis of potential outcomes of an investment banking deal and provide clients with a probability assessment that a deal will be profitable or have a return that exceeds a certain dollar amount or percentage return.

The goal of *Monte Carlo analysis* is to simulate the process for a particular investment and run the analysis over and over again to obtain a range of likely outcomes to assess the attractiveness of a given investment. The investment banker and client can then make a more reasoned decision regarding a specific investment opportunity.

With Monte Carlo analysis, the key is, of course, the financial model. The model should provide estimated ranges and probabilities for key variables — such as sales, interest rates, and the like. The model should also have important interrelationships (or correlations) between various inputs embedded in it. For instance, in certain industries when interest rates are high, sales may be low, or when interest rates are high, fuel prices may be high.

In Monte Carlo analysis, the financial model is run literally thousands of times — ten thousand or more "What if?" simulations being generated is typical — and the results are summarized in a *probability distribution* of returns. This probability distribution is likely to look like what we all know as a "bell curve," often associated with education and grading on the curve. The client and investment banker can make a more informed decision about the likelihood of success of a particular project. More important, perhaps, they can see the likelihood of failure and the potential cost of failure in terms of dollar amounts. They can also assess whether they're willing to accept a worst-case scenario.

What Can Go Wrong Will Go Wrong

The poet Robert Burns once wrote that "the best laid schemes of mice and men often go awry." He obviously wasn't referring to investment bankers' cash flow forecasts, but he certainly could have been. Investment bankers are often prone to making overly optimistic projections regarding cash flow forecasts and underestimating the risks of things not turning out the way they would like them to. Investment bankers often talk about pro forma financial statements. *Pro forma* simply means "for the sake of form." But how often do things go as to form?

How does an investment banker take into account the unexpected? After all, if you could anticipate something, you would input that into your model. Investment bankers aren't required to be omniscient regarding unanticipated circumstances, but recognition that things likely won't turn out as expected is important. There is no systematic or quantitative methodology to factor in the unexpected — remember, there are elements of both art and science to investment banking. The best remedy for the investment banker is to adopt a conservative bias in estimating cash flows. This may involve slightly tempering assumptions — perhaps something as simple as making a sales forecast a percentage point or two lower.

Adopting a conservative bias in making estimates will lessen the chance that the client and investment banker will be negatively surprised and a relationship either strained or severed. Clients rarely complain when a deal turns out better than expected. Unless, of course, the client is a firm whose IPO immediately doubles in price and the firm believes that it left a lot of money on the table.

It's Tough to Make Predictions, Especially about the Future

Many wonderful quotes have been attributed to that great American baseball player and philosopher Yogi Berra, but none more fitting to the investment banker than "It's tough to make predictions, especially about the future." While Yogi was more at home behind home plate than in an investment banking war room, investment bankers should consider his sage wisdom.

Many financial spreadsheets manipulated by investment bankers involve estimating and discounting cash flows for 5, 10, and even 15 years into the future. They involve assumptions about future sales growth that can be accurately characterized as nothing better than "wild guesses." In fact, much of the value of the Internet companies that sold shares to the public in the late 1990s and early 2000s was estimated to be realized from cash flows that were only going to turn positive several years into the future. In the case of these firms, the positive cash flows never materialized.

Most analysts agree that it's very difficult to project a company's earnings over the near term — the next quarter or year — much less several years into the future. In fact, the accuracy of financial forecasts — like other forecasts — decline with their time horizon. It's much easier, for instance, to estimate Coca-Cola's earnings next year than three years from today. Too much can change in the economy and industry that make yesterday's forecasts wildly inaccurate. Imagine trying to predict the future earnings and cash flows of mortgage lenders in, say, early 2006.

The takeaway for investment bankers of the difficulty of predicting the future is to shorten the time horizon of many models. Focusing on the near term — the next three years — and simply making a conservative assumption about long-term future growth will serve the analyst better than projecting cash flows over an extended time period. In the case of financial models, simpler is often better.

The Investor of Today Doesn't Profit from Yesterday's Growth

Investment bankers want to view the world out of the windshield instead of the rearview mirror. Yet, there is so much historical information available and the easiest assumption to make is that the past will continue into the future. It may seem as good a place as any to start in coming up with a sales growth estimate for next year for a firm that realized 18 percent sales growth last year is 18 percent, but such an assumption is fraught with peril.

What simply extrapolating past growth into the future fails to take into account is a simple truism in economics: High returns in a particular industry often attract new competitors, and the influx of new competitors drives down returns in that industry. Quite simply, that's the basis of the competitive free market economic model.

Now, the influx of new competitors is driven by how easy it is to enter and succeed in a particular market — in effect, how high are the economic barriers of entry in a particular industry. Some industries have lower barriers to entry than others. For instance, if a particular kind or style of food becomes popular, you'll see many restaurants serving that kind of cuisine springing up and the returns in that industry tend to fall. On the other hand, the aerospace and nuclear energy industries have very high barriers to entry due to the investment in plant and equipment and the long lead time it takes to enter a market and compete.

Justifying abnormally high growth rates in industries with high barriers of entry is much easier than it is in those industries with lower barriers to entry.

As shown in Chapter 14, those barriers to entry may also involve brand names, as well as physical investment. Coca-Cola and PepsiCo have built huge economic moats. These economic moats — big advantages the companies have that are difficult to copy, like brands — make it very difficult to compete with those two goliaths in the soft drink industry. Economic moats can be huge barriers to new competition, even though the physical barriers to entry in the soft drink industry are quite modest.

Garbage In, Garbage Out

With all the detailed financial models and computing capacity available to investment bankers, how can they make mistakes? How have financial pros been so wrong about valuing the complex real estate securities — mortgage-backed and asset-backed financial instruments — that were central to the recent financial crisis? How did investment bankers and the ratings agencies (like Moody's and Standard & Poor's) miss the boat on the valuation of these securities and not anticipate the housing bubble disaster that ultimately befell the residential real estate market?

The simple answer is that the valuation models that both investment bankers and the ratings agencies used to value and rate these securities had a fatal flaw: They failed to take into account the likelihood that one mortgage will default is related to (or *correlated* with) the likelihood that many mortgages will default.

In statistical terms, the likelihood that you'll default on a mortgage is not independent of the likelihood that your neighbor will default on a mortgage. They're positively correlated — and highly positively correlated at that. This is due to the fact that, among other factors, the valuations of real estate in a particular area are very much related to each other. When the market in a particular area softens, the valuation of all properties in the region falls even though some properties may decline in value more than others.

When various entities were valuing these securities, they relied on the same principle that insurance companies use to price car insurance. That is, insurance companies know that some policyholders will experience losses, but that the large pool of policyholders allows the company to diversify and predict fairly accurately the level of claims. This is because auto insurance claims typically aren't highly related to each other. This is not the case with valuing a large pool of mortgages. The probability of default on any one mortgage is related to the probability of default on other mortgages.

The complex financial models employed by many of the firms involved in the financial crises failed to take that relatively simple relationship into account. And the results were disastrous. The moral of the story is that no matter how intricate the financial models are, if they're flawed then it's simply the case of "garbage in, garbage out."

Rates Are Falling — It's a Better Deal!

The mathematics of valuation seem to make it clear that when interest rates are low — or are in the process of declining — investment banking deals look more attractive. The cash flows are in the numerator of the valuation equation, and the discount rate is in the denominator. When interest rates are low or are falling, the analyst is dividing the cash flow by a lower number and — *voilà!* — the valuation is higher.

But, the linkage between interest rates and valuations isn't as direct as it seems, and lower interest rates aren't always better for the investor and the investment banker. In fact, investment bankers are often seduced by lower interest rates, and the volume of investment banking deals generally rises with falling interest rates.

Investment bankers need to be very careful and recognize that the level of interest rates affects *both* the numerator and the denominator in the valuation equation. Falling interest rates are a reflection of a lower level of economic activity, which may be a signal for the investment banker to rein in the often overly optimistic cash flow estimates.

There are two types of analysis that many stock analysts employ — *top-down* or *bottom-up* analysis. Oftentimes, the analyst adopts one orientation at the exclusion of the other. In top-down analysis, the analyst starts first with a projection of general economic activity, proceeds with an industry or sector analysis, and, finally, does an analysis of a company. In bottom-up analysis, the analyst begins with the company. Neither type of analysis is right or wrong — they're simply different ways of getting to the same place. However, the danger of ignoring or mitigating the broad economic effects is that the analyst may ignore why rates are low and fail to adjust cash flow projections accordingly.

Read Your Putt from Several Angles

Investment bankers often have a vested interest in making a deal happen. After all, they're paid to generate ideas for deals and to shepherd them through to fruition. If investment bankers can convince a client firm that the best course of action is to acquire another company or to spin off a division of the existing company, this leads to investment banking deals taking place, generates fee income for the investment banker, and results in higher year-end bonuses and larger bank accounts for the investment banker.

However, just like a golfer who is well advised to read the break of a putt from several angles, the investment banker is well advised to look at the attractiveness of a deal from not only the investment banker's perspective but also the company's perspective.

Too often, the cash flow estimates from proposed deals are developed under very rosy assumptions — those that make the deal appear more attractive and, thus, more likely to happen and benefit the investment banker in the short-run. Investment bankers may appear to win if they can convince clients to do deals — and, to some extent that's true in the short term. But these investment bankers may win the battle and lose the war. In other words, they may sully their reputations by encouraging firms to engage in ill-conceived deals. The investment banking industry is a pretty small community, and firms' reputations follow them. It's better in the long run for investment banking firms to pass on some potential deals by developing cash flow forecasts that are more realistic and less optimistic.

The Weighting Is the Hardest Part

After cash flows from a firm or project are determined, they must be discounted back to a present value at the cost of capital. That is the method by which value is estimated and drives the entire valuation process. Chapter 12 describes the concept of weighted average cost of capital (WACC) and how it represented the average cost of a firm's sources of financing. The concept of WACC is very simple — the average cost of capital is a weighted average of the individual component costs. But things are rarely as simple as they seem. Investment bankers can and do differ upon the weights of each component cost of capital and how those weights are computed.

Most analysts agree that basing the computation of WACC on book values of debt and equity is flawed. A better weighing scheme is based upon market values instead of the historical book values that you'll find on financial statements. So, if the market value–to–book value ratio is two-to-one for a given firm, that firm actually has twice as much equity as it would seem by simply looking at historical book values listed on the financial statements. Likewise, if interest rates have risen substantially since debt was issued by the firm, the book value of debt could overstate the true amount of debt in the capital structure of the company.

A second point of contention among investment bankers centers around using current weightings in the computation of cash flows versus using *target weightings* — weights the firm is likely to have in the future. If the investment banker believes a firm is changing its capital structure — and investment bankers are often well informed as to this fact because they often work with the firms on altering their capital structures — then using target weights makes the most sense to generate a WACC estimate.

Chapter 21

Ten (Or So) of the Best Online Resources for Investment Bankers

In This Chapter

▶ Finding online resources for investment bankers

▶ Understanding the roles of professional systems and websites

▶ Locating government statistics important to financial markets

▶ Tracking down important financial information

*L*et's face it. Investment bankers are armed with some of the best technology and financial tools available on the planet. Traders, underwriters, and investment bankers of all sorts are likely to have access to some high-powered information system on their desk. Just about any banker's desk would be bare without a Bloomberg or Reuters terminal, or access to professional online services like S&P Capital IQ.

But here's the rub: These high-end professional services are priced well beyond the means of the curious, regular investor who wants to peer into the world of investment banking. That doesn't mean all the information that investment bankers use is locked up behind the walls of premium priced services, though.

Investors who are curious about the data that matter most to investment bankers, but aren't prepared to pony up thousands of dollars a month to access high-end systems, can still get a glimpse. Several advanced financial websites provide access to many of the same pieces of data that investment bankers stay glued to regularly.

Bloomberg

Bloomberg is one of the world's leading providers of financial data. The company maintains data on just about any security, debt, or equity, that's been sold. Investment bankers use Bloomberg, running on a dedicated machine or on their existing PCs to monitor every move in the financial markets. But Bloomberg is not designed to be used by individual investors, as it's priced at levels only large firms can really afford.

But, for those interested to see what's inside these machines, Bloomberg operates a very powerful and capable website at www.bloomberg.com. The website provides a valuable slice of the data that's on its full-fledged system, including:

- **Market data:** If you want to get prices of just about any security that trades on the planet, Bloomberg.com will provide that to you. Not only can you find prices of all the stock market indexes, but investors can also get up to-date-prices on foreign markets, currencies, bonds, and *futures contracts* (financial contracts to buy or sell assets at a preset time in the future at a preset price).

- **News:** Markets can move very quickly based on developments in the capital markets. Bloomberg News highlights news that is relevant to the markets. News is organized into categories, including information about stocks, bonds, and currencies.

- **Company-specific data:** The full version of Bloomberg contains almost limitless data on companies, including just about any financial ratio you can imagine. A good portion of these data are also at Bloomberg.com. Many of the more common financial ratios, such as price-to-earnings, are calculated for you.

- **Interest rates:** Monitoring interest rates on securities sold by companies, governments, and cities is a critical element of investment banking. Securities are sold so they're competitive with other comparable securities, so monitoring rates is essential.

Reuters

Reuters and Bloomberg are archenemies and are constantly battling for desk space at the offices of the nation's investment bankers. But the two also have a strong rivalry online, which is a benefit for anyone interested in getting more data but not paying for premium professional services.

Reuters is perhaps best known as being a news service that covers all sorts of events, not just financial developments. But the website (www.reuters.com) also contains very valuable information for investors.

One of the website's strongest points is its excellent database of company-specific financial ratios. Not only does Reuters calculate the ratios, but it also compares a company's ratios to the industry and sector the company operates in.

If you want to get comfortable with financial ratios, but some of the formulas seem a bit onerous to calculate just from the financial statements, get started at Reuters.com. The ratios are a bit hard to find, but these steps should help. From `www.reuters.com`, enter the company's name in the Search News & Quotes box in the upper right-hand corner of the screen. Wait for the company's name and ticker symbol to appear in a pop-up menu that displays below the Search News & Quotes box and click the ticker symbol. Next, select the Financials tab and you'll be treated to a treasure-trove of data.

Standard & Poor's

S&P Capital IQ is a web-based tool that's a hit with investment bankers. This tool allows investment bankers to dig deeply into the financials of companies, see who the big players are, and monitor business transactions.

Separate from S&P Capital IQ, though, S&P operates `www.standardandpoors.com`. The site, which is largely free as long as you register, allows you to access some data that's collected by financial-data juggernaut, Standard & Poor's.

The website is especially strong in two key areas: debt credit ratings and index research. S&P is one of the largest providers of credit ratings on debt issued by companies and governments. If you register for the service, you can see how high, or low, various debt issues are rated. Knowing the credit rating of a company can be very important when comparing the interest rates on different securities.

Meanwhile, S&P is also one of the largest providers of stock market indexes through its S&P Dow Jones indices unit. At `www.standardandpoors.com` you can get all sorts of information about important market benchmarks like the S&P 500.

Renaissance Capital and IPOScoop.com

Initial public offerings are among the more important functions that investment bankers provide. Allowing young companies to sell stock for the first time, for instance, allows entrepreneurs to tap the capital markets.

But the IPO market is a very fickle one and investment bankers must monitor it closely to understand whether investors currently have an appetite for new companies. Two excellent online resources for all things IPO related are Renaissance Capital (www.renaissancecapital.com) and IPOScoop.com (www.iposcoop.com). Both of these websites provide tools to help you understand what kinds of companies are going public, how much money they're raising, the sort of multiples of earnings they're commanding, and what kinds of interest they're getting from investors.

Some examples of IPO data you can get from these sites include the following:

- **IPO Calendar:** The IPO calendar is the much-watched list of companies that are very close to selling stock in the IPO market. Both Renaissance Capital and IPOScoop.com gives a list of the companies that are expected to *price,* or sell shares to investors at the offering price, in the coming week.

- **Performance data:** IPOs are very cyclically driven. As soon as investors' desire for new companies starts to open up a bit, investment bankers are eager to sell more shares to the public and bring more companies to market. Investment bankers watch closely how IPOs are doing in their trading on the secondary market compared with the offering price. When they're doing well, investment bankers bring out the deals.

- **Market data:** It's one thing to understand how individual IPOs are doing, but quite another to get a feel for the whole market. Renaissance Capital provides comprehensive data on the number of IPOs that are being conducted.

The Securities and Exchange Commission

Just as anyone who plays a sport knows, it's only possible to win if you know the rules. And when it comes to investment banking, the rules and the rule maker mostly come from one place: the Securities and Exchange Commission (SEC).

The website of the SEC (www.sec.gov) is a bonanza of financial and securities market data. You read about using the site's EDGAR system in Part I of this book. EDGAR is a free way to obtain all the financial statements filed by companies and other investors and borrowers.

But the SEC website has more information that's useful to individual investors. You can also use the site's search tool to find any rulings or settlements that came from the SEC. For instance, the site contains the details of the massive settlement against investment bankers for their research during the Internet boom.

Moody's

If you were going to lend money to someone, you'd probably want to have a decent idea ahead of time if the borrower was reliable. Rating the credit worthiness of borrowers is exactly what Moody's (www.moodys.com) does. The company employs armies of analysts who are supposed to dig into the financial records of borrowers to tell investors how likely those borrowers are to repay the loans.

Moody's provides most of its data and information to paying subscribers. But the website can be a useful resource because it provides, for free to registered users, broad trends on companies' financial strength in addition to data on the macro economy.

For instance, registered users can look up companies that Moody's rates and see their credit ratings. Additionally, Moody's provides most of its broad economic information, charts and forecasts on the website.

FreeStockCharts.com

Understanding the pricing trends of securities is a good way for investment bankers to sense the mood of investors. And when it comes to tracking movements of stock prices, it's hard to beat a good old-fashioned stock chart.

Most financial websites provide stock charts. And the tools on S&P Capital IQ, Bloomberg, and Reuters professional services are tough to beat. But as far as web-based stock chart tools go, FreeStockCharts.com is tough to beat. The site provides powerful tools that allow users to quickly pull up stock charts. Another key feature of FreeStockCharts.com is the ability to download stock price data going back decades into a spreadsheet for further analysis. This function can allow investment bankers to perform historical ratio analysis on data.

Index Fund Advisors

Investment banks have a much longer history than many people appreciate. But the same could be said about various investments.

The Index Fund Advisors website (www.ifa.com) is kind of a history book of the annual of financial performance. It's mainly designed for individual investors looking for financial guidance. But investment bankers can find an impressive collection of historical data on stocks, bonds, and foreign market stocks by selecting the Calculators tab at the top of the page. Investors can see not only what the returns on stocks and bonds have been going back all the way to the 1920s, but also how risky they've been.

Morningstar

Morningstar is one of the leaders in providing analysis on mutual funds and other investments. The company offers its data in many forms, including premium-priced data services aimed mainly at professional financial advisors.

But the Morningstar website (www.morningstar.com) is also a valuable resource for investors looking to dig more into investments being pitched by investment bankers. One of the most powerful tools of the site is the ability to enter the name or symbol of any mutual fund and get a complete rundown of that fund.

For mutual funds, for instance, Morningstar shows you how the fund has performed over different time periods and how it has fared against the market and other similar funds. You can also see what the fund's biggest holdings are and what dividend it pays to investors.

Bureau of Labor Statistics

Investment bankers who only pay attention to the security they're trying to sell or the company they're trying to pitch are exposed to great risk.

Investment banking is highly sensitive to trends in the broad economy. During a soft economy, investment bankers find a muted appetite for many of their offerings. It's a bit of an occupational hazard.

That means tracking the broad economy is part of an investment banker's job, even if it's not in the job description. The Bureau of Labor Statistics website (www.bls.gov) is home to many of the key data points that investment bankers monitor.

There's nothing to stop you from jumping on the BLS site the second a piece of data is to be released and getting the number. But sometimes, that number in itself doesn't tell you much. It's important to look at how the piece of financial data changed and how that change diverges from analyst expectations.

For instance, more important than the overall unemployment rate is the change from the previous period. Similarly, investment bankers like to compare economic data points to what was expected. Briefing.com (www.briefing.com) is a helpful source for investors looking to know what economists were expecting from various indicators. Using the Briefing.com estimates will tell you if the numbers from the BLS are better, worse, or in line with expectations.

Department of Commerce

The U.S. Department of Commerce maintains a variety of data sources important to investment banking activities. A number of Commerce Bureaus are of upmost importance, including the following:

- **Bureau of Economic Analysis (BEA;** www.bea.gov**):** If you're looking for any data having to do with the economy, it's likely to be kept and tracked by the Bureau of Economic Analysis. You can find data on everything ranging from gross domestic product (GDP) to personal income and corporate profits. The BEA also maintains statistics on industries and geographic regions.

- **Economics and Statistics Administration (ESA;** www.esa.doc.gov**):** This portion of the Commerce Department is in charge of collecting and spreading national economic indicators. The unit generates a variety of economic reports including retail sales, international trade, and manufacturers' shipments.

- **Bureau of Industry and Security (BIS;** www.bis.doc.gov**):** This bureau is in charge of examining business activities to make sure parties are adhering to treaties and that export controls are working. The site contains information about international commerce and proposed business rules.

Federal Reserve

Investment banks like to think they're all-powerful. And to some degree, they're right. After all, investment banks have a big hand in determining which businesses, cities, and other ventures get the money to expand and grow, while others don't.

But if there's a body that even investment banks defer to, it's the Federal Reserve. The nation's 12 Federal Reserve banks, and the Fed's leadership, are the overriding force that controls investment banking activities. The Fed is given the task of making decisions to increase or decrease the money supply with several goals. Specifically, the Fed is tasked with keeping employment up, prices stable, and long-term interest rates reasonable. When the Fed makes a move, it can have seismic effects on the investment banking world. Investment bankers would be foolish to ignore the Fed.

The Fed operates somewhat secretly, which isn't a big surprise, given the importance of its decisions. Even so, the Fed maintains a public website at www.federalreserve.org that contains limited information of value to those monitoring the government's moves.

Who owns the Fed?

Given the amount of power handed to the Federal Reserve, it's not surprising that it's often the subject of questions of intrigue and mystery. Given the Fed's regular business dealings with investment banks, for instance, many people believe that the Fed is somehow beholden to them.

There is an undeniable link between the Fed and investment banks, because they all work together to ensure the free flow of capital. The real question, then, is: Who actually owns the Fed?

The answer is somewhat complicated. The Federal Reserve System is composed of 12 regional Federal Reserve Banks. These banks are created using a structure similar to private businesses. And it's true that these banks sell stock to banks that are members of the Federal Reserve System.

But what's important to realize is that while member banks own shares in Federal Reserve Banks, these shares don't bestow power. The members are required to own stock in the Fed, as a stipulation of being part of the Federal Reserve System. But the stock cannot be sold or traded. It's Congress, though, that oversees the Fed and governs its mandate.

The Fed's website maintains data on the issuance of *commercial paper*, which are short-term loans sold mainly by large companies. The Fed also provides data on interest rates and industrial production. You can see all the data provided by the Federal Reserve in one area of the website at www.federalreserve.gov/econresdata/statisticsdata.htm.

Trefis

The website of Trefis (www.trefis.com) was cooked up by several engineers from the Massachusetts Institute of Technology (MIT), who also have experience with financial markets.

The site's mission is straightforward. It tries to use financial analysis to show investors what is driving a company's stock price. The site culls financial data to break down what factors are driving a company's valuation.

Trefis is primarily designed for investors who are trying to figure out how much a hit product may help a company's stock. But the tool is useful enough to warrant an examination from the perspective of an investment banker.

To start using Trefis, enter the name or ticker symbol of a company you're interested in. Trefis displays a breakdown of all the areas that the company derives its market value from.

Appendix

Where Investment Banking Came From

*I*nvestment banking may seem like a modern innovation, but that's not the case at all. Many of the financial products and services pitched by investment banks today trace their history back to the days of maritime commerce during the age of the Renaissance.

That's right: Investment banking existed even before the high-speed computers and cellphones that the profession is so closely associated with today. The profession of investment banking arose out of the long-standing need of investors to find interesting opportunities to get a return on their money, and dreamers and merchants to get money to make their businesses a reality.

Understanding the historical background of investment banking may seem like a massive waste of time. After all, there's no question that the business has changed dramatically over the centuries, as investors' and merchants' needs have changed and the economy has evolved.

But the background of investment banking is important to understand nonetheless. As you'll see, after reading this appendix, many of the quirks and unique qualities of investment banking today are the result of rules and methods of financing from days long past. And much of the role of the investment banker has been defined over the ages as money, currency, trade, and commerce have blossomed.

This appendix gives you a greater appreciation for the role investment banking has had during the ages. You see how investment banking has changed and how that evolution explains the role it plays to this day. You also get a sense of the complicated relationship between investment banks and traditional banks over time, and see why that interaction is so important.

Above all, understanding what investment banking *was* is one of the best ways to understand what it *is* now and how it may change in the future. Investment banking is a constantly evolving business, one that must adapt to changes in the economy in order to survive.

Exploring the Roots of Investment Banking

Investment banking became famous in the minds of many during the 1980s, thanks to Gordon Gekko and his enormous cellphone. It became infamous in the late-2000s with the financial crisis. But investment banking actually dates back well before Wall Street even existed.

Investment banking has somewhat of a tortured past, rising out of what was originally traditional banking services. And although investment banking serves the same primary role as traditional banks, getting money from those who have it to those who need it, the route by which investment banks make this happen creates a distinctly unique industry with its own culture, characteristics, and dynamics.

Going way back: Evolving out of traditional banks

If you've had a savings account since overstuffing your piggy bank for the first time, you may think that banking has been around forever. But that's not the case. The development of banking remains one of the greatest accomplishments in history, and one critical for accelerating the rate of progress through the ages. Banks were the first real institutions that had the job of getting money into the hands that needed it most.

Scholars figure there was some semblance of banking going on in Ancient Greece, the Roman Empire, and even before. Most of these banks were essentially lenders to businessmen and leaders of commerce. There is evidence that these early bankers took deposits and stored the valuables in temples. Some of these early bankers are also believed to have verified the value of currency and converted monies into different currencies.

The Renaissance of banking

Banking really got cooking during the age of the Renaissance, spanning from the 14th to the 17th centuries in Europe. After the world was shaking off the funk that was the Middle Ages, the globe was alight with new ideas. Certainly, the art of the period — created by Leonardo da Vinci, Michelangelo, and their peers — is still considered some of the finest ever created. But developments in the financial world were equally a masterpiece.

The innovation of banking is widely thought to trace its roots to the Italian cities of Florence and Genoa. Two wealthy families, the Bardi and Peruzzi families, quickly set up banks to finance the burgeoning activity at the time, including maritime commerce and other business activities. This practice of private lenders offering loans to customers, usually businesses, gave rise to the concept of a *merchant banker,* which is still in existence today.

The lenders of the Renaissance financed all sort of ventures, including wars. It's believed Italian bankers floated loans to kings and princes of the period. The Medici bank, created by the powerful Medici family in the 14th century, was even the banker to the pope. Being a lender to royalty proved a difficult task, because it was hard to force a monarch to repay loans and equally hard to decline lending to a deadbeat king. Making such bum loans along with a string of other complicated events resulted in the failure of the Medici bank in the late 15th century.

The role of the Catholic Church in high finance isn't as obscure and academic as it may seem. The church played an unintentional but significant role in finance, one that partially explains some of the more convoluted financial instruments today, including particular bonds. The Catholic Church considered *usury* (the collection of interest in exchange for a loan) to be immoral. The pope's ban on usury made collecting interest a sin. Bankers, therefore, had to cook up some crafty financial instruments that allowed them to get paid for their loans, without looking like they were collecting interest payments. These ancient rules explain why some financial instruments, even today, are so darned complicated. A classic example of usury-ducking investments are zero-coupon bonds. With *zero-coupon bonds,* investors pay below the face value of a bond (say, $90) but then get the full face value (say, $100) back when it matures. Investors got interest, but it was disguised. (For more information on bonds, turn to Chapter 11.)

Banking starts to spread to Britain

Although the Medici bank didn't survive, the ideas of banking and finance caught on. As economic prosperity and expansion spread throughout Europe, banking needs grew and radiated through the continent as well. Italian banking practices made their way to England in the 17th century.

The rise of the bill of exchange

One of the financial instruments to make its way to England is the bill of exchange, which was a breakthrough in the financial world. A *bill of exchange* was a document that allows the holder to hold a promise that a certain amount of money would be paid in the future. These documents would be critical in fueling the rampant international expansion taking place. It was a boom for banks in Europe, as young nations hungry for cash were eager to borrow.

IOUs turn into a medium of monetary exchange

Another significant development in Europe was also a breakthrough. Goldsmiths in London were artisans that held gold on deposit. They would give people who deposited gold with them a deposit receipt. The goldsmiths found that they could start lending out gold and hold IOUs in exchange, which would be repaid with interest. But in a major development, it turned out that these deposit receipts, could be exchanged between people in exchange for goods and services instead of commodities, like gold itself. This development opened brand-new ways for money to be exchanged.

The rise and fall of Barings

Barings Bank remains one of the greatest cautionary tales in all the history of investment banking and finance. The bank is one of the oldest European merchant banks, with its hands in some of the most momentous events in finance of the British Empire, including helping to finance Britain's role in World War II. Many rival investment banks had come and gone during Barings' impressive run, but the bank founded by John and Francis Baring was one of the most storied financial institutions in Europe.

In 1995, the 233-year-old firm was snuffed out at the hands of Nick Leeson, a 28-year-old trader in the Singapore office of Barings. Leeson was instructed to use *arbitrage,* a financial maneuver to take advantage of short-term price differences between different markets. Specifically, he was to trade on temporary price anomalies between Japanese financial instruments and those in Singapore. But instead of playing price changes off each other, which would have had minimal risk, Leeson placed large lopsided bets on the Japanese market. Due to a lack of supervision from the London headquarters, Leeson was able to hide his loss and keep gambling, hoping to break even. Following the Kobe earthquake, though, Asian markets tanked sending Leeson's losses soaring. By the time the fraud was discovered, Leeson had racked up trading losses north of $1.3 billion. Barings Bank collapsed and was bought by Dutch bank ING for roughly $1. Talk about a rise and fall.

The rise of key British banking powerhouses

Some of the iconic British banks arose in the 1800s. Barings Bank, founded in 1762, was created to work in the import and export business and later evolved into a merchant bank. The bank was heavily involved in financing some of Britain's biggest military engagements; it also handled the financing of the Louisiana Purchase. Ultimately, Barings yielded its influence to the institution of Rothschild & Son, founded in 1811, as the latter firm helped create an international bond market.

Banking Catches On in the United States

Up until 1863, the Europeans had dominated the global banking system. That changed, though, with the passage of the National Bank Act in the United States. All of a sudden, the federal government had the power to allow the creation of banks. Demand for banking erupted, first to finance the costly Civil War and the railroads. By the turn of the 20th century, major banking powerhouses were in full swing. It was around this period that some of the most well-known investment banking powerhouses were consolidating their influence, including J.P. Morgan; Bear Stearns; Kidder, Peabody; Goldman Sachs; Lazard Frères; and Lehman Brothers. These investment banks were financing the Industrial Revolution, one of the more progressive and capital-intensive periods the United States has ever seen.

Witnessing the development of modern investment banking

Investment banking as we know it today is in large part the result of the banking system's failure in the 1930s. Widespread speculation and aggressive lending was the norm in the early 20th century. Following the stock market's crash in October 1929, rampant runs on the banks sparked a record-breaking period of bank failures. At the height of the crisis, a number of pieces of legislation were passed that forged the modern investment banking era. Perhaps most important, the Banking Act of 1933, known as the Glass–Steagall Act, banned commercial banks, which took deposits, from engaging in investment banking.

The ban precluded banks from selling stocks or bonds. Similarly, the investment banks were banned from owning banks. Banks and investment banks couldn't have it both ways — they had to choose banking or investment banking. This was a pivotal moment in financial services.

The new rules were designed to rope off the risky business of investment banking from banking, preventing a collapse in an investment bank's bets from causing a financial panic on Main Street with bank depositors. One of the best examples: J.P. Morgan remained in the commercial banking business, but a former member of the bank left to form the investment bank Morgan Stanley.

The passage and ultimate repeal of Glass–Steagall remains one of the most definitive shifts in modern investment banking. The safeguards created during the Depression, and repealed in 1999 created a perfect environment for problems that lead to the financial crisis of 2007, some say. With Glass–Steagall out of the way, large super-sized banks were able to engage in increasingly risky businesses that were usually the domain of investment bankers. Some academics, of course, disagree and think that banks and investment banks would have engaged in similar behavior even if Glass–Steagall were in force. The debate will take years to sort out. But the financial crisis, no matter the cause, served up a reminder of why government plays such a strong role in overseeing and supervising banks and investment banks. Investment banking, even today, is considered a risky business. Keeping it separate from the savings of widows and orphans was a goal of early lawmakers.

Seeing how investment banks were threatened by banks

Investment banks blossomed during the 1950s and 1960s. Even big companies outside the finance game wanted to get into the lucrative business. The 1980s was a time of some strange mergers, including the Sears purchase of Dean Witter Reynolds, the Shearson/American Express purchase of Lehman Brothers, and the General Electric purchase of Kidder, Peabody. Each of these deals ended in disaster and eventually dissolved through spinoffs and sales.

Investment banks then went into their next phase, of being stand-alone, often publicly held, companies. The behemoths Bear Stearns, Morgan Stanley, and Goldman Sachs all sold shares of themselves to the public in the mid and late 1990s. But just as investment banks were able to stand on their own two feet, the commercial banks were grabbing more of their business as they found ways to provide more investment banking services themselves.

That would change in 1999. The Gramm–Leach–Bliley Act, also known as the Financial Services Modernization Act of 1999, turned banking and investment banking upside down. The Gramm–Leach–Bliley Act repealed a big chunk of Glass–Steagall, allowing banking companies to encroach on the turf of investment banks by selling securities. Banks were so eager to jump into the investment banking business that one, Citicorp, bought Travelers Group (which owned Smith Barney) even before the Gramm–Leach–Bliley Act was signed.

Feeling the pain: The financial crisis of 2007 changes everything

Facing stiffer competition from the traditional banks, who largely encroached on the lucrative business of selling stock and bonds for companies, the investment banks were pushed into riskier ventures. Large investment banks got heavily involved with a number of exotic and highly complicated financial instruments, including many tied to the housing market. Some of the most infamous financial tools that investment banks got wrapped up with included *mortgage-backed securities* (debt instruments tied to mortgages) and *collateralized debt obligations* (financial instruments that allowed financial institutions to buy and sell pieces of loans).

Meanwhile, investment banks — which were pushing for profit in an age in which banks were soaking up much of the high-end business — searched for ways to make money. And that meant taking on more risk. Investment banks found what they were looking for in the subprime housing market, where they financed loans to homebuyers with low credit ratings and little or no down payments.

The fall of Bear Stearns and Lehman Brothers

These bad bets started to haunt the investment banks when the housing market collapsed, bringing the value of the financial instruments down with it. In March 2008, the first major investment bank to fall was Bear Stearns. The failed institution, swamped in losses from bum bets, was sold to JPMorgan Chase for $10 a share.

Lehman Brothers was the next major investment bank to be claimed by the financial crisis. Large amounts of subprime loans and related investment soured, and Lehman couldn't stay afloat. The company filed for Chapter 11 bankruptcy protection in 2008.

More shotgun weddings in finance

The crisis only widened from that point to historic proportions. In another defining moment, Merrill Lynch, one of the best known investment banks, dating back to 1914, was choking on its own massive portfolio of investments tied to bad housing bets. As trading partners lost faith in Merrill Lynch, that choked off the company's access to capital, which is the oxygen to investment banks. With its options dropping off, Merrill Lynch agreed to be bought by Bank of America for about $50 billion.

Hoping to fend off another Great Depression, the federal government agreed in 2008 to buy troubled assets from the banks and remaining investment banks to prevent the financial system from collapsing. This historic bailout, called the Troubled Asset Relief Program (TARP) turned into a defining moment of the financial crisis, as taxpayers found themselves in the position of saving some of the nation's most powerful financial institutions.

Investment banks stay alive by becoming . . . banks

The wake of the financial crisis marks the end of the standalone American investment bank. In September 2008, both Goldman Sachs and Morgan Stanley, the two last independent investment banks, turned into bank holding companies. This move allowed the companies to accept deposits, which they needed to do, because they were no longer able to get enough cash by selling securities. But they also had to adhere to banking standards, which, in theory, would rein in their ability to chase after any risky ventures in the name of profit.

Not only did Goldman Sachs have to tap TARP to get adequate operating capital (to the tune of $10 billion), but it also sold $5 billion in *preferred stock* (a unique type of shares that gives its owners typically oversized dividends) to Warren Buffett's Berkshire Hathaway.

Index

• J •

• K •

About the Authors

Matt Krantz: Matt is a nationally known financial journalist who specializes in investing topics. Since 1999, he has been a writer for *USA TODAY,* where he covers financial markets and Wall Street, concentrating on developments affecting individual investors and their portfolios. His stories routinely signal trends that investors can profit from and sound warnings about potential scams and issues investors should be aware of.

Matt also writes a daily online investing column called "Ask Matt," which appears every trading day at USATODAY.com and in *USA TODAY.* He answers questions posed by the website's audience in an easy-to-understand manner. Readers often tell Matt he's the only one who has been able to finally solve investing questions they've sought answers to for years.

Matt has been investing since the 1980s and has studied dozens of investment techniques while forming his own. As a financial journalist, Matt has interviewed some of the most famous and infamous investment minds in modern history. Before joining *USA TODAY,* Matt worked as a business and technology reporter for *Investor's Business Daily* and, prior to that, was a consultant with Ernst & Young.

Matt has spoken for investing groups, including at the national convention of National Association of Investors Corporation, and has appeared on financial television.

Matt earned a bachelor's degree in business administration at Miami University in Oxford, Ohio. He is based in *USA TODAY*'s Los Angeles bureau. When he's not writing, he's spending time with his wife and young daughter, running, playing tennis, mountain biking, or surfing.

Robert R. Johnson, Ph.D., CFA, CAIA: Bob is a full professor of finance in the Heider College of Business at Creighton University. He teaches in the Master of Security Analysis and Portfolio Management Program and serves as the editor for the *Quarterly Journal of Finance and Accounting.* He also serves on the board of RS Investments, a San Francisco–based investment management firm that is majority-owned by The Guardian Life Insurance Company.

Bob was formerly Senior Managing Director and Deputy CEO at CFA Institute, responsible for all aspects of the CFA Program for the majority of his 15-year tenure. In 2013, he received the Alfred C. "Pete" Morley Distinguished Service Award from CFA Institute in appreciation of his leadership, stewardship, and outstanding service.

Prior to joining CFA Institute, Bob was a professor of finance at Creighton University from 1984 through 1996. Throughout his academic career, Bob won several teaching awards and, in 1994, earned the university-wide Robert F. Kennedy Award for Teaching Excellence. Bob has over 60 refereed articles in leading finance and investment journals. His publications have appeared in

The Journal of Finance, Journal of Financial Economics, The Journal of Portfolio Management, Financial Analysts Journal, and *Journal of Banking & Finance.*

Bob has extensive media relations experience both in the United States and abroad. He has been quoted in *The Wall Street Journal, Financial Times, Barron's, USA TODAY, Forbes, The Globe and Mail* (Toronto), *South China Morning Post, The Straits Times* (Singapore), and *Le Temps,* among others. He has appeared numerous times on ABC World News, Bloomberg TV (Europe and U.S.), CNN, and China Business News, among others.

Bob received his BSBA in finance (summa cum laude) from the University of Nebraska–Omaha in 1980, MBA (with a concentration in finance) from Creighton University in 1982, and PhD in finance/investments from the University of Nebraska–Lincoln in 1988. He earned his CFA charter from the Institute of Chartered Financial Analysts in 1991. He earned his CAIA charter from the Chartered Alternative Investment Analyst Association in 2011.

Bob lives with his wife in Charlottesville, Virginia. When he's not working, he enjoys cycling in the Blue Ridge Mountains, hiking with his wife and dogs, and rooting for his beloved Nebraska Cornhusker football and Creighton Bluejays basketball teams.

Dedication

This book is dedicated to my wife, Nancy, who has supported the project from the very beginning. The book is also dedicated to my daughter, Leilani, who inspires me with her hard work and dedication.

—Matt Krantz

This book is dedicated to the love of my life, Heidi, and my son, Jack. They are both sources of great joy in my life.

—Bob Johnson

Authors' Acknowledgments

Matt Krantz: Working with co-author Bob Johnson was an absolute joy. He was always prepared with suggestions to make the book better and eager to share his keen insights in finance. My mentor and friend, Rob Golum, has long been a big help in my writing and business knowledge. Rob was a big help again with this book as he guided my thinking about the best way to approach it. My editors at *USA TODAY* supported the book from its genesis and encouraged me along the way. My assignment editor, David Craig, as well as other *USA TODAY* editors, supported this book and my development as a writer and reporter.

Wiley personnel have been tremendous to work with as well, including our acquisitions editor, Erin Calligan Mooney, and our project and copy editor, Elizabeth Kuball, who found ways to make this book a real resource for readers. A big thanks to Matt Wagner, my literary agent, for thinking of me for the project and presenting it to me. Thanks to my mom and dad for instilling, at a very young age, a curiosity in investing, writing, and computers (and for buying me my first computer well before having a PC was common). And thanks to my grandparents for teaching me the power of saving and investing.

Robert Johnson: Thanks to my co-author, Matt Krantz, for inviting me to participate in this project. It was a lot of fun to work with a consummate professional. I echo Matt's acknowledgements about the wonderful folks at Wiley.

My dissertation chairman and friend, Dr. Thomas Zorn, taught me that a good academic could take something complex and make it simple — an ability that I have tried to cultivate throughout my career. My good friend and trusted advisor, Gary Cook, has been instrumental in shaping my career path and helping me achieve my life's goals. Creighton University College of Business Dean Anthony Hendrickson has supported this project and continually reinforces the notion that business is an applied discipline, a simple concept that all too many business school academicians forget.

Most of all, thanks to my mother for inspiring me to continue learning throughout my life. And thanks to both of my parents for the simple gift of love.

Publisher's Acknowledgments

Acquisitions Editor: Erin Calligan Mooney

Project Editor: Elizabeth Kuball

Copy Editor: Elizabeth Kuball

Technical Editor: Kenneth Washer, CFA, CFP

Project Coordinator: Melissa Cossell

Cover Image: © iStockphoto.com/
Danil Melekhin